REME BEING, INFINITE IS THY GLORY.

MW01677697

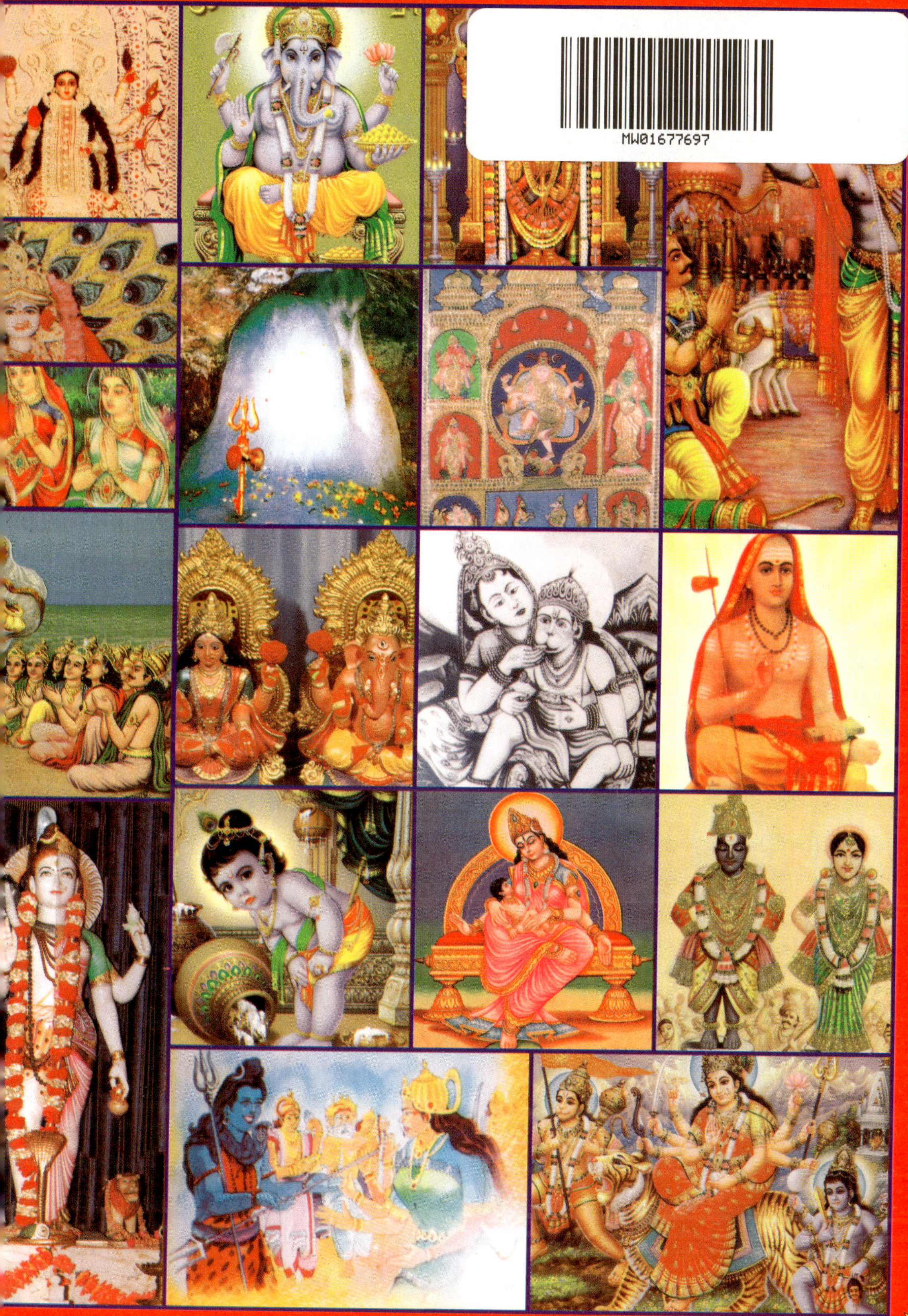

YOU ARE OMNIPRESENT, OMNIPOTENT, OMNISCIENT

STATIONS, NAMES, FORMS, EPITHETS

To dear Pankaj, Canada.

Mother Divine
the
Supreme Being

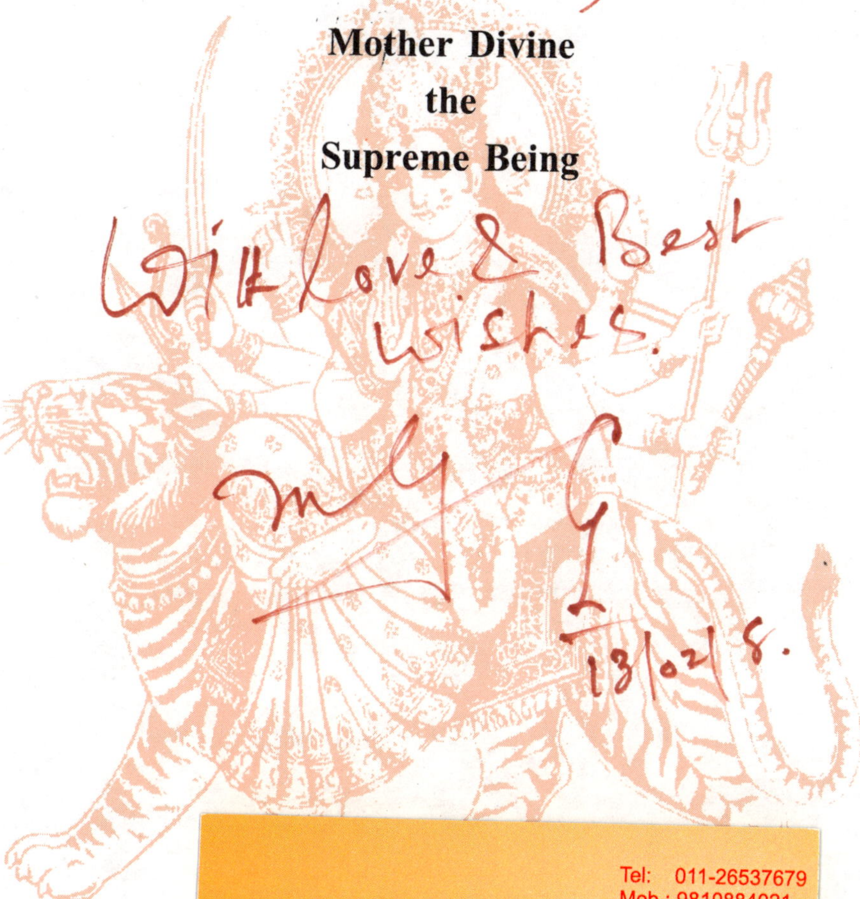

With love & Best wishes.

13/02/18.

Tel: 011-26537679
Mob.: 9810884021

Chaman Lal Kaushal

Author of

परमसत्तात्मक आद्यशक्ति

(मातृशक्ति के रूप में परमसत्ता का तात्विक विवेचन)

MOTHER DIVINE THE SUPREME BEING

(Meditation on the vision of eternal Presence)

K-56, Green Park (Main), New Delhi - 110016

E-mail: clkaushal21@gmail.com

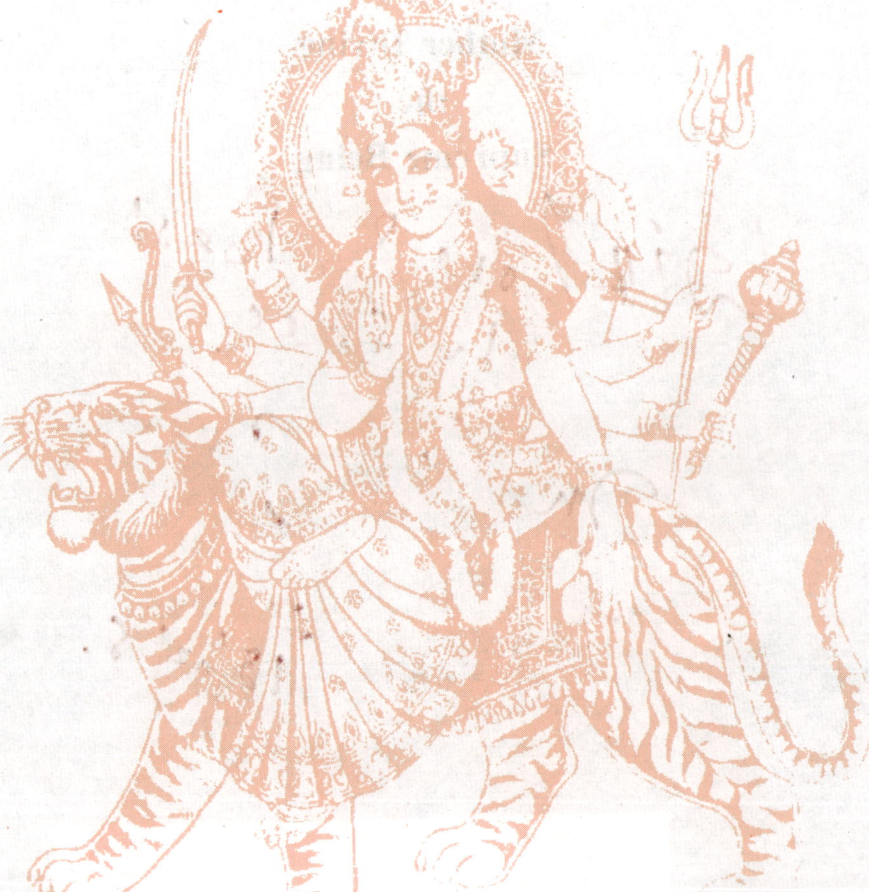

MOTHER DIVINE the SUPREME BEING

Meditation
on the vision of the eternal Presence
(An Exposition of Personal Faith and Choice)

Chaman Lal Kaushal

Foreword
by

Prof. Vachaspati Upadhyaya, Vice Chancellor,
Shri LBS Rashtriya Sanskrit Vidyapeeth (Deemed University),
New Delhi.

❄

Aravali Books Internaional (P) Ltd.
New Delhi-110 020

ISBN 81-86880-97-6

First edition : 2003

© Chaman Lal Kaushal : 2003

MOTHER DIVINE, THE SUPREME BEING

Rs. 800/- US $ 60/-

Illustrations : **Courtesy :**
National Museum, New Delhi

Publisher : Aravali Books International (P) Ltd.,
W-30, Okhla Industrial Area, Phase II,
New Delhi-110 020
Phones : 26388830-32, 26389736-38 Fax : 26388829
E-mail : Aravali@nde.vsnl.net.in
Website : www.Aravalibooks.com

Printer : Aravali Printers & Publishers (P) Ltd.,
New Delhi-110 020

या देवी सर्वभूतेषु मातृरुपेण संस्थिता
नमस्तस्यै नमस्तस्यै नमस्तस्यै नमो नमः।।

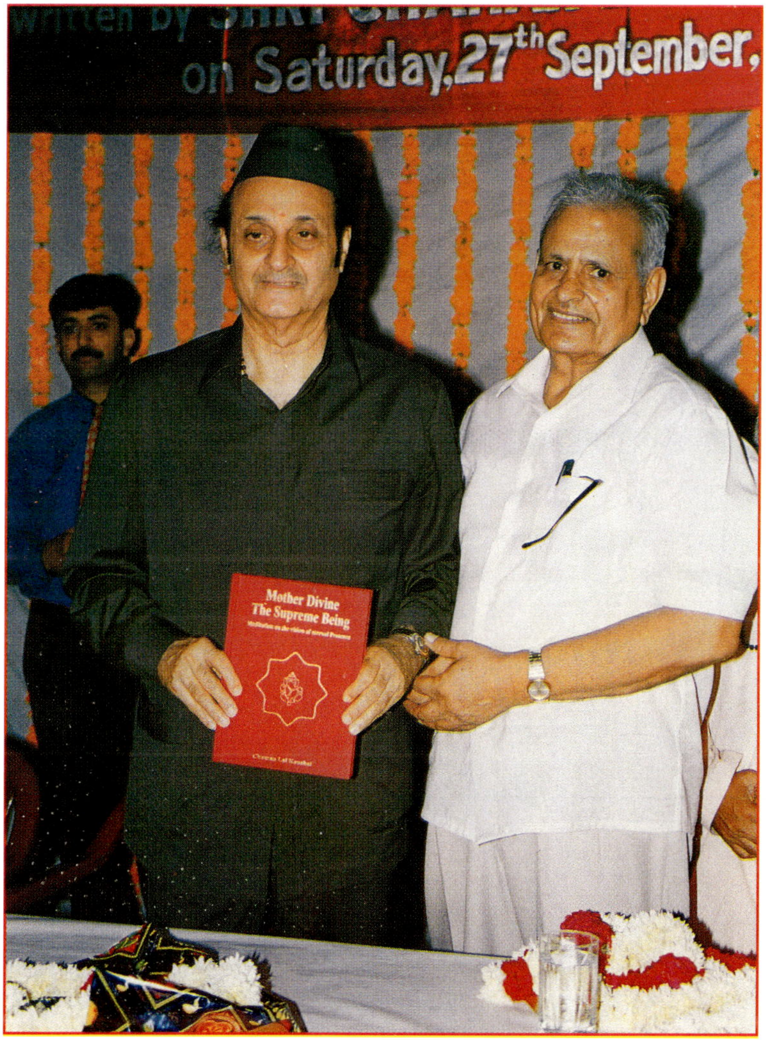

Hon'ble Dr. Karan Singh, M.P. (Rajya Sabha)
released the book (लोकार्पण) on 27-9-2003

या देवी सर्वभूतेषु मातृरुपेण संस्थिता
नमस्तस्यै नमस्तस्यै नमस्तस्यै नमो नमः।।

मुझे बड़ी प्रसन्नता है श्री चमनलाल कौशल जी ने बड़ी श्रद्धा से बड़ी लगन से बड़े समर्पितभाव से भक्तिपूर्णभाव से इन्होंने यह पुस्तक तैयार की है Mother Divine the Supreme Being इन्होंने अनेक उदाहरण दिये हैं, अपने भाव से अपनी रट में तैयार किया है। वधाई के वो पात्र हैं।

Dr. Karan Singh, M.P. (Rajya Sabha)

CONTENTS

Invocation

या देवी सर्वभूतेषु मातृरुपेण संस्थिता
नमस्तस्यै नमस्तस्यै नमस्तस्यै नमो नमः ।।

Yā Devī Sarvabhuteṣu Matṛ Ṛūpeṇa Saṃsthitā,
Namastasyai, Namastasyai, Namastasyai, Namo Namaḥ

SALUTATIONS TO THE MOTHER DIVINE WHO ABIDES IN
ALL BEINGS IN THE FORM OF MOTHER.

O *Māṃ* SARASVATI,
Source of all-learning,
This hymn composed of words that are Thine,
is addressed to Thee.
PRAY
Condescend to sanctify this song of Thy praise.
Whether my effort overflows with full fruition or with none,
Thou art my sole resort, O *Māṃ*.

"I do not know, O Supreme Being, who you are, what you are, where you are. Whether you are He or She, a Person or a Presence, manifest or hidden, attributed or without attributes. None can grasp you though your grasp is on everything. Without doubt, you are all-pervasive, all-knowing, all-powerful, substratum of all that exists. Wherever I see, I see your Presence. How to address you? Being your child, I fascinate the Absolute as Mother. So dare I call you *'Māṃ'* (Mother). It seems to be the most appropriate address to evoke a response from you. Hope, you are listening. Your real face is veiled by your own dazzling effulgence. You are the sun which illumines the inner darkness of the ignorant.

Eager to see your gracious form, O Mother of the universe, Chaman, your own child, thus prays: "May, the virtuous and genuinely motivated readers of this book attain their cherished desires fulfilled " by the grace of Mother Divine, the Supreme Being,

Jai Māṃ Jai

THE COSMIC TREE

ऊर्ध्वमूलमधःशाखमश्वत्थं प्राहुरव्ययम्।
छन्दांसि यस्य पर्णानि यस्तं वेद स वेदवित्।

(Ūrdhva-mūlam adhaḥ-śākham aśvathaṁ prāhuravyayam
Chandāṁsi yasya parṇāni yastam veda sa veda-vit)

Material life is described by Lord Kṛṣṇa in Bhagvadgītā as a tree, the holy Aśvattha tree, whose indestructible roots are upward, branches spread below and the leaves likened to *vedik* hymns - a reflection of the spiritual world, a shadow of the Reality. This tree is known for its huge size and long life.

Later, however, the Lord advises us to cut and destroy this tree which has a non-changing appearance despite its being subject to constant change. This seems to be a fit analogy for the material world whose roots are in the invisible and imperishable *Brahman* and the way to know the Truth is through *vedik* hymns described as the leaves of the tree.

Those who are attached to the pleasures and pains of living on the tree (material world) will be allowed to continue to undergo the wheel of transmigration (*saṃsāra cakra*) and remain in bondage. But after cutting down this firmly rooted tree by the mighty sword of non-attachment one attains the goal from which there is no return. The tree ceases to bind those who are intent on reaching its source (Grace Divine) in search of eternal peace. Once *vairāgya* becomes a living inspiration and nothing seems to belong to them, the illusory nature of the world comes to the surface. The detachment disentangles them from the tree and gives them the right to climb higher up and slip into the lap of the Mother Divine, the Supreme Being.

Alas! only when the day shuts its dazzling eye and the light casts its dark veil, man's quest for Light begins.

DEDICATION

This

song of glory is sung,

with humble and respectful obeisance to

MOTHER DIVINE,

THE SUPREME BEING

(श्री माता)

who made me instrumental

to gather these pearls of love and wisdom

and

dedicated

with love, reverence and obeisance,

to

the cherished and ever-lasting memory

of my loving and revered mother *(jananī)*,

late Smt. Bhāgwanti,

who always loved me, inspired me

and

blessed me.

▲

(I have nothing to offer but love and tears,

for all else is thine)

Humbly Yours,

clk

❄

Mother in Her most pure form symbolises unconditional love, divine dedication and invincible powers. Her love and blessings are cherished and sought after by all. At Her feet lies the secret to eternal bliss.

To Dear Devotees

या देवी सर्वभूतेषु मातृरुपेण संस्थिता
नमस्तस्यै नमस्तस्यै नमस्तस्यै नमो नमः

Blessed fellow devotees,

Where there is the basic acceptance of one's limitations in knowledge and of one's need to know more, there alone one will seek knowledge, the true hallmark of a seeker of Truth. Nobody is more conscious than myself of my weaknesses and limitations in this regard.

I submit this bouquet of the choicest flowers (*Māṃ's* blessings), the essence of spirituality, with great humility, reverence and sincere love. For this I claim no credit. But I do seek your head and heart, for, in the eternity of our seeking the Divine Grace, you and I have a rendezvous in Her Majesty's *darbār* (royal court). The audience with the Supreme Being has to be in the harmonious blend of body, mind and spirit.

God is not the object of perception. Everybody is ignorant of Its abode, Its nature, Its form. Everybody knows Him by certain 'Name' only. The highest *yogis* do not recognise any distinction between male and female address either. If you wish to know and worship divinity, develop a relationship with God, sing praises of glory and meditate. I address God as *Māṃ* (Mother), a matter of personal choice and faith. It seems to be the most intimate and informal mundane relationship. The true value of devotion lies in the *bhāva* (disposition) of the devotees.

This treatise is intended to be treated as a foot-way to inner penetration. Nobody can define Mother Grace. You will have to make an effort yourself to know Her. Spiritual growth is gradual, yet desire to aspire inspires.

I also dedicate all my shortcomings, omissions and commissions unto the lotus feet of my beloved *Māṃ*. She forgets and forgives because Her nature is compassion. Pray we all remain at peace with ourselves at all times. Grace Divine, bless us all.

the author.

FOREWORD

by

PROF. Vachaspati Upadhyaya, Vice Chancellor,
Shri Lal Bahadur Shastri Rashtriya Sanskrit Vidyapeeth
(Deemed University), New Delhi.

WHAT is the greatest boon God has given to all living beings? It is mother's love, undoubtedly. It must then be the unique quality of mother-child relationship that worship of God as mother became so wide-spread. In the Vedas the goddess Uṣas is identified as the goddess of Dawn, the coming of light to the world. The concept expands to include Prithvi, the Mother Earth; Aditi, the mother of *aditya-s*; Vāk who reveals herself through speech, and Rātri associated with Night, besides many minor goddesses.

The worship of Devī is enriched through various hymns. In the Kena Upnishad Devī Umeshvari imparts knowledge as a *Guru.* In the Rāmāyana we see Rāma worshipping Durgā for success in battle. In the Mahābhārata, we see Pāṇḍava-s doing the same at the instance of Krishna. In Srimad Bhāgavata, *gopi-s* pray to Devi: "O Katyayani, Thou who art Mahāmāyā ! Deign to make the son of Nanda my husband. Prostrations to You." The image of Devī is further highlighted in various *Purāna-s* such as Markandeya *Purāna*, Srimad Devī Bhāgavat *Purāna*. She is portrayed as the Creator, Preserver and Destroyer of the universe and ruling the Trinity. In the *tāntrik* scriptures the concept of *Śakti* as the Supreme Principle, gains fullness. Durgā Sapatśati and Saundarya Lahari further elevated the rank and image of Devī.

The aim of the religious and devotional writings is to inspire love of God in human beings, and raise them step by step to the level of Self- realisation. This treatise under review comes very close to serve this purpose. Through the study and practice of this work, we seek to free ourselves from the chronic diseases like *moha* (attachment) and *ahaṅkāra* (ego) by expanding our awareness beyond the material world.

Mr. Kaushal has clearly brought out the teachings and practices of a multitude of enlightened souls in a concise and comprehensible volume in an easy and flowing style.

The thematic contents of this book make one believe that they are entirely based on the personal experiences of the author. The book will not only inspire and help the aspiring devotee but will also be of immense service to the novice reader. In the Invocation the author draws inspiration from *Māṃ* Sarasvati. He glorifies the Divine Being with all his heart and soul and suggests that each one of us should emulate the same. He is very clear in his mind that *Ādyaśakti* and *Brahman* are not two separate entities but one and the same.

The book is neatly and methodically divided into six Parts, each Part is sub-divided in a number of chapters. Part One meant "For the Inquisitive" is "humbly definitive". Here the author makes us well acquainted with some very important concepts e.g. *brahman*, *saguṇa-nirguṇa*, *śraddhā* (faith), *Anūraga* (divine love), *Kṛpā* (divine grace), *Svarūpa* (divine form), *Jyoti* (divine light), *Iṣṭa-devatā* (chosen deity) &c. The treatment of each topic is exhaustive and all the concepts are carefully set forth.

Part Two is "For the Upcoming Aspirants". The thrust area of this Part is to discern such important aspects like Purity of Mind, Ego, Illusion, Time, Harmony, Silence and Surrender. Those who are desirous of attaining the final beatitude will surely appreciate the usefulness of the material provided in this part of the book.

Part Three deals with a catalyst: "Know Thyself" *(ātmabodha)* leading to God-realisation. Self-realisation, he says, is not attainment or achievement but a discovery of the Self in one's own heart. The knowledge of the Self is *sine qua non* (indispensable) for attaining *summum bonum* (the highest perfection) of spiritual ends of life. "It is this 'I' which is the essence of man and this 'I' is never seen".

In order to make his points clear the author takes cue from very interesting and instructive anecdotes, parables and stories. To him, Knowledge *(jñāna),* Devotion *(bhakti)* and Action *(karma)* are equally important for God-realisation but he does hint that the path of Knowledge is suitable for the intellectuals who are adept in making proper use of rhyme and reason; the path of Devotion for those who are emotional and sentimental; and the path of Action for those who are practical in life. The three paths of course, are not mutually exclusive. Each is complementary to the other two. The accomplishment of one is at once the fulfilment of the other two.

Part Four deals with the actually designed feature of the book, "*mātṛdevobhava*." Mother is none other than God. Spread into fifteen chapters under headings like *Māṃ* And Me, God As Mother Divine, Śiva-Śakti, Mercies of Divine Mother, In Praise of Mother Divine, Durgā Sapatśati &c. the glory of the Absolute is sung in a dedicated manner. To the author the universe is the mother-heart whose manifestation can be easily seen and realised in the cosmos. "Divine Mother could not be everywhere, so SHe made mothers". The amount of careful thought given to each one of the topics deserves all praise.

Part Five "Towards Soul Emancipation" raises certain issues for the advanced aspirants and resolves them in a convincing manner with a touch of experience. It is meant to serve as a word of caution as well as of encouragement for the "now-grown-up" aspirant.

Part Six "Wisdom Dispensed" covers a vast treasure of practical moral and spiritual knowledge in the form of Thoughts and Quotes which mothers a vision of the One beyond the beyond.

The book undoubtedly embodies the results of a long and devoted study undertaken by the author and is a very valuable addition to the world of literature on the "Faith in the Absolute". In fact with his intimate knowledge of the subject he has succeeded in giving a full and connected account of the chosen theme. He writes in a simple, facile and precise manner and his exposition is interspersed throughout with face renderings into English of *śloka-s* from the original source. Another noteworthy feature of the book is the examples which he now and then gives from the teachings of saints and savants.

In the religious life of Hindus today there is no need to resuscitate the Great Goddess referred to by the author as Mother Divine, *Ādyaśakti*. Most of the topics are based on "Devī Mahātmyam" which is recognised as a text of unique significance to Hindu religious traditions. In a lecture delivered in 1840, H.H. Wilson ranked it "amongst the most popular works in the Sanskrit language" and to this day its hymns are recited with great devotion and dedication by a vast number of people all over the world. The verbatim repeated recitation of the hymns, believed to possess an eternal power, not only helps the mind to get rid of its dross progressively but also pleases the Deity the most. The ultimate Reality in the universe is here understood to be feminine, the Goddess Devī.

There has been the need for a reliable and readable book on the subject for Mother's devotees and the present meets that need exceedingly well. The English-speaking devotees will benefit the most from this text. I heartily recommend "Mother Divine, the Supreme Being" to all those who are desirous to dive deeper in search of Truth.

Vachaspati Upadhyaya

New Delhi,
May, 2000.

> Immanence is God's presence within the whole of creation. We can see God only if SHe turns His light on Her own face. Let's behold Her in all these names and forms. Let's remember Him in all these names and forms.

INTRODUCTION

by

ACHARYA SHARAD CHANDRA KUSHAL,
President,
Manav Vikas Niketan (Regd.), New Delhi.

I CAME in contact with Shri Chaman Lal Kaushal through my father, Late Pt. Amir Chandra Shastri, about 12 years ago. He would come to my place whenever my father was in Delhi, and discuss with him concepts like *brahman, saguṇa, nirguṇa,* universal Consciousness and above all, the concept of the *Ādyaśakti*, the Supreme Being, the Mother Divine. They would sit for hours together; Shri Kaushal putting forth his queries persistently and my father replying to them very serenely and patiently. The quest for the substance was so great in this man that I, sometimes, wondered what has this businessman to do with metaphysics and spirituality. Unable to control my curiosity, once I asked my father what he thought of this man and he replied: Here is a true devotee of the Mother, who aspires to achieve Her blessings and affection and that is why he is more concerned about the *tattva jñāna* and not just the manifestations of the Goddess Durgā, since he wants to know Her in totality. At that time naive as I was I could not understand the import of this statement. By and by both of them allowed me to peep into their spiritual world by letting me take part in their discourses.

Later on when Shri Kaushal approached me with the manuscript of his book 'MOTHER DIVINE, THE SUPREME BEING' under review, I was taken aback by the thought that he even considered me worthy of it. Here before me was humility personified. As I went through the pages of the manuscript I was astonished to find the clarity of his thoughts, the purity of his vision and the depth of his faith. Herein is an author who neither claims originality nor erudition, yet in a very subtle and simple manner establishes the Supreme Being, the God as Mother, as against the common belief that He is a Father. For him the reality ought to be She as SHe includes He, and thus together they constitute the neutral *brahman*, the Absolute.

But for the sad demise of my father, I would not be writing these lines. Instead it would have been my father himself who would have showered his blessings on this great piece of remarkable work, because the intellectual chemistry between the two of them was par excellence.

I have been with this work from the very hour of its conception and I have seen it growing step by step, stage by stage, into a glorious and magnificent bunch of flowers. Shri Kaushal welcomed suggestions from all quarters and gracefully incorporated them in his work. As my knowledge was bookish and his was inherent, I would be hesitant in expressing my views at times but he would goad me to say something which might be contrary to his basic idea. Thus, he, by inviting negative criticism, comes across as a man who in reality is a seeker of Truth, and for whom the opposite is complementary as it constitutes the whole.

There is no attempt on his part to start a new school of thought or a sect or philosophy. Instead it is a saga of faith and total conviction in 'that' faith; that is why he rightly calls it 'An Exposition of Faith'. This is an outcome of long years of contemplation and meditation on the part of the author on the 'vision of the eternal Presence'. He bows before the God as *Māṃ*, a matter of personal choice as it is the most 'intimate and informal mundane relationship'. Thus he starts with God as a mundane reality and through the course of the book establishes Her as the only transcendental Reality, without going into the jargon of philosophical terminology, lexicography of definitions, denotations and connotations, and makes his point of view crystal-clear by his simplicity of expression and honesty of quest.

He has quoted extensively but his presentation of the quotations is not verbatim. They have been put forth in a manner as he understands them. He does not preach sermons about values or morality or religion or chastity, nor does he insist upon performance of rituals like *Yajñās* or *Ārati.* He does not want an aspirant to go through the nuances of controlling breath and thus elevating oneself to the higher stages of yoga. He does not refer to the twenty four *tattva-s* of Sānkhya, yet is able to differentiate between the Manifest and the Unmanifest *'Prakṛti* and *Pradhāna'*. He is neither a rationalist like Descartes who gropes in the dark with his meditations of a 'thinking thing' nor does he try to differentiate between transcendental and empirical reality in the Kantian way. His *'esse est percipier'* is his *'esse est percipi'*. That is why he sees a mundane mother in God and is able to establish Her as a Supreme Transcendental Reality without any doubt or dogma, for his approach is that of love for, of faith in, and of inquisitiveness about Truth and Truth alone.

His method to seek the ultimate Reality leading to Self-Realisation is simple but entails certain sacrifices like 'give and take'. Spiritual unfoldment is *nāma-rūpa tyāga.*

One starts with the query into the Absolute, the Divine Player *(brahman)* that is related to our very existence, with the faith of a child. Faith is the pointer of the soul that leads to the divine abode. Chant the divine *nāma* with love and devotion to qualify for the divine Grace. Divine Form is the hidden Light, the eternal Presence perceived everywhere and conceived in everyone and everything. The seeker experiences a glimpse of the vision of that Form and establishes a bond of relationship with the Divine. The mind thus is freed from all impurities, the ego takes to its wings, the illusion behaves in all modesty, the harmony prevails and makes its mark resulting in silence (the language of Truth) and complete surrender (the transcendence of ego).

The aspirant is now ready to get closer to embrace divinity, the Mother Divine, the embodiment of love, compassion, mercy, grace and glory. He traverses through sixteen chapters comprising some hundred pages describing all aspects and facets of Mother Grace, the *Ādyaśakti* and takes off to the unfathomed heights of a dreamless world of bliss and bliss alone, in a state of transformation and sheer ecstasy.

In my humble opinion Shri Kaushal's Treatise 'MOTHER DIVINE, THE SUPREME BEING' deserves a careful reading and silent contemplation by all those who seek to know the *Summum Bonum* of all that was, of all that is, and of all that shall ever be, in consonance with time and space and beyond it. The devotees of Mātṛ-*Śakti*, stand to gain a lot more in terms of a brush with divinity.

Let's pray together :

> "O Divine Grace, Thy goodness is Infinite. Be gracious to Thy children who have taken refuge in Thee. Shower on us Thy grace and grant us faith, devotion, love and protection. We bow before Thee in gratitude, Amen."

Sharad Chandra Kushal.

The divine form we worship is an embodiment of the attributes that reveal the supreme Principle. This knowledge should evolve into an intense awareness of the Reality that is at the root of all creation.

PREFACE

THIS STUDY is an endeavour to offer an exposition of the nature of the ultimate Supreme Power, the *Brahman,* worshipped as Divine Mother in Its infinite manifestations.

The conception of the Infinite as Mother is ages old. The Ṛgveda bears testimony to the fact that even in ancient times, there was the persistent belief that the Ruler of the universe is the All-Compassionate Mother, *Adyaśakti,* the Primordial Power, the Supreme Godhead. Mother is synonymous with *Śakti*, the Divine Power that manifests, sustains and transforms the universe as the one unifying force of Existence. She conceives, bears, produces and nourishes the entire universe. Mother is the personality that appeals most to the human heart.

Although God in the transcendental realm is beyond conceptualisation in terms of gender, It is commonly referred to with the male pronoun 'He'. Why should God be addressed only in masculine terms as Father? Why not speak of God in feminine terms, too, as Mother? The fact remains that God is a personal being with whom we can truly choose to have any relationship. Our *ṛṣi-s* expressed God by using the neuter pronoun 'That'. Calling God as Mother is not at all meant to show any distinction of sex in Divinity. It is just a matter of appeal and devotee's faith and choice.

An ignorant villager was travelling by train. The ticket checker thought of having some fun with him and told the villager that he could not travel on the ticket which was for ladies. The villager changed his dress. The ticket collector at the gate joined the ticket checker. "It is a male ticket," he said. The villager got angry and said, "Well, if it is a male ticket then surely I can travel on it as I am only dressed like a lady." A ticket is just a ticket. It is neither male nor female just like Truth. Truth is One. Expressions differ.

The doctrine of *Śakti* as Divine Power is one of the greatest doctrines evolved through spiritual intuitions by human mind, and is the manifestation of the Divine Consciousness Itself. When anybody needs protection from an imminent danger, is it not the word '*Māṃ*' that comes out spontaneously from his mouth?

It is one of the greatest contributions of Sri Rāmakṛiśna to Indian religious tradition that his spiritual experience has identified *Śakti* (Mother Divine), not as a mere female counterpart of the Absolute, but as the Absolute Itself.

The appellations of God are as endless as the attributes. Since *Śakti* cannot be worshipped in its essential nature, the mind must have an image, a form, a vision, a Personal God *(Iṣṭa)* to contemplate upon. Ram Prasad, a staunch devotee of Kāli, says, "My Mother is formless. What then is the use of your making images of metal, stone or clay? Make an image out of the stuff of your mind and install it on the lotus seat of the heart." Fatherhood and motherhood are mere distinctions of address and just two aspects of the selfsame Reality.

The Supreme Self is known as Universal Mother because the universe with all its organism evolves in the womb of that Mother. There is a pulse of the Mother-heart. Our sages discovered that pulse of Energy behind *Prakṛti* in the tangible universe. So they sang of God as Mother, as *Prakṛti,* as the Supreme Energy, the Supreme Nature. Mother Grace hearkens all our prayers and meets all our wants. And when She seems to deny what seems our right, in denying She grants. The Supreme Ruler manifests Herself in all Her glory to shower Her blessings upon Her progeny. She fulfils the worthy ends of man's life: *dharma, artha, kāma* and *mokṣa.*

God whom we call Mother has certainly a form. Sweetness has no form but sugar has. Qualities have no form but the things that possess these qualities have form. Similarly, peace, bliss, purity are formless but their possessor does have a form. Therefore God who is an inexhaustible source of such characteristic qualities, virtues and attributes has surely a form and an abode. It is left to us to realise God rather than describe Him.

❄

Nothing that is being written today on metaphysics, can claim to be original or anybody's own. Our scriptures provide wholesome knowledge leaving no margin to additions or subtractions. Adi- Śaṅkarācārya explains that the Gītā is a modified version of the Vedas and that Lord Krishna is only a narrator. Truth always existed much like the geometrical truth that three angles of a triangle are equal to two right angles. The preceptors and great messengers from the High Above are only narrators. Sages alone seem to be the actual founding fathers of the noble Truth.

The idealistic thoughts given by the mystics and seers and by the scriptures are real only when we make them real, otherwise they remain closed books to us. We may be fortunate enough to come in contact with the highest and the holiest, but we must have the openness, the readiness and the receptivity to be blessed.

Search for Truth is as old as man. Whence we come from and where we go to is a mystery that has intrigued mankind. How the universe came into existence and what will be its end has been the enigma of the ages. We must recognise therefore the state of our ignorance and the nature of our beliefs and adventures as our own.

No two schools of thought are identical in their approach to Reality. There is always a grain of truth or a useful doubt in the reasoning. However, the message replete with knowledge, albeit borrowed or plagiarised, always inspires and is welcome. The fortunate one does not entangle himself in the complex labyrinths of philosophy. Without trying to find differences where they do not exist, the earnest seeker should apply the infallible test of the peace of mind brought about by different modes of expressions of the Reality and be convinced and satisfied.

A nobleman who was a student of Gautama, the Buddha, went to the Master and said, "Sir I will practise meditation, the technique of total liberation, that you have taught, only if you answer all my questions." And the student asked a long list of questions including "where does the universe begin, where will it end and who created the same?" Buddha replied: "O foolish one, I have taught you all that you need to know. If an arrow has pierced you, would you immediately try to pull out the arrow and end your suffering, or would you ask endless questions, such as, what the arrow was made of, or who made the arrow or who made the bow and who shot the arrow?"

There is an area of our thinking where the mind and the spirit seem to come closer. The views invariably discussed in this volume have been experienced by the true seekers while exploring into the vast expanse of the Spirit with a searchlight. These crystallised thoughts have been brought out here for the benefit of aspirants in their pursuit of higher goals.

❄

Every man is at war within. While the Spirit wishes to soar high, the flesh pins him down. Life is a flash of a firefly in the night. Man in the world passes suddenly like dust borne on the wind. We come and we go. And in between we try to understand. Once one knows oneself, one is lost in One. If you know your Self, all coming and going ends.

Death has always been a mystery to the mankind. Yet the living ones think and act as if they were immortal. Measureless is the world's misery. Yet man has stuck to it! Desire and hope motivate him at every stage of life. One day all old and dear ones will part with; goods and riches obtained by rigorous efforts will be left behind. The spiral of prosperity will break down because the price of pleasure is pain and both are destructive when they exceed their limits.

This human body, a ship for that matter, has been purchased by us against payment of sacrifices, good deeds and great suffering of several past lives. Success in one's spiritual endeavours should be achieved before one drops this body.

❄

My thoughts on the subject are neither original nor novel. They are part of the eternal Truth as propounded by sages, saints and prophets of yore. The worth of any writing consists in its ability to convey the intended message. Sometimes an exact explanation of a single word involves a wholesome variegated experiences and wisdom. But a different direction strikes and resolves the issue.

Many thoughts, quotations, sayings, verses, parables, anecdotes, illustrations etc. are the result of my own collection from various sources such as newspapers, magazines, books, discourses, discussions, over the last more than 25 years. Unfortunately, sources were seldom noted. Hence my inability to accurately acknowledge the same. Regardless of the sources, however, I wish to express my gratitude to those who may have contributed to this treatise, even though anonymously. This collection, at its best, results in a synergy that, I believe, can be reasonably productive and equally effective. I highly value interdependence rather than dependence or independence.

The basic urge to pen this treatise is twofold: one, the satisfaction of my own soul, to dispel the darkness and to probe into the inner depths of the mind in search of Truth. Two, to carry the message of the sages and saints which revolutionised my outlook towards the world and life as such, to those late risers, in particular, who may be eagerly aspiring for spiritual knowledge. I am grateful for the inspiration and words of wisdom of all those great thinkers and saints who might find them included in the text. The approach is purely of a seeker and not that of a teacher or a preacher. The core of my faith has been that there exists an intangible Power, the Supreme Ruler, whose nature is grace, love and compassion and that life's fulfilment is the realisation of that eternal Presence.

❄

When and how must one start? What happened to that holiday-maker who waited on the sea-shore for the waves to subside so that he could take his bath comfortably? Don't wait anymore on the shore of life. Plunge in and sail across the ocean before it proves too late. Without an aspiration from below, there will not be an answering call from above. Remember, 'now' alone is the all-auspicious occasion to initiate our new plans. This is the only secret of all great achievements - secular or spiritual.

Our advantages fly away. Gather flowers while you may. Defer not till tomorrow for, tomorrow's sun to one may not rise. Pray, Mother Grace bestows Her grace on all Her devotees.

The essence: bridle your passions, curb the desires for gratification of selfish ends, abstain from the base thoughts, display forgiveness, exercise charity and realise the Presence in you showing signs of promise.

Ever since the worshipful Mother assigned this job to me, I have been keen to bring out this song of Her glory and share it with fellow devotees 'at the earliest'. However, She willed a longer and sustained exercise. I bowed to Her Will. She dictated, I jotted. She edited, I recreated. She approved, I treasured and executed. A period of over twelve years has elapsed since. Another guy could have done it much faster. My fortune, however, is greater. While I struggled to think and comprehend, my mind lingered longer in the contemplation of Her resplendent Person and Presence.

C.L Kaushal.

I forget what I was taught; I only remember what I have learnt.

BLESSINGS

(आशीस)

The Enlightened Soul, Sant Baba Nagpal Ji of Shri Adya-Katyayani Shakti Pith Mandir, Chhattarpur, New Delhi.

Dr. Karan Singh
Sri Amir Chandra Shastri (late)
Swami Sarvananda Ji
Prof. Vachaspati Upadhyaya
Dr. Veeracharya Shastri
Swami Satyamitrananda Ji
Mahant Surinder Nath Ji
Swami Bhoomananda Ji
Prof. S.P. Singh
Sri M.P.K. Kutty
Prof. Makrand Pranjape
Acharya Prabhakar Mishra
Pt. Subhash Chandra Shastri
Pt. Lakshmanacharya
Sri Mohan Lal Chopra
Sri Moti Lal Pandit
Swami Pragyananda Ji
Swami Brahmananda Giri Ji
Swami Vishvas Ji
Dr. Vijay Shankar Shukla
Sri Satyanarain Bansal
Sri Narinder Chanchal
Swami Rupnarain Ji
Brig. Dr. Kapil Mohan VSM (Retd)

Smt. Sushma Swaraj
Swami Gokulananda Ji
Dr. Kireet Joshi
Swami Anubhavananda Ji
Swamini Purananda Ji
Swami Adveshananda Ji
Prof. S.R. Bhatt
Prof. Ram Janam Sharma.
Swami Bodhananda Ji
Sri Sharad Chandra Kushal
Sri Vishwanath Ramesh
Sri Shrikrishan Semwal
Dr. Badri Narain Pancholi
Pt.Vijay Shankar Chattarvedi
Sri Sri Maddhobi-Maa
Swami Nityananda Ji
Dr Balbir Singh
Pt. Siyaram Saran
Swami Asanghananda Ji
Sri R.S. Bhardwaj
Swami. Raghvindrananda Ji
Prof. Kripa Narain Misra
Swami Atmachaitanyapuri Ji
Swami Namonaryanji

❄

Sing a song to the unfailing grace of Mother Divine.

THIS STUDY

This study endeavours to offer an exposition of the nature of the Absolute, the Supreme Being, and seeks Its proximity as Divine Mother. God is both our Mother and Father. Motherhood being more intimate and loving, the devotee chooses to address the One without a second as Mother and confides his faith in Her. Calling God as Mother is not at all meant to show any distinction of sex in divinity. It is only a matter of appeal in his approach and faith.

> *"The aim of the religious and devotional writings is to inspire love of God in human beings, and raise them step by step to the level of Self-realisation. This treatise under review comes very close to serve this purpose."*
>
> Prof. Vachaspati Upadhyaya
> in the Foreword.

There are as many paths to God as there are faiths. Every individual has his or her own way to realise God. It is wrong to force one's beliefs on another. The perspective of tolerance and acceptance helps overcome sectarianism. All quarrels and disputes concerning religion simply show lack of spirituality. There is no single mode of behaviour which is absolutely right because all people are not of the same nature and bent of mind. You cannot administer one medicine for all ills.

> *"There is no attempt on his (author's) part to start a new school of thought or a sect or philosophy. Instead it is a saga of faith and total conviction in 'that' faith; that is why he rightly calls it 'An Exposition of Faith'.*
>
> Acharya Sharad Chandra Kushal
> in the Introduction.

❄

Truth Is One, Expressions vary.

PART ONE

For the Inquisitive

(humbly definitive)

"The beginning of all knowledge is the definition of terms. The best aspirants are those who want to know, not those who want to show."

This Part, I earnestly hope, should benefit the novice spiritual seeker a great deal. It will introduce him to the basic spiritual concepts and inspire him to take to his wings to fulfil his aspirations. Even if you have been a seeker for a while, you will be duly compensated for the time spent in gliding through these chapters. You will undoubtedly pick up a few useful cues and shortcuts for enhancement of your spiritual knowledge and wisdom. A fair amount of knowledge of these concepts cannot be over-emphasised in the context of a steady spiritual progress.

"O Bounteous One, You are our Mother. You are our Father. We pray for your Grace. You are the embodiment of infinite energy. Shower on us Thy Grace, endow us with virility, armour us with fortitude."

Realise the divine Presence. Faith transcends reason.

CHAPTER ONE

BRAHMAN, THE ABSOLUTE

THE INDESTRUCTIBLE, transcendental, living entity is called *brahman* and His eternal nature is termed Self. This Supreme Personality of Godhead who is greater than all, is attainable by unalloyed devotion. He is all-pervading and everything is situated in Him.

Bhagavadgīta.

THE ABSOLUTE TRUTH is indestructible. Being indestructible, it is eternal. Being eternal, it is Self-existent; it is Infinite. Being Infinite, it is vast and deep, it is Transcendent and Intelligent. It is because it is vast and deep that it contains all existence. It is because it is Transcendent and Intelligent, that it embraces all existence. It is because it is Infinite and eternal that it fulfils all existence. In vastness and depth, it is like the earth. In transcendent intelligence, it is like heaven. Infinite and eternal, IT is the Infinite itself.

Tsesze.

BRAHMAN is both transcendent and immanent Spirit of the cosmos, pure Consciousness beyond time, space and causality. As the unchanging reality in the individual is called *ātman* (Self), the unchanging Reality in the universe is called *brahman.*

Since the Absolute is the sole substance and ground of the world, It must also be conceived as the seat of infinite energy, power, knowledge and wisdom, beauty, happiness, love and mercy, for we see the manifestation of all this in cosmic system. Thus the Absolute must be conceived as One Omnipotent, Omniscient, Omnipresent, Magnificent, Ever-active Divine Personality.

The Ultimate reality is believed to be a state of equilibrium. The divine Energy is all-pervasive, all-encompassing. This universe, before it was created, existed as Spirit, as *brahman.*

The Absolute does not become. It is ever Itself, never an object, never a subject, and therefore eternally invisible, indivisible, imperishable. *Brahman* is Being, harmonious and complete, whose spirit embraces the whole creation and yet remains apart as Self-sufficient Being.

The absolute Truth is non-conceptual. The moment one begins to think about it, there are only words. The Truth can never become a word. This indeterminate Real is God, the object of pious meditation and highest devotion. We superimpose our impressions and ideas of the higher Being upon the symbols and images. The *rūpa* of Bhagavān (form of God) is beyond our comprehension. Spirit has been called *brahman* but that does not explain what Spirit is, nor does it explain what *brahman* is. God makes his existence known to us through creation and is revealed by his grace to one who seeks him.

The Absolute is a bewildering and indescribable Reality. We coin innumerable names symbolic of the innumerable forms of his manifestation. God manifests in an infinite diversity of ways and also in one integral whole. I see and behold its beauty, the true divinity, everywhere. These are just imaginative approaches. The whole universe is a temple, no doubt. In one sense it is the shrine of the Supreme Being. One can adore anything as God.

We can merely say and think that "God is" but not "what God is like". The divine Essence is imperceptible. God is hidden in all beings in his subtle form. God is present in occult form as oil in oilseeds, as silence in the midst of sound. What the true One in essence is, no one knows. God's reality and man's concept of Reality are two different things.

We cannot catch God. We have to tune ourselves to him in his Omnipresence. Our techniques do not grasp things which have neither dimensions nor weight.

To label is to define; to define is to confine; to confine is to limit; *brahman* is beyond all that. He is Infinite.

Upaniṣads describe the Ultimate Reality by the expression *brahman*, beyond and outside of which nothing exists. *Satyam* (truth), *jñānam* (knowledge) and *anantam* (infinity) are stated to be the nature of *brahman*. These terms signify only the *lakṣaṇā-s* (attributes) which refer to the very nature of the Thing-in-

Itself that is unique to it and without which it would lose its distinctiveness. Unlike an adjective, a *lakṣaṇa* (characteristic mark) cannot be separated from the entity.

He moves because the objects of his creation move. He does not move as he stays pervading the whole universe. He is near as he dwells in the hearts of all beings. He is far as he is beyond the reach of mind and intellect.

Man in his essential nature is divine. Behind the finite, man is *ātman,* ever-free, ever-pure and perfect. This leads us to discover that the same divinity is the basis of the universe as well. The sages termed this as *brahman* - the totality of the Self and the not-Self.

"Whoever knows Him not, he alone knows:
Whoever knows, knows Him not!

The unknowing thinks He is within knowledge,
The knower knows He is beyond knowledge."

Kena Upaniṣad.

IF THE UNDIFFERENTIATED ONE appears manifold to us, it is because of the power of *māyā* or delusion which obliges us to see things as separate rather than as unified in a single field. All humanity is one. We may number the various waves in the sea as separate lines of force but they all represent unfolding of the same tidal water.

ॐ

> The phenomenon is not mysterious. It is the Reality itself which is, to our limited mind, a mystery. This mystery, the reason must accept.

CHAPTER TWO

GOD IS

DOES GOD exist? It is like the story of the fish and the water. Among the fish arose a question as to what the water is. The grandma was asked if there was anything like water and she replied: "Tell me where there is no water and I shall tell you if there is such a thing as water. Similarly, if I can be told where God is not, I can tell you what God is like."

THEY PROVED to me by convincing reasons that God did not exist and I believed them. Afterwards I saw God, for It came and embraced me. And now which one am I to believe? The reasoning of others or my own experience.

Śri Aurobindo.

LOOK at the harmony and rhythm expressed in various laws of nature. Who is that eternal Law-giver who orders these laws to function in strict perfection, obedience and reverence. The sun, the moon, and the earth are hung like electric bulbs. Where is the thread of suspension? Every phenomenal existence has surely got a hand behind it. Each element is true to its nature. Each planet is true to its allotted course. Truth is the law of the entire universe. A single Intelligence must govern all. One unchanging substratum persists in all its splendour behind all this seeming multiplicity of existence.

This infinite Being, the One and the Only spark of life that pervades everything, that glows in everything, resides within us in the form of an indescribable substance. This one Existence is spoken of differently using a host of names.

The making of an earthen pot requires a potter, clay, skill, means and effort. How can we dispense with these requirements for the creation of the universe? Could there be a book without an author, a child without parents, a clock without a maker?

Who created the sun, moon and stars? And who regulates their movement? We believe that nature plays this role. Is not the word "Nature" synonymous with God? God is unknown and imperceptible but immanent.

What if God goes on strike? How good of him that he has never done so despite the fact that he is not treated fairly in things being done on earth. If only once he so decides and orders the sun to cut off the supply of heat and to the moon to stop light and run the oceans dry and finally turns off the oxygen supply ! But he continues to show his mercies. He is One without a second, absolute Perfection (*Pūrṇam)*.

Whether the owl believes or not in the existence of the light of the sun, the sunlight always shines. Whether a person believes or not in the existence of God, the self-effulgent *brahman* shines eternally in the chamber of his heart.

There lived a famous astronomer and another famous scientist who did not believe in God. Both were personal friends. Once the scientist saw at the astronomer's house a model of the solar system installed on a table. The planet could be switched to go around the sun on its own by turning a handle. The scientist was amazed and asked his friend as to who made the model. "Nobody, really. It made itself", answered the astronomer. "Don't be funny, tell me the name of the person who made this model", gestured the scientist. "I am not funny; rather you are funny. Is it not strange that you cannot believe that this model made itself? And yet you believe that the real sun, moon and the whole universe came into being of their own without any maker." The scientist went away with a good dose of food-for-thought and later turned a believer in God.

THE DIVINE PLAYER has been playing his delightful game from eternity. Attune yourself to the divine Designing for harmony. The universe is the outward visible expression of the Truth and the Truth is the inner and unseen reality of the universe.

❄

I THINK TOO MUCH OF MYSELF. HOW CAN I THINK SO MUCH OF GOD?

God is a nameless and formless phenomenon - the universal consciousness. The *avatāra-s,* messengers and prophets who manifest as God on earth, do get names e.g. Kṛṣṇa, Rāma, Śiva, Buddha, Jesus, Mahāvira, Guru Nānak, Mohammed &c. But the names are names. Behind these names is only one Consciousness which is universal and nameless.

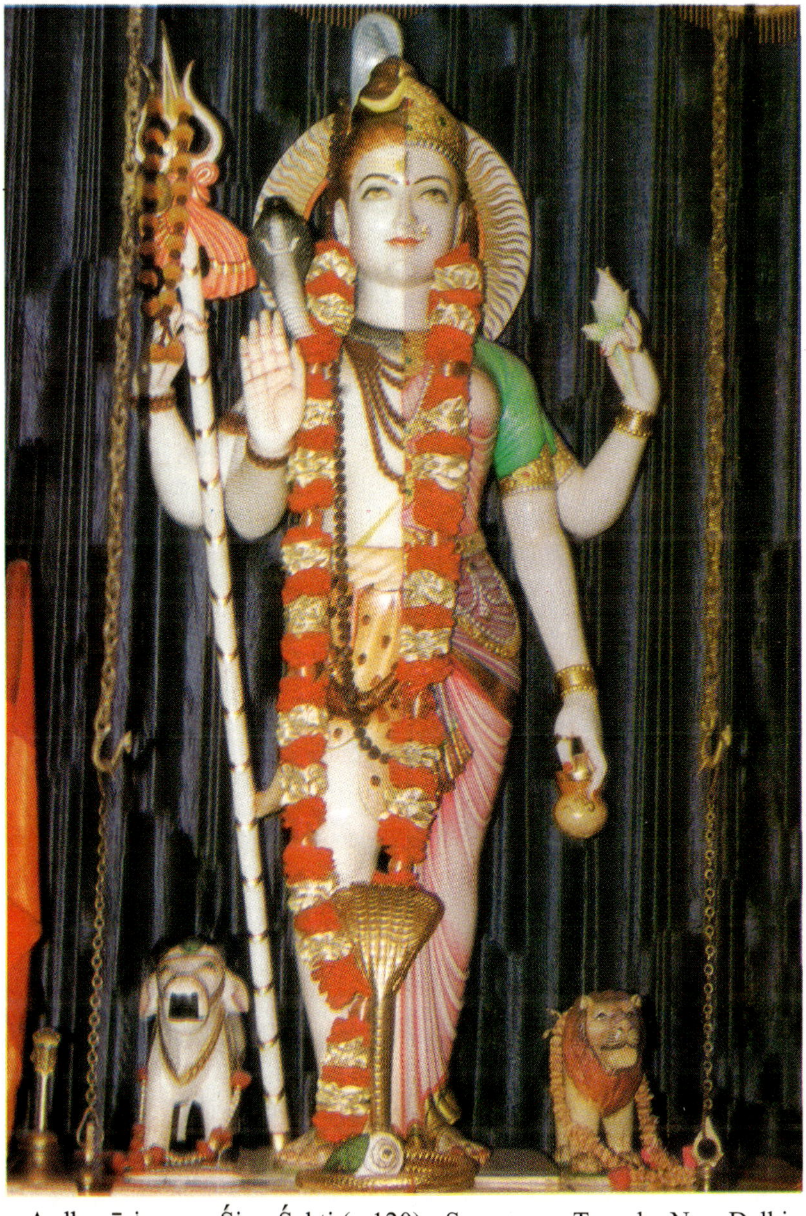

Ardhanāriṣvara : Śiva-Śakti (p.120) - Saraveṣvar Temple, New Delhi

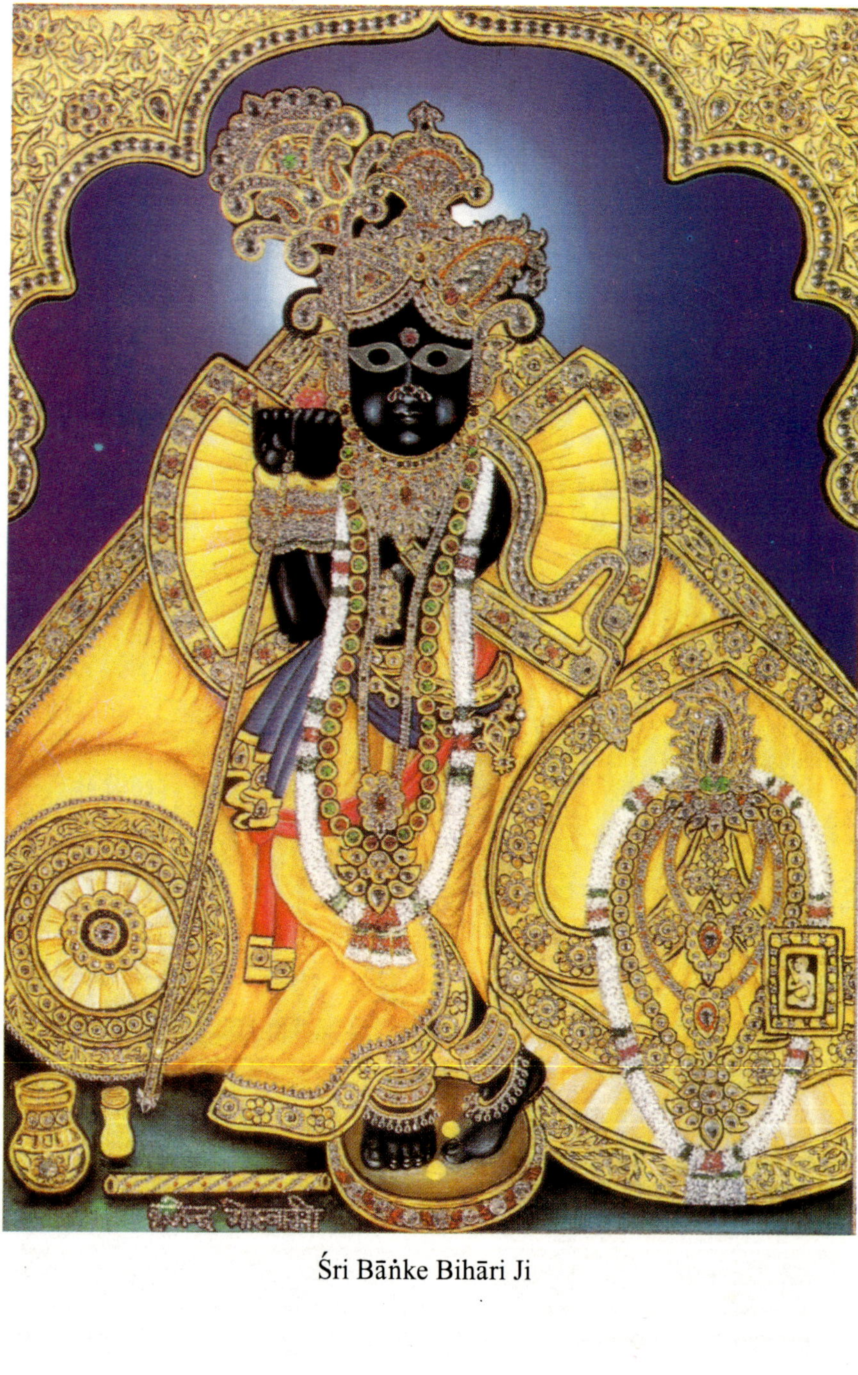

Śri Bāṅke Bihāri Ji

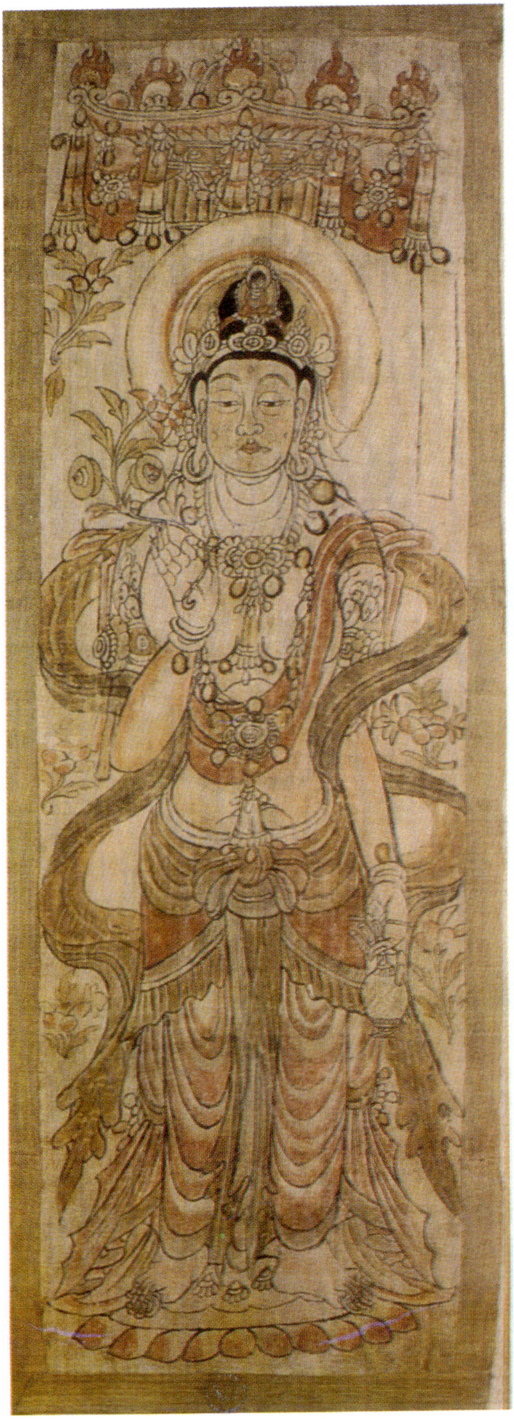

Avalokītesvra

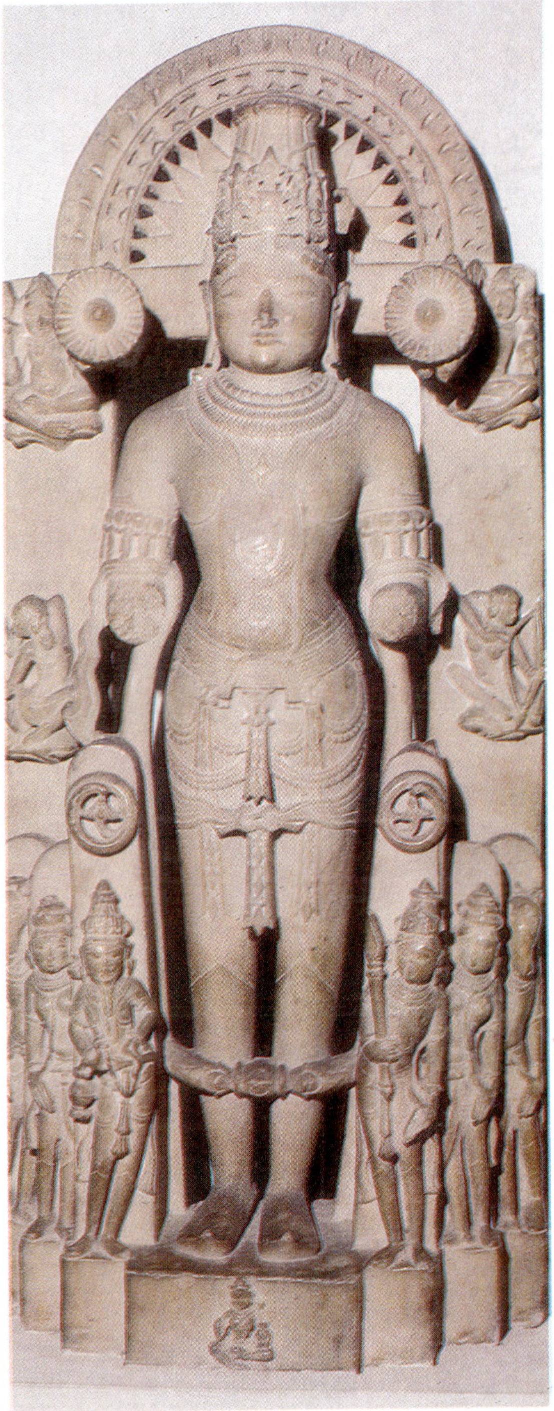

Sūrya

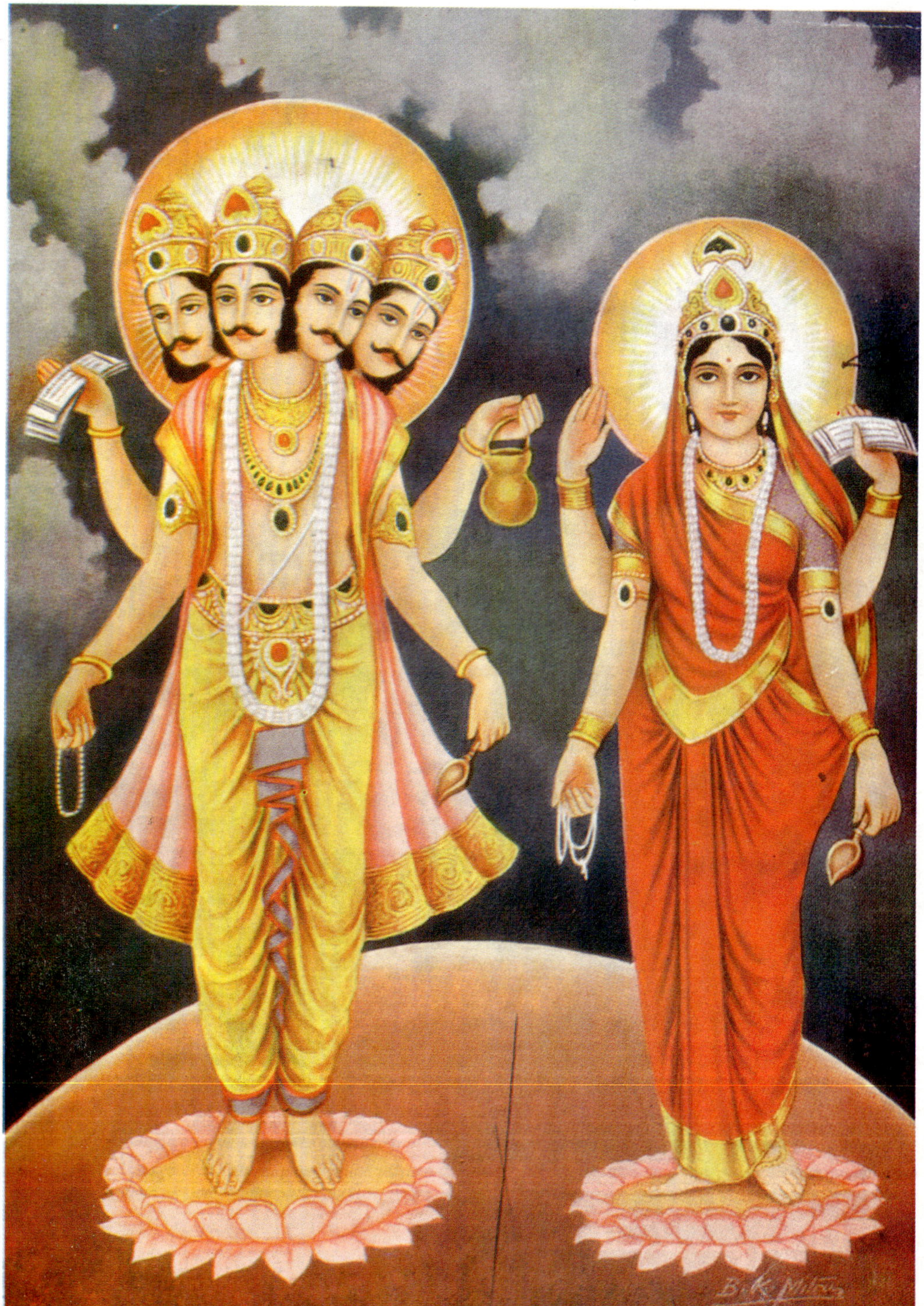

Shri Savitrī - Brahamā

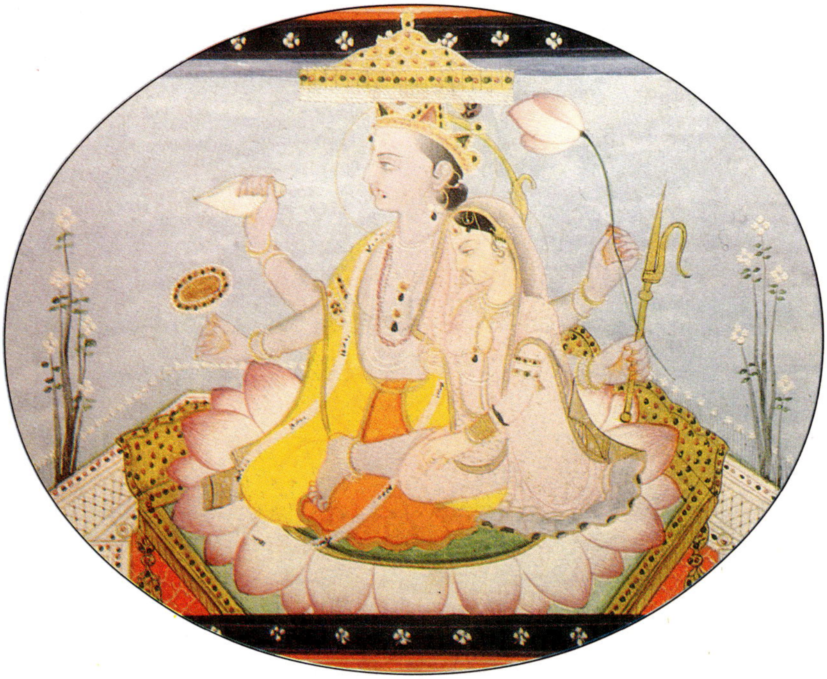

Vishnu and Lakshmi

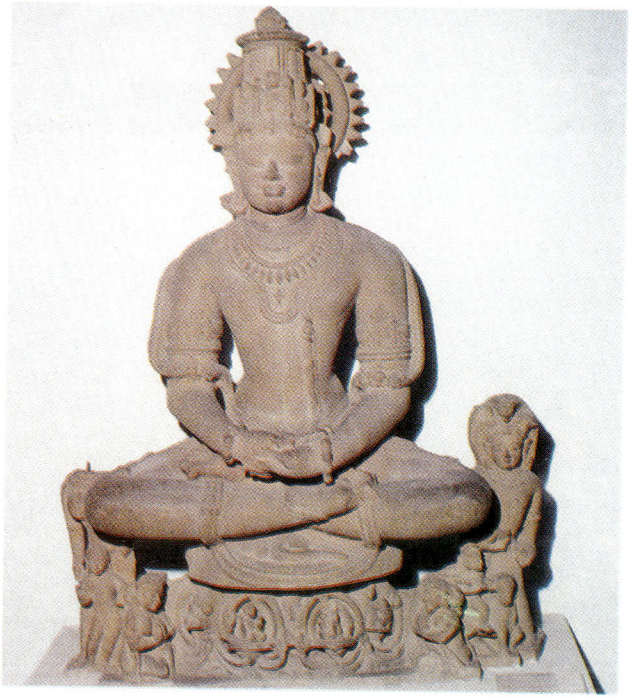

Yoga Narayana

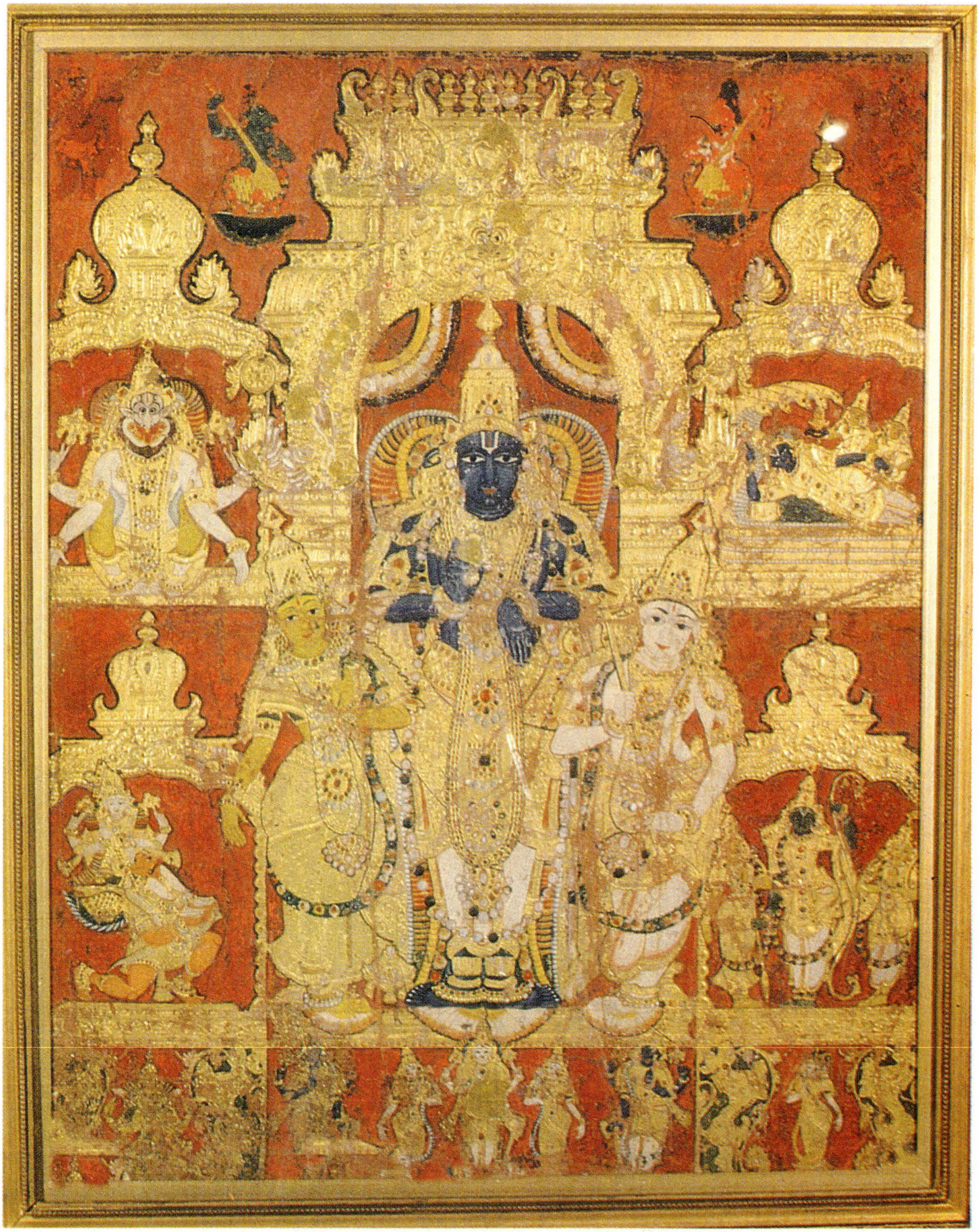

Viṣṇū and His Incarnations

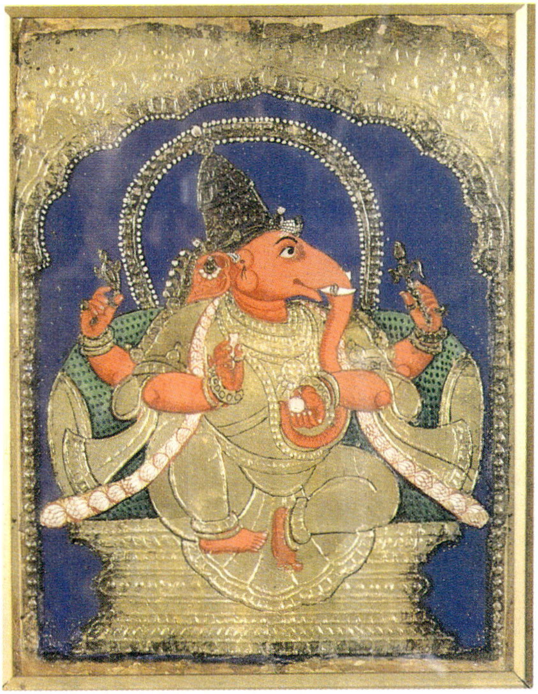

Lord Ganeṣa

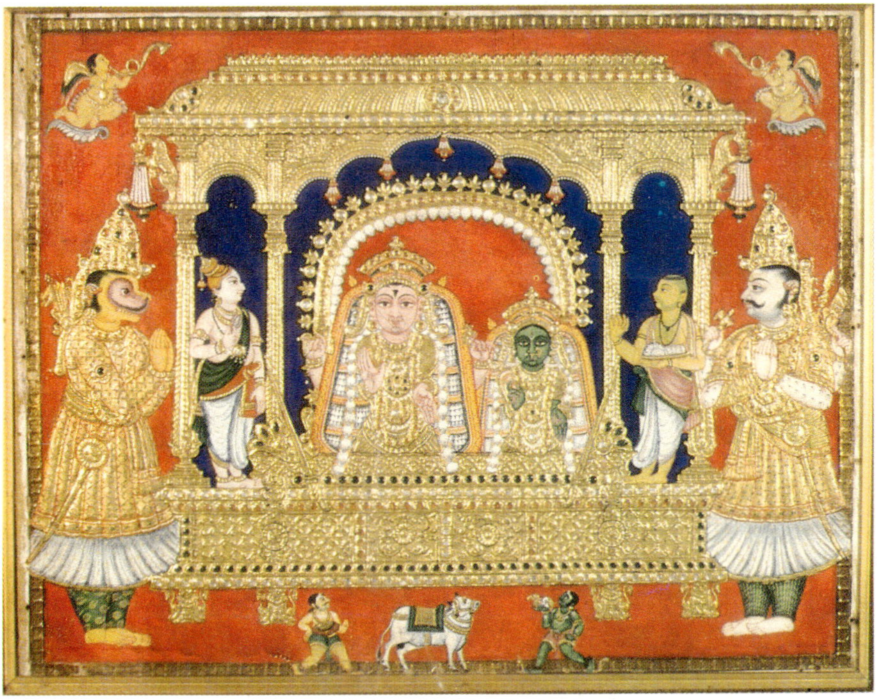

Worship of Śiva-Pārvatī (p.127)

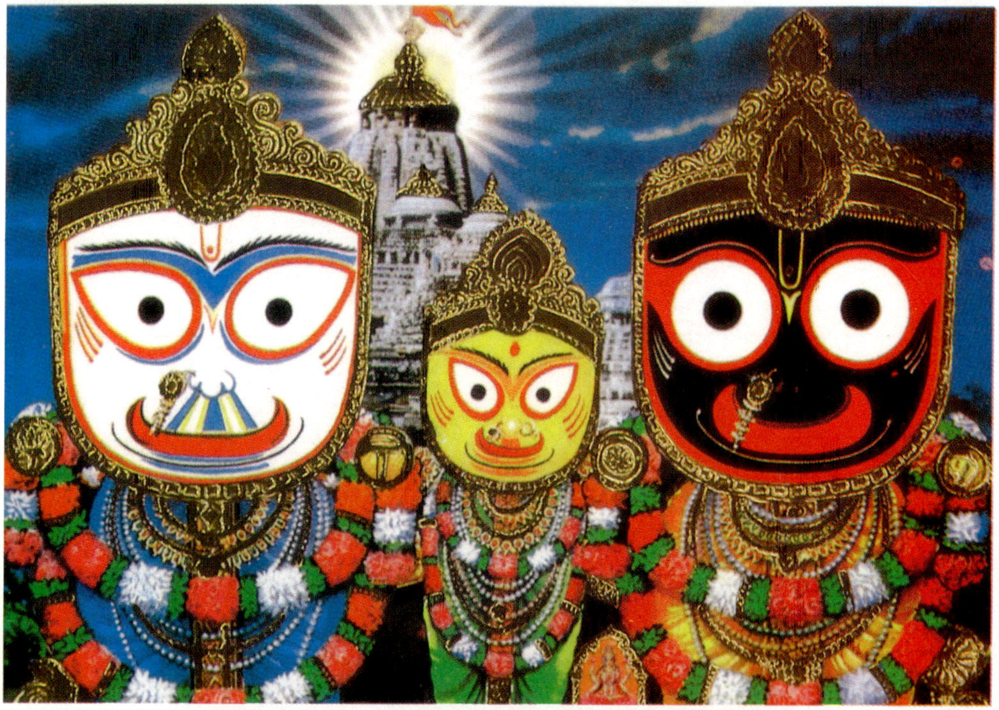

Bhagvān Jaganath

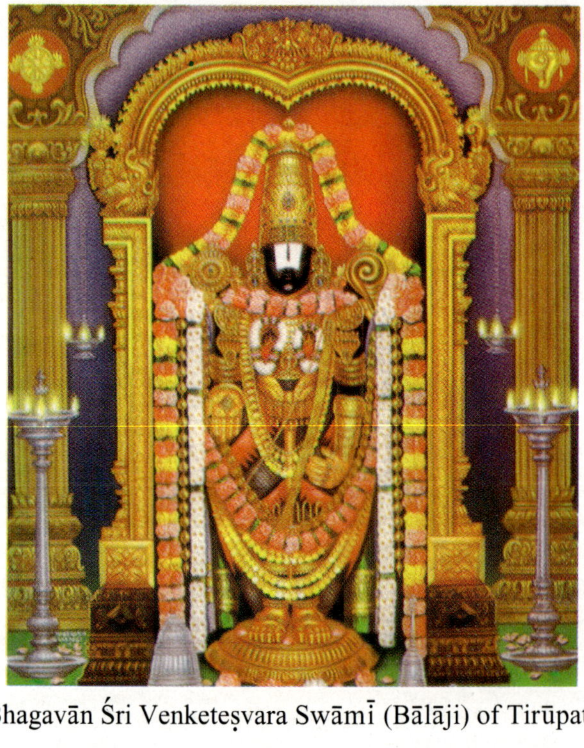

Bhagavān Śri Venketeșvara Swāmī (Bālāji) of Tirūpatī

CHAPTER THREE

PERSONAL-IMPERSONAL GOD

(*Saguṇa - Nirguṇa Brahman*)

> How does it matter whether God is Personal or Impersonal, *saguṇa-sākāra* or *nirguṇa-nirākāra,* so long as there is none second to Him? I visualise the unknown in terms of the known. Do not project any image upon God. Just fill any image with the Spirit which is God, (*sat-cit-ananda*).
>
> Śri. Rāmakriṣna Paramahansa.

> "THERE is only *nirguṇa brahman. Saguṇa brahman* is a mere appearance for the sake of pious meditation of *bhaktas* (devotees)."

GOD, though one, has been recognised to have two aspects: the manifest aspect and the unmanifest aspect. The manifest aspect of *Paramātma* is united with *māyā* (*guṇa-s*) and is known as *saguṇa* (with attributes) and *sākāra* (with form). The unmanifest aspect of God, devoid of *guṇa-s,* is the *nirguṇa* (without attributes) and *nirākāra* (without form). The All-pervasive *nirguṇa brahman*, although continuing in its formless state, also manifests itself in this world with attributes and form. But there is no difference in the two states. Everything in this world is said to have a *nirguṇa* aspect behind it.

The relation between the Absolute and the relative as also between light and shadow is not of mutual dependence. A shadow depends on light but light does not depend for its existence on the shadow. Manifestation of the Absolute implies a Being and a Becoming. The Being is the supreme Reality (the Self) and the Becoming is the phenomenal reality.

From the concrete, man can proceed to the abstract by constant practice. The manifestation of the Personal God is often a spiritual form seen only by the purified soul. In whatever name or form one desires to know God, in that very name and form he will see God.

To attribute a body to God is to recognise His omnipresence. He is thus brought within the grasp of our mind more easily than when He is described in terms beyond comprehension. Thus a devotee can usefully think of a concrete deity and call him by any name..

To draw an analogy between the state of *nirguṇa* and *saguṇa brahman*, a comparison may be made between the radio receiver detecting sound from a perfectly silent radio wave and the human mind converting the *nirguṇa brahman* into colourful and lively *saguṇa brahman*.

Devotion expressed through formal image worship is a sort of aesthetic approach to God. Men of devotion who yearned for the holy vision of the adorable Deity, naturally wanted to keep His memory ever fresh in their minds. Accordingly, they made images or idols of the most Beautiful. The ideal Idol was thus always present before the eyes. The devotee invokes God to come down from His celestial abode and dwell in the image in order that he can offer oblations to Him. He offers flowers and fruits not to the inanimate image but to the Indwelling divine Being.

Saguṇa brahman and *nirguṇa brahman* should not be considered as antagonistic, though the reasoning faculty tries to see a difference between the two. What in fact is the true nature of the *brahman,* whether He is *saguṇa-sākāra* (possessed of qualities and form), or *nirguṇa-nirākāra* (devoid of qualities and form) is known only to *brahman* Himself. The devotee's mind must have before him an apparent object of worship representing the invisible Absolute. Attributing a body to the formless does not limit the Unlimited. It only helps the devotee to have a glimpse of something which he cannot see otherwise.

Every object of creation is a symbol of infinity and infinity may be reached through the worship of any one of its finite symbols. To enjoy flowers for their captivating loveliness is one thing, but far greater is to see behind their beauty and purity, the face of God. God is immanent in the infinite beauties of the finite.

Worship of the *nirguṇa-nirākār brahman* is extremely difficult for embodied beings. Constant contact with the world of objects has nurtured the *jīva-s* to see things in concrete forms only. Hence the need for a *saguṇa* God.

Śaṅkarācārya seeks to render clear the distinction between *nirguṇa* and *saguṇa brahman* by reference to an ordinary example. A shepherd comes to the stage in the role of a king, engages in warfare, conquers the territory and becomes the ruler. It is evident that the shepherd is the king only from the audience point of view and not so in relation to the actual mode of his being. Similarly, the description of *brahman* as the very essence of "Being-Consciousness-Bliss" seeks to bring out what it is in its real nature whereas its description as the cause, creator etc. of the world brings out what is true of it from the relative or human point of view.

Our scriptures proclaim that there are two types of knowledge to be acquired by men: *Parāvidyā* (higher knowledge) and *aparāvidyā* (lower knowledge). The lower knowledge consists of the sacred *Vedas*, the phonetics, grammar, etymology, code of rituals, etc. *Parāvidyā* is that knowledge by which the ultimate Reality is realised.

THE INFINITE is like the fire implicit in the wood. The finite is like the explicit flame which all can see.

The Absolute without form is my Father and with form is my Mother.

Kabīr.

卐

He made all things visible and Himself remained invisible.

CHAPTER FOUR

MAN NEEDS GOD

> DIVINE BELOVED, I have nothing to offer Thee, for all things are Thine. I grieve not that I cannot give, for nothing is mine, nothing is mine. Here I lay at Thy feet my limbs, my life, my thoughts and my speech; for they are Thine, they are Thine.
>
> *Swami Yogananda.*

MAN needs God more than a baby needs mother. Baby 'outgrows' the need of the mother. The man 'in-grows' the need of God, whatever his achievements or age, whether he is aware of it or not.

God is man's elemental need to reach the fulfilment of his life as a tree which requires sunshine, air, water for its same purpose. There is a kind of nourishment our souls crave for. Unless this nourishment is provided for, the souls remain wanting. God alone can fulfil this want and make our lives happy and blissful. We may fail to realise and appreciate, or pretend not to do so, but all of us do need God.

To live without God is really dying while living because when disease and old age are creeping on, you feel that the end of your joys has come. But when you love God, you have a different experience. You see that life is not ending but beginning with Him, and that endless romance with the Infinite is in store. Those who love God will make death their footstool.

Old age is waiting like a tigress. Life ebbs away as if it were water from out of a broken pot. Darkness is not dispelled by the mentor of the word 'lamp'. What then is there to be done? Realise God. It is never too early to start. It may otherwise prove too late.

When God created universe, His inmost spirit entered into all that was created. It is given to man, rare among created species, to know Him. If a man dies without realising the unity of the Self, the *brahman*, he never reached the true goal of life and will have to come back. The cycle of birth and death continues.

There is an urge to be happy. There must be something to satisfy this urge. This something is God - an ocean of happiness.

If God did not exist, it would be necessary to invent One.

God is not bribed by beautiful edifices. He comes to the tear-washed altar of the heart that is continuously calling unto Him.

When God is realised, the world never appears empty. Believing firmly in God makes us feel that we are not isolated and certainly never alone.

What is the source of energy which impels life to the world of names and forms while Itself remains nameless and formless? Seek therefore the true source, the God, the Absolute. You are here only to complete this mission.

It is faith in God that sustains life. God is a psychological necessity. Almost instinctively man turns to God in times of crisis.

> MY SON, a time will come when you are enveloped by darkness after the joys of life have passed away. Then you will need a refuge to find peace. Let's realise therefore the need for this Refuge, that is God.
>
> Śri Rāmakŗśna.

SEEK THE SUBTLE AND INVISIBLE. TRANSCEND HUMANNESS TO REALISE GOD.

A Prayer

O Adorable Lord of Mercy and Love!
Salutations and prostration unto Thee.
Thou art Existence-Consciousness-Bliss Absolute.
Thou art Omnipresent, Omnipotent and Omniscient.
Thou art the Indweller of all beings.

Grant us an understanding heart,
Equal vision, balanced mind,
Faith, devotion and wisdom,
Grant us inner spiritual strength
To resist temptations and to control the mind.

Free us from egoism, lust, greed, hatred, anger
and jealousy.
Fill our hearts with divine virtues.

Let us behold Thee in all these names and forms.
Let us serve Thee in all these names and forms.

Let us ever sing Thy glories.
Let Thy *nāma* be ever on our lips.
Let us abide in Thee for ever and ever.

Swami Śivānandaji

God in fact has left nothing for us to want. All what is required e.g., earth, water, fire, air, ether, sun, moon, stars, are there.

❄

The Truth which is God cannot be expressed in words, but it is that Truth which enables us to speak whatever we say.

CHAPTER FIVE

Faith in God

(*Āstha - Śraddhā*)

He who has faith has everything, and he who lacks faith, lacks everything. It is faith in the *nāma* of the Lord that works wonders; faith is life and doubt is death.

Śri Rāmakṛśna

Without faith there is no knowledge, without knowledge there is no virtuous conduct, without virtues there is no deliverance, without deliverance there is no perfection *(nirvāna).*

Uttaradhyāyana Sūtra.

Something deeper in us becomes aware of a Truth which is not palpable to the physical senses. This awareness is the starting point for an aspirant. This faith is the vehicle that carries the devotee to the deity. Like life, faith is also a growing process.

Faith in its spiritual context does not mean an unquestioned surrender or an emotional tribute at the altar of a symbol or idea. Faith means that psychological and intellectual understanding without which not even our day-to-day life business could be efficiently transacted. Faith in ourselves is the nucleus of all our achievements.

Faith is the odour of divinity that reaches man before he discovers it. Faith in God is the foundation of spiritual life. It is a positive attitude and not superstitious acceptance of the unknown. It is made of noble and sacred feelings.

Is it possible for us to know, by reasoning, things beyond our sense-perceptions? Not exactly. Belief is the result of experiments done by elevated divine souls. True knowledge, they say, is not in thought but in intuition. Even scientific results are the outcome of intuition only. Things which are inconceivable should not be subjected to the canons of logic.

A course of destiny is ordained by God for every living being. If you put faith and be one with the chartered course, you will at once embrace harmony and be at peace. That will release at least some pressure of your tension and sorrows. Faith and reverence generates a unique energy which continues to give strength to the seeker and enables him to attain his goal by virtue of that strength. Through a clay image of Dronācārya, a teacher of archery, and by dint of faith and reverence alone, Ekalavya, the Bhīl youth, acquired proficiency in archery, which caused wonder to Arjuna, nay, to Dronāchārya himself. True discipline stems only from reverence and faith.

There is no uniformity of opinion on anything - material, philosophical or spiritual. Why? Man wants proof of evidence, a concrete perception of the subject of belief. Is it possible to prove anything to the satisfaction of everybody? It is only the belief in the 'subject' that takes one forward in its quest.

Faith is like a fond mother who can never fail to save her trusting child from dangerous situations. Faith removes anxiety, brings peace and joy, earns grace, leads to true wisdom. It can directly hold on to the Truth vouchsafed in the *śruti-s.*,

Emotions will not weigh with the intellectuals. The intellect must go via reason and emotion via faith. Emotions cannot doubt, reason cannot trust. Even if reason is able to trust, it trusts only because there is no reason to disbelieve. The trust is just a logical conclusion. Descartes used doubt as a technique to move towards faith. "I must not trust until there is no reason left for any doubt"

I do not know who the Lord is, where the Lord is. Whether It is He or She? But I do see His glories. I see the sun, the moon, the order in the creation, the unchanging substratum in all its splendour, the glitters in the flame of the lamp, the light of my intellect. This makes me a believer in the existence of the divine Absolute: I become an *āstika.*

Faith is a prerequisite to *jñāna* (knowledge) leading to the practices of *karma* and *bhakti yoga.* It means trust in God who will fulfil one's wishes. Faith is thus the carrier of the desire to the deity on whom the devotee relies for the fulfilment. *Śraddha* is the feeling that elicits *bhakti* (devotion) in the hearts of the devotees.

Bhakti suffuses the actions of those devotees who express their faith.

Faith is the first and last word. If one has faith, the goal is almost in sight. Blind faith is the only kind to have, for it is not faith if it is not blind.

Faith is not a possession. Faith is a decision, faith is an action. By placing our faith in God does not mean that we are going to eliminate all our troubles and tribulations. On the contrary, our test may be harder than that of others. However, when we acquire faith in the Eternal and experience the Reality, the sorrows of the world do not disturb us. Man begins to achieve when he begins to believe.

"How clear is the path of one who believes?
He lives with honour and with honour he leaves.
Through faith, the mind and intellect find concentration,
And to the seeker are revealed all the stages of enlightenment.

Through faith one will not receive blows in the hereafter,
nor be subjected to death's terror."

Two yogis were practising austerities with a view to realise God. One day Nārada, the divine sage, was passing by their hermitage, when one of them asked him, "Are you coming from heaven?" Nārada replied, "Yes, that is so." The yogi said, "Do tell me what you saw the Lord doing in heaven." Nārada replied, "The Lord was playing by making camels and elephants pass through the eye of a needle." At this the yogi observed: "There is nothing in it to marvel at. Nothing is impossible with God." But the other man exclaimed: "Nonsense! That is impossible! It only shows that you have never been to the Lord's abode."

The first one had the faith of a child. Unless we become like little children we cannot enter this holy kingdom of faith.

"The faith of every man, O Arjuna, accords with his nature."

Bhagvadagītā.

Faith is the pointer of the soul that leads to divine abode. True faith does not suppress doubts. There are no laid down rules for faith. Questions determine the origin of faith.

When a person is ill, he calls for a doctor because he has faith in him. Whenever we are in need of human assistance, we call on those who can fulfil our needs because we have faith in them. Similarly there are souls who have unquestioning faith in God, and naturally in their hour of need, they call on Him for assistance.

Faith in the Divine is the root of our being. We owe a certain obligation to our spiritual Being and when we do not fulfil it, we weaken our spiritual fibre. We cannot have a true sense of balance unless we have an increasing measure of spiritual consciousness.

The marks of faith are peace and hope. As faith springs up in the heart, it clears five negativities (*vikāra-s*): lust, ill-will, mental sloth, spiritual pride and doubt.

> "We need wings of love, not of logic. Logic pulls you downwards. Love takes you towards the stars. Allow the mystic in you and you have found what is worth finding."
>
> Osho.

"I love you, I adore you, I trust you, I believe you. I need you. I seek you, I beseech you. I salute you, I look forward to meet you. I bow to you, Glory be to you. Praise be to you, O Mother Grace, the refuge of all. "

MOST PEOPLE believe in God because God represents the perfect Ideal of mankind. Faith is a divine gift. Believing firmly in God makes us feel that we are not isolated and certainly never alone. When faith is granted, an individual effort is indispensable to hold on to it.

❄

The Supreme Being as the infinite ocean can also be understood from a different angle by the spiritual aspirants. The various gods manifest as Its waves and the mortals attached to their bodies are like the bubbles.

CHAPTER SIX

DIVINE NAME

(nāma kī mahimā)

"I sing to Thee,
O Singer of the Ages !
Thy name, O Love, is ineffable !
And Thy glory is unthinkable !
Thy abode is in the heart of man
And in the cycle of the universe !
A worm though I be born
May Thy name be ever in my mind.
That one boon I ask of Thee,
O, the Creator of the
universe."

❄

There is no *sādhanā* easier than the repetition of *nāma.* It can take you to the highest spiritual eminence by giving you the all-comprehensive knowledge of God. *Śri* Rāmakṛśna had gone through various *sādhanā-s* for years. And ultimately, whenever anybody went to him for spiritual advice, he would ask him to take only to *nāma* of God. This is the essence of all *sādhanā-s.*

Swami Rāmdāsa.

The form of an object may be known but it cannot be recognised apart from the name, whereas it is possible to meditate on *nāma* without seeing the form and have the attendant feeling. *Nāma* is greater than both, the named and form, and brings them under sway. Rāma redeemed only one woman, Ahalya, but his *nāma* has shown light to the millions.

Nāma and the named are One. It is the *nāma* that makes the named intelligible and thus superior to *rūpa* (form).

Every form is His form. Every name is His name. He can be invoked in any name and in any form. Repetition of *nāma* purifies the mind, intellect and senses, fills one with abundant spiritual energy, takes the *sādhaka* nearer and nearer to God. Drink the nectar of divine *nāma* constantly. The immaculate *nāma* of God is immortal.

Nāma is the mediator between the abstract Absolute and the personified Absolute. *Nāma* is effective whether it is uttered with love or with spite.

We think of God through his *nāma* but we have to ultimately realise the Reality behind the *nāma*. The Ultimate is a bewildering reality and is unnameable. But we coin names to make it real, names derived from the numerous forms of his manifestations and emanations. Mystic visions are created though God's attributes will only be partial because every word uttered will be an imperfect image of the Reality.

Nāma uttered knowingly or unknowingly burns the sins of man as fire burns fuel. Like a strong drug taken by mistake or a *mantra* uttered unknowingly, *nāma* has its effect on persons uttering the same.

Chant His *nāma* and your life will be sublime. *Nāma* is filled with countless potencies of *śakti*. The power of *nāma* is ineffable, infinite.

The Absolute must be conceived as One omnipresent, omnipotent, omniscient, divine Personality. Call It *Viṣṇu*, *Śakti*, *Śiva*, Rāma or *Kṛṣṇa*. Any suitable name might as appropriately be applied to this nameless One conveying the same significance.

The power derived out of the recitation of God's name which reveals His attributes, will root out the gloom in one's heart. Devotion should be cultivated from young age in order to reduce the workload in old age. *Bhakti* is a universally accepted emotional approach to the highest Truth.

Mahatma Gandhi spoke of Rāma *nāma*, a sovereign remedy and an unfailing panacea for all ills. *Nāma* itself is the *rūpa* (form). *Nāma* is not only the *upāya* (means) to reach the Lord, but also an *upeya*, (the end), the holy goal itself.

When you say "milk", ideas of the properties of milk come to your mind. Name stands for the absolute Reality whose nature is pure bliss. Attune your mind with the Name and you are filled with bliss.

Repetition of *nāma* leads to meditation, cleanses the filth of ego.

The divine Name can bring you face to face with the Lord and make you love all beings and creatures. The Name is the foundation of spiritual and ethical life.

"The sky is the platter,
The sun and the moon are the lights,
The sandalwood's fragrance is the incense,
What a wonderful *ārtī* it is!
The wind is the fly whisk
And all the forests Your flowers.
Oh, You destroyer of life and death!
It's an unending strain,
the melody of
Your *nāma*."

Guru Nanak.

God is intangible but this intangible Being is present with us in one tangible aspect and that is *nāma*. The *rūpa* of God is beyond comprehension but *nāma* and *nāmī* (named), the Lord and His name, are identical. In Him are woven the heavens. In Him the life-webs are fastened like the spokes to the nave of the chariot. Realise the vision of the scenario.

When we worship the names, we worship what is behind the names, the transcendental. The seen may be true and may not be true but the seer is always true. The dream may be true or untrue but the one who saw the dream is true.

> I DO NOT ask of Thee, O Mother, riches or salvation. I seek no happiness, no knowledge. My only prayer to Thee is that as the breath of life forsakes me, I may still chant Thy Holy name.
>
> Ādi Śaṅkarācārya.

❄

I wish to have a purpose in everything I do, even in my eating, drinking and sleeping, to do all to the glory of God.

CHAPTER SEVEN

Divine Love and Devotion

(*Anurāga and Bhakti*)

> He who created us yearns for our love. We shall never be happy till we give it to Him. The feet of the Lord and the hands of the devotee are all that is required to consecrate this act of love.

In divine love the Lord is the beloved in the eyes of the devotee and the devotee is the beloved in the eyes of the Lord. When you love God, you have to place yourself mentally in the presence of God Himself as if the Almighty is looking at you. Will you then commit any mistake or do any wrong? You will be just right and true to yourself.

Divine love *(anurāga)* is an important part of spiritual life. It is not to be shown off. It should be nurtured in secret. Allow it to grow into the heart. People 'fall' in love ! They could very well 'rise' in love. Earthly passion is not love; it is *kāma* (lust). Love is the core value from which all values flow. It is an emotion which is highly intense and soothes the heart, a feeling of one's own.

The majesty of love lies far beyond the reach of intellect. The greatest law of God is love which is the key to all problems. Love is a gift from the God to man. One who loves and obeys is the beloved of the Beloved.

Pure love arises in the heart of the aspirant to the form of descent of Grace Divine. As soon as he is ready to receive, the Grace descends. The Divine is always on the lookout for the soul who deserves the descent of grace in whom the grace will fructify.

Devotion *(bhakti)* is cultivation of a 'friendly' sentiment for the Lord, the Supreme Being, who is beyond all desires. *Bhakti* is both a feeling and an action. Pure love is verily devotion.

Devotion is the steady remembrance of that which one seeks to find when all his thoughts, words and actions align themselves in the direction of Supreme will.

Devotion is not different from divine Grace. Love pours itself without reason, without being called for and devotion galvanises the two.

The love of God is the greatest virtue that a man can ever cultivate. The path of love is like the relationship between a child and the heart of his mother. Without love and devotion, awareness of the Divine cannot be experienced.

The nature of a devotee's love for the Divine has been likened to that of

- a fish for water, without which it cannot live.
- a moth for flame in which it strives to consume itself.
- a *chakor* (bird) for the moon which it constantly gazes.
- a faithful wife for her husband who is all-in-all for her.

In his own heart the devotee mentally materialises his love for the *Iṣṭa* (his chosen deity). Divine love rests in the mind. Where there is love in the heart, no language is necessary.

True devotion asks only for the divinity, not anything through It. Divine is the soul of the cosmos. Anything which stirs the soul from within can be regarded as a manifestation of God.

Love is a supreme force which the eternal Divine sent down into an obscure world so that it might bring Its beings back to Him. There is no substitute for love divine.

When you think of the Lord, you are a devotee. Devotion is a feeling of the deepest love and supreme attachment to God. The flame of divine love burns in the heart of the thirsting devotee day and night.

The supreme deity to be loved is the indwelling Spirit, pure consciousness, which animates and activates the body, the mind and the intellect and is within and without.

For those who seek to attain the Lord, Love alone is the highest discipline. Love consists in harnessing all one's enjoyments for the gratification of one's highest object, purging himself of all the cravings for the enjoyments of the world. A devotee endowed with such unalloyed love attains supreme peace.

Prema bhakti (loving devotion) for the Divine, like the way a fish loves water, is considered best. She lives not a moment without water.

Love does not manifest in human beings alone. Its presence is there in plants, in the very stones, in birds and in animals. It is so easy to detect its presence!

Love grows in silence like the bud blooms in the stillness of the night. This love *sans* murmurs, *sans* music, *sans* words made by His unseen hand through His unsung lullaby, mingles with the promise and love of the Divine.

God is love, Love is His name, Love is His essence, Love is His colour, Love is His presence. A single moment of love is Eternity itself. To be in a prayerful mood is to be in love with the Absolute.

Only a few hearts are tailored for love; only a few hearts are ready to receive the gift of love. The heart of a lover constantly burns with the fire of love. Love is that music which can be played on every instrument.

To have an object is not a necessity in the love-play. You can walk in love, sleep in love, eat in love, drink in love. Everything that comes in contact with you receives your love. A flower may be on a path where no one passes but still it exudes perfume. Play with God. Sing His glory. Enjoy the fun. The greatest romance is with the Infinite.

Love in essence is the joy of identity. It finds its supreme expression in the bliss of union. Love alone can put an end to the sufferings of the world.

If the child gets lost, the mother runs like a mad person in search of him. Did you ever cry for the Mother in your grief of separation in the same manner? Man's quest is lukewarm. It has not reached the boiling point.

The mother forgives her son even when no one else will. That kind of love exemplifies God's love. He forgives his children no matter what sins they might have committed.

Without faith and devotion all virtues and blessings are insipid as is any quantity of condiments without salt.

Vain indeed is all struggle for spiritual life if there is no love in one's heart. True love is the yearning to be free, to be one with the Infinite.

Liquids keep their level; yet water in two separate vessels does not seek to establish the same level. Both the containers must be connected together. Then only the scientific truth comes to play. Unless the aspirant establishes his contact with God, no divinity can flow in him. The 'contact' is a precondition for the spiritual growth to flourish.

Dhruva and Prahlāda are outstanding examples of devotion which give hope to the devotees. Prahlāda affords an example of perceiving God in all creation.

> 'I love dark colour because the Mother who enchants the world with dishevelled hair is dark-coloured.
>
> Ramaprasada.

The *bhakta* sports in the Self, rejoices in the Self. He hugs the great Beloved, kisses Him and passes his days and nights with Him in His bosom. Separation makes him mad.

God Himself gives equal regard to His devotees. *Śrī* Kṛiṣṇa says: "To my devotees, I act as if I have no control over myself and they hold sway over me. I love my *bhakta-s* very dearly. They have taken entire possession of my heart, over which I have lost all control."

Rāma and Lakṣmaṇa visited Pampā Lake. Lakṣmaṇa saw a crow very eager for water. Again and again it went to the edge of the water but would not drink. He asked Rāma about it. Rāma said: "Brother, this crow is a great devotee of God. Day and night it repeats the name of Rāma. Its throat is parched with thirst but still it won't drink it for fear of missing a repetition of Rāma's name."

Just as the burning fire reduces fuel to ashes, similarly the devotion to the supreme Spirit destroys all sins completely. The true value of devotion lies in the mental attitude and not in the outward action.

When I sit calm and silent in the hour of dawn, there comes my Mother. She talks with words of Love which I alone can hear. "You are my divine Lover, O *Māṃ*, dye me in your own hue."

Meera's object of her devotion is the paramour par excellence: "My love! He is here inside. He does not leave, He doesn't need to arrive".

Divine love is unlimited in essence and expression because it is experienced by the soul through the soul. The more you feel this love, the more you will be intoxicated.

God is love. He who abides in love abides in God and God abides in him. Where there is love and protection, can the face of divinity be far behind?

WHAT IS lasting, eternal, immortal and infinite, is indeed worth having, worth conquering, worth possessing and worth loving. It is divine Grace, divine Name, divine Light, divine Love, divine Life, supreme Peace, perfect Joy.

The pathway of love is the ordeal of fire. Those who take the plunge into the fire, attain eternal bliss. Those who stand afar, looking on, are scorched by the flames. Love is a priceless thing only to be won at the cost of death.

CHAPTER EIGHT

DIVINE GRACE

(Kṛpā)

(To get more than one qualifies)

THROUGH grace She reveals Herself. We can see Her only if She turns Her light in Her own face. The accumulated sins of countless lives vanish by a single glance of the Lord. The wind of Divine Grace is incessantly blowing. Lazy sailors on the sea of life do not take advantage of it. Kālīdāsa, from the state of an ignorant rustic, became a poet at once through the grace of Mother Sarasvati.

Śri Rāmakṛṣna.

CONTRARY to common notions, the Divine Grace comes to us in the form not only of plenty but of scanty also. The devotee must comprehend this subtle truth and be prepared to face life as it comes. Destitution and misery are also the manifestations of Her Grace and one should love to learn it sooner than soon.

INNUMERABLE persons were lifted by Mother's grace. It is the nature of water to flow downwards but the sun's rays lift it up towards the sky. Likewise, it is the very nature of the mind to go to lower things (objects of enjoyment), but the grace of God can make such minds go towards higher objects.

The conflict between the role of personal effort and the divine Grace is solely a mental conundrum, and the moment one enters into the realm of experience, the problem is no longer there. One comes to realise that the effort itself is the result of the Grace and the achievement is the fruit of a long-sustained endeavour, seen and unseen. An act of Grace is preceded by the state of grace. In that state one builds up a climate that invites Grace.

Lord's grace is paramount. Without it nothing is achieved. Pray to Her unceasingly for the grace. Grace is the fruit that one expects for his sincere and humble efforts and it dawns when She wills.

We do not start our life with an awareness of God but only with an awareness of the external world. Awareness of God comes only by divine grace. It is only through divine grace that a man can withdraw his mind from external world and fix it on Her holy Feet.

Divine grace is the Consciousness-pull or the attraction of the part (*jīva*) towards the whole (God) which is more powerful than the part. He who meditates attains progressive salvation passing through the different planes of the higher consciousness. That is what it is believed to be.

Grace is one of those high spiritual mysteries that cannot be explained in terms of everyday human experience. It is not subject to conditions and does not depend upon any qualifications. The Lord's favours cannot be bought or borrowed. Some, even when awake, attain them not. On others She confers these, shaking them awake.

Grace does not pause to consider if Its beneficiary is virtuous or sinner. Consider when Lava and Kuśa came face to face with Rāma to fight for the sake of the pious horse of *Aśvmedha Yajña,* Rāma felt love for both of them without recognising them as his offspring. Then he pondered 'why this feeling?' and at once asked why should he think of the reason behind the feeling? To feel love and search for its reason is self-contradictory. Grace dawns spontaneously.

If birth, youth, beauty, power, wealth, knowledge do not cause arrogance, take it that the divine Grace is ever pleased with you.

Divine grace is like the flow of water. Even a tiny space in the devotee's mind will make grace to rush in. In the very word *Kṛpā* (grace, love) there is a sense of flow, for, love for juniors is *Kṛpā* while love for equals is *maitrī* (friendship) and love for seniors is *satkār* (reverence).

Mother's grace is always there but we have to be receptive. When it pleases Her, She showers and the *jīva* goes to bathe in the pool of Truth and becomes free.

Just as the gentle dew falls unseen and unheard of, and yet brings into blossom the finest of flowers, so is the divine grace ever ready to rain upon the votaries to extinguish the fire of their sins and sufferings.

Have you ever heard of a lady who had a fall from the top floor? Underneath was a heap of fencing wire. She was miraculously saved. She expressed the experience thus: "I felt the warm embrace of some invisible hands which laid me on safe grounds." Grace is a thing that surpasses all comprehension.

Doctors often express their experience thus: "Sorry, there is no hope. Meditation, not medication, may help." And the patient survives!

Look again how the Divine bestows the grace and blesses the devotees. Thatched roof of Kamban's (the Tamil Poet) hut flew in the storm. It was raining. Praying to Durgā, Kamban fell asleep. When he woke up, the newly thatched-up roof had been substituted. God's grace is for him who prays for love and devotion and for nothing else.

Rous Peter, a Briton, was Collector of Madurai in 1812. It was his wont to go round the Mīnākṣī Temple every day. One night it was raining very heavily. He was suddenly woken up from his fast sleep by a small girl unseen before, and beckoned by her to get out of his room. Implicitly, he complied with the instruction. Hardly had he left the chamber, the entire structure, struck by lightening, came down. The girl also vanished. He realised that his escape was providential by the grace of Mīnākṣi.

A human being through remembrance and practice aspires to 'reach out' towards God, but it is the divine grace that 'draws in' the questing soul.

Grace is a vision of Truth, not a sentiment. Do not crave for the attainment of grace, discover Its Presence. God can be seen the moment Her grace descends.

Divine grace is a thing that surpasses all comprehension; it is the expression of the Supreme. The grace is something that pushes one towards the goal to be attained.

It is often believed that nothing had the power to wipe away the consequences of *karma-s.* But Grace can do it. Faith in the Divine Mother and Her Grace are required to live a fearless and bold life.

The conclusion to be drawn: The Divine Mother appears in diverse forms to shower Her grace. You don't bring space or sunshine into the room. You only open the window to let it come in. Grace is all compassion and mercy. She pours Her grace on any person who opens his heart to receive it.

God is the charioteer of our existence. The world is Her Play. SHe is present in the hearts of her devotees and every one has a claim upon her Grace and infinite Bliss. Her grace may fall on us anytime. There is no definite rule of regulating it.

None can resist *Māṃ's kṛpā*. Through Grace is Truth revealed.

SOMETIMES God acts as the magnet and the devotee as the needle. God attracts the devotee to Herself. Again, sometimes the devotee acts as the magnet and God as the needle. Such is the attraction of the devotee that God comes to him unable to resist his love.

The Grace is always there. You are neck deep in water and yet you cry out that you are thirsty!

CHAPTER NINE

Divine Form

(Svarūpa)

O how can I express the secret word?
How can I say ?
"SHe is like this, SHe is not like that?"
SHe is neither manifest, nor hidden.
There are no words to tell what SHe is.
"You have hidden your light in every one, O Lord,
Wherever I see, I see your Presence!"

Kabir's God is without a symbolic form, subtler than the flowers' fragrance. Such an essence is SHe.

The divine Beloved is essentially invisible. But does that make him any less real? Love has no form. Wisdom has no form. Joy has no form. Yet we experience them. They are more real to us than form. Well, that is what God is. In the ultimate sense SHe is infinite love, infinite joy, infinite wisdom. Nevertheless some devotees find it helpful and spiritually captivating to think of him in one of his divine aspects such as Lord Chaitanya and Meerā worshipped God as Lord Kṛṣṇa, Tulsidāsa worshipped Him as Rāma, and one of the greatest exponent of *bhakti, Śrī* Rāmakṛśna Paramhansa worshipped God as the Mother Divine named Kālī. God-vision is only the vision of the Self objectified as God of one's own faith, the *Iṣṭadevtā*. It involves emotional comprehension as well as physical perception.

God is both existent and the state of existence. We call the existent God, the Personal God and the state of existence, the Impersonal God. There is no difference between these except the play of our consciousness.

The distinction between the Impersonal God and Personal God is also well recognised. The former is God as SHe is in Herself and the latter is God as SHe appears to the devotees in an idol. When we address the Absolute in the manner we choose, It becomes a Personal God for us. Ideal is identical with the ultimate Reality. If the spiritual eye is open in one's inner silence, the Invisible becomes visible.

As a matter of fact God is personal. He is always the first person 'I' ever standing before us. Since man gives precedence to the objects of the world, God appears to have receded to the background.

A devotee does not worship the idol. He worships the divinity through it. In the idol he beholds his own beloved deity, the essence of existence, knowledge and bliss. The chosen deity, the object of worship *(Iṣṭa),* is God-incarnate in that particular form.

You respect the photograph of your mother. The photograph itself cannot be your mother. She is not present in it. You just see her image. God's image is therefore as good as God himself as you do believe God in some form. In bowing to the Image we bow to the God in that form.

Attach yourself to all-perfect divine *Puruṣa,* through your entire emotional power. Let all your love be centred upon the perfect divine Ideal. This divine personality which a devotee chooses is termed as *Iṣṭadevtā.*

The personal and manifest aspect of God is conceived by different sects and creeds in different forms and is called by different names. The practitioner may select any name and form according to his own liking, belief and mental outlook. In reality, whichever form or name the devotee worships, he is adoring the One Supreme Being.

Worship that aspect of God which is in harmony with your own inclination. The *saguṇa* is SHe, the *nirguṇa* is SHe. Choose that which calms your distracted mind and frees it from agitations and doubts.

All the forces of Nature have their origin in the same Śakti (energy) though they are represented by separate gods. However, as long as we believe that the divine form we have chosen for worship is the personification of all virtues and attributes that reveal the supreme Principle and the Indweller of all beings, we are on the safe path. This knowledge should develop into an intense awareness of the supreme Reality that assumes the forms of the various deities in response to the wishes of the devotees who supplicate.

In the course of one of his lectures, Swami Rāma Tirtha referred to God as 'He' and another time as 'She' and yet another time as 'It'. This way of talking about God surprised some of his listeners. One of these stood up and asked, "Swamiji, you speak of God sometime as 'He', sometime as 'She' and sometime as 'It' and I should like to know whether your God is Mr., Mrs., or Miss?" Without a moment's pause the Swami shot out the answer: "My God is neither Mr. nor Mrs. nor Miss but a mystery." Verily God is a mystery.

> There can be as many gods as there are devotees. There can be as many spiritual paths, as there are aspirants. As long as the central fact that these gods are the doorways leading to the one Godhead is not forgotten, polytheism and any theism is acceptable. The bewildering variety of the Hindu gods should be viewed from this angle. We can only understand and see God as we create Him in our mind and thus we begin by creating God in the image, in the idol.
>
> Śrī Rāmakṛśna Paramhansa

Let the Self be sought and had. The world then be unsought and at last lost.

CHAPTER TEN

DIVINITY CALLING

NATURE'S beauty is an art of God. Let's feel the touch of God's invisible hands in everything beautiful. By the first touch of His hand the rivers throb and ripple. When SHe smiles, the sun shines, the moon glimmers, the stars twinkle, the flowers bloom. By the first rays of the rising sun, the universe is stirred, the shining gold is sprinkled on the smiling buds of rose, the fragrant air is filled with sweet melodies of singing birds; the dawn is the dream of God's creative fancy.

In the blue of the sky, in the green of the forest, whose is the hand that has painted the glow? In the pattern of the blooms of the flowers, SHe is woven.

Sri Aurobindo.

ALL the attraction you see in the world is but the true divinity. Flowers are known for their fragrance and loveliness but far behind their beauty and purity is the face of God. The candle does not talk but shines and sheds light all around. The jasmine does not speak but wafts its fragrance all around. Even so the Unseen beats no gong but Its omnipresence is felt by the dispassionate all around. The Supreme is the vital content in every particle of this world.

Divinity is immanent in the finite beauties of creation. The way to know God is to study Nature. God makes Himself known to us through the beauty that is manifest in nature and the rest of the creation. The study leads us to God-realisation.

You hear a bird singing, see a flower, look at an innocent child, witness a sunset - it does not matter what it is. Suddenly something overwhelms you, an emotion so deep, so intense! There is something behind this perceptive world and that is Divinity. Realise it.

In nature we see Him, in nature we hear Him speak, in nature lies the essence of joy and peace.

REALISE THE DIVINE PRESENCE IN :

- the chirping of birds.
- the blossom of the flower.
- the coolness and music of the gentle breeze.
- the effulgence, the warmth of the sun's glorious rays.
- the whiteness of the snow on the mountain.
- the smile of the child.
- the savour of food.
- the sweetness of water.
- the melodies of music.
- the tender smile of blooming buds.
- the joyous squeaks of infant children.
- the many-hued beauty of the jungle.
- the flavour of the fruit- juice.
- the ecstatic streams of birds in the sky.
- the cool breeze, clouds and rain.
- the dawn and the dusk.
- the painted butterfly.
- the colours and magic dance of the pea-cock.
- the fascinating hues of rainbow,
- the heart of a bud of jasmine in the form of fragrance.
- the calm moonlit nights.
- the potency in the pill.
- the devotion of worshippers.
- full blown mango blossoms bowing low.
- honey bees in rows.

The list is endless. Look around and marvel at the vast expanse of Nature, the divine beauty, nay, the divinity Itself.

What is that which gives lustre to my eyes, lends bloom to my cheeks and glory to my person; shines through my eyes, lends life and light to my senses and my body? It is the *ātman* (the Self). It is the divinity. It is the Mother Grace. See that divinity in everything. Feel that divinity everywhere.

O, cool gentle breeze strolling leisurely and humming silent songs in the night, what are you whispering so sweetly in my ears? Is it a lullaby or a sweet story of my *Māṃ*?

"These harps
that sound Thy Beauty,
Thou hast made; Why then
dost Thou conceal Thyself?
Thou hast worn the robes of Beauty,
Why then dost Thou Thy lovers escape?"
"O Beloved Mother, Thy Light doth shine
On herb and grass, on flower and fruit,
On drops of dew, on beauty of the clouds,
On running streams, on falling rains,
On winds and on wheeling fires,
On every silence of night
and sleep."

Beauty is Nature's effort to awaken man to the universal harmony and divinity.

Beauties of nature are but waves of the divine bliss, the invisible Spirit of beauty.

❄

A DIVINE VOICE:

"THERE IS A BEAUTY which is all-comprehending. It knows neither ugliness nor shortcomings. It is sublime. It is manifest as storm and as peace, but is beyond these. This is the beauty of the Soul. Of all attractions, I am the Centre, I am the Magnet; all other things are iron filings, some drawn this way, some that way, but all are drawn - irresistibly. There is a Light which no other lights can outshine. I am that Light. I am the Spirit in all forms that are. I am Silence within the Sound of Life. I am

Eternity woven on the warp and woof of Time.

"I am the Dweller of the Innermost. I am Spirit untouched by thoughts or form. I am *ātman.* I am *Paramātman.* I am *brahman.*

"I am in you. Can you be apart from Me? I am thine, you are mine. Nay, You and I are One. Nature itself is at peace. Let the senses and their activity subside.

"Take life calmly. Be at peace with you at all times. It is only by complete extinction of one's personality that the Sublime Impersonal can be understood and realised. When you do realise *brahman*, all planes and spheres and conditions of Consciousness are made one. Accept all truths and worship all aspects of the Divinity. See the whole universe as permeated with the divine Life. Let every form and soul have a spiritual message for you."

BLISS, delight and procreation are not all what one should desire. Know also the discerner of bliss, delight and procreation.

THE MOST BEAUTIFUL and most profound emotion we can experience is the sensation of the mystical. It is the essence of the true science. He to whom this emotion is a stranger, who can no longer wonder and stand rapt in awe, is as good as dead.

Albert Einstein.

SEE IN THIS SCENE OF CHANGING SHOWS, THE CHANGELESS ONE THAT GLOWS.
A BIT OF FRAGRANCE ALWAYS CLINGS TO THE HAND THAT GIVES YOU ROSES.

CHAPTER ELEVEN

DIVINE LIGHT

(Brahmjyoti)

THE *ātman* is the Light. The Light is veiled by ignorance. When the Light of *ātman* drives out the darkness (of ignorance) It shines forth a sun in splendour, the revealed *brahman*.

Bhagavadgītā.

"We bow unto Light divine,
It shines in every heart that is awake.
This Light is benediction of Spirit;
This Light is unending joy;
This Light is the peace that passed understanding;
This Light is the Wisdom that knows all;
This Light is boundless, beyond space and time.
It is the Light divine,
Unto It we bow."

THE Lord is spiritual and the rays of His transcendence are called *Brahmjyoti*, the spiritual effulgence. Everything that exists is situated in the *Brahmjyoti*. But when the *Jyoti* is covered by illusion (*māyā*), it becomes material.

Silently that Light is observing everything that is going on. It observes our physical activities, knows what is going on in our hearts and minds. It also knows what we do not know. And it is this silent Light of consciousness that observes all three states of waking, dreaming and deep sleep.

The Light as described in *Veda-s* is symbolic of the eyesight. The seer's light of *Agni* (fire) of divine origin has tremendous power to remove darkness of ignorance. This *Vedik* light has been associated with Aditi who is prayed to protect mankind from sin and bestow on them the heavenly light. This prayer for the light of consciousness for the redemption of mankind suggests the presence of the supreme Light above the physical light.

Only one effulgent glow is hidden in every creature. Without the glow of this Spirit, nothing will exist, nothing will operate.

God has Its own imperishable existence, a point-of-light. Each being has within himself a latent spark, a divine flame *(Jyoti).*

Agni is the flaming aspiration in the heart of the man. This mystic flame within represents that articulate urge for Divine. This flame is ever burning. Feed this inner flame with the appropriate fuel of right thoughts, right feelings, right activities. When the flame gathers momentum and shoots up, the mind is purified, illumined, and raised above its human limitations. The call then goes forth to the Infinite. The man's consciousness widens and he spontaneously observes the law of Truth. *Agni* is there in each of us as the non-worshipped god, the immortal in mortals. *Agni* rises and carries our aspirations to the Lord. When one lights a lamp before the deity, one also lights a flame *(Jyoti)* inside the heart and thus offers one's obeisance to the Almighty.

Intellectuals and aesthetes are deluded by the outward beauty and attraction of relative truth. They are unaware of the spiritual Spark *(Jyoti)* which is both truth and beauty. The spiritual Spark is so significant that as long as it burns in the body, the man is alive and there is warmth. When however it extinguishes, the body is cold to the touch. *Jyoti* is no more. The body perishes.

By constant meditation is kindled the flame of knowledge which completely burns the impurities of mind. That is the purpose of spiritual discipline.

In dense darkness you cannot see your hand in front of your eyes. Yet, you know that you are there. By what light is your presence known? That is the light of Consciousness, the divine spark that is always burning there in the deep quietude of the heart. Hear its voice, follow its dictates.

Life is light, the manifestation of divinity, the stream of eternal Being, a flow of existence, intelligence, purity and bliss. Light *(Jyoti)* bestows the power of perception and gives a mainspring to all beings.

At sunset Hindu homes will lit a *dīpa* (lamp) and worship the flame *(Jyoti)* as

Divine, thus calling for brightness and illumination (inner light) before darkness sets in.

God made man in His own image. That was not said of the body which is mortal, but of the soul which is immortal and consists of His Light. Where does this Light come from? The Buddha answers: This is the light of the Heaven of heavens. That Light has no roots. It is boundless.

Consciousness is termed *Jyoti* (Light) because it is self-effulgent. Through this Light the body and its organs are activated and gain momentum.

Brahmajyoti is the divine flame, emanating from the supreme spiritual Planet *(manidvipa);* all other lights are its derivations, manifestations and reflections. Until one surpasses the glare of the *Brahmajyoti*, he cannot realise and perceive the abode of the Mother Divine, the Supreme Being.

On Devī *Jāgaraṇa*, Mother Divine is worshipped in the form of a flame *(Jyoti)* that is lit and consecrated. The flame in particular has been chosen to represent the Deity as She is manifest at *Jawalāmukhi. Jyoti* is a symbol for the divine Light, a glimpse of which the devotee perceives during introspection and contemplation. May the sacred flame shine bright in our souls. There is only one Divine Light behind the creation of the universe.

HOLY FLAME,
Ever-burning in our hearts,
Salutations, Salutations, Salutations,
unto Thee.

The light of Truth inebriates the heart of the beholder.

CHAPTER TWELVE

Relationship with God

(Sambandha)

Thou art our Mother and Father Supreme,
Benevolent Thou art, our Friend Supreme,
Thou art our All, O Giver Supreme.

Relationship is the lever. The memory of the worldly relations recurs so frequently. We have built these bonds so strong. Each relationship is tied up with certain privileges and obligations which must be accepted and abided by in order to really enjoy the thus-established relationship.

Our personality blossoms amidst loving relationships. A loving relationship creates love and harmony. Love is light. If a child is taken away from the mother's care, he would not be the same person that he could have been in the care of the mother. Something that grows with the mother-child relation will not grow otherwise.

What if this memory of relationship is switched on to God, the Ruler of the world? And that directs us to build a relationship with our *Iṣṭadevatā*, the chosen deity.

The *Vaiśnava-s* look upon *parābhakti* as the end in itself. So the main thing in these devotional attitudes being love of God, the chosen deity is looked upon as their parent, a master, a friend, a child or a sweetheart.

One such attitude is known as *śānta bhāva*, which we generally find among the saints who consider God as the All-pervading, All-conclusive supreme Power. *Śānta bhāva* is the placid attitude of peace and serenity towards the divinity in which God's presence is felt but no definite relationship has been established between God and the devotee. The ascetic believes that God resides in the heart of everyone. He withdraws his senses from the objects of the world and concentrates the mind on God as the only Reality.

The second is *dāsya bhāva.* Here the devotee considers himself a servant of God and God as his Master. This *bhāva* is represented by Hanumānji towards *Śri* Rāma in Rāmāyana.

The third is *sakhya bhāva.* In this relationship there is equality and oneness, a friend to friend attitude. Kṛṣṇa regarded Arjuna both as a friend and a devotee. It is also illustrated by the case of the cowherds and Sudāmā who treated *Kṛṣṇa* as their friend.

The next is *vātsalya bhāva*, which is love towards one's own child as found in Yaśodhā for Kṛṣṇa, and in Kaushalya for Rāma. There is no element of awe in it, really, for, the devotee looks on the deity, the object of his love, as his own child and feels privileged to act as his well-wisher and guardian.

Another one is the *madhura bhāva,* the relationship which exists between two lovers, the beloved and the lover, and even between the husband and wife. This is the most intense form of attachment. The idea of least separation is unbearable. The sweetness of the relationship matters most. The oneness with the beloved achieved by the lover even produces physical transformation in the devotee. The milkmaids of Vrindāvan were mad for Kṛṣṇa, the embodiment of beauty, to whom they had surrendered their body, mind and soul. The perfect devotee of this type is obviously one who looks only to the comforts and interest of the Beloved regardless of his own. Meerā loved Lord Kṛṣṇa in this *bhāva.*

Still another unique relationship with the Absolute is the Mother-child feelings. Here the child is the devotee and Divine Mother is the deity. This relationship of Mother and child is that of love and compassion alone. Variety of words and names are used to express this relationship of love and devotion. Love alone forms the link between the two. *Śri* Rāmakṛśna Paramhansa had genuine and profound love for the Divine Mother. Though he was worshipping an idol, he began to feel that he was worshipping a living Goddess. He became actually Her child and began to behave like one. We have roots, though invisible, just like trees. The child's roots are in the mother and the sap flows from her towards the son, unknown to both.

These are the *bhāva-s* or feelings of emotional ardour towards an object of love and devotion to which we feel attached. We will not be able to think of God in any other manner than in terms of one of these emotions.

For any relationship with God other than the one described above, e.g., *mātṛdevobhava* (Mother is God), an aspirant has to make lot of adjustments, mental as well as intellectual. But the worship of God in the form of Mother Divine is very spontaneous. The mother is our most intimate relation. Translate this intimacy, this *bhāva,* in terms of Mother Divine and you are in the proximity of God.

In my relationship with God, the Supreme Being, I like to think of the Divine in the aspect of Mother and hence call It Mother Grace. God is a concept. Mother is a Reality, a Truth. None can deny this.

THE human body is like a cosy ship to take one across the ocean of sorrow in the shape of mundane existence. Cherish a true spirit of service to God. Then every action will turn into an act of worship to the Lord and life will be crowned with success. Be scrupulously devoted to Mother Grace.

ॐ

The grace from the Transcendental Consciousness is like the flash of lightning which for a split second breaks through even the thickest cloud and illumines the path of the pilgrim. All doubts are then cleared.

DURYODHANA AND YUDHISTHIRA

Once the disciples of Dronacharya asked their Guru, "How is it that Yudhisthira is recognised as an embodiment of virtue and Duryodhana as a wicked man?" The Guru explained that the reputation enjoyed by the two was not without foundation and in order to demonstrate his point he called Duryodhana and said to him, "O Duryodhana, find out a virtuous man." Duryodhana went far and wide in search and came back after some time. He told his Guru that he could not find even a single virtuous man in the whole world. Rather he saw men of evil nature everywhere. Duronacharya then called Yudhisthira and asked him to find out and bring a wicked man. Yudhisthira also travelled far and wide and came back after a long time. He said to the Guru, "My worthy Master, I could not find even a single wicked man."

Thus the reports of the two disciples were of a conflicting nature. All the other disciples of Dronacharya were surprised at these contradictory reports and could not make out which was correct. Dronacharya then said, "One sees one's own mind reflected in the world. Therefore the whole world appears to be full of virtuous men to Yudhisthira and abounding in evil to Duryodhana. He who suffers from jaundice sees the whole world tinged with yellow colour. As is the mind so is the vision."

❄

If my heart had wings and you gave it the strength to fly soaring heights above, I would have been with you !

CHAPTER THIRTEEN

THE FOCAL POINT

MAN IS BORN to achieve and regain the lost awareness of his divinity. His life is incomplete if he has not achieved the tranquillity, equipoise, and equanimity of mind. The aim of life is fullness of life.

A CHILD comes into the world. The spirit enters therein. The 'Dame' Nature readily welcomes the 'Prince', provides milk in the mother's breast, shelter in the mother's lap and an army of attendants to his bare needs. She mobilises all its forces to claim the child as its own. But as the child grows and begins to feel the life-impulse, the Foster mother, the world, claims him as hers and the child fondly clings to it and to its toy-gifts totally oblivious of his true nature and original home. And thus he continues to live for a 'while'.

Then begins a continuous battle of life fought within and without, in the mind and in the world. Man keeps rushing restlessly, preoccupied by soaring desires and misty instincts, fully absorbed and fully involved in search of 'happiness'. He craves for things he does not possess. A sort of happiness is undoubtedly experienced when he acquires the cherished objects of his desire. An object gives pleasure only when it is desired. So the pleasure belongs to the desire. Health, wealth, intelligence, name and fame do not determine lasting happiness either. The fulfilment of continuous desires through acquisition of material things also is no way out to a lasting happiness.

The fire-fly runs towards the lamp and gets burnt. Even so the passionate man runs towards a false worldly object thinking to find real happiness but gets burnt in the fire of lust.

The present world is steeped in rank materialism forgetting all moral and spiritual values. It believes in the satisfaction of desires and advocates cultivation of means and methods for satisfying them. A person suffering from scabies experiences a relief of sort by scratching, but makes it worse later on!

Does man realise what he has wrought for himself in the worldly pursuits of life? It is his vanity, his ego, that prompts him to run up and down. Driven by desire he is arrogant to those below him in rank and envies those above him, earning nothing for himself in the bargain.

Suffering is no illusion. Buddha located the cause of pain in human desire and laid emphasis to eliminating the suffering by ceasing to desire. Even if you acquire everything to meet your needs and wishes, you will always find that you still suffer due to something which you did not want to. When you do not need anything, you have everything.

Man is more inclined towards the world and its material objects than towards God because the searchlight of his senses is directed outward. Never does he behold the inner world unless that searchlight is reversed and directed within.

Why a desire for a car is stronger than that for the God? Our understanding of God is so poor! If we give a gold necklace to a cow, will she be really happy to put it on its neck? The cow wants only grass. The appreciation of the value of a substance depends on one's comprehension of what it is.

Too many of us end up feeling that we have wasted our lives and that instead of happiness, peace, harmony and fulfilment, we have earned depression, disgust, anxieties and miseries. At this late stage though, only a person of some inner strength can resolutely turn away from the glitter and attraction of sense-objects that keep on enamouring his mind outward.

Happiness *(sukha)* has always been the chief commodity sought after by one and all. Various ways and means are devised for the purpose. Our *ṛṣi-s* (saints) dwelt on the highest happiness called *ānanda* (bliss) which can be experienced by those who look forward to the Supreme Being and meditate on Her. Mundane happiness is related to the sensual and the material, and the bliss is concerned with the spiritual and eternal. The common man can hopefully attain the moderate happiness.

The human nervous system is so marvellous that a person can make himself happy or miserable regardless of what is happening outside, simply by changing his attitude and awareness. The sage does not wish to dominate the environment. He just manages to live harmoniously with and within it.

We experience the greatest happiness, the deepest sense of peace during the moments when we cease to want.

True happiness can be attained by taking refuge in God. Man is part and parcel of God. A little child is crying and no one can pacify him. But as soon as he is put in the lap of the mother, he is at once happy and consoled. The bliss attained by realising a sense of unity with the Divine replaces worldly sorrows. For those who abide by the eternal Law, the winds are full of cool and sweet melody.

A turning point in the course of one's life is often a crisis which does at times prove to be auspicious and a blessing in disguise. True human spirit grows out of it. An illness gives us time to be holy, to think and reflect on the purpose and direction of life.

God is merciful and benevolent. When one cultivates this faith, one will attain peace. You will perceive supreme benignity in every dispensation of His. Pin your faith in God and be one with His chartered course. You will at once derive consolation and peace, which in turn will release pressure of your miseries on you. Faith and reverence generate a unique energy which continues to give strength to the seeker and enable him to attain his goal by virtue of that strength and harmony.

Indisputable is man's urge, conscious or unconscious, to realise a higher life. The *jīvātman* passes through lacs of lives, yet only as a man can he obtain the Truth and redemption. The Lord dwells within the lotus of each heart.

Before embarking on a spiritual quest, however, it is imperative to apply certain ethical norms and practise moral values in order to qualify oneself for true meditation on God:

Purify the mind. Eradicate the recognised vices. Virtues will automatically start pouring in. The body is cleansed with water, the mind by truthfulness, the intellect by sacred learning and the soul by practising the true knowledge. Nothing in this world purifies like spiritual wisdom. Transform your negative thoughts into positive ones. Thoughts order the mind into a definite pattern, and this determines the texture, efficiency, sincerity and quality of action.

Destroy the Ego. The renunciation of ego and vanity is a must for spiritual growth and it does not mean any loss to the individual. Give up anything that props the ego and perpetuates its existence. As long as our ego separates us from God, we continue to be unhappy.

Contentment is an active aid in overcoming the wandering tendencies of the mind. It helps to acquire true tranquillity of mind. As one travels on the road of spirituality, he reaches a point when he realises the absurdity of the passions to accumulate possessions. Unhappy are those who live under the influence of lust, anger and pride.

Humility and simplicity exalt man to the heaven of glory and power. The lower scale of a balance is always heavier.

Selfishness is a big hurdle in getting closer to God. **C**ompassion for others annihilates selfishness.

Above all pin your Faith in the Almighty God. The more complete your faith, devotion, sincerity and surrender, the more will Grace be with you.

One night a man dreamt that he was walking along a path with the Lord. Across the sky flashed scenes from his life. For each scene, he noticed two sets of foot-prints on the path: one belonging to him and the other to the Lord. He also noticed, however, that certain portions of the path bore only one set of foot-prints and those scenes happened to belong to the saddest times of his life. This really bothered the man and he questioned the Lord about it. "O Lord, you said that once I decided to follow you, you would always walk with me all the way. But I have noticed that during the troublesome times in my life there is only one set of footprints. I don't understand as to why you left me alone when I needed you most." The Lord replied, "My dear child, I still stand to my words. I would never leave you alone. In fact during your bad patch of life where you see only one set of footprints, I carried you." Know that you are not just the child of God, but His heir, too.

The pilgrimage to God is full of ups and downs - ups consisting of flashes of God's grace and the downs consisting of depths of despair. We may not be able to change the events, but we can change our attitudes. Qualities in man determine the quality of his life, his peaceful or sorrowful state. All our efforts to make the world a better place to live in, would be of no avail until and unless there is transformation in our inner nature and behaviour. For facilitating this self-transformation, one has to have intimate and continuous contacts with pious souls and a love-link with God.

Become like a child, give yourself up to the Divine Mother. Let Her take care of you. Once you turn to the Divine Mother, saying, "I want to be yours", you have nothing to worry. She will carry you. Live constantly in the presence of the Lord. Live in the feeling that it is the Presence which moves you and is doing everything you do.

Chanting the *nāma* of God has a magnetic effect on the mind. The life becomes sublime. The power derived out of the recitation of God's *nāma* reveals His attributes and roots out the gloom in one's heart. By chanting and singing God's glories, the *saṃskāra-s* are purged from within through dreams, visions and thoughts.

"What is the secret of your song?" the river was asked. The river replied: "I would lose my song if I took the rocks away!" The river knows that ocean is both its original home and final abode. In the natural course the river will join the ocean one day. Life too is a river. As it flows on, it strikes against the rocks of suffering, sorrow, trial and tribulation. Man can also achieve his goal if the river of life joins the ocean of Divine Existence. The hurdles on the way will have to be crossed before the light is seen in the tunnel.

To know oneself is not enough. This knowledge must bring a conscious self-control. There must be an aspiration at every moment. The path to Truth-realisation is long and difficult, strewn with snares and obstacles. It is absolutely important to observe and practise the needed austerities of life while on way to the goal one has set before him. Spiritualism advocates limitation of wants, self-discipline and renunciation of the unwanted.

The aspirant is required to change the quality, the quantity, and the direction of his thought-flow. Then alone he becomes eligible for true meditation on God. Devotion to God *(bhakti yoga)* is the means by which the quality of the heart is improved. The heart only feels. The feeling of love is the vehicle which enables a man to advance on this path. The path of dedicated action *(karma yoga)* controls the quantity of thoughts. If we work in the spirit of dedication and surrender to the Lord, the mind becomes peaceful. Action for self-gain creates bondage and should be abandoned. All our actions and their fruit should be offered to God as we offer flowers. The direction of thoughts can be shifted inwards by the pursuit of knowledge *(jñāna yoga).* It is a delicate path. One must know that the world is not real even though it appears to be. Spiritual knowledge develops equanimity of mind. The state of mind thus attained leads to God-realisation.

Yoga is a methodical effort towards self-perfection by giving expression to the potentialities latent in the man. We see a union of the human individual with the universal Existence partially expressed in man and in the cosmos.

We are as though debarred from direct experience of our own Self. This calls for our attention in this direction. Contemplation on the perishable nature of creation will begin to take the aspirant's mind to some deeper reality underlying the ever-changing phenomena of life. The sap in a tree indicates that there is 'something' which remains constant at different levels. That 'something' reveals to the aspirant that the ever-changing world is based on a never-changing state of Presence devoid of form and phenomena.

The fusion of subjective wisdom and objective reality is what is called realisation of the true nature of life and is the same as attaining enlightenment. This is what was attained by Buddha. The enlightenment comes only when we are totally free from attachments, desires, personality-hang-ups and ego.

Do not worry if your mind spins. So many clouds come and go but the sky remains the same. In the same way thoughts arise and disperse in the mind, but the Self is not disturbed.

On an honest assessment of one's inner being one will realise that he is an *asura* full of cravings, disturbing emotions and an agitated mind. Until and unless one is true to oneself, one cannot humanise his passions and sublimate his thoughts and emotions.

A person who neither rejoices on achieving something pleasant nor laments upon obtaining something unpleasant, who is self-intelligent, and who knows the science of God, is to be understood as already situated in Transcendence.

Bhagavadgita

WHEN ALL THE DESIRES that surge in the heart are renounced, the mortal becomes immortal. When all the knots that strangle the heart are loosened, the mortal becomes immortal. Here in this very life.

Bṛhadāraṇyaka Upaniṣad

THE FLUTE OF KRISHNA IS STILL PLAYING IF WE HAVE THE EARS TO HEAR.

❄

That which has risen will set,
That which has blossomed will wither,
That which has been built will fall,
He who has come to this world will depart.

Kabir

An ant was trying to cross a stream on a leaf. The leaf overturned due to strong winds. The ant cried, "Help, help, the world is drowning." A frog close-by said, "What rubbish! The world is not drowning, you are drowning." "Well," cried the ant, "Once I drown, the world as well will not exist for me." All existence is within you.

THE GENDER SYNDROME

Forgive *the simple-minded if they assume God to be male. Masculine pronouns litter the scriptures conceiving God as male. While discussing God it is impossible to avoid some sort of personal pronoun - 'He', 'She' or 'It'. The Sacred, however, could never be grasped and contained within a human system of thought. The Reality is above and beyond all gender syndrome.*

❄

The Divine *is, in some profound sense, a product of the imagination rather than a matter of fact. The process of 'God-making' in the factory of man's mind cannot be seen better elsewhere. In the masculine form of Sri Kṛṣna and in the feminine form of Sri Devī, is personified the idea of the Paramātmā, the formless Existence, Bliss Absolute. In the ultimate sense God is impersonal without form (nirguṇa nirākāra).*

Śakti is symbolically female but it is neither male nor female.

PART TWO

For The Upcoming Aspirant

(Supplementary Reading)

These following chapters should make an excellent supplementary reading for an upcoming aspirant in order to broaden the outlook and transform the mind. He who practises, attains progressive spiritual wisdom. Topics discussed are:

Purity of mind:
May this mind of mine resolve on what is noble.

Ego:
Empty your ego, you will be filled with divine. Lose your personality, you will realise God.

Illusion:
Māyā is the power that creates the delusion: 'I am born, I am enjoying, I am suffering.'

Time:
Short as life is, we make it still shorter by the careless waste of time.

Harmony:
In nature there are neither rewards nor punishments. There are only consequences. The true life of man is rest in identity with the Supreme Spirit.

Silence:
To be alone with silence is to be alone with God!

Surrender.
Reduce yourself to a zero and humble yourself at the feet of the Lord. That is the way to attain grace. Self-surrender means that the little 'I' has merged into the Supreme 'I', the Divine Mother.

CHAPTER FOURTEEN

PURITY OF MIND

(*Viśuddha Maṇ*)

ARJUNA: The mind is very fickle, O Kṛiṣṇa, it is impetuous, strong and obstinate. I think it is as difficult to control as the wind.

Kṛṣṇa: Without doubt, Arjuna, the mind is restless and difficult to curb but it can be controlled by constant practice and non-attachment.

Bhagavadgītā.

REMOVE *Ahantā* (I-ness) and *Mamatā* (My-ness), the two poisonous fangs of the mind. The result is pure mind. Pure mind is Supreme Self.

THE MIND dwells upon the objective world. To make it free and calm, the worldliness has to be unloaded from it. To achieve this end, the mind should be given an alternate choice to play with. Turn it inward and focus it on the invisible Self. It should rejoice with the change. Affliction comes from the outward propensity which if kept aside deliberately, the mind finds repose and the inwardness will grow decisively.

The mind wanders because it does not find a suitable subject to absorb itself in. Material things bring a bit of comfort but they do not stay for long. The mind is not like a monkey, as it is often believed to be. In fact it is like a king who will go to places he likes most and do what pleases him. So the mind, like the king, will not stay at any place unworthy of him. When withdrawn from its extrovert fascinations and offered a better alternative to indulge in, the mind may not like to return to its earlier favourite rendezvous. The intuitive power is nothing other than the mind turned inward and held in attention. The effort at all times must be to gain more purity and wisdom. It is purely an inward process. That is a state of equilibrium and tranquillity which one must cultivate for oneself.

Do not let your mind become a dirty pool by degrees in the belief that the overt action alone matters and that no one will know what passes in the mind; otherwise all your life's actions will become evil beyond redemption. There is no greater *gurū* than your mind. When the mind has been purified, it will direct you from within.

Purity of mind is the basic need for Self-realisation. The impurity of mind is bad thoughts. By *śravaṇa* (listening), the knowledge dawns and the flame is lit. *Manan* (reflection) plays the role of a wind-screen, protects this flame and does not let it extinguish. The unwanted thoughts thus are not allowed to overwhelm the right ones. By *nidhidhyāsan* (spiritual discipline) the flame is kept burning bright and the wick duly trimmed. Knowledge has thus been compared to Light *(jyoti).*

We must exert our control over the mind without allowing it to feel that any pressure is being exerted. Why is it that the mind is distracted? The reason is that the heart and the head are not co-operating with each other.

It is the clean mirror that reflects the shining sun and not the wall built of mud and stones. One learns only when the mind is receptive. This is true of knowledge as well.

Just as a physical disease arises out of neglect and carelessness towards the body, there are subtle and causal 'diseases' that build up in the subtle *(sūkṣma)* and causal *(kāraṇa)* bodies through ignorance and carelessness in our approach to life, that is, the way we feel, think, act, react, and interact in life.

The saint *(yogi)* masters the mental waves *(vṛtti-s).* He encounters many difficulties on his way, for the waves of the mind are stronger as compared to those of the ocean. He gives a stiff fight and puts an end to the mental waves by continued concentration and consistent efforts, thus finding the other shore where peace and happiness reign.

One must not waste time and confuse the mind by pedantic discourses. Our little intellect is like shallow water in a little pond. If we stir it too much, the mire comes to the top.

The bliss manifests only in a steady and pure mind. The experience of that bliss is liberation. It is in our power to eradicate ego, the cause of all misery, by steadying all mental activities born of ignorance.

"A dog is given a tail to keep away the flies or whatever. As long as the dog wags the tail, it is fine. But suppose the tail starts wagging the dog! Then the dog cannot afford to have a tail. As long as our mind is an instrument helpful to us, it is nice to have it. If the mind determines my lot, it is not good to have it. The world cannot touch you unless you so desire."

Swami Dayānanda.

Try to hear with your ears. Stop hearing with the mind. Taste things with your tongue not with your mind. Your mind will be automatically disciplined. Our reactions are governed by our possessed minds. There is nothing wrong with the senses. They perform their natural functions. It is the mind which dilates the information supplied by the sense organs and distorts our vision of reality.

We have an ally in our mind. Utilise it. All sorts of *sādhanā-s* (spiritual practices) and austerities aim at removing the distraction of mind and focus it to bring about a state of one-pointedness *(ekāgaratā).* The restless mind does not fix at one spot. Like a goat, it must nibble at tender shoots. When the mind is free from restlessness and becomes steady, it behaves itself and extends full co-operation. It experiences joy and peace. This makes our horizon distinct, our path clear and we move towards a greater certitude.

It is the conscious mind that should be taken care of. It is the instrument which, when serviced, will enable us to explore the hidden depths of the subconscious mind and burn out negative tendencies (*saṃskāra-s*) which, now and then, rush up from beneath the surface. And by this same conscious mind, the highest super-consciousness may be attained.

When desires, aversions and cravings do not disturb the mind, it may be inferred that mental conditioning has been set right and the aspirant is on way to his goal.

Mind is like milk that gets easily mixed up with water. But by churning, it is changed into butter which floats on the water. Likewise a mind purified by divine knowledge may dwell in the world but it will not be involved in the worldliness.

Ignorance is like coal-dust in the eyes. A man travelling in the train got coal-dust into his eyes causing irritation. The man became restless. He tried to remove the dust by rubbing the eyes but the speck of dust could not be dislodged. He got down from the train, reached home and asked his wife to remove the dust. The wife poured some medicine into the affected eyes. The dust came out and the irritation stopped. The man was happy. Did he really get any happiness or did he only regain the happiness that he had lost for the time being? It is certainly the later. So, in the case of an ignorant soul, the removal of ignorance means the regaining of divine consciousness which was obsessed by illusion and thus lost.

The mind is like the void. The void emerges only if you get rid of the conceptual thoughts and eliminate objects of perception. The pure mind shines forever but we are not aware of it. We are afraid to empty our minds lest we are lost in the world. The void in fact is eternal. There was nothing before it existed.

The secret of our mind is that the moment it is observed keenly, it calms down. It is to be decontrolled before it is controlled.

> SPIRITUAL progress needs observance of mind and its activities. Inauspicious propensities of mind block this progress.

Eliminate negative thoughts and experience the joy, the bliss.

CHAPTER FIFTEEN

EGO

(Ahaṅkāra)

> IN the secret cave of the heart, the two are seated. By life's fountain, the ego drinks of the sweet and bitter stuff liking the sweet and disliking the bitter; while the Self drinks both sweet and bitter neither liking this nor disliking that. The ego gropes in the dark while the Self lives in light.
>
> Katha Upaniṣad.

Vedānta visualises the notion of witness (sākśi) as that part of our being which quietly watches the other parts in action. All the actions of the latter are watched and recorded by the meditative and detached silence of the former. In other words the quiet Self guards the restless ego.

When the soul identifies itself with the modes of Nature, it forgets its own eternity and uses mind, intellect and body for egoistic satisfaction. A gap is thus created between the Absolute *(brahman)* and individual soul *(Jīva)* by the 'I' sense which stands in between the two, like a stick on the surface of the lake making the water appear divided into two parts while in reality the water is one. This sense of 'I' is the stick which separates man from God.

The ego is an impostor whose status is as precarious as that of a bridegroom's friend in the story: "During a marriage in former days lasting for several days, a stranger had a very good time for a day or two, as the bride's party took him for a groom's friend. But when an enquiry was started about his identity, he disappeared discretely."

Swami Chinmayananda.

Ego is the feigned self-forgetfulness of the Reality of its own eternal nature. So long as the ego remains, finite exists. The acquisition of the finite world will not do. Ego disregards the prompting of the Spirit. It believes in living for sensual pleasure and self-glorification aided by greed, lust and anger.

I-identity is known as *ahaṅkāra.* We are all victims of this *ahaṅkāra* and consequently suffer from this I-identity syndrome.

It is only on account of the ego that one relates oneself to the things around. If there was no ego, you would be just like a plant having no knowledge of your existence. This is the paradox of creation. On one hand ego binds you to the plane of objective experience and on the other hand it exists as the nucleus which has to be exploded to awaken unified existence.

Just as the ghost has no existence apart from the post, so too, the ego-centre has no existence other than the supreme Self. The vision of the post and the ghost can never coexist at one and the same time. So, too, a glimpse of the Self will make the ego-centre disappear at one stroke as readily as at the touch of the intellect dream-world rolls off.

Ego is consciousness boosted by the props of wealth, status, learning, beauty, accomplishments, talents, name and fame. Egotism, pride, greed, anger and other outgrowths of self-centredness are barriers to spiritual development and prevent man's escape from the misery of soul ignorance. Once these adjuncts are removed what remains is true Self. Transformation of the ego is the goal.

It is this ego, the mistaken self-identity, that is the cause of all problems! The wretched 'I' is almost indestructible. It is like the *pīpal* tree that grows from the rubbish of a dilapidated house. You may cut it down today, but tomorrow you will find it growing from the roots again. It is like the strong odour of garlic which does not leave the pot even after several washes. The liberation lies in uprooting this I-thought.

Ego in man dies hard. Śri Rāmakṛṣṇa therefore advises man not to engage himself in destroying ego but in transforming it by acts of disposition and dedication.

The ego keeps its grip by making us feel needy and powerless. Renunciation of ego is thus necessary for spiritual advancement and it does not mean any loss to the individual. Man and Nature are manifestations of the same entity. He who has realised the insignificance of his ego, realises the basic unity of the universe.

The Self, which is of the nature of intelligence, has no sense of 'I'. The insentient body does not possess the sense of 'I'. The appearance of a delusive ego between the intelligent and the insentient is a mystery. Only when it is destroyed by whatever means, the Truth will be seen as It is.

A human being has many personalities because the ego has many faces. In the *sātvik* state the ego is the true knowledge of Self; in the *rājasik* state, ego is a desire for power; in the *tāmasik* state, it is mere selfishness. The true ego is the 'I' that knows Itself and has an honest assessment of its abilities and limitations.

Ego wants to be independent. Sometime it 'appears' stronger than God even as darkness of the night may appear to overpower the brightness of the sun. As long as our ego separates us from the Lord, we shall continue to be unhappy. All the gross and subtle manifestations of this ego should be ignored so that nothing stands in the way to spiritual growth.

Ego is the acquired nature of man. It contains the accumulated knowledge of the mind. The egoist is very proud of this knowledge. So long this knowledge of pride speaks, the voice of the wisdom cannot be heard. But when the pride drops away, there comes the grace of wisdom, the gift of the Unknown, the light from Beyond. What we need to experience is the conscious presence of the Self.

Realising God means melting the ego and draining it away, even as the ball of ice held before the sun melts and loses its form. When you love God, the ego does not show its head.

The Spirit operates at all levels of beings. Each plane of our being has its own surface thoughts, its habitual ways of feeling, thinking and acting. The ego should not be let hold the sway over the obscure and limited consciousness. I shall be free when the 'I' ceases to be !

"The Lord is seated in the heart of all beings, O Arjuna, and being seated there, He is making them move as if mounted on a machine. When one recognises this fact, he withdraws his 'I' and says, 'I am not doing anything. Thy will, O Lord, not mine. Thou art the doer of everything. I am only a tool in your hand. You are the wielder of that tool."

When the ego thus becomes separated, one at once finds that his mind has assumed its right dimension. Gradually the spiritual practices will scrub the ego. That is of course a matter of practice and experience.

The 'I' casts off the illusion of 'I' and yet remains as 'I'. Such is the paradox of Self-realisation. The effort to dissolve the 'I' notion and then to make the Self revealed is the great penance.

Mahāṛṣi Ramana.

In the case of a *jñānī* (enlightened soul) the existence of the ego is only apparent. He continues to enjoy his unbroken transcendental experience in spite of this, keeping his attention always on the Source. This ego is harmless; it is like the skeleton of a burnt rope which though looks like a rope but has lost its utility.

The ego has to sacrifice itself so that man's divine nature can manifest itself. 'Mine' is death; 'not mine' is immortality. Renunciation results in peace.

Sathya Sai Bābā.

"Pain is hard to bear". But with patience, day by day, "This will pass away". Fame is but a silent decay. "Even this will pass away". Life is done? But what is death? Death is a dream. "Even that will pass away."

CHAPTER SIXTEEN

ILLUSION

(Māyā)

> THIS world has its appearance due to ignorance like the illusory silver in the mother of pearl, the snake in the rope, the water in the mirage, blue-ness in the sky, city in the clouds.
>
> Swami Sivānanda.

> METAPHYSICALLY, *māyā* is the creative principle or the power of the Supreme. In its subjective form *māyā* is false egoism (cloud of spiritual ignorance) which manifests itself in the form of attachment, lust, desire, anger, power, fraud, deceit, heresy and other passions.

Māyā is usually translated as illusion, but this can be misleading. *Māyā* is the surface reality, representing materiality. It also stands for the divine power which forms Nature. As the product of the divine creative power, Nature and material world cannot be denied, but there is always a danger that appearance restricts us to the divinity behind everything. Only in this respect *māyā* is regarded as illusory. *Māyā* is an inherent and inexplicable power of the Supreme which is as inseparable from Him as heat from fire, as sunshine from the sun.

Māyā is likened to the snake and rope illusion: In the dark of night a rope is mistaken for a snake. The rope does not really become a snake; it has no other reality than the rope itself. In the same way this universe has no real existence. It is the Self, pure Consciousness and supreme Bliss in which this universe is seen to exist.

The pull of *māyā* is very powerful and extremely difficult to be understood, leave aside abandoning or conquering it. Those few who must have mastered their senses may claim to do so. She enchants even the wisest though she does not possess any form. The whole world is under the magic spell of this unborn and incomprehensible *māyā*. No one can escape from its clutches.

A mysterious delusion dwells in the mind of man by which his pure reason is blunted, by which he is again and again made to cling and go back to those very objects and persons from which he is subject to so much pain and suffering. This mysterious veiling power termed *māyā,* is really a wonderful divine energy. The Lord causes all beings to revolve round as if they were mounted upon a wheel.

Māyā's ways are mysterious. It resides everywhere in the universe. Its nature consists of the three *guṇa-s*: *sāttva* (good), *rājas* (good and evil) and *tāmas* (evil). These three qualities are never in a state of admixture. There is an unceasing tussle between these three *guṇa-s* for gaining supremacy over one another. Their proportion varies from individual to individual and in the same individual from time to time. This takes place in all the shades and depths of all walks of life.

As a musician makes the wooden dolls dance to his tunes at his will, so this world-enchanting *māyā* is making this world dance from *Brahmā* down to the blade of grass including human beings.

The *Devī* (in *Śrimad Devī Bhāgavatam*) says:-

"I have an inherent power called *māyā.* This *māyā* is not existent nor is it non-existent, nor can it be called both. *Māyā* can be destroyed by *Brahma-jñāna*, so it cannot be called existent; again if *māyā* doesn't exist, the practical world cannot exist. So it cannot be called non-existent. Of course it cannot be called both, for it would involve contradictions. This *māyā* arises naturally as heat comes out of fire, as the rays come out of the sun and as the cool rays come out of the moon."

"*Māyā* has one *doṣa* (defect) - It hides Me, its Originator. I am *nirguṇa* and when manifested I become *saguṇa,* the great Cause of the world. *Māyā* is classified into *vidyā* and *avidyā. Avidyā* hides Me. *Vidyā* reveals Me. Man transcends both when he realises *brahman*, the supreme Reality. *Māyā* united with Consciousness is the efficient cause of this universe; whereas *māyā* reduced to and united with five *bhūtā-s* (original elements), is the material cause of the universe."

"This *māyā* is conceived in Me. It is not in reality different from Me. Viewed practically, it is known variously as *māyā*, *vidyā, avidyā;* but viewed from the point of *brahman*, there is no such thing as *māyā*; only the *brahman* exists."

How the finite arises out of the bosom of the Infinite is an incomprehensible mystery and that is why it is called *māyā*. The phenomenon of the universe is therefore beyond reasoning. This is divine Play.

The entire world is caught up in the vast net of attachment *(rāga)*. This attachment is an amazing delusory phenomenon often termed *māyā*.

Māyā is *brahman 's* power; in this sense, *māyā* is inseparable from *brahman* as heat from fire. In another sense *māyā,* as cosmic illusion, is a superimposition upon *brahman. Māyā* veils man's vision of *brahman*, as a result of which man perceives the manifest universe instead of the one Reality. Life is a flowery mystery and every exposure is beautiful.

In the cosmic dimension God takes a universal form which is Omniscient, Omnipotent and Omnipresent. This energy of God governs the entire process of evolution over which we have no control. We feel that we are controlling our life-stream, but in fact the cosmic energy laughs at us. "*Māyā moha ṭhagni ham jānī*" (*māyā* is a great enchantress), says *Kabīr.*

Māyā is the veil of transition in Nature, the veil that each man must lift in order to see behind it the Creator, the eternal Truth.

Just as the magician's tricks delude the audience alone and not the magician himself, so also the veiling of *māyā* affects the creatures and not the Creator. This *māyā* is the dynamic aspect of the latent self-sufficiency of the Supreme and is unfailing.

A farmer, married for many year, was blessed with a son who was named Haru. Naturally the parents loved the boy dearly. The farmer was of religious nature and well respected by the villagers. Once the farmer was working in the fields when a villager brought the bad news that his son suffered an attack of cholera and died. All the members of the family were aggrieved but the farmer kept his cool. "How heartless you are? You have not shed even one tear for the child," said his wife to him. The farmer consoled the other family members who were weeping and crying and spoke thus:

"Shall I tell you why I have not wept? I had a very vivid dream last night. I became a king and the father of eight children and was very happy. Then I woke up. Now I am so amazed and perplexed! Should I weep for those eight sons or for this one Haru?" The farmer realised that waking state is as unreal as the dream state. There is only one eternal substance and that is *ātman.*

WHAT is not known, that is *Māyā*.
It alone shines as many forms:
Vidyā, Avidyā, Parā, Aparā,
Tāmas, Pradhāna, and *Prakṛti.*

The world appears from the ignorance of the Self and disappears with the knowledge of the Self, just as the snake appears from the non-cognition of the rope and disappears with its recognition. ✡✡✡✡✡

CHAPTER SEVENTEEN

TIME

(Kāla)

FROM Time all beings emerge. From Time they advance and grow.
In Time do they come to rest. Except Time all things are created.
Time is the creator. It has no limit, neither top nor bottom.

A Persian saying.

TIME is a concept of mind. Annihilate the mind, you will go beyond time. In the Absolute there is no time. Time is a measure or duration of experiences. Where there is only one homogeneous experience of Self, how can time be there!

While everything sleeps, Time keeps vigil. None can transgress the movement of Time. Time moves within every being equally, freely, with nothing to obstruct it.

Life is measured by actions, not by time. Time and space are the factors of division in the world. Of these, space refers to the location of objects and time to the sequence of events.

The whole phenomenal existence can be reduced to three distinct concepts: space, time and causality. Space is infinite, time is without beginning. And so is causality. Therefore time, space and causality are no real objects at all. They are shadows around everything which you cannot perceive. They have no real existence yet they are not non-existent.

As a matter of fact *Puruṣa* (God) Himself is designated as *Kāla* (Time). In this way the Lord Himself abides unaffected within and without all beings as *kāla,* as their inner Controller.

The great *kāla* (Time) fashions the universe. All the *jīva-s* are subservient to Time which cannot be ruled over. None can fathom it. Time is passing by, independent of what is happening elsewhere.

When did 'Time' come into being? The concept of time was conceived only on the emergence of mind or consciousness. Time is passing? (do we pass the time?) Time is running? (does it ever stop?) Time is relative to the state of mind. Time stretches? Time contracts? Time runs?

In all things time plays a vital role, a period of preparation and the hour of fruition: Take birth, childhood, youth, old age and death, for example.

The Indian concept of time is circular, coming back to itself. The wheel symbolises time. This seems more natural. Every movement is circular. Time is nothing but a medium of movement. If things are static, we will not feel time. Time alters perception. Time swallows everything.

Time goes, you say. Alas, Time stays, only we go.

Nothing but time really belongs to us. Even he who has nothing else has time.

Yesterday is beyond repair. Tomorrow may not come. Today alone is ours. Make the best of it.

Nature, time and patience are three healers of all ailments.

Nature speaks the voice of dissolution. The highway of history and of life is strewn with the wrecks that Time has made.

The time which has neither beginning nor end blossoms from the flower bed of our mind.

> THE PLEASURE of leisure is the ability to live in the moment, forget about time and give yourself over to an activity. If you are perpetually saying 'what next' you are almost never living in the moment.

> The world is a thorny thicket. One gets entangled and lost in it.
> I shall be free when the 'I' ceases to be.

CHAPTER EIGHTEEN

HARMONY

(Tālamel)

THOSE who abide by the eternal Law, the winds are full of sweetness; the rivers pour sweets; so may plants be full of sweetness for them.

Ṛg Veda.

THERE is a rhythm of life but man's ignorance is creating problems which start when he fights with nature. The happiness depends upon one's capability to realise this rhythm and abide by the unwritten laws of nature.

NATURE's intelligence functions with effortless ease. The creeper just grows without trying to grow. The fish just swim; they don't try to swim. This is the law of Least Effort. Minimum effort is needed if our actions are motivated by Nature's ways. To get back to Nature is to live an easy, simple and carefree life. The life flows with effortless ease in harmony with Nature.

Our physical well-being depends upon our living in harmony with the physical environment, obeying the laws of health and nature. Similarly, if we ascertain the laws governing our mental and moral life and endeavour to live in harmony with them, we shall enjoy the well-being of the whole personality. These physical, mental, moral, intellectual and spiritual personalities must all be blended into one harmonious whole.

To get satisfaction out of life we must believe that it has a purpose. The aim of life is fullness of life. We crave for it and we are free to choose and meet that purpose. Not merely physical needs require satisfaction but inner needs do as well. Happiness arises from the harmonious blend of the two. We seek harmony, an ideal, a purpose in which we can lose ourselves.

The sufferings and obstacles in life are often the mysterious efforts of nature to help us in our work. That which is to be shunned is pain not yet come. Nature performs its duty regularly and perfectly but still we complain. Our complaints arise because of our maladjustment with the ways Nature *(prakṛti)* works.

The ignorant lives in a world of disharmony, division and conflict; yet in his heart of hearts there is a faith that in the centre of this vast and dynamic universe, a substance like harmony is at work. A glimpse of that harmony so satisfies him and makes him feel as if the very purpose of creation was fulfilled and that the whole labour of the cosmos is justified. This awareness awakens man to the universal harmony.

With every selfish action we create certain results from which we cannot escape. It is an interference with the balance of things, with the harmony that exists amongst the objects. The system cannot tolerate any kind of interference from any quarter. We generate a poison in the system by our wrong thoughts and actions which must culminate in disharmony and consequent ills. Nature as a whole maintains its equilibrium.

Nobody can deny the existence of conflicts in this world. But if a state of harmony is created and maintained in the mind, the disharmony around is seen from a new angle of detachment. The conflicts are thus understood and resolved.

The being, knowing, and doing must fuse into one harmonious unitary process right from the moment one wakes up from sleep and moves into the working world. Harmony stands for happiness and is the road to self-achievement and Self-realisation

"Oh Rāma, he truly is the great man, the most exalted soul, who is enriched by the ornament of equipoise. That man is really pure. His feet are sought after and prostrated by even the great sages of the world."

Yoga Vasiṣṭa.

The rhythm of our body, mind and spirit is akin to Nature's rhythm. The main reason for all our conflicts with others (the external world) or even with ourselves is the lack of understanding of that rhythm, the essential nature of the world. The harmony of the cosmos is an experienced truth in higher minds and it may be glimpsed by those who can rise above a mechanistic conception of the cosmos. A spiritual approach can heal the psyche and lead to personal growth, peace and happiness.

We have the freedom to live up to saner dictates, or to be misguided by inner insufficiencies. Our response (fight or flight) is always to 'go towards happiness' or 'getting away from unhappiness'. Thus when we hold on to the changing moods of the mind, we miss appreciating the innate joy and peace experienced by a quiet mind. The rhythm of the body, the melody of the mind and the harmony of the soul make the symphony of the life.

All is burning with the fire of lust, hate, sorrows, lamentations, pains, grief, despair, delusion, ageing and death! Who can deny that? This suffering cannot be abolished as long as the individual is inconsistent with the Infinite. The human being is always attached to the immediate concerns of life. He is grieved about the past, doubtful about the future and worried about the present. He is always dis-eased in his thoughts due to his violation of the eternal law. Take opportunity to understand and realise the Eternal law and follow the right path.

Mental harmony is the true spiritual attainment. Nature has provided us with all possible hints, clues and suggestions in all matters and events. Only we lack the understanding. It is better to try to work with the Mother-wit (Nature) rather than against it. The aim is attainment of inner harmony with the help of universal consciousness. Life without any inner conflict represents the process of perfection. Harmony has to be felt in every stage of life.

To live in harmony with the external world is not to be construed as a life of idle acceptance or unintelligent surrender. A man is living in harmony when his dancing steps on the path of pilgrimage are tuned to the constant hum of the Eternal.

Harmonise emotion and reason in a unifying outpouring of action that is appropriate to the end to be achieved. Harmonise body, mind and spirit to experience happiness.

Harmony between two people will not come about by insisting on uniformity.

It is possible only by their admitting the differences between them and showing equal respect for each others' rights and faith. A harmonious society is formed by tolerating various view points

Life is a rhythm and one who 'knows' this rhythm can stay healthy, live long and feel happy and achieve his goal of life.

Equality is prior to inequality. It is also prior to diversity. It is eternal and shows the way to harmony. The universe is restless and will continue to be so until it coalesces into the eternal Absolute. Let's leave it to Nature to perform the best. She understands better than we do.

The flute in the hands of Kṛṣṇa can be 'you' or 'I'. The Lord fills us with breath and life and plays the melody He likes. But we, in our stupid ego, try to sing our own song and thus bring wrong notes in His Music divine. Result: disharmony, conflict, sorrow and suffering, all in bad taste. Be a faithful instrument of the Lord. Listen to the uninterrupted and enchanting flow of His melodious grace in gay abandon within. And lo! the Lord's message of love is knocking at your door. Harmony resolves all your problems.

We are passing through a period of crisis and hypertension. Spirituality leads us to rise above our narrow ends and thereby strengthens us to bear with our day-to-day difficulties. It helps us to build character and practise the core values like truth and peace which are universal in nature. Spirituality does not relate to any particular religion or sect. It is the power that guides us to know the truth - what is right and what is wrong.

LIFE is to enjoy but who does so? Everyone is struggling. What is the end? Only suffering and dying? Why not then try the real spiritual path?

❄

Harmonise everything in your consciousness. Express the inner change in your outer activities.

CHAPTER NINETEEN

SILENCE

(Mauṇa)

GOD is the ocean of utmost silence. This silence, the voice of God, can be heard only in the silence of the soul. The Grand Silence is the Reality, the Truth, the God.

SILENCE is gold for an ignorant person. And if he understands it, he is no more ignorant. When one realises God, he is silent. The object is to achieve the inner quietude.

THERE is a hidden silence altogether unknown to all but for those who taste it, its sweetness is of the heart, not of the flesh.

SILENCE is the language of the heart. Silence is immense strength. Silence is great eloquence. Silence is Reality. The goal of life is silence. Behind all noises and sounds is silence. Silence is Infinite. Silence is intuitive experience. The message of the Himalayas is silence. When the heart is full, when it is overjoyed, there is silence. Who can describe the glory of this silence? The silence that one enjoys during deep sleep and the silence that he experiences at dead of night marks the existence of that Ocean of silence (the innermost soul). Silence is not a thing we make. It is something into which we enter. It is always there. All we can make is noise, more noise.

Silence is the innate nature of the mind. When the mind does not think, it is all silence. We need not do anything for silence. Silence is the state of mind when it has nothing to think about. Silence is natural. However agitated the mind may be, it does become silent now and then. What is really wanted is silence of the bubbling mind. With the practice of *mauṇa*, the energy of speech is slowly sublimated into spiritual energy.

Sarasvati (Divine Mother) is manifest in all beings as speech (*vāk*). Therefore to conserve speech through regular periods of silence is also an adoration of the Mother Grace.

The seeker is advised to meditate upon the smile of the Lord. He will then realise that to meditate upon the smile is to live the smile and its silent message. A profound silence is only the right attitude which the soul should adopt towards the Absolute. What is important is how we are able to communicate with God through silence. Silence and modesty are very valuable qualities in the art of conversation. The direct silent communication with the Divine can go on for all times, not just during the meditation.

Experiencing love in its pristine pure content is spirituality. The experience can never be communicated fully through words. Words suffice only for the mind to speak to the mind. When the mind transcends its limits, it falls silent. Then one hears the music of Silence, the rhythm of the inner voice, the murmur of the soul.

As your mind becomes silent, serene, calm and quiet, you start understanding your own consciousness, the inner being becomes more and more centred, and your actions will reflect morality quite naturally, as naturally as the sun rises in the morning.

Love grows in silence like the sleeping child in the cradle, whose mother is gazing at him with fond tenderness but is too careful to fondle him. This love *sans* murmurs, *sans* music, *sans* words, mingles with the love of the divine expressed by His unseen hand through his unsung lullaby.

Mauna (silence) is constant speech. A holy thought is a voice which speaks when the tongue is silent. Silence does not involve us in controversy. Where there is no fuel, there is no fire. Silence helps in getting rid of ego.

Silence is another technique for discovering Truth. Practising silence means to silence all your desires that try to percolate into your consciousness from outside; so you can go deeper within to feel your soul.

Silence is ever speaking. The words obstruct the mute language. The most befitting attitude to the knowledge of the Absolute is silence. Speech and thought cannot find it.

He who speaks noble truths and gives utterances to the word of God, observes the vow of silence. Silence is restraint of speech.

Be silent so that the Lord may speak. The language He most listens to is that of silent love. Nothing should be spoken unless it is absolutely necessary to do so.

By silence is not meant the stillness of speech or dumbness of the tongue but quietude of mind. The silence acts as a great force to the soul and one feels relaxed as a result.

Man spoils matters much more by speech than by silence. An armour of silence will surely protect him from the onslaught of nasty encounters.

In silence there is a luminous pathway for special enlightenment and mystic realisation. Let us learn to savour the sound of silence and the tenderness of its touch and cultivate the art of silent communion to express our devotion to the Almighty. Silence and solitude are the cherished possession of a realised soul. Silence helps disentangle confused thoughts.

> LOOK within, enter the silence, listen the silence, see the silence, feel the silence and realise your eternal union with God, the Supreme Silence.

In silence we can hear the birds singing, the sound of the wind blowing, the silent repetitions of the *mantra-s* in the mind. Silence is healing. Silence is a path and also a goal.

CHAPTER TWENTY

SURRENDER

(Śaraṇāgati)

ABANDON all supports and look to Me for protection. I shall purify you from the sins of the past; do not grieve.

Bhagavadgītā.

THE wise should surrender his words to his mind; and the mind he should surrender to the Knowing Self; and the Knowing Self he should surrender to the Great Self; and that he should surrender to the Peaceful Self.

Kaṭha Upaniṣad.

WHEN can one be Mother's? When one loses oneself completely, when there is no thought in the heart other than that of Hers. Through practice, determination and love, place yourself as an instrument in the hands of the Almighty who carries on her work in her own way.

Self-surrender is not so easy. It needs constant practice to come to that point of intense feeling. So long as meekness, purity and love do not adorn one's expressed life, self-surrender is not real. It is only after we have struggled and failed to pull through our problems, and find ourselves helpless, that we realise the need to surrender and take shelter of the Supreme Being. It is through Her grace only that the mind and intellect attain light. The Beloved awaits you. You have only to call Her name and SHe runs to you.

It is the soul that surrenders itself to the Mother Divine in joy, love and admiration for Her in the first instance; the surrender of *tan, man, dhan* follows in its wake as a matter of course. Taking refuge in Her Majesty itself means freedom from all sins and sorrows. SHe is bliss. Even the happiness we derive from prayer is merely the fruit of our contact with the Divine.

There is a tendency to equate surrender with inactivity, a sort of 'let God do it' view. But it is only our 'ego-sense', the idea 'I am doing' that we surrender. We have to do without this ego in order to hold God responsible for our actions.

Just as a dry leaf is tossed here and there by the wind not of its own choosing, so the man of knowledge is guided by his destiny without the least vestige of egoism in him. 'Everything happens' is his common belief.

A father was once passing through a field with his two little sons. He was carrying one of them in his arms while the other was walking along with him holding his hand. They saw a kite flying and the latter boy giving up his hold on his father's hand, began to clap his hands with joy, crying, 'behold, papa, there is a kite' But immediately he stumbled down and got hurt. The boy who was carried by the father also clapped his hands with joy but he did not fall, as his father was holding him. The first boy represents self-help and the second self-surrender.

Śri Aurobindo prescribes a constant self-surrender to the divine Force which alone has the power to affect in man the irrevocable transformation. This divine Force, in the form of a secret evolutionary force of Nature, is constantly working in man so that he can transcend his imperfections.

Once the Lord spoke to me thus: "Dost thou come to Me in a spirit of self-surrender? " I replied, "Lord, to Thee I surrender my I-ness, my ego and all that I have." "Remember, My child, If you have renounced your all to Me, I too shall renounce My all to you," assured the Lord. Surrender is the transcendence of ego.

> Love seeks union with the beloved. Obedience seeks the pleasure of the beloved. Surrender seeks nothing.

❄

Surrender and insistence on one's own will cannot go together.

PART THREE

TRUTH REALISATION

(Satyajñāna)

ULTIMATE, unheard, unconsidered, unbowed, unseen, undifferentiated and unspoken, albeit listener, thinker, seer, speaker, discriminator and fore-knower, of that Interior Person of all beings, one should know that 'He is my Self'.

Aitareya Āraṇyaka

The secret of the cosmic game is that God hides His bliss behind the temptations of the world. He knows that man made in His own image with supreme joy hidden within him, will not forever wallow in the mud of the senses. Disillusioned by non-satisfying sense pleasures, man is haunted by the memory of his lost soul peace. Hurt by the poisoned honey of pleasures, he ultimately seeks the pure divine nectar. God's game of hide and seek with His sons in this cosmic dream would be pointless if He had not made it hazardous with pain and pleasure. He blindfolded men with ignorance and hid His perfect blissful face. The surprise goal to be achieved by His children, one by one, is consciousness of identity with Him.

Paramahansa Yogānanda.

Self-Realisation, Who Am I? *(Ātmabodha)*
God-Realisation, The Goal. *((Brahmajñāna)*

As long as you run with the running mind, you cannot discover the Self. The silence of the Self is ever there waiting within.

CHAPTER TWENTY ONE

SELF-REALISATION, WHO AM I?

(Ātmabodha)

THIS *ātman,* hidden in all beings, is not manifest to all. But it can be realised by all who are accustomed to inquire into subtle truths by means of their sharp and subtle reason.

Kaṭha Upaniṣad.

SELF-knowledge is the primary *sādhanā*. The Self, O dear, is to be seen, listened to, reflected upon and meditated upon.

Mahārṣi Ramana was asked by his student, "What is man's principal duty in life?" The sage responded, "A man who aspires for the highest ought to know his own true nature".

Who am I? The body is not the Self for it does not exist either before birth or after death. The vital airs is not the Self because it is devoid of consciousness. Mind is not the Self because it has desires and is moved by pain and pleasure.

The notions 'I am this', 'I am that', 'I do this', 'I did that' are accompanied by the sense of doer-ship and enjoyer-ship. When we question these fundamental beliefs, we discover that these beliefs are born out of ignorance. This knowledge may not result in immediate happiness but the illusory sorrows are certainly shown the exit. The ego takes to its heels and thus at least a bad dream ends.

Mistaken self-identity (I-thought) is the foundation of all our problems. The means to peace lies therefore in uprooting this I-thought. It is not that until all the gross confusions like seeking sense pleasures, emotional gratification, attachments and other passions, are significantly reduced, if not totally removed, the enquiry 'Who Am I?' comes to the fore. It results in just the seeker's turning inward. Normally we are extrovert. The revelation of Self is God, the Ultimate Reality. You cannot objectify the Self as you can objectify your eyes before a mirror. The Self cannot be the object of experience. The Self is self-revealing. The Self cannot be negated. Being all-pervasive, the Self *(brahman)* cannot be limited by Time and Space. 'That' which makes things subject to our perception and understanding is Self, is Consciousness. It is Infinite.

Self-realisation is not an attainment or achievement. It is the discovery of the Self in one's own heart. If the Self is not there, how can you raise a question? 'I think I think', 'I think I act', but It is another one who thinks and acts in me.

When other thoughts arise, one should enquire: 'To whom do they come?' The answer would be 'to me.' Then 'who is me?' The mind will go back to its source and the thoughts will subside. Self-realisation requires absolute purity of mind. The realisation of the Self is in a way like the shining of the sun when the clouds no more cover him.

The battle for Self-realisation is a tug of war between the Self within and the world without. The best and easiest way to defeat the opponent is to leave the rope so that the enemy falls by his own force. The answer is renunciation.

There is no agent to know the Self nor any light to lead to it. The Self Itself flashes its Self-luminosity. The delight of the Self is the delight of the Being. It is the Bliss of Consciousness Absolute.

Patanjali includes physical exercises, moral practices, and exercises of attention in his eight-fold method (*yama, niyama, āsana, prāṇāyāma, pratyāhāra, dhāraṇā, dhyāṇa and samādhi)* for attaining this Perfect state. As soon as all movements of the mind are arrested, the Self shows in its pure state and this staying in the pure state is what is meant by Self-Realisation.

Everyone is conscious of his existence. 'He is', 'I am'. That is the Self which speech cannot express but that which makes us speak, that which cannot be felt but that which makes the mind feel.

The great sage, the most eminent of the Enlightened, Bhagavan Śri Ramana Mahārṣī, who always abided in the Self in human form, spoke thus:

"The nexus of the body and the Self is called *granthi* (knot). It is only by this connection with the Self that one is aware of the body. The connection between the two is deduced through the intellect. Even as the subtle forces like the electric current pass through visible wires, the light of awareness flows through a *nāḍi* (vein) in the body. As the light pervades the entire body, one gets attached to the body, mistakes the body for the Self and regards the world as different from oneself. When the discerning one renounces attachment and identification of himself with the body and pursues one-pointed self-enquiry, the Self gets separated and shines forth. He from whom the *ātman* alone shines, within, without and everywhere, as clearly as objects to the ignorant, is called one who has cut the knot. As a heated iron ball appears as a ball of fire, this body heated in the fire of Self-enquiry shines as the Self. The old *vāsanā-s* are destroyed, no sense of doer-ship remains and the *karma-s* completely destroyed."

"Lay aside this corpse-like body. Do not even murmur 'I' but enquire keenly within what it is that now shines within the heart as 'I'. Transcending the intermittent flow of diverse thoughts there arises the continuous, unbroken awareness, silent and spontaneous, as 'I', 'I' in the heart. If one catches it and remains still, it will completely annihilate the sense of 'I-identity', and itself disappear as a fire burns camphor. Sages and scriptures proclaim this to be liberation."

It is this 'I' which is the essence of man, and this 'I' is never seen. 'I' pass away. 'THOU' alone dost endure.

Divine is your essence. You are Its expression. If That would not be, I would not be, nor you would be.

We use the pronouns 'that' and 'this' to indicate two things, one at a distance and the other nearer. What if the distance narrows down to nil and 'this' is no more 'that'. In Self-Realisation it is only the Self seeing the Self.

The Supreme Spirit is the vital content in every particle of this world. There is neither life nor light in the absence of this Spirit.

In truth, the Self, the mystic spiritual Presence, alone exists for all times. To know this, to be so, and to find one's fulfilment in that knowledge, is one aim of all spiritual disciplines and *sādhanā.* God is at hand for anyone to realise. Only one needs to be.

We have experience of determinate consciousness but our aim is to realise that Indeterminate Consciousness which is real Self, which is hidden but not non-existent. 'I see' does not mean the 'eye sees'. But 'I' endowed with eye.

"Blend the wakefulness with sleep. The blend will mean the birth of a new state which is neither wakefulness nor sleep, nor dream. This is the key to the entire mystery about Self, about God."

Swami Bhoomānanda Tirtha.

Where Light, which is life and truth as well as peace, shines forth, there the time is blotted out, the physical and mental consciousness is dispersed, all dreams end, desire is extinct, life and death no more exist, the struggle ceases. In the stillness the heart throbs with quiet rapture. In the Self there is no sense of self. It is all 'That'. It is only when man realises his *ātman's* permanent relationship with the Supreme Reality that he becomes liberated.

"As fragrance abides in the flower,
As reflection is within the mirror,
So does our Lord abide within us,
Need we search for Her without?"

Our ancient seers and saints have opined that to realise Self, the mind, *antāhkarṇa,* must subjugate the three major undesirable hurdles, e.g., *mala* (impurities) by *karma* (actions performed in the name of God), *vikṣepa* (tossing and agitation of mind) by *upāsanā* (mental worship) and *āvarṇa* (veil, ignorance) by *nidhīdhyāsan* (meditation, contemplation).

Self-realisation, the ability to commune directly with God, can be done only by shutting the sense communication and opening thc instrument of silence within. Practice silence. It is a vital part of one's *sādhanā.*

Self-knowledge is a progressive evolution and it starts from being true, honest and sincere to oneself, which, of course, needs courage. Often we keep lying to ourselves, refuse to own our follies, to admit our failures. That we fear ourselves is a great irony. When one fears, one refuses to know. One's strength is in proportion to one's being honest to oneself. *Upaniṣad-s* designate as *dhīra* (the courageous), the one who sets his heart at Self-knowledge.

Self-realisation could also mean Self-engrossment but a self-engrossed person cannot be selfish because a selfish person does not know his inner Self. Higher one moves towards the state of self-realisation, lesser will be the degree of selfishness.

Self-enquiry is the shortest road to *vairāgya* (renunciation). Passions and attachments are in the mind. When the mind is controlled, they are subdued and that is *vairāgya.*

Self-Realisation is Self-manifestation. A person will benefit by spiritual realisation to the extent to which he is able to integrate his inner illumination with outer brilliance.

> THE FLUIDITY that is not water, the limpidity that is not air, the Light without fire and the Spirit without body 'That Thou Art'.

Enlightenment is a state of maturity in which one's self is unshakeable by any circumstance. Come what may nothing can rob you of your smile.

CHAPTER TWENTY TWO

GOD-REALISATION - THE GOAL

(Brahmajñāna)

Some realise Him after great effort;
Some find Him without seeking;
Some long for Him with no response;
With some He ignores dealing.

FOR THE ETERNAL object of your quest within your soul, enough have you wandered during the long period of your quest. Dark and weary must have been the ages of your searching in ignorance and groping in helplessness. At last when you turn your gaze inward, suddenly you realise that the bright light of faith and lasting truth was shining around. With rapturous joy, you find the soul of the universe, the eternal object of your quest. Your searching mind at last finds the object of your search within your own heart. Your inner vision is illuminated by this new realisation.

Yajurveda.

HE whose mind is tranquil without support of any object, whose breath is controlled without effort, whose gaze is steady without looking up at anything, has attained the goal. What else does one obtain by realisation of God? Does one grow a pair of horns? Our mind becomes pure, and through that mind, comes enlightenment. The fruit of the achievement of God-realisation is not in some paradise beyond, but here on earth, in life. What is sought for is secured and enjoyed here.

Is the Divine inaccessible (transcendent) or approachable? Whichever way you turn, there is the face of the Lord. Adore him as though you did see him, and if you do not see him, SHe, nonetheless, sees you.

All the processes meant to lead us to Truth-realisation are limited, not perfect in themselves. Just as those who do not know the spot and walk over the hidden treasure of gold again and again, but do not find it, even so all those beings who visit day after day that abode of *brahman* but do not realise him, for, truly, they are ignorant.

The path to realisation is long and arduous, scattered with innumerable hurdles and doubts. It is like an adventurous mountaineering expedition on Himalayas through dark virgin jungles in quest of the ascent of the Mount.

Various methods of *sādhanā* are prescribed in the scriptures and by our saints and preceptors. In fact there can be as many spiritual paths as there are spiritual aspirants. Each path is an approach to the Absolute. Move and the way opens. Choose the one which appeals to you most and practise it.

Realisation is in fact a sudden experience. But the preparation for it is gradual and can be accomplished only through a steady and ceaseless practice.

Superimpose divinity on everything. Make the whole mind filled with thoughts of your chosen deity by feeling that whatever you see, taste or hear, is divine. There is nothing other than the divine.

Silence is another technique for discovering the Truth. Practising Silence means to silence all your desires that try to percolate into your consciousness from outside. Thus you can go deeper within to realise the Self.

The divine Presence within us, the soul, is ever seeking to express its perfect qualities and powers. As our consciousness becomes attuned to the divine Consciousness, we are able to absorb the impact of our melancholy and maintain tranquillity of mind. What is needed is to dig out the mind from the transient world objects where it is rooted, and transplant it in the divinity of Being which is its true source.

This awareness of the ultimate Reality destroys *māyā* (the finite aspect) and the individual is liberated. Guru Nānak wants us to have a spiritual experience of feeling the presence of God in the form of an all-pervading Spirit.

Buddha said, "I do not care to know your theories about God. What is the use of discussing all subtle doctrines of the soul? Do good and be good. This will take you to freedom and whatever truth there."

Remember God in the same way as:

- A lover remembers his lady-love.
- A pauper thinks of a few coins he has collected and which he counts every now and then and forgets them not even for a moment.
- Like the mad attachment of the moth which he has for the flame - he burns himself to death but does not shrink from hugging the fire.
- the love which the fish has for water.
- A musician is ever aware of the base-sound while he sings.
- A mother is ever in attention of her child in the cradle even though she is engaged in the domestic activities.

Sādhanā aims to remove the distractions of the mind and bring about a state of *ekāgaratā*, (concentration, one-pointedness) in order to integrate the life. This in-gathering of the mind is the beginning of the spiritual acquisition.

Mahārājā Parikśit attained perfection by *śravaṇa* (listening), Sukhadeva Gosvami glorified the Lord by *guṇagān* (singing glories), Prahlād remembered the Lord by *japa* (recitation) and realised Him. Ākrūra offered *stuti* (prayers) to the Lord. Hanumāna served the Lord *(dāsya bhāva).* Arjuna enjoyed friendship with the Lord (*sakhya bhāva*). Meerā loved the Lord *(bhakti, mādhura bhāva).*

The goal was attained by cow-maids (*gopī-s*) through love, by Kaṇsa through fear, by Śiśupāla through hatred and by Pāndavā-s through friendship and numerous others through devotion. Never is devotion to Lord fruitless.

Give up all desires that stand in the way of your fulfilling the chief objective of human existence. To overcome this array of desires, generate a greater desire for divinity, a strong desire for perfection, for realisation, to make your life sublime, ideal, holy and sacred.

It is the offspring of thoughts that has veiled the infinite Reality. The attempt of all spiritual seekers should be to check the on-going flow of thoughts and maintain that state till the Truth reveals Itself. The mere elimination of our weaknesses, negative forces, meanness etc. is no worthwhile achievement, for, if the bosom is empty, they will enter again by the backdoor. To remove the obstacles in the way of spiritual growth, renounce the objects of the world. Or, learn the technique of using them as means. In this case attitudes need to be transformed.

"Think of space in your heart and in the midst of that space think that a flame is burning. Think of that flame as your own soul and inside the flame is another effulgent light and that is the Soul of all souls, God. Meditate upon that."

Swami Vivekananda.

"I went to pray with the devotees but did not feel in place. I went among those who mortify themselves, who observe fasts and other austerities and still did not feel in place". I said, "O my God! What then is the way to Thee?" And the answer was: "Abandon thyself and come".

Having a vision of the *Iṣṭadevatā* is not true realisation of the supreme Reality. The true realisation is the understanding of its real nature. The true vision is the experience of peace and bliss in one's heart.

Realise the changeless Reality by constantly noticing and observing what keeps on changing. Observe the changing and you will observe the Changeless. Notice the changing without getting trapped in it and you will realise the Changeless.

Four vital themes that should help realise the Ultimate:

- Self-observation: It is your own nature. Observe your silly as well as good thoughts with a detached mind.
- Self-integration: After self-observation, you will find a lot of guilt, fear and compulsive habits. You are not slave to them. Check them out and integrate yourself.
- Self-appreciation: Appreciate the moments you feel content and full, just as when you hug your child or take a cup of coffee or enjoy nature. Let these feelings saturate your entire being in such a way that the appreciating mind gets lost in its own world.

- Self-realisation: When the mind thus gets lost, you hit the crucial point of self-realisation. There is no one to appreciate and nothing appreciable.

To realise God, man has to conquer first of all the beast in him, and later, the ego in him. The next fight with passions *(asura-s)* is on a much higher level and is a never-ending struggle. These *asura-s* never die. Slain in one form they rise in another and renew the attack. Beware of their return ! Keep them at bay.

The short cut to Self-enlightenment is to cut your ego and surrender before the highest One with utmost humility.

God reveals to those whose eyes yearn only for his Presence, whose tongue, like the swan, gathers pearls of His perfection, whose head bows down and adores His feet, whose feet take him to holy places, who mutter His Name, who desire devotion to His feet, who know no lust and work for the goodness of all his beings, who look upon others' wives as their mother. May the Lord of lords bless them.

Listen to the praises and sing the glories of God and His creation. Understand what you hear. Perceive or gain a concept of what you have understood. Realise the nature of what you have perceived. Know the Reality. This will go a long way to help you to experience divinity.

Pūjā and *Japa* done with love and devotion works wonders. The seeker begins to understand how the mind, often vicious, can experience blissful calmness during devotional practices. A mind which dwells on God, derives inner strength and rises above disturbing situations.

When the *jñāna jyoti* (the lamp of Knowledge) lights up in the chamber of the heart and tries to loosen the knot, the soul obtains its desired object. But when *māyā* sees this act of untying the knot, it creates many obstacles and tries to put out the lamp by a side-puff. If the man is intelligent and well-informed, he perceives and ignores the *māyā's* hostile intent and design. If, however, the blast of sensual air penetrates the chamber of the soul, it forthwith extinguishes the lamp. To light it again, the same cumbersome course will have to be repeated.

A disciple once asked his Master, "Sir, please tell me how I can see God". "Come with me," said the Guru, "I shall show you God." He took the disciple to a lake, and both of them got into the water. Suddenly the teacher pressed the disciple's head under the water. After a few moments he released him and the disciple raised his head and stood up. The Guru asked him, "How did you feel?" The disciple said, "Oh! I thought I would die; I was panting for breath." The teacher said, "When you pant like that for God, then you wouldn't have to wait for long to see God."

Make your mind the funeral ground, burn into ashes all the desires. Bold steps are needed in the spiritual life as also in the temporal life. He who risks not can never hope to gain. Make the Infinite your horizon. Let the whole universe be the field in which you wander! No one can realise for you, no one can renounce for you. You alone will light your own lamp.

Bhagavadgītā prescribes some methods of God-realisation: Meditation (*upāsanā*) for those who can control their *antāhkaraṇa* and senses and are endowed with the ability to concentrate. The path of knowledge *(jñāna)* for intellectuals who are adept in making proper use of rhyme and reason. The path of devotion *(bhakti)* for those who are emotional and sentimental; and the path of action (*karma)* for those who are practical in life activities and believe in *dharma.*

In Śaṅkarācārya's view deeds can only cause the purification of mind. Persons endowed with a pure mind can directly have recourse to knowledge and can attain the *summum bonum* of human life. *Karma* is a means to the attainment of knowledge. In Rāmānujācārya's view devotion is the primary means; knowledge and actions remain its subsidiaries. Śaṅkara holds that a person having devotion alone, is entitled to obtain scriptural knowledge from a preceptor. However, for reaching the ultimate goal of release one must have recourse to the path of knowledge. The path of knowledge is very rigorous and exacting. It requires a moral discipline of the highest order.

True knowledge is the practical wisdom of fully enlightened beings. It purifies the mind and intellect. The *jñānī* experiences God-consciousness within himself. To him the whole universe is illusory. Like a dream he is always established in the reality of the Self. But with the lover of God (*bhakta*) the case is different. *Bhakti* in essence is the path of divine love and devotion, path of emotions attuned to God conceived as the beloved. To make it tangible, the human imagination must personify the divine Essence, endow it with loveable attributes and develop an attitude of fervent love towards the Divine. His ideal is the Personal God *(Iṣṭadevatā).* Of all the conditions required for release, devotion is deemed most important. *Śaṅkarācārya* defines *bhakti* as the search for the nature of one's own self.

Bhakti yoga suits most people as man is essentially a creature of feelings, sentiments and emotions. To the man of head it will hardly carry an effect.

God-realisation is the highest *sādhanā*. One may banish the fire of sin by *karma upāsanā* (worship through noble works) but good works alone do not necessarily destroy ignorance. Without *jñāna* (true knowledge that destroys ignorance) one cannot know God. But *jñāna* is not independent of *karma* (actions) any more than work can be independent of *jñāna*.

The divine energy, known as Spirit, is in everyone but we are not aware of it. The Spirit is the link between the individual and the divine. It is the realisation and experience of the Spirit which links the individual with the universe. Once this realisation takes place and one is able to live in that state, nothing else remains to be known or experienced.

Philosophers, intellectuals, preceptors and theologians have written tons on ways to realise God. Innumerable means and paths have proliferated. Prolific descriptions of *ātman* are being advanced. God is beyond verbal teaching. The divinity in man is clouded and veiled consequent upon his lustful desires and attachment *(āsakti, moha)* to the objects of the world. These strings can be eliminated. "Among thousands of men scarce ones strive for perfection; of the successful strivers, scarce one knows Me in essence."

THERE are hundred and one channels of the heart. One of these passes up to the crown of the head and leads one to immortality. The others depart in various directions.

Chāndogya Upaniṣad.

We suffer because we seek the Self in the not-Self, the subject in the object. The true Self is devoid of any self-image. Even to call it Self is misleading because it belongs to none and none belongs to it.

God-realisation is a question of individual effort and consistent struggle to experience the Omnipresence in every thing perceivable and non-perceivable. Happiness is spiritual experience born of love and truth.

The human mind, in its evolved stage, has been considered to be the crowning achievement of this world but how often do we dive deep to know its Source? It is sadly ignored.

The image of the child is the symbol of purity, innocence, simplicity and humility. Reject erudition, annihilate ego and live as a child. You will realise the goal.

> WISE, self-controlled, and tranquil souls, who are contented in spirit, and who practise austerity and meditation in solitude and silence, are freed from all impurity, and attain, by the path of liberation to the Immortal, the truly Existing, the changeless Self.
>
> *Muṇḍaka Upaniṣad.*

❄

I come from the Infinite. Infinite is my home. I go back there and become the Infinite. You would not seek Me if you did not possess Me.

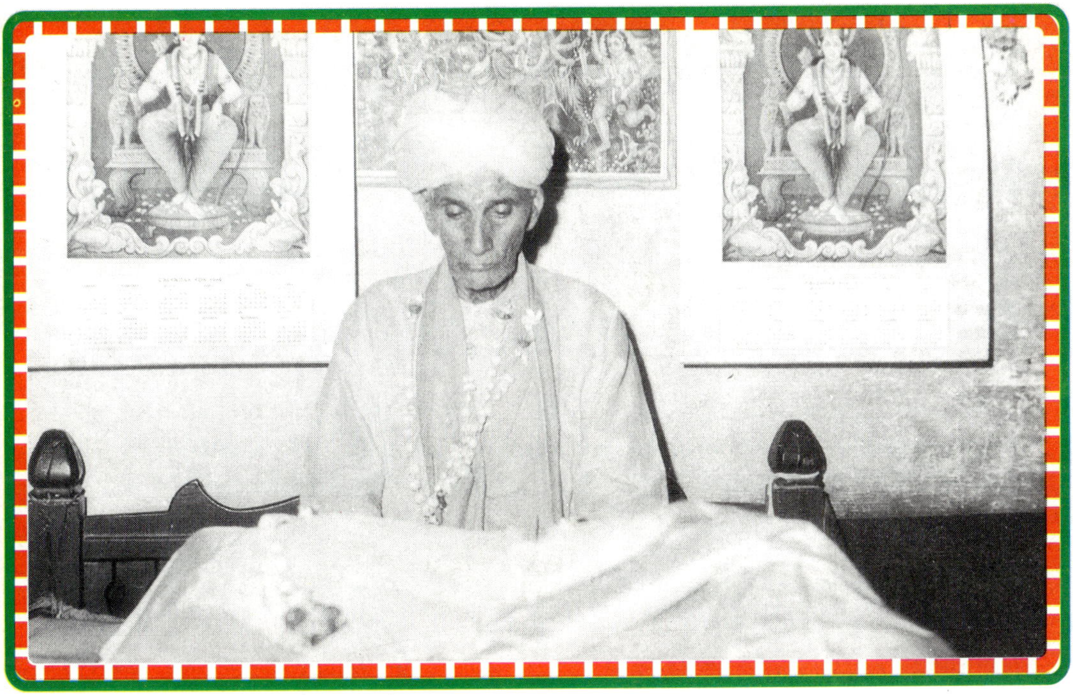

Pūjya Sadgurū Śri Śri 1008 Sant Sadhu Ram Ji,
Mansa Ram Mission, Nurmahal (Punjab)

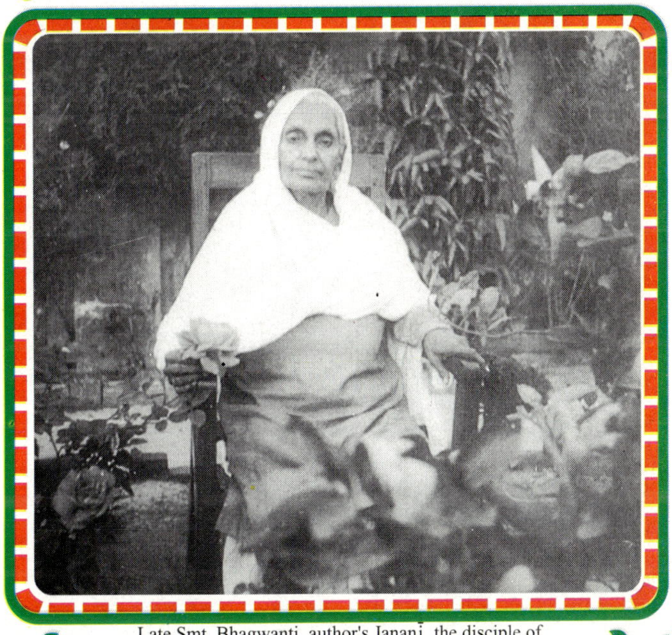

Late Smt. Bhagwanti, author's Jananī, the disciple of
Puja Sadguru, and the divine inspiration behind this text (p.101)

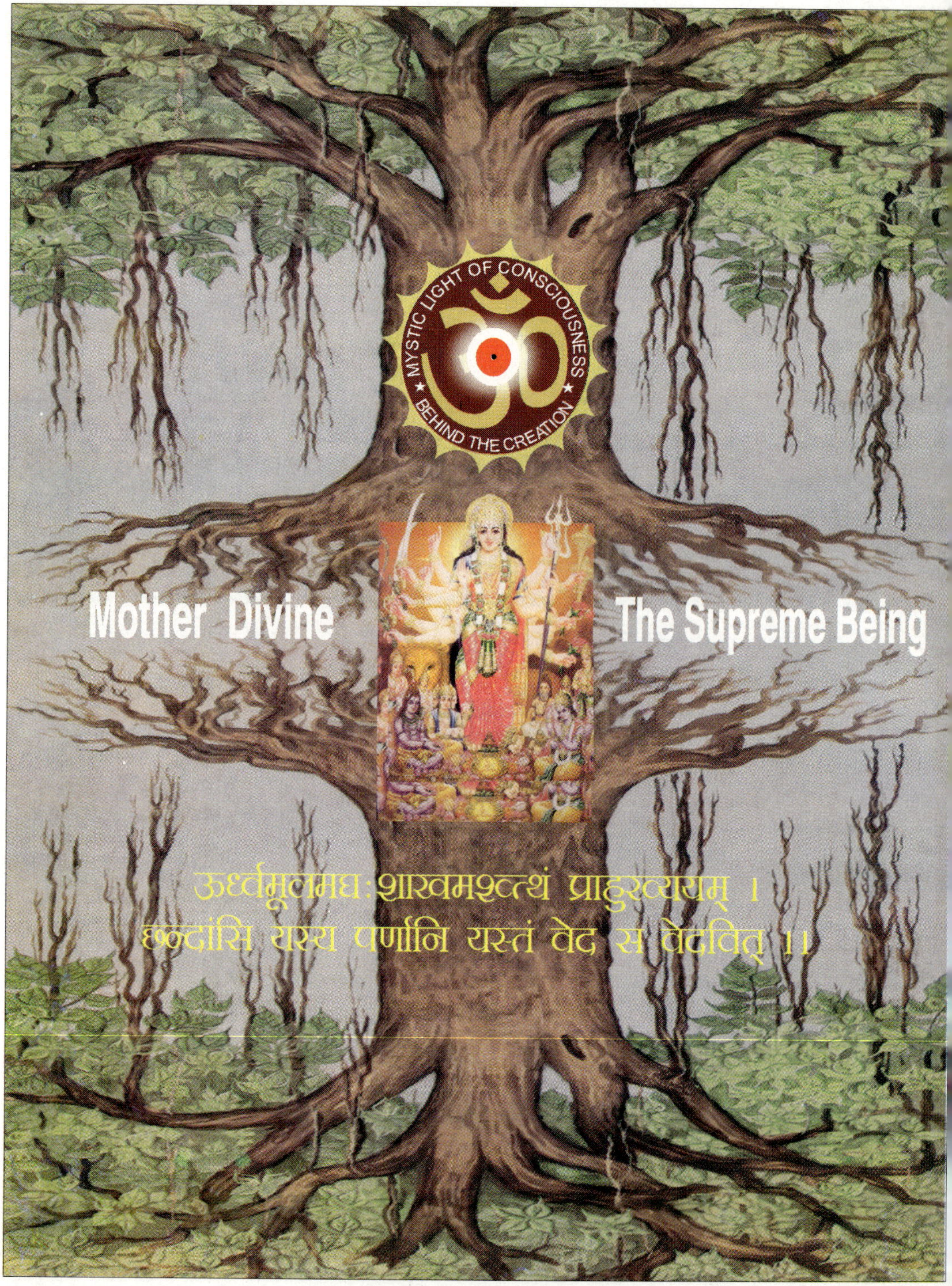

The Cosmic Tree

PART FOUR

Glory Of The Mother Divine

(Māṃ kā Guṇgāṇa)

या देवी सर्वभूतेषु मातृरुपेण संस्थिता
नमस्तस्यै नमस्तस्यै नमस्तस्यै नमो नमः।।

Salutations to the Mother Divine who abides in all beings in the form of Mother.

Obeisance to You, Salutations to You, O Māṃ Maheṣvarī.

ĀDYAŚAKTI

MOTHER DIVINE, the SUPREME BEING

THE ONE whom we adore as MOTHER DIVINE, the Supreme Personality of Godhead, is the divine CONSCIOUS FORCE *(Adya Śakti)* that dominates all existence. That we call Nature or *Prakṛti* is one of Her executive aspect. MOTHER DIVINE is ONE but many are Her powers and personalities. Her emanations and *vibhūti*-s only attend to the allotted works in the universe. To address the Supreme Being as Mother Divine is not against the common belief that God is divine Father. The Reality ought to be 'SHe' as 'SHe' includes 'He' - He for God and SHe for God in it. SHe is the charioteer of our existence. SHe marshals and establishes the harmony of Her forces, and processes and impels the operations of *Prakṛti*.

THE OBJECT OF MEDITATION

Meditation implies a *jīvātman* and an object of meditation. There is a cherished desire and constant effort to reach the perfection of the object. Choose the object of meditation you love most, the one which delights your heart and arouses your emotions and feelings, an object which is considered to be 'all-in-all' capable of granting everything we want, a 'total' object, not just one of the many. That object is not a symbolic form like a dot, a triangle or an image but a representative of the Supreme Being. We have to become truly friendly and intimate with the object since we seek union with it. That iconic object of worship inspires and exudes confidence. Men of vision see in their hours of meditation the symbolic image of their faith and choice which may precede an experience and realisation. You can embrace God, you can interact with God through that object. The object carries the message of the devotee to his Beloved. As one can reach the ocean through any river, so also one can reach the Ultimate through one's chosen object of maditation. God as Mother Divine is one such object of meditation.

> Everything that exists is situated in the *Brahmjyoti*. But when the *Jyoti* is covered by illusion *(māyā)*, it becomes material.

CHAPTER TWENTY THREE

ASPECTS OF THE MOTHER DIVINE

Ekam sad viprāha bahūdhā vadanti. (Ṛg Veda)
(Truth is One, the wise call it by many names.)

The Hindu mythology has personified the abstract and active power of the divinity, and has ascribed sex to these mythological personages. The *Śakti* (Energy), an attribute of God, is female and is fabled as the consort of that personified attribute.

Śakti that we call Mother Divine is said to have first assumed sixty different forms, each of which is believed to have a great many modifications. Each of these secondary manifestations of the Śakti is again said to have taken a variety of forms, and so on almost without end.

Śakti is also identified with the Supreme Being: "Thou are predicated in every prayer. Brahmā and the rest are all born of Thee. From Thee this whole universe proceeds and in Thee, is the asylum of the world". The Śakti of Śiva being identified with *Śaktimān* (the deity), is declared to be not only superior to Her Lord, but the Cause of him. Śakti gives strength to Śiva. Without Her, he could not stir a straw.

Our great sages and saints realised the pulse of that *Śakti* of the *prakṛti*, the Mother-heart, behind the universe. So they sang of God as Mother, as *parāśakti* (the supreme *śakti)*, as *prakṛti* (the supreme Nature), and her unique manifestations as Durgā, Kālī, Rādhā, Sitā, Devī &c. Some of the known western writers also have expressed their views on the Presence of that pulse behind everything.

Mother Divine is the same as Brahmā (the Creator), Viṣṇu (the Protector), Śiva (the Destroyer), Kāla (the Time spirit), Yama (the god of retribution), Manu (the Progenitor of the human race), Vāyu (the wind-god) and Agnī (the god of Fire). SHe constitutes (all) created beings. SHe is the source of happiness, destroyer of darkness, mitigates the sufferings of Her devotees. SHe is all-pervading and all-enveloping (like space), the basic energy behind all forms of matter and energy.

In short, SHe is *brahman*, the Absolute, the Supreme Being. The deities supposedly appearing to be different and independent, are in fact the emanations of the same Mother Divine, the Supreme Being, *brahman*, the Absolute.

An American philosopher invokes the Divine Mother thus:

> Dark Mother, always gliding near with soft feet,
> Have none chanted for Thee a chant of fullest welcome?
> Then I chant it for Thee, I glorify Thee above all,
> I bring Thee a song that, when Thou must indeed come,
> Come unfalteringly.

Goethe's last line in his book *Faust* reads:

> "The eternal Feminine leads us on and on."

An overwhelming majority of the goddesses of Hinduism are aspects and variations of Pārvati, e.g. Haimavatī, Girijā, Dakṣayānī, Rudranī, Sarvanī, Umā, Gaurī, Ambā, Ambālakā and so on. All the female deities are called *śakti-s* of their male counterparts. The words *Śakti* and *Devī* are more exclusively understood to denote Śiva-Śakti (discussed elsewhere in this treatise). Appended below are a short and descriptive representation of the most popular and widely worshipped goddesses of the Hindu pantheon.

Durgā

Durgā is the most widely worshipped and popular aspect of Śakti. She is the personification of the totality of the powers of gods, the Mother of the universe. The *sādhaka* is advised to turn to "Durgā-śapataśati" (an exclusive chapter) where three aspects of Devī are depicted as Mahālakśmī, Mahākālī, Mahāsarasvati.

Lakśmī

Lakśmī is elevated to a position of supreme divinity. She is eternal and pervades the cosmos. Also she is said to be *prakṛti*, the principle of nature which makes the material reality. If Viṣṇu is speech, Lakśmī is its meaning. She is also named as Padmā, Kamalā, and so on. She is the goddess of wealth and fortune. She is seated on a lotus throne. Owl is her carrier.

Kālī

The most enigmatic goddess, stands on a fallen body of her own spouse Śiva, wears a garland of human skulls and holds a chopper in her hand. Kālī once destroyed all demons in a battle and started a terrible dance out of sheer joy of victory. All the worlds began trembling. None could make her stop. At last Śiva lay like a corpse down under her feet and she suddenly realised her arrogance and became still. She is termed *digambara* (clad in space). The Divine created this universe and then entered into it. So the universe becomes a cloak for the divinity. When the veil is unveiled, the divinity stands exposed. She is the goddess of time that destroys everything.

Sarasvati

Sarasvati is the procreatrix, the mother of the entire creation. She is also described as Śārdā, the giver of essence; Vageśvarī, mistress of speech; Brāhmī, wife of Brahmā; Mahāvidyā, knowledge supreme; and so on. Clad in white apparel and seated on a swan, She holds and plays a *vīnā* (lute).

Bhadarakālī

One of the several aspects of Kālī. She is said to have sprung up from Umā's wrath when Dakṣa insulted Śiva. SHe fought along with Virbhadara to destroy Dakṣa's sacrifice (*yagnā*).

Cāmuṇḍā

Kālī is also named Cāmuṇḍā since she killed the demons Caṇḍa and Muṇḍa. She is the force of concentrated awareness, the power of spiritual awakening in the heart that devours the ceaseless activity of the immature mind and uplifts it to the highest level. Rakatabija is actually the mind, each wave of which gives rise to other waves. Killing of Rakatabija by Cāmuṇḍā means the destruction of the mental modifications by the awakening of spiritual consciousness.

Kātayayānī

She is described as Durgā *(Mahiśasurmardinī)*, Kameśvarī (mistress of desires). Rājarajeśvarī (supreme ruler), and so on. She is the goddess in her supreme form.

Sitā

Primarily the wife of Rāma, the hero of the epic Rāmāyana, is revered as the model Hindu wife who although the victim of injustice always remains loyal to her husband. Rāma and Sitā became identified as manifestations of the god Viṣṇu and his consort Lakṣmī. It is an important example of devotional model and suggests a significant trend towards worship of feminine dimension.

Rādhā

Rādhā has been associated with the god Kṛṣṇa. She represents the human devotee who gives up everything for the Lord. The aim of Kṛṣṇa's devotee is to develop the Rādhā dimension within himself. The theme of love in separation is dominant in his relationship with Kṛṣṇa. Kṛṣṇa, the ultimate Godhead, includes within himself various *śakti-s*, powers, through which he reveals himself. The most important *śakti* is the *hlādini śakti*, the *śakti* of bliss, and this *śakti* is identified with none other than Rādhā herself. If Rādhā is Kṛṣṇa and Kṛṣṇa is Rādhā, then Rādhā is divine and worthy of the devotee's adoration. She is an essence of the Godhead. Rādhā has thus assumed the eternal *śakti* of Kṛṣṇa.

Daśamahāvidyā-s

Dashmahavidyas are the representations of transcendent knowledge and power, the sources of all that is to be known. They are a group of ten goddesses believed to be a version of Viṣṇu's ten *avatāra-s.* It is also a reflection of Ādyaśakti's tendency to manifest in a great variety of forms. The origin of these ten *Mahāvidyā-s* called *mahāśakti-s,* is read in the context of the story of Satī. Satī's father Dakṣa ignores to invite his son-in-law, Śiva, to attend a great *yagnā* (sacrifice). Though Śiva does not feel offended by this act of Dakṣa, Satī could not bear this great insult. She loses her temper, visits the site of *yagnā*, assumes a dreadful form and multiplies herself into ten forms, named *daśamahāvidyā-s.* They are:

Mahākālī

Kālī is the goddess of time. She has a terrible countenance. Her Kālrātrī aspect is considered most destructive. She has four arms, sports a garland of human skulls and dwells in the cremation ground. Kālī liberates the worshippers from all fears and grants their wishes to be fulfilled.

Tārā

She is the power of the embryo *(hiranyagarbha)* from which the universe evolves. She is also known as Ugratārā (energy of the sun). She is dark, rests her foot on a corpse, wears a tiger skin and garland of severed human heads. Her four arms are coiled by snakes.

Ṣoḍaṣī

Ṣoḍaṣī is also known as Tripurasundarī, the śakti of Śiva. She is the personification of fullness, of perfection.

Bhuvaneśvarī

Bhuvaneśvarī represents the forces of the material world. Her breasts ooze milk. She holds noose and a goad. Her other name is Rājarājeśvarī.

Chinnamastā

The naked deity holding her own severed head in her own hand and drinking her own blood. She represents the continued state of self-sustenance of the created world, continuous self-destruction and self-renewal in a cyclic order.

Bhairavī

Bhairavī stands for desires and temptations that lead to destruction. She is of reddish complexion, wears a necklace of severed heads, holds a rosary and a book. She is worshipped for peace.

Dhūmāvatī

Dhūmavatī personifies the destruction of the world by fire. She is dressed like a widow, has no teeth. She is affiliated with thirst and hunger and rides a crow.

When propitiated She bestows peace and freedom from worldly ailments and calamities.

Mātaṅgī

Mātaṅgī is the embodiment of the power of domination. She has black hue. Her eyes roll in intoxication. She redeems the devotee from all worries and bears fruit of all actions.

Bāgalāmukhī

Bāgalā represents the ugly side of the living creatures like jealousy, hatred and cruelty. She has two hands, one hand beats the enemy with a club while the other hand is pulling the enemy's tongue. She is endowed with far-sightedness and recognises foe from friend.

Kamalā

Kamalā, the pure consciousness of the Self, bestowing boons and allaying fears of the supplicants, has beautiful golden complexion, is surrounded by elephants pouring trunk-full of water over her. She is seated on a lotus.

***Sapta-Mātrkā-s* (Seven Mothers)**

According to Durgā-śapataśati, when Durgā was fighting the demon Rakatbija whose blood, when spilled, could produce innumerable demons similar to him, she manifested out of herself seven emanations called *Sapata Mātrikā-s* or Seven Mothers. They are Brahmnī, Vaiṣnavī, Narasimhī, Varāhī, Maheśvarī, Kumarī and Aindrī.

Vaiṣṇo Devī (*Śeraṅvālī,* the Lion-rider)

Vaiṣṇo Devī is today the most popular and widely worshipped goddess with utmost devotion. She is enshrined in a cave in the bosom of Trikuṭ hills. She is worshipped in the form of three *piṇḍi-s* (stone outpourings) which represent the three cosmic aspects of Śakti - Mahākālī, Mahāsarasvati, Mahālakṣmī.

Vaiṣṇo Devī is considered to be a virgin Mother often choosing to manifest herself in the form of a virgin girl. Thus all *kanya-s* (virgin girls) are regarded as her representatives and worshipped ceremonially. She is known as the universal Mother because the universe evolves in the womb of the Mother. Devotees worship Māṃ Vaiṣṇo Devī out of love and devotion and pray for the fulfilment of their wishes and desires which She grants. She too, is the personification of the totality of the powers of gods and goddesses.

Jāgran-s, an all-night vigil of constant devotional singing in praise of Mother's glory, are held by the devotees. Waking is a form of self-denial (of sleep at night). The goddess is involved in the form of a *jyoti* lit in the beginning of the ceremony.

She is Durgā. She is Kālī. She is the Supreme cosmic Power. The Trinity owes its existence and allegiance to Her. Her names run into thousands. She is armed with various weapons. Her facial expression is calm, serene, divine, benign but determined to punish the wicked.

Navdurgā-s

I bow down at the lotus feet of the nine emanations of the Mother Divine, the Supreme Being: Śailputrī, the Goddess of Inspiration; Brahmacāranī, the Goddess of Sacred Study; Caṅdrghaṅṭā, the Goddess of the Delight of Practice; Kuṣamāṅḍā, the Goddess of purifying Austerity; Skandamātā, the Goddess who nurtures Divinity; Kātayāyānī, the One who is Ever-Pure; Kālarātrī, the Goddess of the Dark Night; Mahāgaurī, the Goddess of the Great Radiant Light; and Sidhadātrī, the Goddess who grants Perfection.

> Spiritual experience is not realisable through scriptural statements (Śruti) alone. Śruti is only informative. It is through personal will and determined endeavour (puruśartha) that one can realise spiritual unity and harmony.

❄

Traditions evolve, faiths vary. Spirit alone endures

CHAPTER TWENTY FOUR

MOTHER DIVINE - THE THING-IN-ITSELF

(*Svarūpa*)

TAKING the form of the void in the robe of darkness wrapped, seated alone in the shrine of *samādhi*, who art Thou? O Mother Divine.

THE essential nature of a thing makes it what it is. Sweetness is the essential nature of honey, you cannot take it away. You cannot take away the burning property of fire, the hardness of the rock, the coolness of water, the fragrance of sandal paste. Illumination is the essential nature of light. You cannot take it away. The essential nature of a thing or being is that aspect or that factor which is permanent to it, which is without a beginning or an end and therefore it is the Thing-in-Itself *(svarūpa)*.

The Supreme Being, in Its transcendental aspect, is beyond conceptualisation in terms of form or gender. When we think of It we cannot truly form any concrete opinion about Its form. There are no attributes in terms of which we can describe It and make It an object of our understanding. We can therefore merely say that 'IT IS' and not 'WHAT IT IS'. This is obviously the notion of *nirguṇa-nirākāra brahman* (Absolute - without form, without attributes) of *Vedānta*.

Nevertheless some devotees find it helpful and spiritually captivating to think of the Supreme Being in one of His/Her divine manifestations such as Viṣṇu, Kṛṣṇa, Rāma, Śiva, Durgā, and so on. Lord Chaitanya and Meerā worshipped Lord Kṛṣṇa, Tulsidāsa worshipped Rāma, and one of the greatest exponents of *bhakti, Śrī* Rāmakṛṣṇa Paramahansa, worshipped Mother Goddess named Kāli as God. God-vision is only the vision of the Self objectified as the God of one's own choice and faith. It involves physical perception, emotional comprehension as well as spiritual experience.

One such vision the poet-devotee describes here is the enthralling form of Divine Mother *Tripurasundarī*, part by part, for enhancing the devotional fervour of eager aspirants who cannot realise the *nirguṇa-nirākāra brahman*. While describing an ideal beauty, he is conscious that the object of his praise is the cosmic Person conceived as a woman (Universal Mother). The Goddess praised here is not a mere anthropomorphic deity, but the Mistress of the whole universe, to whom all Nature is an embellishment.

The Goddess is seated in a lotus or riding a lion. Her face beaming with joy, radiating a golden hue, and sporting a golden lotus in one hand. Adored by all celestials, She is the very embodiment of *vidyā* and tranquillity. She is rosy like the dawn, a 'treasure house of beauty'. Her breath has the perfume of camphor. She is fond of flowers like *champaka, aśoka.*

"The golden crown on Thy head, set densely with precious gems, constituted of the twelve suns, gives the impression that the crescent moon on Thy head is Indra's bow."

The braid of Her locks resembles a forest of full-blown blue lotus flowers. The vermilion adores the parting middle line of Her braid and looks like the rays of the rising sun. The jewels She wears compare with stars in their splendour. Her face, having the orbs of the sun and the moon as a pair of ear-pendants and surrounded by the curly locks, mocks at the celebrated beauty of the lotus flowers. Her forehead, shining with the brilliance of its divine beauty, is a second crescent moon.

Her eyes move like fish in the stream of beauty flowing from Her face. All glory to Her wide auspicious eyes shedding a continuous flow of grace, offering protection to the world. The expression of Her look is characterised by the sentiments of love and compassion for Her devotees. The opening and closing of Her eye-lids mark the creation and dissolution of this universe.

Her shapely nose is like a fresh-blown *champaka* bud. The nasal ornament set with a jewel excels the brilliance of the planet Venus. The cheeks are far fairer than mirrors of ruby. Her rows of teeth resemble the sprouting of pure knowledge *(Śri vidyā).* Her chin is peerless in beauty.

Her naturally red lips: even the *bimbā* fruit will feel ashamed to stand before these lips, a mere reflection of which has made that fruit red.

"O *Devī*, below Thy neck are Thy naturally white cluster of pearls necklace. The comeliness of Thy four creeper-like arms decked with armlets and bracelets of gold, resemble the stalk of lotus in beauty."

Indescribably unique is the glory of Her naval, which is verily a still whirl-pool on the surface of the sea.

The splendour of Her hands surpasses the brightness of the morning lotus blooms. She has eight hands and they hold weapons representing different qualities that the devotees seek. They are conch, disc, sword, bow, mace, lotus, trident. One hand shows signs of 'refuge' *(abhay)* and 'boon' *(vardān)*.

Her lotus feet, adorned with tinkling anklets set with jewels, a delight to watch because of their ever lasting brilliance, are undoubtedly far superior to the common lotus flowers which perish in snow. The upper part of Her feet are the seat of all excellence worthy of praise and they are the panacea for all dangers. The illuminating splendour of Her toe-nails dispels the darkness of ignorance in the votaries prostrating at Her feet. Her gait is slow and gentle like the morning breeze.

She wears round Her hip a deep red garment. She is adorned with a girdle having many bells set with precious stones.

> To friend and foe Thy lotus eyes are even. Ever Thine animating touch brings fruit to fortunate and unfortunate alike. The shade of death and immortality, both these are Thy grace, O Mother Supreme. May Thy gracious face be never turned away from me, Thy child.
>
> Swami Vivekananda.

The attribute-less is the Absolute. It is devoid of all opposites.

CHAPTER TWENTY FIVE

REMINISCENCES AND INSPIRATIONS

(A Short Life Sketch of my *Jananī*)

> IT is not so easy to be the mother. As mother, You have to understand the anguish of your son's heart, O *māṃ*.

BORN in a village Kishanpura Kalāṃ, Ferozepur district, (Panjab), she was the youngest and only sister of four brothers in a well-to-do *brahmin* family. She was the darling of all and was addressed as *'bibi'* by all out of respect and loving care. She was the *Śri* in the family and virtually ruled the parents' family, thus I was once told by my maternal uncle.

The exact date of her birth or of marriage is not known. It is however presumed and roughly calculated from several landmarks described by the elders that she was married in 1905 or 1906 when she was about twelve years old. She had absolutely no schooling though she learnt Hindi script at her own and could read Gītā printed in bold letters and also write her name.

My family lived in a village called Uppal Jagir (Nurmahal) in Jalandhar district, (Panjab). My father was a petty businessman and also owned a small piece of land for cultivation. The family was one of the most respected and honoured one in the village.

I lost my father and my elder brother during riots in 1947 when the country was partitioned. At that time I had just completed my Matriculation. I had known my mother truly from that time onward when she happened to play the double role of both a mother and a father.

The sudden death of my father and eldest brother during riots completely changed the complexion of the family. I was so eagerly awaiting to join the college for further studies, but that was not to be. My mother was rendered helpless. It is a pathetic tale to recall when she called me and said, *'Beṭā*, I am extremely aggrieved to tell you that I shall not be able to afford to send you to the college. Rather, I expect you to contribute your bit to support the family.' I could well understand the plight of a widowed mother who had three young daughters to marry. And then she added, "May *Māṃ* bless you. The *Mahārāni* (Mother Divine) alone will quench your thirst for further education. *Māṃ* Rānī demands harder work from you! Have faith in Her. May you be happy, prosper and live long. I have nothing but blessings to give you."

Hence this poor being left home in search of a living and did get one by Her grace. It was a matter of do-or-die, learn while you earn and in this process it took me as long as twelve years to complete my Post-graduation. Behind all this was hidden the love and blessings of my revered mother and grace of the Supreme Mother.

She was an embodiment of piety, love, wisdom, compassion, devotion, and of very serene temperament. There used to be day-long rows of village folklore coming to her for advice on all kinds of domestic and personal matters. She loved all and in turn received respect and regard from everybody.

My forefathers worshipped Mother Goddess and the *paramparā* continues till date. One extreme corner of a room in the native house was assigned to the deity. *Jyoti* was lit and *ārtī* performed every evening. My uncle *(taojī)* was a *siddha pandit* and a staunch devotee of *Māṃ* Durgā.

My mother was initiated by a saint Guru named Sant Sadhu Ramji who lived in the neighbouring town. She would go there for *darśana* and attend discourses on days of all festivals. During summer I used to be told by her to visit Guruji's *Āśram*, draw water from the well and fill the clay pitchers kept there for the thirsty.

She was very keen to visit holy places like Mathura, Vrindavan, Paryāga, Haridwar, Rishikesh and always took me to accompany her.

Once, during a visit to Haridwar, she insisted to climb the steep hill to Mansā *Devī Mandir* for *darśana.* Hardly had we covered some hundred yards distance when she felt tired. I carried her on my back for the rest of the distance to the temple. The pilgrims on the way were heard whispering "Sarvan Kumāra-s are still there in the world"! Feeling proud of listening to praises showered at her

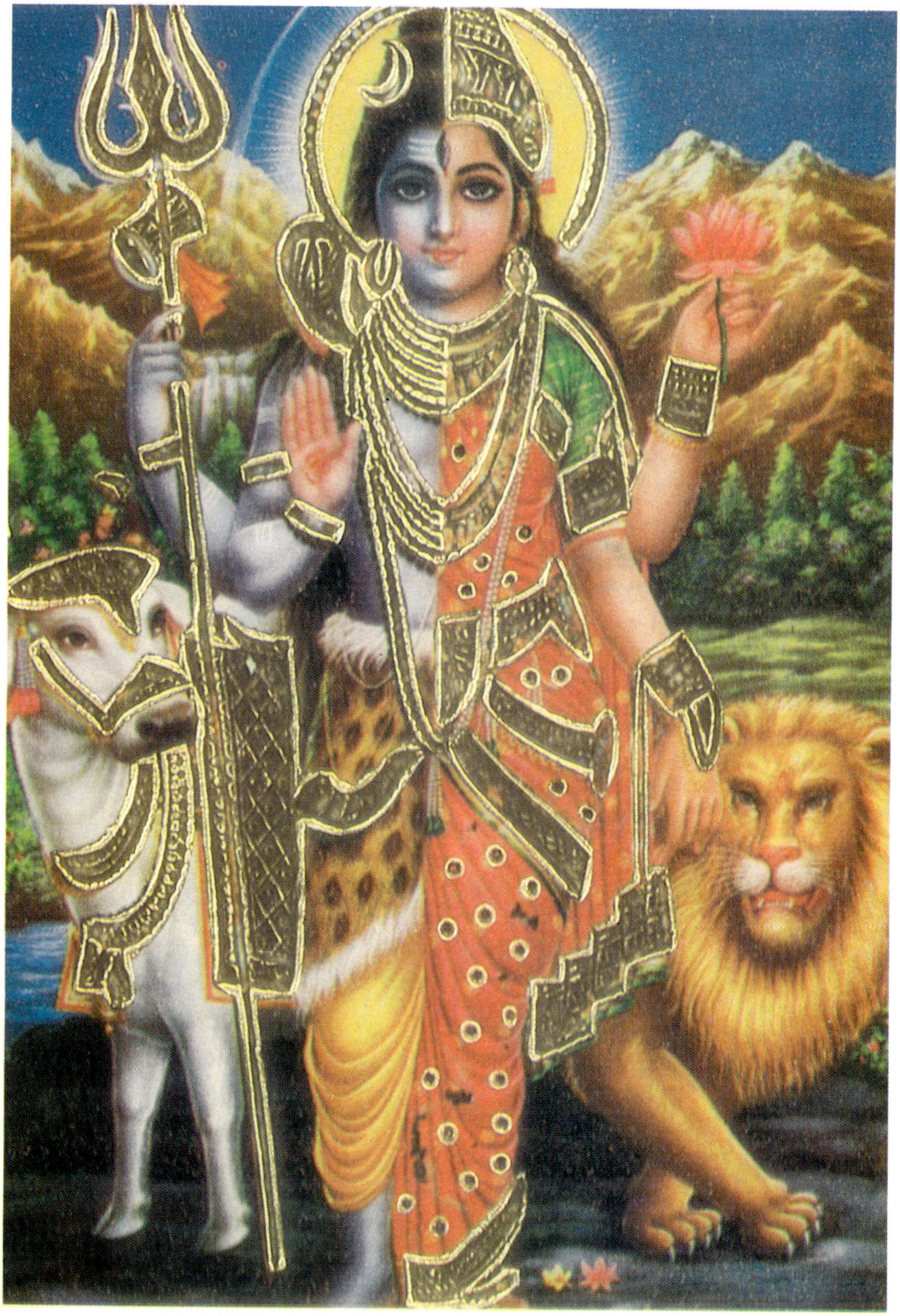

Ardhanārṣvara : *Puruṣa-Prakṛti* (p.120)

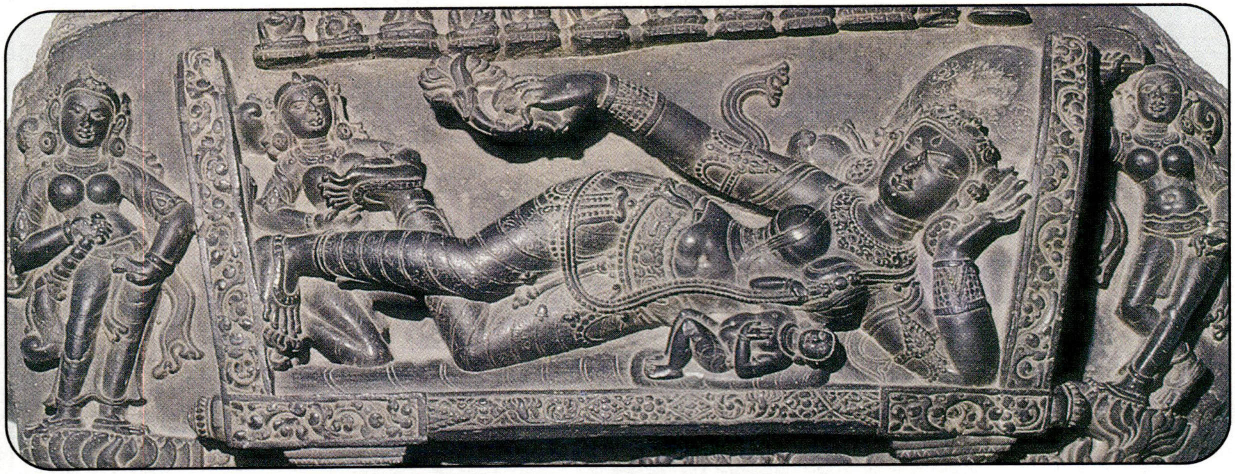

Mother and Child : Māṃ and Me (p.115)

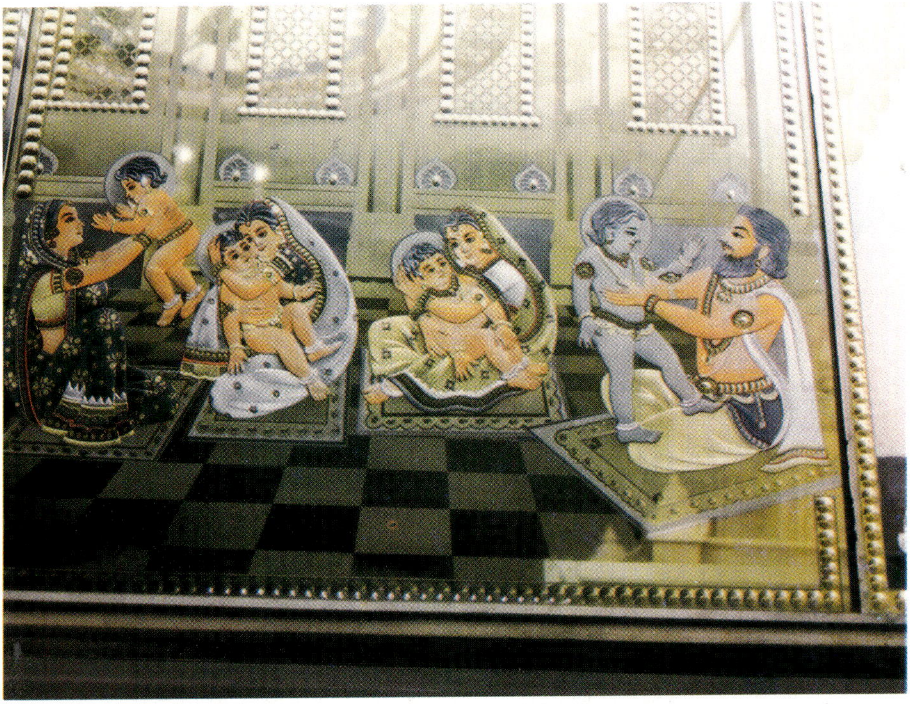

The Filial Love

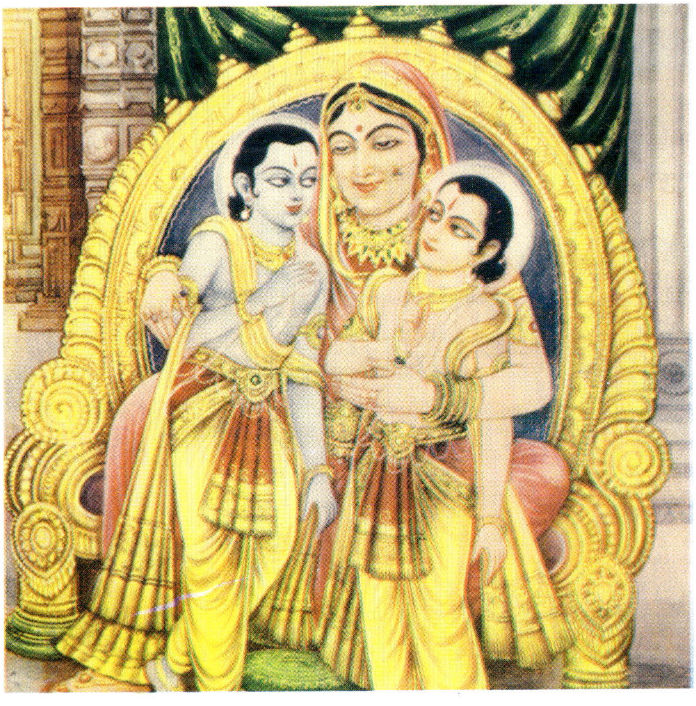

Woman as Mother (p.107)

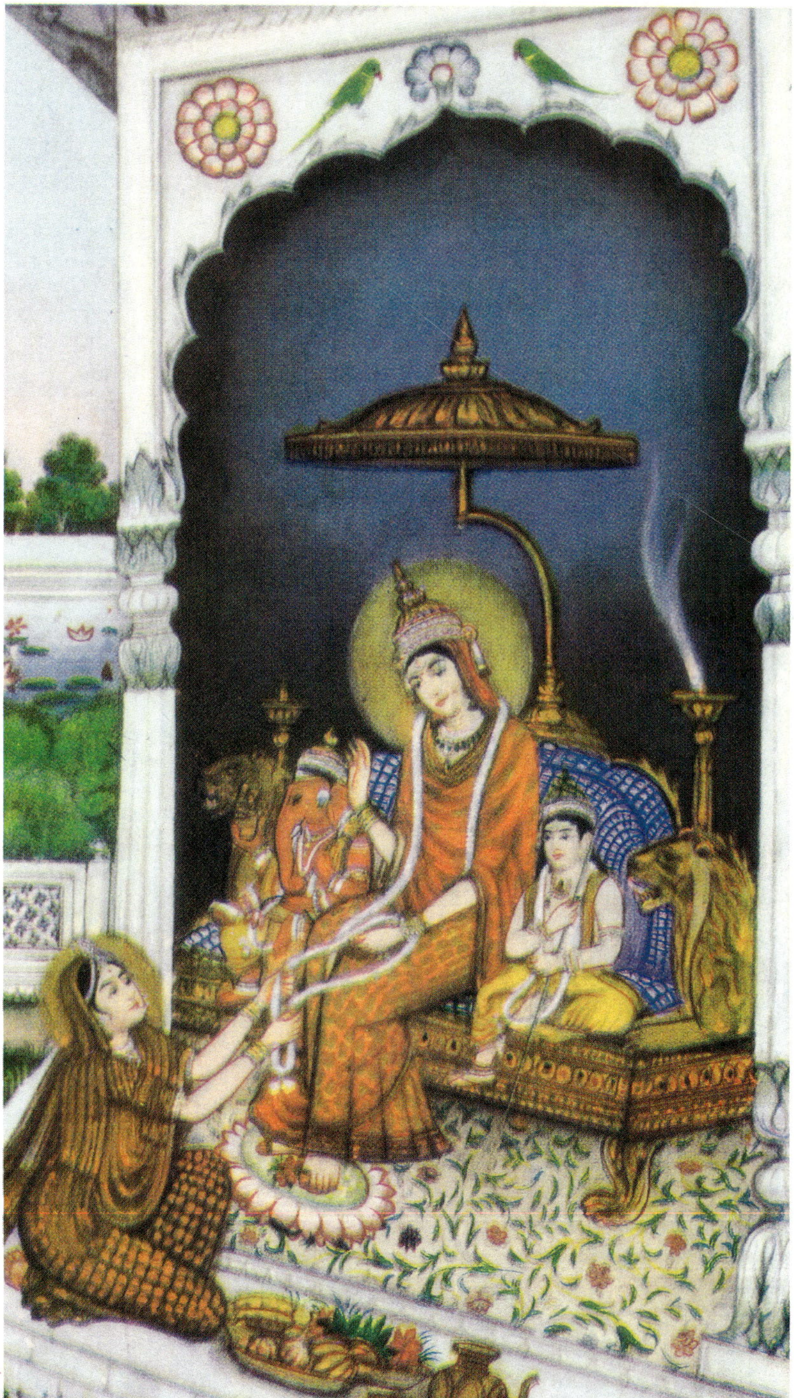

Sita ji worshipping Gaurī, Mother Divine (p.127)

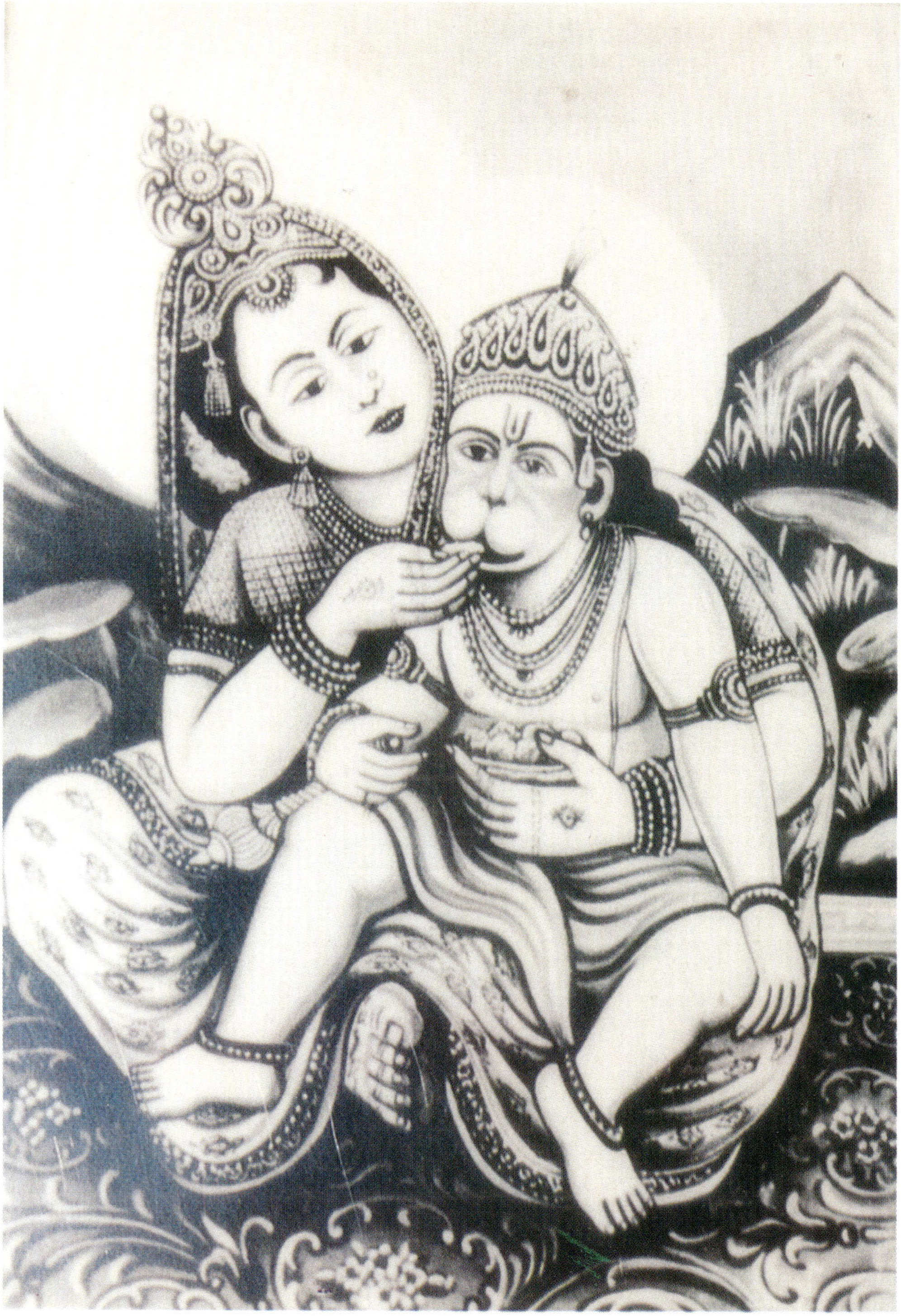

Mātā Anjanī rearing the babe Hanumān (p.107)

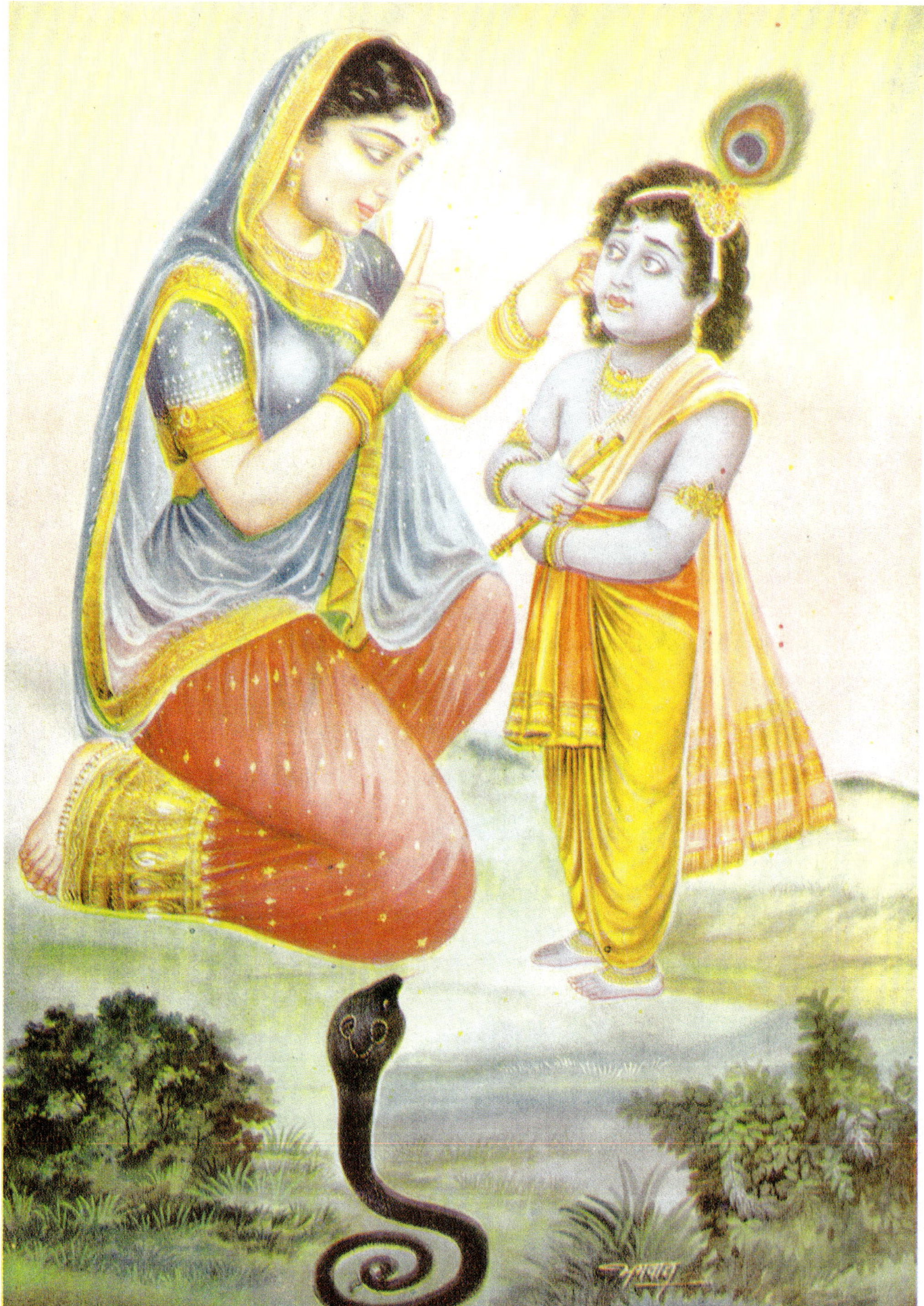

The maternal discipline (reprimand) (p.107)

Daśamahāvidyā-s

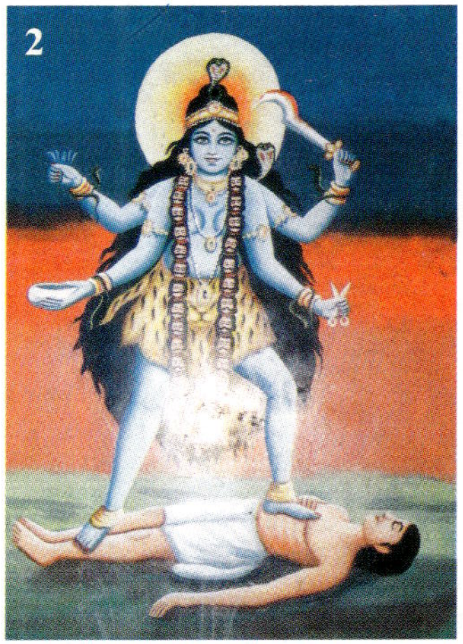

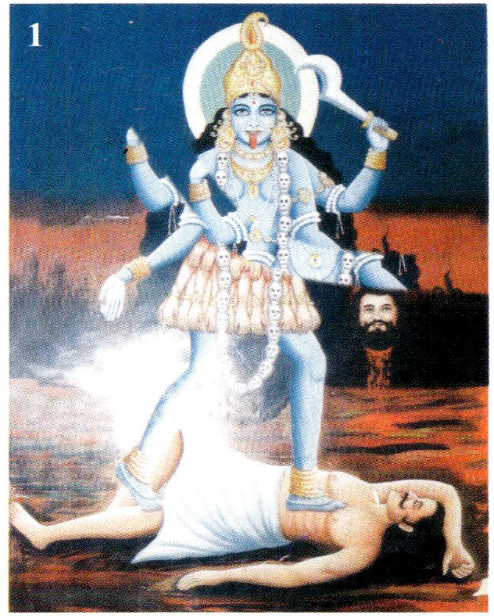

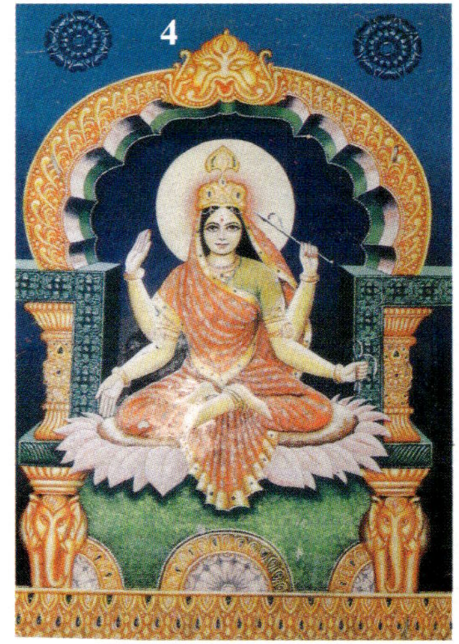

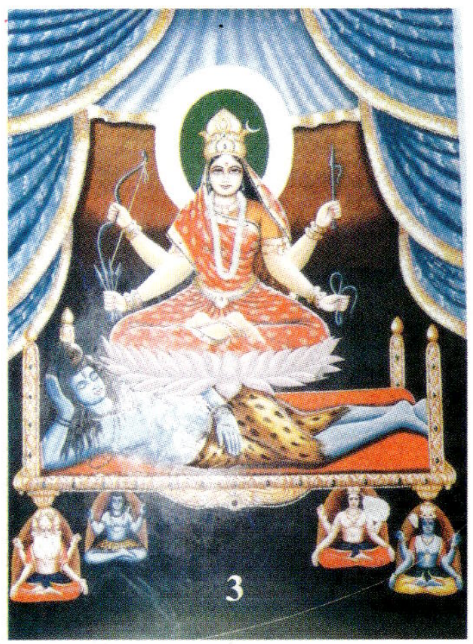

1. Mahākālī

2. Tārā

3. Ṣoḍṣī

4. Bhuvaneṣvarī

5. Chinnamastā

(p.92)

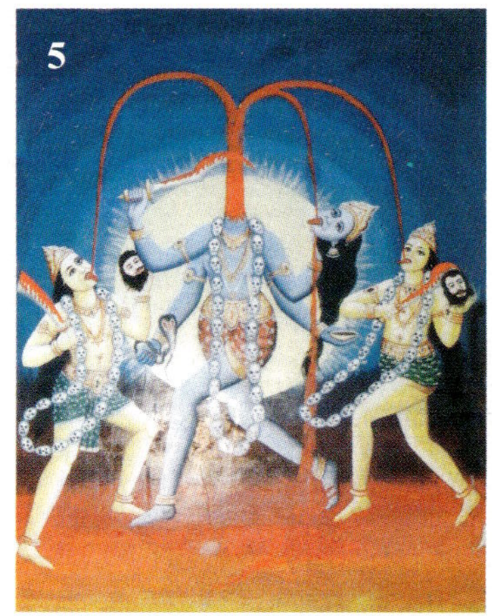

Daśamahāvidyā-s (contd.)

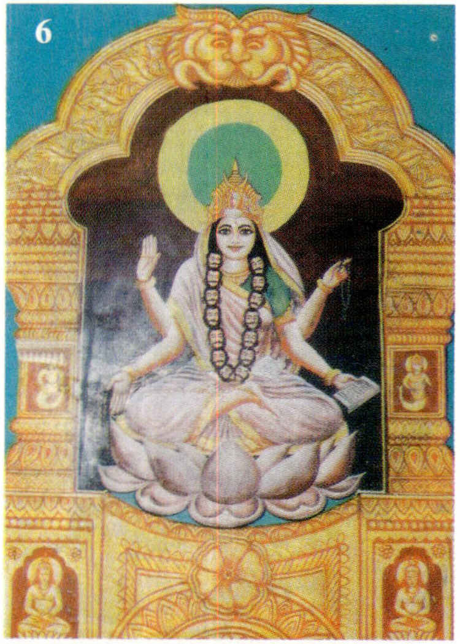

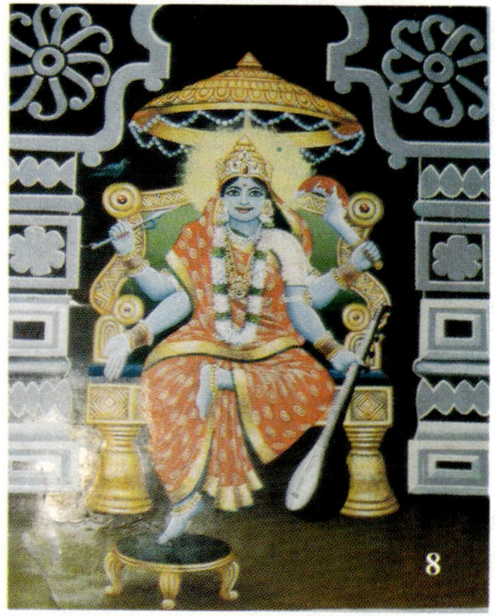

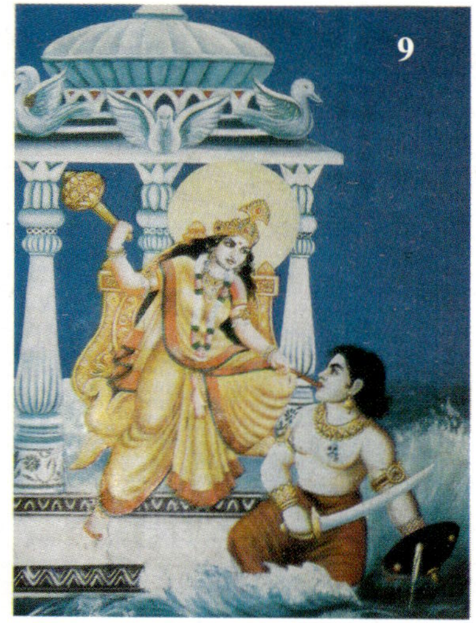

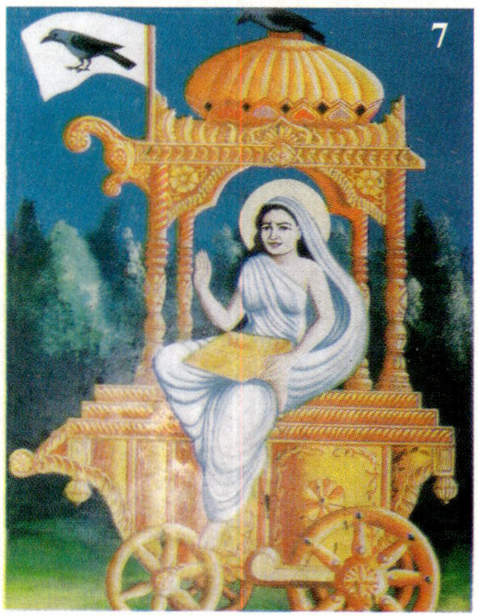

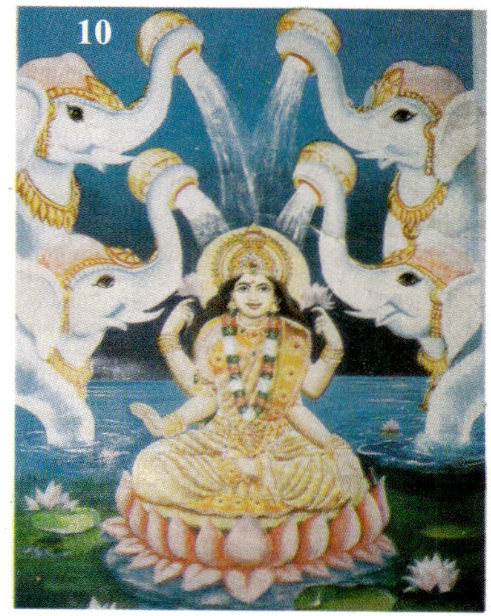

6. Bhairvī

7. Dhūmāvatī

8. Mātungī

9. Bāgalāmukhī

10. Kamlā

(p.92)

son, She offered obeisance to the Mother and prayed with humility, "May one such son be born in every family; if not in every family, at least one in every *kula* (lineage)."

She always kept a smiling face and a loving gesture. Whosoever came close to her was impressed by her presence and motherhood. I have yet to recall an occasion when she was seen scolding somebody. It used to so happen sometimes that I came home very late at night. She would express her anxiety and prefer to stay awake waiting in the balcony till my arrival. I knew her nature so well. The moment she opened the door from inside and before she could utter a word, I would pass on a small wooden stick to her, saying, "*Māṃ*, I don't like your son! He is an errant child. Tell me, is it the time to return home? He needs thrashing left and right and today is the day for it. Go ahead. The *daṇḍā* (a wooden stick) is in your hand." How she used to be elated at that time that she would kiss me and hug me with that loving motherly warmth which is beyond description.

Once in the late sixties I incurred a handy sum of money on car repairs and was a bit perturbed. She noticed it from my face and asked me the reason. When she was told about it, she reacted in this manner: "*Beṭā*, if you befriend a camel, the doors must be kept high." What a way to appease?

She was very fond of planting saplings of trees and plants and grow vegetables wherever she found a suitable vacant piece of land in or around the house premises. A big grown-up Eucalyptus tree which she planted in front of the house in Delhi in 1970 continues to inspire and remind us of those sweet and warm days.

Once a couple of travellers passing through the village late in the evening knocked at our door. They showed their desire to stay for the night and leave early next morning. Besides providing them with cots and sheets, she offered them food which was prepared for the family. As a result she was left with no food for herself. "The guest is an *Iṣvar svarūpa* and should not sleep hungry", she told us later. She was an ideal host.

She had an inner healing power. It was often seen that people suffering from common ailments like headache or stomach ache were relieved of the pain by the sheer touch of her hand. Her very presence would at times suffice for the purpose.

She was particularly attached to children. During winter she would accommodate as many as five children in her specially made bed and keep them warm and comfortable at night. Is it devotion? I now realise the true meaning of *vatsalya.*

She treated everybody alike in the family though she was softly inclined towards the daughters and showed them favours of sorts. "Daughters are *'parāyā dhan'* (others' property) and deserve better treat", she would often proclaim. And for that matter the servants would get a better deal over the sons. Everybody in fact believed that she loved him most although she loved all alike.

She taught us more from example than from precept. Day in and day out she kept herself busy on the spinning wheel. It was her solitary hard work which provided sustenance to the family after father's death in 1947. Cheerfully did she carry out the household duties single-handed with little support from any quarters. The struggle continued till I was able to share the burden. She was happy when I took over the entire responsibility and freed her from all domestic worries and anxieties. She lived a very peaceful life thereafter.

'Matṛdevobhava'. An ideal mother is God Itself. She is greater than God in mortal form. Who says God has yet to come in *Kālīyuga.* God is born in the guise of a mother as *saguṇa sākāra brahman* (God with form and attributes). The saint who uttered *"Matṛdevobhav"* must be born to an ideal mother. He must have tasted the nectar which flows from mother's heart. A country where ideal mothers reside has a bright future.

Mother is Brahmā, mother is Viṣṇu, mother is Śiva. Brahmā creates the universe. The mother gives birth to a human being. Does Brahmā undergo any pangs in creating the world? Perhaps he cannot think of the pains and self-sacrifice experienced by the mother in giving birth to a child. Viṣṇu sustains. Does he put in any labour of the kind? The mother brings up the children by the sweat of her brows. Śiva performs double role. He sustains as well as destroys. The mother cultivates good things in the children and destroys their wrongful doings. She uplifts us from beasts to human beings. Is not mother greater than gods?

Anything said in regard to the self-sacrifices and renunciation of a mother will not be sufficient to prove the real truth. The mother spends the most valuable moments of her life on her off-spring without any selfish motive. She only wishes to see them prosper.

Mother's silent love is not a matter of words. One has to experience her deep emotions to understand it. There is no substitute for mother and absolutely none for her love. The only tribute we can pay to our mothers is to practise the ideals shown by them and live a pious and truthful life.

That 'tears and smiles meet' and that 'joys and sorrows also meet' I had heard of but never experienced. Both were witnessed and experienced when she breathed her last. She died a peaceful death in 1974. Did she pass away? 'Not passed away, but absorbed' in the words uttered by Mahāṛṣi Ramana when he was told that his mother had passed away.

❄

> "By your grace alone all my senses are in harmony with your celestial orchestra of fragrance, beauty and joy playing their refrain in the eternal symphony of the cosmos. Prostration unto Thee."

❄

A CHILD REMINISCES

She is humble. She is sweet, kind, generous, simple, charming, innocence personified, honest, truthful, hard-working, dedicated, always washing, cleaning, cooking, teaching, helping. Who is she? She is my dear mother, of course.

She embraces me, consoles me, loves me, nurtures me, values me. She is like the sun who gives light and warmth to all in the family.

The word mother gives me courage. She taught me how to crawl. She gave me her finger that I may hold and walk. She is bold, brighter than gold. She helps me to study, so that I am better than anybody.

I love you, O dear mother and bow my head to you. You gave me birth and I came on this earth. You gave me love with which I grew up. You teach manners and give us knowledge. Thank you Mother Grace for this invaluable gift.

MOTHER is the maker of this heaven.
If I am a pot, she is the potter.
If I am a book, she is the author.
If I am a flower, she is the florist.
She is my Mother.

SHE was humble and sweet.
She was talented and dedicated.
She cheered me, embraced me
and consoled me. She was my mother.

"**M**" is for the **M**illion things She gave me,
"**O**" for **O**nly that She is growing old.
"**T**" for the **T**ears She shed to save me.
"**H**" for her **H**eart of the purest gold.
"**E**" for the **E**yes with love shining.
"**R**" is for **R**ight and right She always is.

Much of the bonding between mother and child takes place during the early period after birth. The moments after birth are vital for the these bonds.

> O māṃ, we invoke thy power in temples but we rarely care to acknowledge the role of a woman in real life. "Like Śravankumār, I would carry my parents on the pilgrimage and demand nothing from them in order to be called a worthy son".

"There is no other like you, O *Māṃ*."

CHAPTER TWENTY SIX

WOMAN AS MOTHER

IN Hindu *dharma*, the *strī* or feminine energy is the executive divinity of the universe. A woman is considered as the embodiment of cosmic Energy. Since she is the concrete will of the Lord, she is a mystery, a wonder, the representative of the protective forces, the queen of the home. Women are thus the repositories of divine Energy.

The first manifestation of God is the hand that rocks the cradle. She is the mother. There is no substitute for mother. The mother is the treasure of love and affection. A son may not emulate Rāma, but every mother definitely plays Kauśalyā for him. In the thought of Divine Mother's loving and tender compassion, every human heart knows that there is an opportunity for forgiveness. She stands by the child through thick and thin. Wife and children may desert man but mother never. Mother again is the impartial energy of the universe because of the colourless love that asks not, desires not, cares not for the evil in child.

It is a woman who teaches humanity finer values of life. The feeling of being a mother is the sole privilege of a woman. The sensitivity of a mother for her child is remarkable. Like the mother-hen she would have under her protective wings the other members of the family. She takes care to bring them up in the best traditions of the society.

The first cry which almost every quadruped or human being utters is the beloved name of *'Māṃ'* and this word remains with him for life whether it is a moment of sorrow or joy. The mother sacrifices her all for the sake of her children. First word of the child is mother; first thought of the child is mother. First guru of the child is mother.

The mother is thrilled by the first cry of the child. The cry hurts her not, nor fills her heart with pity. Instead, it gives her joy and she is moved by a blissful sense of fulfilment.

The word 'mother' is so prevalent in every language of the world. She gives birth to a life, nurses him, brings him up, gives her all to him, does anything for him, walks on fire, fights the storm, faces every challenge and difficulty. She is the friend, philosopher and guide. She is there when children need her. She is most pleased when the child grows up and stands on his feet and if the child does anything wrong, she takes the blame on herself. But what does she get in return?

The mother comes up like a teacher in our childhood to make and mould our character and guide us through life. She is as important in the home as the soul in the human body, a source of light and delight, consolation, and compassion, health and happiness. Mother is a very sacrosanct word which means 'a woman in authority'.

Mother is the image of the earth, the earth itself, *mātṛbhūmi*. To honour the mother we term our language as mother-tongue.

Watch how a loving mother intelligently comes to control her child in its mischief! Persuasion by offering something quite attractive and winning his attention. The child is tempted to renounce the play. If this fails, another weapon comes to the fore. She would offer the child greater freedom at another period of time: 'If you would now come and sleep, I shall send you to the Children Park in the evening when you can play for longer period.' The child cannot resist the tempting proposal.

None can match the intensity of emotions in a mother: the loving care of Yaśodā *Mātā*, the wrath of *Māṃ* Kālī, the jealousy of Kaikeyi and Śrupanakhā, the faith and patience of Sītā, the self-sacrifice of Gaṅdhāri, the soothing touch of Mother Teresā, the strength and will-power of Jhāṅsi ki Rāni, the courage of the soul's nobility of Sāvitri.

The woman first appears as daughter, then as wife and then as earthly mother. As a daughter, wife and mother, she has kept the universe going. Let Mother Grace bless our mothers and let our mothers bless us, her children.

It is pure grace in her mind that makes her sublime. The man has to move heaven and earth to achieve this divine character. A mother will not forsake her child, no matter what other attractions and inducements are offered. That is the very natural grace of motherhood in a woman. Whatever be the achievements of a woman - a leader, a politician, a musician - her pride as a mother is unique. It makes her worthy of worship.

Woman has been known for such desirable human values and virtues as affection, dedication, forgiveness, sacrifice, devotion, charity, modesty, patience, self-denial etc. She tamed the wild man and made him useful to the society. The attributes of a woman are the expressions or manifestations of the attributes of the divine Consciousness.

The spiritual woman emerges as *Śakti*, the quintessence of female power. Through her spiritual power she commands respect and awe of society, attracting equal reverence from men and women. Meerābāi, Anḍāl combined social transgression with spiritual transcendence.

What should I take you for? Just 'a woman'? *Śakti*,? Or the Mother-form of the Great Creator? Can any one see the light of the day without you? Can anyone be born on this planet without your maternal grace? Can we imagine any creation without a mother?

If our mothers had punished us for every mistake that we committed, we would have been dead long ago. A child grows into man under the fostering care of the mother. Of course, there are moments when 'spare the rod and spoil the child' too comes into play. The mother not only cautions the child, but executes the threat strictly. In sheer fright, the child comes to his senses and quickly gets over those wrong tendencies. The effort is meant to secure the future.

When you see a woman of striking beauty, praise the Creator and look for the Divine Mother in her. The thought and sight will lit within you the love of the Great Mother of the universe.

By woman we are conceived; from her we are born and with her we are married.

She keeps the race going. When one woman dies, another is sought after. With her we are positioned in the society. From woman is also born a woman.

He whose mother and father are not properly served and honoured, meets with worries and woes; while he whose mother and father are held in high esteem, achieves bliss and wins admiration among his friends and virtuous people.

The idea that man and woman are equal, is a western concept. The Indian concept is that man and woman, *puruṣa* and *prakṛti*, Śiva and Śākti, are one and indivisible. Wife is *ardhāṇgini* (better half) and dwells in her husband.

Love involves the willingness to sacrifice the self for the loved one. Sometimes the love of a mother for a deformed child is stronger than that of a normal child capable of returning that love in full measure. The absolute dependence of a deformed child and the absolute necessity of a large measure of sacrifice by the mother strengthens the bond of love.

Mother is a radiant nurse bandaging the cut finger of her errant child and whose sweet voice and presence gives strength to the sick child. Mother is an angel of mercy, a watchful guardian waiting well past midnight for the child to return home and a compassionate attorney with the dad not to punish the child.

Is woman weaker because she does not possess the brute instinct in the same measure as man? Remember, if she is weak in striking, she is strong in suffering, as a mother.

Mother's role of child's character-building does not start after the child is born. It starts the day she conceives. This is an established fact today that the *saṃskāra-s* (impressions) accumulated by the expecting mother through whatever source, do cast their shadows on the child in the womb and are carried by him in real life. Even the surroundings leave their impressions on the child through mother during pregnancy.

An American lady gave birth to a child whose features were resembling a Negro. The family became suspicious. A careful study based on various aspects of the matter was undertaken by psychologists and others. The study revealed that the lady had been occasionally looking at the picture of a Negro hanging on the wall of her bedroom and that was the real cause behind the resemblance. What if she had the Lord's portrait instead?

There is a popular story from our scriptures to prove that the child assimilates the teachings imparted to the mother when the child is in the womb. When Subhadrā was on family way and Abhimanyu was to be born, Arjuna once started describing the design of the *Cakravyuhā* (battle array) to her. She learnt up to the entry plans and fell asleep and therefore did not listen the way to exit. Consequently, Abhimanyu in his real life did enter the *Cakravyuhā* laid by the enemy in the great battle of *Mahābhārata* but could not get out of the same and was captured and killed therein, being unaware of the passage to exit.

O Parents, mothers in particular, please take stance: you will have to bear the burden of your guilt consequent to your over-indulgence during the period of pregnancy. The quality of food, the quality of pastimes, the activities of mind and body indulged in during the period, have a direct bearing on the character build-up of your new born. You can make him a saint, a king, a preceptor or a vagabond. You are the architect. Follow the footprints of Madālsā.

Madālsā was a queen, very learned and religious woman. She gave birth to her sons and brought them up as saints. She sang divine songs and lullaby while inducing the children to sleep. She read the scriptural stories to them. The children imbibed with the milk of the mother and the Vedānta teachings. The first seven children became sages. But on the request and advice of her husband she taught politics to her eighth child who became a good king.

The mother moulds the child, right or wrong. She feeds the child with her breast, and thus fuses the vices or virtues in her child. It is said that through mother's faults a child is lost and makes its life accursed. Various personal defects in the child are the result of wanting association with mother, which cannot be procured for any amount of money.

The education of the woman, therefore, cannot be over-emphasised in order to achieve this mission. Only mothers who are strong and sound physically, intellectually and spiritually can do it. If you educate a man, you educate one person but if you educate a woman, you educate the whole family.

The great Indian heroes like Śivāji, Netāji, Bapūji, Bhagatsingh and so on grew into heroes because of their mothers' foresight and will-power. Guru Gobind Singhji's mother wanted to make her son a warrior and she made him so. The hand that rocks the cradle is the hand that rules the world. The status of women reflects the progress of any society or culture.

Today the old folks speak so loud blaming their children for paying them little attention. Who is actually to blame? The elders themselves cannot be absolved totally. They will have to understand the aspirations and the psyche of the present generation and adapt themselves accordingly before looking forward to the fulfilment of their expectations.

Today we are talking of equality of woman! But are they really separate from men? One has no existence without the other. Both men and women are the two sides of the same coin. There is no difference, only a distinction.

In her younger years, a woman is escorted by her father, after marriage by her husband and in old age by her sons. She cannot live separate at any stage of her life.

Both Viṣṇu and Lakśmī constitute a single entity called *Puruṣa.* The difference between the male and female energy lies in that the former constitutes static and the latter kinetic energy. Apply it to the actual world experience. The male energy provides the seed and the female energy performs the function of soil, accepts it, fertilises it and brings out the species as part of its nature. The tree thus grows and spreads to its limits. Its deeper bonds of relations are rooted in the soil (female energy) which help it to sustain.

Gārgi, Maitreyi, Ahalya, Anusūya, are all worthy of worship. Did they ever move to seek equality with men? And were they not a happy lot then?

The mother's endeavours to elevate the children, to make them perfect men and brighten their prospects in life, do deserve rewards. It becomes therefore, the foremost moral duty of all of us not to neglect our parents. Keep them happy, serve them to their hopes and aspirations, and remain ever grateful and indebted to them. There is no substitute for mother and none for mother's blessings. Mother's love serves as a tonic.

The rank of the mother has been considered thousand times higher than that of the father. Even the saints to whom all people pay obeisance, pay obeisance to the mother. 'Where women are honoured, there verily the gods dwell. Whoever disgraces a woman falls irretrievably from grace of the Lord.'

In the 20th century we have the unique examples of mother Śāradā Devi, Aanandamai *Māṃ*, Mother of Pondichery and Mother Teresā who occupy positions of spiritual distinction.

Women are revered for they are the mothers of the human race. The maternal instinct, the love of children, the gentle virtues of the hearth and home, give women an abiding place in the scale of ideal humanity. Service to earthly mother and father is service to Divine Mother.

The procreative faculty generating new beings and the link of the altruistic love connecting the offspring to the parents is personified in the mother.

Motherhood is a *sādhanā*. To us therefore even the God is revealed as the Mother of all creation, *Śrī Mātā,* the Great Goddess.

Motherhood comes from true sacrifice and integrity of purpose. Gāṇdhāri in Mahābhārata gave birth to one hundred sons but she failed to imbibe the true spirit of motherhood. Shivāji was known for his fearlessness and assertion of self-respect. His mother's role cannot be over-estimated. Mahātmā Gāndhi was equally impressed by the spirituality of his mother, Putli Bāi. Ramakriṣna, a known monk, said, "There is nothing comparable to divine love except motherhood. Every debt of this worldly life can be paid off if the person is willing but the sacrifice of motherhood cannot be compensated."

Motherhood is considered the most pious and selfless feeling on the earth. Its concept is close to God's love for the human beings.

A mother can be all (mother, father, friend, teacher) but none other can. She alone can console a child in moments of pain and distress.

The word Mother reminds us of a loving, protective and renewing deity ever active in the world, encompassing both material and spiritual realms, so as to bring about an orderly and beautiful universe.

A woman's pride and place as a mother is unique in society. Even the greatest of saints will have to reverentially bow before the woman who bore him and suffered the pangs of childbirth for his sake

Culture transmits through the family. No one can escape from the sort of culture which he acquires sitting in the lap of the mother. What is precious to the child then is not the price but the value. The mother teaches him to live a value-based life. The mother is thus the teacher of the family. Parents are also the best carriers of infinite love of God. In their selfless love and compassion is envisaged the unconditional nature of divine love.

THE future destiny of the child is always the handiwork of the mother. One good mother is worth hundred teachers. We bow to the mothers.

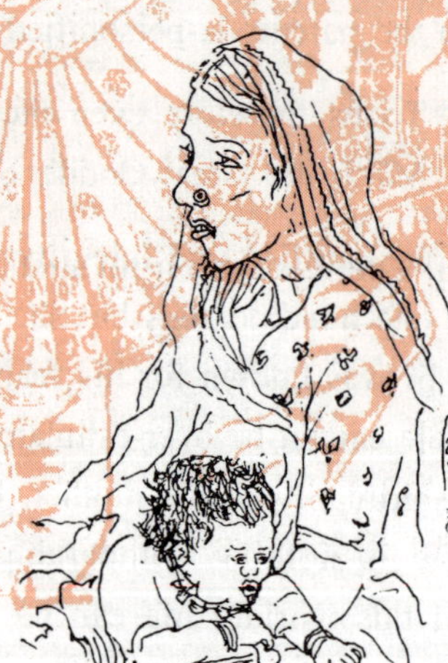

।। गोद में खेलता भविष्य ।।

Woman is gifted with the motherly instinct to save mankind.

CHAPTER TWENTY SEVEN

Māṃ and ME

HUMAN relations are to be idealised not idolised. If you consider the love of your worldly mother as the unconditional love of the Divine Mother, you should not be aggrieved when she leaves for her heavenly abode.

YOU will really fulfil the duty of a son if you can help your mother to gather the means for her final journey. You have grown by suckling her milk. How much suffering she has undergone to raise you to manhood? Service to her is worship of the Divine Mother.

MY sincere and dedicated love for my *jananī* (earthly mother) who was the base of my true devotion to the Divine Mother. The mother is an expression of the true and selfless love. Every woman to me is a representative of the Divine Mother. I see my mother in all women and the Cosmic Mother in all mothers.

The worst kind of tragedy in human life is 'not to belong to anybody'. Worst still is 'not to have a mother'. My heartfelt sympathies to those who have not known and experienced the love of a mother. They have been deprived of a great experience of life. My mother was everything to me. I loved her, respected her and worshipped her till she breathed her last. I lost her and I missed her very much. Then began the search for my lost mother in a mad fury. Where has she gone? I asked everything around, the flowers in the garden, the birds on the tree. The mad search continued. And lo! the Mother began to show herself to me in the blossom of the flowers, in the chirping of the birds, in the smile of the children. The horizon widened. I could see her all around in everything. And one day I met her in my dream. She raised her hand and blessed me saying (as if), "Don't despair, my child, be blessed. I am always with you." Who she could possibly be? Was she my lost mother? Nevertheless, I believed my dream to be true and realised that she could be none other than my lost earthly mother appearing in the cosmic form.

I now recognise my mother in every woman, in all gods and goddesses, in Sītā, Rādhā, Pārvati, Lakśmī, Sarasvati and in all *avatāra-s* and saints. I never feel her absence. I am not alone. She is always with me. She is not lost to me. She was in fact sent by the Divine Mother to mother me for a while.

One's earliest memories of childhood are mingled with the warmth of mother's bosom, the gentleness of her cares and the music of her words. Love, compassion, sacrifice and sweetness unite in the form of mother making her the beloved of all.

To the child there can be nothing so sweet and so pure as his mother. The very mention of the mother raises holy thoughts in the mind and drives away all that is impure. It is for this reason that no epithet that you can adopt in addressing God, will so much move your sentiments as the epithet of 'mother'. The idea that God is your mother always keeps the heart cheerful and acts as a safeguard against temptation. Realise the motherhood of God in the universe and everything around you will reflect the purity of her countenance. A smile, a hug, a murmur and a caress and a pat on your back. You are moved, your ego cracks. It rolls down in the form of tears. You feel consoled, tranquillised, transformed and sublimated.

My mother was so good to me ! She loved me when I was good. She loved me when I was bad. She loved me when she punished me. I didn't like her to punish me but it would not hurt me. It hurt me most to see her crying !

Mother means benefactor. To be a worthy son, I must also be, like my mother, a benefactor, seeing not the defects of others but picking up only the jewels.

Mother has always been an object of love, adoration, compassion, respect and regard. Mother is everything to the child. When we become helpless, we become humble and submissive and beg like children. The relationship of mother and child is quite natural and unique. This relationship also holds good with Divine Mother. She is the embodiment of all the fine qualities combined in one. We should therefore develop this relationship with the Divine.

The mother is bound even to the most erring children by a kinship that no misdoing on the part of the child can break. If the human tie be indissoluble, shall the divine one be less so? The soul that worships becomes a little child and finds God often as Mother.

She is termed *jananī*, because She gives birth. She is *Ambā,* because she fondly fosters her children, makes them grow and ever sweetly cares. No cooler relief from the scorching heat, no refuge, no protection, no love is greater than what is found in that one word "mother".

God is both infinite wisdom and infinite feelings. When the Almighty manifested himself in creation, he gave his wisdom the form of a father and his feelings the form of a mother. The father is moved by reason, whereas the mother is moved by the feelings. The father wants to govern the child by reason, the mother by feelings. Every father should strive to temper his reason with love and every mother to temper her love with reason. Pure reason and pure feelings both have intuitive qualities.

Look at the torture the mother bears in bringing up the child. Surely, she enjoys it. Why? Because there is no selfishness. She holds back nothing, desires nothing, and considers no sacrifice great. Her award is the well-being of her children. Let us hold a grateful thought for all mothers who nurture their children with affection.

The great Śaṅkarācārya had promised his mother while taking *saṃyāsa* that he would come back and be at her bedside if she thought of him at the time of death. And he was at her bedside at the time of her passing away to perform the obsequies.

There are several instances in the life of Śrī Rāmakriśna Paramahansa of the most tender concern for his mother, Chandrā Devi. Once he went on a pilgrimage to Vrindāvan and was so taken in by the spiritual atmosphere there, that he wanted to stay there itself. But he had a consideration for his old mother who would be left without care if he stayed there. So he returned home. Another instance showing his concern for his mother is recalled here. One of his brothers died quite young. Śrī Rāmakṛśna was afraid that the news would break the heart of his mother, he went to the Kālī temple and prayed to Divine Mother to give his mother necessary strength of mind to bear the loss.

Coming to the most recent time, think of the extraordinary and tender relationship between Mahāṛṣi Ramana and his mother. The undercurrent of love and regard *Mahāṛṣi* had for his mother and the regard and love she had for him are very evident. The mother went to Tiruvannamelai to persuade Ramana to return home as she could not bear the separation. Ramana however declined to accede to the mother's persuasion and instead gave her the appropriate piece of advice. Once his mother fell seriously ill and Śri Bhagvān had sought divine intervention for changing the course of events. He invoked the power of Arunachala as the conquror of death to cure his mother's fever.

"Oh Conqueror of Time
Your lotus feet are my refuge
Let them protect my mother from death
What is death if Scrutinized?"

This is the only known instance of prayer to change the course of events. The mother recovered. So deep was the mother's love for Śrī Ramana that she spent her last few years with him. At the time of her death Śrī Ramana sat by her side with his right hand on her head, and she attained *samādhi*. When somebody told him that she had passed away, he corrected the person with a curt remark, 'not passed away, absorbed'.

And in the prayer Sri Raman addressed Arunachala as "Mother" instead of "Father" as he always used to do.

"Oh Mother of those who seek refuge in you
Is their a better shield than you from fate's blows?"

Certain forms we admire; others we love. To Mother we belong. Whether we realise it or not, we are Her children. 'Whom else should I cry to, O Mother? The child cries for its mother alone.' Mother is dutiful, compassionate, considerate. She loves, blesses and also coaxes at times when considered necessary. She may avoid but shall not hate. If you remain child-like, the tomorrow would be looked after by the Mother. I salute unto Her lotus feet.

The universe is the play of the Divine Mother. Behind the universe is the mother-heart whose manifestation can be seen in the cosmos. *Māṃ* ! Grant me a drop from the sea of Thy radiant love.

In my relationship with God, I like to think of that divine One in the aspect of Mother. One can approach the Mother aspect as a child, and claim Her love as his own, regardless of personal merit.

Who is divinity in flesh? One's mother, of course. Mother alone can console a child in moments of pain and distress.

We are children of the same Mother, belong to the same family and the same fate awaits us all.

I love *Māṃ and Māṃ* loves my loving her.

Mother in her pure form symbolises unconditional love, divine dedication and invincible powers. Her love is cherished and blessings sought after. At her feet lies the secret to eternal happiness.

मां परम ब्रह्म
कल तक तू ईश्वर था। आज तुझ में "मां" है।
हर ॐकार ध्वनि में मां है। हर ईश्वर छवि में मां है।
मेरे नयनों से कोई देखे। पुरे ब्रह्मांण्ड में मेरी मां है।
कल तक जो मेरी मां थीं। आज वह जगतजननी है।
कल तक जो ममत्त्व का झरना थीं।
आज अमरत्त्व का सरोवर है।
मां परम ब्रह्म

❄

For long I had forgotten my home and my *Māṃ*. Now I prepare for the return journey, as its end seems quite in sight. The return ticket only awaits endorsement. Life is like a dream which of course ends in death but that is not the end. The man rises again. I await the moment when I will return to *Māṃ* and rest in absolute bliss in Her loving caresses. I am the moth surrendering on the flame of Her love for me.

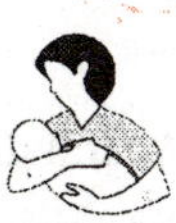

She was humble and sweet. She was talented and dedicated. She cheered me, embraced me and consoled me. She was my mother.

CHAPTER TWENTY EIGHT

ŚIVA-ŚAKTI

(Śakti is Śiva, Śiva is Śakti)

"WHO is 'I'? That is *Puruṣa*. Who is *Puruṣa* ? That is 'I'. The difference between force and the receptacle of force is because of delusion."

Mother in *Śrimad Devī Bhagavatam.*

गिरा अरथ जल बीचि सम कहिअत भिन्न न भन्न।
बंदउ सीता राम पद जिन्हहि परम प्रिया खिन्न।

I revere the lotus feet of Sita and Rama who, though stated to be different, are yet identical just like a word and its meaning or like water and the waves on its surface, and to whom the afflicted are most dear.

THE source and sustenance of all creation at all levels of matter, life and mind is One without a second. It is *brahman.* This Supreme Consciousness manifests Itself as a twin Personality, Śiva and Śakti. Śiva is quiescent consciousness with neither evolution nor involution. Śakti signifies the dynamic aspect of the Divine. If Śiva is the coiled serpent in sleep, Śakti is the same serpent in motion. If Śiva is like fire, Śakti is its burning power. The two are inseparable like the word and its meaning. *Brahman* is thus Śiva-Śakti *(aikya svarūpam).*

Matter is involved Spirit. Spirit is evolved matter. There is only One indivisible Reality. Gītā speaks of two entities: *puruṣa* and *prakṛti,* the static and dynamic Spirit, only for the sake of making people understand things. In fact these are two aspects of the same Truth.

If one believes in an *Iṣṭadevatā* (Personal god, chosen deity), Its divine power is taken for granted. When we distinguish between Śiva and Śakti, the divinity is conceived as divided into two aspects. However, Śiva and Śakti are complementary, no more different than fire and its burning action. Better call Śiva-Śakti as Śakti of Śiva, Śakti of Śakti or Śakti-Śakti. Śiva is Śakti and Śakti is Śiva. The concept of Śakti is of primary importance. The power is related to Śiva as the rays to moon, as the heat to fire, as waves to ocean, as whiteness to milk, as lustre to gem. The *śakti* (power) and *śaktimān* (possessor of *śakti*) are one and the same.

The supreme Reality is no other than the abstract Intelligence. Intelligence signifies self-luminosity and abstraction denotes infinite nature. Abstraction and manifestation are inherent in the pure Self. These two aspects are given the names Śiva and Śakti. Śiva, the name of the changeless aspect of One whose power of action and activity is Śakti. The two are necessarily associated and therefore acknowledged as Śakti.

Śiva and Śakti are also identified as the two impersonal creative forces, *Puruṣa* and *prakṛti,* responsible for the creation of the universe. In permanent union with his female power, Śiva is also termed *Ardhnāriśvara.* Both make a worthy unit of purposeful existence. The female part has mother functions and the male is father force to enhance the prospects of liveable society. During play Śakti and Śaktimān seem different but essentially Lakśmī-Nārāyaṇa, Sitā-Rāma, Rādhā-Kṛṣṇa, Gauri-Śankara are One and the same. Śiva, the spiritual concept of the Absolute, and Śakti, the ultimate Reality, stand forth as *brahman*, the Supreme Being.

To make the point further clear: the sea-calm is the Absolute (Śiva); the same sea in waves is Mother Divine (Śakti). SHe is time, space and causation. Śiva-Śakti is therefore synonymous with *brahman*., the Supreme Being.

The seeming difference arises from dualistic vision. If this vision is withdrawn and directed into the source, the two become one. Kinetic energy is not other than the static being.

This world of multiplicity and manifestations is in the realm of Śakti. We all live, move and have our being in the Divine Mother, like fish in water.

The divine Power constitutes the Lord's very being and ever inheres in Him. Together they are cosmic Whole. Though intellectually analysable, they are spiritually One and the same.

Śiva rides the bull and Śakti rides the lion. A bull and a lion live together.

Various aspects in which the term Śiva is used and understood:

- total Godhead, the Supreme Reality.
- one of the Hindu Trinity, as Destroyer.
- as the chosen Ideal *(Iṣṭadevatā)*.
- In relation to His power, the creative Mother aspect of God (Śakti).
- the transcendent Absolute, the Mother aspect of the Godhead.
- as the Guru of all gurus.

The term *Śakti* is also used in its various aspects :

- as the total Godhead, the Supreme Being.
- Mother of the Universe.
- Personification of the Primal Energy or power of *brahman*, the Supreme Being.
- Dynamic aspect of the Godhead, that which creates, preserves and dissolves the universe, in relation to which Śiva represents *brahman* (the transcendental Absolute, or Father aspect of the Godhead).
- worshipped as the chosen Ideal *(Iṣṭadevatā)*.

THAT "Śakti is feminine and Śiva (the possessor of *śakti)*, is masculine", is a wrong notion. The Absolute who is the embodiment of the *śakti*, is also the possessor of the *śakti*. 'God-as-Mother' concept tends towards the vision of a holistic Power, *Śiva-Śakti*.

Let the glow of Divine mercy be stronger than the noise of fireworks

CHAPTER TWENTY NINE

GOD AS MOTHER DIVINE

The Indian seers after ages of deep contemplation came to the conclusion that the cause, effect and propelling agent of creation was Power Supreme and called It *Śrī Mātā*, the Benevolent Mother. It was for the guidance and convenience of the aspirants that several methods of its comprehension and conception were suggested by these seers. The Supreme Power responds in whatever form It is invoked.

THE question "why is God thought of as Mother?" can be countered with another one, "why is God called Father?" God is neither He nor She. We often say 'God Itself'. The Absolute is neither male nor female. God is not a person. God is Presence. Śakti, the name we substitute for the Absolute, is symbolically female because It is the productive principle. It is She as Power which plays an active role in generation as also in conceiving, bearing and giving birth to the world child. All this is the function of the Divine as it is that of the human mother.

THE doctrine of *śakti* as 'divine power' is one of the greatest doctrines evolved through spiritual intuitions by human mind, and is a manifestation of the divine Consciousness itself. This conception is wholly identical with the conception of *brahman* in the Upaniṣads. When God is called Mother, the implication is not so much to show a distinction of sex in divinity or to patronise a female deity but to remind us that in her function of redemption *(anūgraha)*, Motherhood is the most adequate of all humanly understandable love and compassion. When anybody needs protection from an imminent danger, the very mention of the name of Mother 'Māṃ', whom we love and revere, raises holy thoughts in the mind. We pray: 'Protect us, O Mother.' The conception of God as Mother Divine promotes within us the feelings of love, reverence, worship and surrender which are the main factors of spiritual knowledge.

In the *Ṛgveda*, Aditi has been described as the mother of gods and all creation. Devī-worship is the worship of God's glory, of God's greatness and supremacy.

It is adoration of the Almighty. *Mātṛdevobhava* (treat your mother as God) was a guideline for the generations gone by. A mother is the holiest person alive.

The *Śakti* element is the integrated manifestation of *brahman* (the Creator). The worship of Śakti (Divine Mother) is the worship of *brahman. Śakta* cult propagates the worship of the Supreme Being as the worship of the Mother of universe because that is the aspect of the Supreme in which She is regarded as the Creator, Sustainer and Destroyer of the universe.

It is one of the greatest contribution of Śrī Rāmakṛśna to Indian religious tradition that his spiritual experience has identified the Śakti not as a mere female counterpart of the Absolute but as the Absolute Itself.

She is called *brahman* in the Vedas, Viṣṇu by the *Vaiṣṇava-s,* Śiva by the *Śaivite-s* and Śakti by the *Śakta-s.* What form of the Deity can be more fitting for worship and contemplation than that of the All-loving Divine Mother?

Śaṅkarācārya appealed to the Divine Mother for Her grace in spite of his shortcomings on the ground that a 'perverse son there can be but a perverse mother never'. As a matter of fact an invalid child is specially a pet of the mother eliciting from her even a preferential treatment denied to those who are strong enough to stand on their own feet. This unique feature reminds mankind that Motherhood is the final word in redemption.

The feeling which is roused by the word 'mother' is not roused by any other name. Śaṅkarācārya addressed Kṛṣṇa as "Mother". Upaniṣads declare *mātṛdevobhava* (Mother is God). In the song *"Vande Mātaram"* there is obeisance to the Mother. Goddess Durgā is also one of the five deities of the rank of God. Srimad Devī Bhāgavatam and Śri Durgā Sapatśati depict the power and predominance of Divine Mother.

Whoever the deity of your choice, it is the *śakti* aspect that you take for granted and then worship. The Power or active aspect of the immanent God is *śakti.* Kṛṣṇa had the *bhāva* of mother even for Pūtanā who came to kill him but he gave her salvation.

Pentium (2) D:\17.11.02\ABI\Kaushal\Kaushal-1.p65

So momentous is our country's obsession with this relationship (motherhood) that we idealise it in our concept as *Bhārata Mātā, Gaṇgā Mātā, Gau Mātā, Gītā Mātā* and so on.

In this world of change, the phenomenon of the love of the mother for its offspring in the form of care, protection, nurture and nourishment, never changes and has been so ever since creation. The supreme Self is known as universal Mother because the universe with all its organism evolves in the womb of that Mother. The Great Mother is the personification of feminine grace, beauty and energy. She is the energy - spiritual, moral, mental, and physical.

When you appeal to the Mother aspect of God, there is no retort. You simply melt the heart of the Divine. There is no greater experience than to be conscious that Mother Grace is with us and thus we feel fearless. It is an immediate reaction to the strength of someone behind.

God is One and we worship Him/Her as Father, Mother, Teacher, Benefactor of the universe. God in the form of Divine Mother is the personification of kindness and love. No predicate is required with the name of God. *'Māṃ'* by Itself is enough.

The soul that worships becomes always a little child; the soul that becomes a child finds Divine often as Mother.

The ancient sages called the Supreme Being as *bhakta-vatsalya*. SHe has *vatsalya* (mother's love for the child) for the *bhakta-s.* And in the context of devotion the Supreme is addressed as: 'You are Mother, You are Father.'

I address God as *'Māṃ'* (Mother). It could be Rāma, It could be Kṛṣṇa. She is Brahmā, the Creator; She is Viṣṇu, the Preserver and She is Śiva, the Destroyer of the universe. God is not a person. God is a Presence.

While the All-pervasive *brahman* is generally alluded to as 'It' (beyond gender), the motive force behind creation, in the ancient Hindu tradition, is referred to as a feminine power. Hinduism is deeply aware that if the divinity is to be worshipped in an anthropomorphic form, it will have to be a combine of the

Pentium (2) D:\17.11.02\ABI\Kaushal\Kaushal-1.p65

male and female aspects with the female taking precedence, similar to that of the mother over the father. Thus Lakśmi is linked with Nārāyaṇa, Sītā with Rāma, Gauri with Śiva, Rādhā with Kṛṣṇa and so on.

Śakti in Her creative aspect is considered as female because it is the productive principle. On the basis of our worldly experience, we conceive the Supreme Being as the Divine Mother. Without Śakti there is no regeneration of the world.

"In my relationship with God I like to think of the divine One in the aspect of Mother. A father's love is qualified by reason and by the merit of the child. But the mother's love is unconditional. Where her child is concerned, she is all love, compassion and forgiveness. So, God as Father we conceive as Almighty, the Lawmaker and the Judge. But we can approach the Mother aspect as a child, and claim Her love as our own, regardless of our merit."

Śri Śri Dayā Mātā.

SEE in this scene of changing shows, there is a changeless One that glows. The supreme Spirit is the vital content in every particle of this world. Realise this eternal Presence.

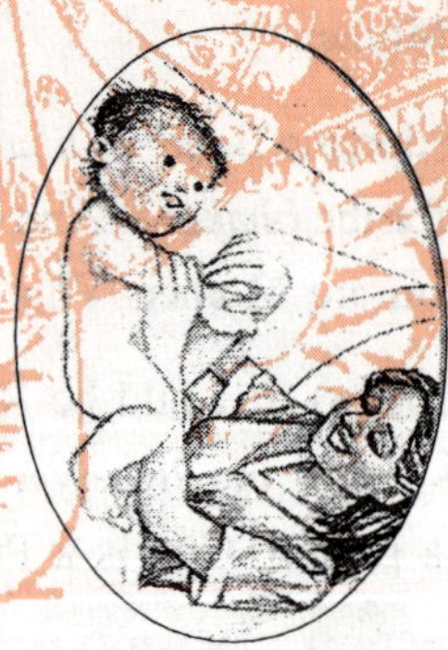

By Thee alone is this world created, sustained and destroyed.

Pentium (2) D:\17.11.02\ABI\Kaushal\Kaushal-1.p65

CHAPTER THIRTY

Worship of Mother Divine

"O Mother, Thou art the operator and I am the machine. Thou art the indweller and I am the home. Thou art the driver and I am the carriage. I move as Thou movest me. I do as Thou makest me do. I speak as Thou makest me speak. Not I, not I but Thou, only Thou, O *Māṃ*."

Śri Rāmakṛśna

Devi worship or Śakti-worship is worship of the Lord's glory, of the Almighty's greatness and supremacy. It is adoration of the divine Absolute.

The origin of *Śakti*-worship can be traced to Vedas. The *Ṛgveda* bears testimony to this. Even in those ancient times, there was the persistent belief that the Supreme Ruler of this universe is the All-compassionate Mother. The concept of the Infinite as Mother had a psychological appeal to the devotees.

In the Mahābhārata, before entering Matsya Kingdom for spending the last year of exile incognito, Dharamputra prayed to Durgā. At the commencement of the battle of Kurukṣetra Śrī Kṛṣṇa asked Arjuna to get down from the chariot to pray to Durgā and Arjuna obeyed. Rukmini worshipped at the shrine of Ambikā before her marriage. Sitā too begged Pāravati for Rāma as husband.

The *Srimad Devī Bhāgavatam* and *Durgā Sapatśati* sing exclusively of the glory and predominance of the Divine Mother. She is described both as benevolent (who grants boons) and malevolent (who destroys and kills the demons).

Truly speaking, all beings of the universe are Śakti-worshippers, for there is none who does not love and long for power in some form or the other. The energy, a form of divine *śakti*, pervades in every form of existence.

The Mother Divine is extolled as all-pervading, subtler than the subtlest, and grosser than the grossest. How can then She be worshipped in an idol? The *ṛṣi-s* say that just as the all-pervading air can be made to manifest by blowing and the fire can be made to manifest by the force of friction, so can the all-pervading Mother be invoked through proper *"āvāhana"* in an idol for the purpose of worship. The Divine Mother is invoked as Durgā, Mheśvarī, Mahākālī, Mahālakśmī, Mahāsarasvati, and so on. The invocation aims to promote peace and harmony.

The worship of the Great Mother as the Grand Multiplier is one of the oldest in the world. The chief divinity was at first in woman form. The human mother is regarded as the giver of life. The Divine Mother alone is truly the giver of life and its joys. Thus the worshipper views her in this form.

The significance of the Mother-worship to a real *sādhaka* is the feeling that he, the individual, and the universe are just the media for the manifestation of One all-pervading divine Power, Śakti.

"Let every hair of mine be a tongue so that I can sing the praises of *Māṃ* as many times. Let every hair of mine be an eye so that I can look at the grace and beauty of my *Māṃ* to satiety. Let every hair of mine be an ear so that I can hear the music and glory of my *Māṃ* till eternity."

The worship of Mother Grace leads us to the attainment of knowledge of the Self. Approach Her with an open heart. Without Her grace the sense organs in the body are mere holes in the flesh, and the outer world of objects is gross inert matter. Mother Grace lends Its potentiality to all our activities of perception, feeling and thinking. "O Mother, but for Thee the whole world would appear lifeless."

"Let's meditate on the Mother Divine, Her Grace, Her Majesty. We shall then be able to understand even the subtlest of truth," thus spoke Śiva to the *ṛsi-s* who came to ask him as to which method is the best to invoke the Supreme Being. Thus invoked, She manifested. Mother Grace explains: "Listen, O sages, I am the abstract Absolute where from the cosmos originates, whereon it flourishes and wherein it dissolves like the images in the mirror. The ignorant know me as the gross universe. The wise realise me as their own pure being eternally glowing as 'I', 'I' within. This realisation is possible only in the deep stillness of thought-free consciousness similar to that of the deep sea free from waves."

The rejoicing in Avadha pleased the gods no more than a moonlit night pleases a thief. The gods called on goddess Sarasvati and fell on her feet with the petition: "Perceiving our sore distress, O *Māṃ,* manipulate things in such a way that Rāma may depart to the forest, relinquishing his throne, so that the purpose of the immortals may be accomplished. You are the destroyer of difficulties. You are the very sea of Mercy. You are the unfathomable sea of learning. You are the dispenser of intelligence."

With folded hands Sītā too addressed the celestial Gangā: "*Māṃ*, pray accomplish my desire."

LONGING FOR THE MOTHER

A picnic party of young men happened to bring an year old child to play with and make fun during picnic. They played with the child and kept him quite happy and cheerful. After some time, however, they found the child getting restless as if he was missing something. The young men made out that child was thinking of his mother. But the mother was far away in the town. So they tried to divert the child's attention by giving him some sweets and toys. He seemed busy and satisfied for a short while, but again looked around and started crying, mother, mother. The young men got frightened as it was not possible to take the child to its mother right then. They brought some more sweets and toys but this time nothing will interest the child. He cried again for the mother, grew more restless and fell on the ground. So, the child had to be taken at once to the town back to his mother. A devotee must be like that child. Without any serious attraction for the objects of the world he plays with and enjoys, he feels at peace with himself only when he meets the Mother.

According to *Bhāgavata Purāṇa,* the *gopī-s* bathed in the Yamunā river and worshipped the Divine Mother in the form of Kātyāyani in order to win Kṛṣṇa's hand. Behind all this lies the power of the sacred voice to arouse the latent spiritual powers of every individual.

We are the radiant children of a resplendent Mother Divine whose song of power resounds through the world and space. Simplicity, humility and child-like nature means true divinity. Words cannot express that state. One has to experience to realise.

Śākta theology worships Śakti as identified with the Great Goddess, the ultimate Reality itself and the totality of all beings. Thus the goddess is equated with *brahman*, the Absolute. The *brahman* has been described in two ways: *nirguṇa-nirākāra* and *saguṇa-sākāra*. As *nirguṇa-nirākāra brahman,* It is the basis of all existence and as *saguṇa-sākāra,* It manifests in the various aspects of divinity. Māhāśakti, the Supreme Being, in Its transcendental realm is beyond conceptualisation in terms of form or gender.

Mother Divine gives to our heart and mind a titan's strength, to our soul and intelligence a god's character and knowledge.

Worshipping the Supreme Being as Mother, the devotee thinks of Her not only in cosmic form but in universal human motherhood also. When we see Her in all mothers as One universal Mother, aren't we all human beings members of one family?

> I know God as the kind of a loving Being whom I visualise as a projection of my Mother. SHe is everywhere. Therefore, SHe does not fall into the category of *avatāra-s.* When we surrender to Her with our head and heart, SHe takes charge and endows us with necessary knowledge and understanding. As sugar is made into various figures of toys and birds and we relish sugar, so do we worship and invoke one sweet Mother Divine in various climes, names and forms.

Even gods invoke Mother, when in trouble

CHAPTER THIRTY ONE

Mother Divine, The Supreme Sovereign

> Yes, my Divine Mother is none other than the Supreme Sovereign. SHe is at the same time the One and the many and beyond the One and many. My Divine Mother says, "I am the Mother of the universe. I am the *brahman* of the *Vedānta*, I am the *ātman* of the *Upaniṣads*. The law of *Karma* in truth exists, but It is I who am the Lawgiver." My Divine Mother is primordial divine Energy. SHe is omnipresent. SHe is both the outside and inside of visible phenomenon. SHe is the parent of the world and the world carries Her in its hearts. SHe is the spider and the world is the web SHe has spun. The spider draws the thread out of herself and then winds it round herself. My Mother is at the same time the container and the contained. SHe is the shell but SHe is also the kernal.
>
> Śri. Rāmakṛsna

Divine Mother who is the indwelling Spirit of the entire cosmic order, is not to be conceived as one of the great deities worshipped as the highest by any particular sect of devotees. SHe is one absolute Being who transcends all deities worshipped by various sects of devotees. SHe is the one Soul of all these deities worshipped in diverse names and forms. This conception of *Śakti* is wholly identical with the conception of *brahman* in the Upaniṣads. SHe is the One without a second, beyond time, space, causality and relativity, and is self-luminous. When we think of her, we cannot truly form any concrete opinion about her. There are no attributes in terms of which we can describe her and make her an object of our understanding. We can therefore merely say that 'SHe Is' and not 'what SHe is'. This is obviously the notion of *nirguṇa-nirākāra brahman* (Absolute without form, without attributes) of Vedānta.

Mother, the divine Player, has been playing her delightful game from eternity. Everything is a part of her game. What a game ! The human intelligence finds itself at bay to appreciate it. But the divine Player goes on playing quite unconcerned. To maintain the balance what we are really required to do is to adjust our attitude with the divine Designing. The subject is Infinite and man's equipment are finite. The man has either to bring down the Infinite to the finite level of understanding, or evolve his finite equipment to transcend and realise the Infinite.

A non-material vital force, exerting vital impulses both at micro and macro level, may be assumed to be causing the changes in visible and invisible world. This vital principle is immanent in Nature and gives rise to the concept of *śakti or māyā*. Man has been curious about creation. In Nature you behold the motherly aspect of God, full of beauty, gentleness, tenderness and kindness - true motherly qualities. We can feel and see God as Mother in Nature. SHe is energy in the sun, Gāyatrī in the Vedas, colours in the rainbow, intelligence in the mind, potency in the pills, will and reflection in the sages, devotion of the devotees. *Vidyā, Śānti,* lust, pride are all her abstract forms. The whole universe is but Her reflection.

"Potency is actualised as the universe and this also is Śakti because the Effect is the Cause modified. What is life? The underlying substance is Being-in-Itself. Life is a manifestation of such Being. The Great Mother is life. Nothing is produced without life or potency of life. What is in the cause is in the effect. The whole world is a living manifestation of the Source of all life, which is the Absolute. Sentiency is a characteristic of all forms of existence."

Sir John Woodroff.

Divine Mother is supreme Will in itself. SHe exercises the will at her pleasure. Power is known by its exercise. We have three attributes of her will: One, *māyā-śakti*, material phenomena, the attribute to create matter; two, *jīva-śakti*, the attribute to produce limited souls; and three, *cit-śakti,* the attribute to exhibit spiritual existence. We conceive of one supreme Power in her realm of eternal Spirit. All these attributes together form the One supreme Power, Māhāśakti, which the Vedas call Parā-Śakti and we call Supreme Being. "Those who try to describe you, are lost in thy depths."

Divine Mother is the life-giving principle of Nature that makes gross body come to life as a living organism - the miraculous touch of *Māṃ*.

Māhāśakti, the Divine Mother, manifests in all beings in various aspects and qualities such as consciousness, intelligence, sleep, hunger, desire, patience, modesty, beauty, mercy and the like.

Many are the aspects of the divine Power which is manifest as action, knowledge and will. The power of *brahman* which manifests itself as Consciousness, is felt in the bodies of all beings. The Potential hides as movement in the air, as hardness in stone, as liquidity in water, as emptiness in *ākāśa.* As a huge serpent is latent in the egg, a tree is latent in the seed, so the world is latent in the *brahman,* the Divine Mother.

Mātṛkā-Śakti is the power of sound inherent in the alphabet, the force that creates words, basis of limited knowledge. Words are responsible for our experience of limitations. With the letters only can we carry on our dealings in the mundane world. Neither language, nor terminology, nor scriptures exists apart from *Mātṛkā-Śakti*.

The Mother is *Ānandalahari* (the wave of bliss), the giver of joy. SHe is *Saundaṛyalahrī* (the wave of beauty). The world is her *līlā* (Play), a free spontaneous activity. Hence Lalitā (Player) is the name of the Mother. She is both Joy *(Ānandamayī)* and Play *(Līlāmayī).*

Śakti is not a handmaid of the Lord but the Lord Itself in Her aspect as Mother of the world. This Śakti is both *nirguṇa-nirākāra* and *saguṇa-sākāra.*

The Mother Is whatever Is. SHe is all-power, all powers are her Play, and therefore all the three dynamic manifestations, Brahmā, Viṣṇū and Maheṣa are modifications of the Mother, *Ādyaśakti.* SHe is also *Brahmaśakti* (Sarasvati), Viṣṇu-Śakti (Lakṣmī) and *Śiva-Śakti* (Durgā). We are not considering here instances where Śakti is associated with a particular god. We understand Śakti as a singular and universal phenomenon.

The Divine Mother brings about harmony and cohesiveness among all things of the universe. SHe is the moving Spirit in all. But for Her there will be only chaos.

The Divine Mother alone is pouring into the human hearts the love of mother for the child, love of child for the mother and love of lover for the beloved.

Our sages and scriptures could not express Her in Her entirety. Therefore it will be presumptuous for us to think that we have understood even a fringe of the veil behind which SHe hides Herself. What we may claim to have known of Mother Divine is only a mite; what remains unknown is like the vast ocean. But it is the love of the child (devotee) that could make an approach and embrace Her.

I am still so far away from Her who governs every breath of my life. Is it the evil passions within that keep me so far away and yet I cannot get away?

नहिं तव आदि मध्य अवसाना। अमित प्रभाउ बेदु नहिं जाना।
भव भव बिभव पराभव कारिनि। बिस्व बिमोहनि स्वबस बिहारिनि।
देवि पूजि पदकमल तुमहारे। सुर नर मुनी सब होहिं सुखारे।
मोर मनोरथु जानहु नीकें। बसहु सदा उर पुर सबही के।

Śri Ramcaritmanas

(You have no beginning, middle or end. Your infinite glory is a mystery even to the vedas. You are responsible for the birth, maintenance and destruction of the universe. You enchant the whole world and carry on your sports independently of others. All who adore your lotus feet, O Shining One, attain happiness, be they gods, men or sages. You know well my heart's longing since you ever dwell in the hearts of all.)

Divine goodness, thy grace is infinite, we bow before thee in gratitude.

CHAPTER THIRTY TWO

Mercies of Mother Divine

"The Divine Mother by whose grace the *sādhaka* realises the divine Power, was already there in him before he entered the path of *sādhanā*. The Mother is Omnipresent and All-pervading. The mother who sits with her child in her lap does not keep her breast milk away from him. The Divine Mother has an infinite supply of milk which SHe is most graciously willing to give to all her children. Every child of Divine Mother has the real and inherent claim on all the treasures of the Mother".

The very name *Śrī Mātā* describes her universal Motherhood. Mother's love for her children is proverbial and peerless. All of us are the children of the universal Mother. The Mother never fails to save her trusting devotees from dangerous situations.

Trials are sent by *Mām* to train us to lead a higher life of strength, love, devotion, purity and wisdom. Pain is the pointer of the Mother teaching us how to bear and grow in raptures. In pain one can be more meditative than in pleasure. Pleasure tends to make us unconscious and forgetful of the cosmic Play. Pain is an awareness. Pain is the reminder. Pain is meditation.

So long the child is busy with his lollipop, he is forgetful of his mother while she attends to her duties, but the moment the child, tired of his lollipop, throws it away and cries for the mother, she leaves everything, runs to the child, takes him in her lap. The *jīva-s* too remain attached to the sensual pleasures of the world and suffer deprivation of the loving care of the Mother Divine till they really wake up and cry for Her.

The child rolls in dirt but the mother takes delight in washing the child and making it tidy and enjoying its freshness. Human beings are prone to commit evil. The Divine Mother absolves them of their sins.

The Divine Mother awards learning, prosperity, charm, longevity and bliss of spiritual realisation to her true devotees.

It is the primary concern of the mother to provide succour to the helpless new born babe. As the child grows, her role becomes moral, ethical and aesthetic. This is not to assume that she slackens her maternal role towards the child. Mother Grace herself initiates her ward into the invocation and worship of goddess Sarasvati (giver of knowledge).

It is because of his confidence in his master that the servant feels quite carefree, so does a child that trusts his mother. The Divine Mother bestows on her children much more than they would pray for. *Māṃ* who is the conscious core of the heart, knows each one intimately.

Just as the child is going to touch fire and the mother stops him and tells: 'No, no, don't touch it.' So the Mother Divine will always guide and protect Her devotees.

Mother Grace loves all her children but specially those who courageously face the difficult in her universe. The mother embodies a unique value that is love. This love that is the urge to care for and protect the offspring even at the cost of one's life, is found in the females of all species. Love knows no fear. Genetic motherhood is exclusively a feminine privilege but spiritual Motherhood is the privilege of the whole humanity. The Creator cannot be inimical to her own creation. SHe is gracious and merciful. Her grace saves them all.

Just as a child carried away by his baser instincts, commits innumerable blunders and falls into the entanglement of *vikarma* (bad actions), the mother after rebuking him harshly, embraces him lovingly in the end and renders him advice. Similarly SHe at once rectifies the mistakes of the devotee, forgives his past errors and guides him to the right path. The devotees are very dear to the Mother.

You play the horse to your son and bottle-feed the doll of your daughter because you love them. Can't the Divine Mother, too, play with you a make-belief game of hide and seek in a finite image that your mind sculptures out of your aspirations? Mother Divine too loves us all despite our dogmatic orthodoxy and narrow beliefs.

Who is worthy or unworthy in front of the Divine Grace? All are children of the one and the same Mother. Her love is equally spread over all of them. But to each one SHe gives according to his nature and receptivity.

Mother Grace hearkens all our prayers and meets all our wants. And when SHe seems to deny what seems our right, in denying SHe grants. The Supreme Goddess manifests herself in all her glory to shower her blessings upon her devotees. SHe fulfils the worthy ends of Man's life: *dharma, artha, kāma* and *mokṣa.*

A story where a selfish son asks for his mother's heart. The mother gives it gladly. While carrying it, the son happens to fall down. The mother's heart asks: Son, I hope you haven't hurt yourself. Do we acknowledge our mothers' sacrifices and dedication and express our gratitude for her mercies? The Mother Grace is All-wise and All-merciful.

Remember: The most important aspect of Mother's nature is compassionate love for one and all.

WHOM do I care in this world when my Mother is the Sovereign? In eternal joy do I live under the direct sway of my ever-joyful Protector.

ON THE THEATRE OF EXISTENCE ALL PLAY IS THINE
ALL THAT HAPPENS IS THY WILL.
I SING TO THEE, O SINGER OF THE AGES.

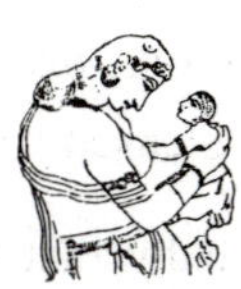

The child believes its mother to be all-powerful and able to do anything.

CHAPTER THIRTY THREE

TO GRACIOUS MOTHER DIVINE

(Interaction with Merciful Mother Grace)

Yā Devi Sarvabhūteṣu Chaitanya Rūpeṇa Saṃsthitā,
Namastasyai, Namastasyai, Namastasyai, Namo Namaḥ

MY ALL-IN-ALL,
To Her I call.
My Storm, My Calm, My Balm, My Rāma.
There is none nearer than *Māṃ*.
None could be dearer than *Māṃ*.

> "TO YOU I address my lament, attend unto it, O Mother Grace: Grant me the grace that mother gives to the son."

We belong to the Mother Divine. We are Her children. We live in Her kingdom and have taken shelter in Her lap. We work for Her selflessly and thereby serve Her. This approach of mind eliminates selfishness and dissolves egocentricity, and the realisation that everything belongs to the Supreme Being, prevails.

"O Mother, the Redeemer of all, I do not know the proper manner of worship. I am lethargic by nature though the job of propitiating you is not so difficult. Therefore, there might have occurred errors and omissions in performing your worship. Being the gracious Mother, forgive all my drawbacks because the children may be unworthy and wayward but the mothers never."

"What should I offer you? The flowers are your own, all beautiful things of the world are your gifts to man. My frailty, my mean selfishness and baseless ego are intuitively mine. May you be pleased to accept them as offering?"

"I have to admit that I am like a baby that can't even walk. But I wish to be a spiritual baby. Which mother's heart has not melted in a tremendous outpouring of love when her two-month old smiles in recognition of her voice and presence? Should you be pleased, do come and take care of me, O *Māṃ*. I am getting tossed about, unable to find the shore. Help me to cross the ever-changing ocean of transmigration. Won't you kindly wash away my afflictions and tears with the waters of your love?"

"*Māṃ*, I know thee, I know thee. In stars, in winds, in flowers; I hug thee and you kiss me. I know thee, I know thee, O Omnipresent *Māṃ*, let thy will be done."

"O Distant One, I am nothing. You are everything. If I have a pair of wings, I'd fly to my *Māṃ.*"

"I adore You with joined palms, O Essence of Mercy, O Compassionate One. Give me refuge, O *Māṃ*. In this world you are the shelter. Forgiving all my wrongs, wipe out the sweat from my brows. I have no support other than your lotus Feet."

"O Highest Being, your love for your children has no parallel. You protect them at every breath and at every step. You are the power of devotion of Brahmā, You are the illusion (*māyā*) of Viṣṇu, You are the *śakti* of Śiva. When your power is invoked, you rush to help your *bhakta-s.* You are the Great Kālī, Durgā, Tārā, *Shāradā,* Gāyatri, Pārvati, Rādhā, Sitā. You are *Vāni* (speech). You take your children in your arms when they sing the glory of your benedictions."

"O Divine Mother, also known as Śakti, Gauri, Nārāyani, Jagdambe, Jagadjanani You are the source of all bliss, all fulfilment. We pray and seek your blessings and protection. We surrender our everything to your lotus feet. Your *śakti* is in Śrī Rāma, Śrī Kṛṣṇa. O *Māṃ*, I am happy with whatever you provide me with. I have nothing which I can call my own."

"*Māṃ,* Your love imparts a divine glow and begets a desire to love the beloved. Reveal yourself to me, O Radiant Divinity."

"Let no counsellor enter in our midst. Just you and my heart alone meet and chat, O Soul of souls."

"To my mind, O Great One, it is no fault of ours that we are immersed in the worldly pleasures and attachments. The delusion created by you is prevailing over us. O *Māṃ*, be compassionate towards your children. Lead us from darkness to Light."

"It is my desperate need for help that calls out to Mother to scare away evil and the ignoble thoughts. O *Māṃ*, Truth Divine, I give you my soulful call. All the wealth and beauty in the world cannot tempt me if your abiding and gracious presence is felt by my side."

"O kind Mother, gladden our hearts through the fragrance, brighten our eyes through light of your Luminosity, delight our ears with the melodies of your Word and shelter us all in the stronghold of your Providence."

"I am calling you. I wish to speak to you. If you had a name, I would address you by it. If you had a size, I would call it 'short one, tall one'. If you had an age, I would say 'young one, old one.' Dare I then call you *'Māṃ'* ? This seems to be most appropriate to evoke a response from you. Hope you are listening, O Omnipresent. I yield, I pray, take me into your own heart."

"O *Māṃ*, I am looking for you and you alone. You have no right to keep me away from you. May be, tempted by delusions of your cosmic play, I have done some wrongs. But being my *Māṃ*, I know, you will forgive me and accept me back."

"O *Māṃ*, unknown Eternity, you remove the sufferings of the supplicants. Be gracious. You are the substratum of the world as Earth. You are the Primeval *māyā*, the Source of the universe. By you alone this world is filled. Salutations to you."

"O *Māṃ*, Glorious Bountiful, my hands were made to pick flowers to offer you, my eyes were made to behold your presence in the shining stars, my feet were made to take me to your temple to sip the nectar of your sermons, my voice was made only to speak of you. By your grace alone all my senses are in harmony with your celestial orchestra of fragrance, beauty and joy playing their refrain in the eternal symphony of the cosmos. Prostration unto you."

"O Divine Mother, may all my speech and idle talk be a *mantra*, all actions of my hands be *mudrā*, all eating and drinking be the offering of oblations unto thee, all lying down be prostration before thee. May all the pleasures be as my entire self-dedication unto thee. May everything I do be taken as thy worship."

"You are the Mother of the universe. We are your children gathered to sing the glory of your names and forms. Banish the darkness of ignorance with your effulgence and reveal thyself unto us. Bless us with your grace. Saturate us with your presence, O Ineffable Unborn. How long this tomorrow and tomorrow and tomorrow? Why not today? Why not now?"

"O *Māṃ*, Brahmā, Viṣṇu, Maheṣ and other gods have not been able to gauge your limits though they are incessantly chanting your praises. I am the smallest of the small, totally ignorant, show mercy on me."

"O *Māṃ*, I cannot live without you. I love you. Reveal yourself to me. To you are known all the secrets of your power. I only crave for a glimpse of yours, O all-wise, all-merciful Mother."

"O *Māṃ*, you annihilate all sorts of poverty, misery and fear. Who else other than you has a heart always melting to do good to all? Being the Mother, forgive all my drawbacks because the sons may be unworthy and wayward but the Mother never."

"O *Māṃ*, have you left me here to die with longing for your vision? The days are passing one by one. All my hopes are pinned on you. Will you also forsake me? I desire to see you. Did I commit any mistake? What could be the possible reason for your not revealing your true form to me? Delay no more, *Māṃ*. Give a drop of your love to my burning heart. Chanting *Māṃ*, *Māṃ*, my mind has forgotten all other paths. I desire only pure devotion to you. Please stop your tests, I can't stand them. Extend your hand and pull me up. Many great souls have adored you and thereby attained your vision and become sternly one with you, O Merciful One. Open the doors of your Merciful Grace for this humble servant of yours also."

"O Mother, why are you taking so much time? I am entrapped in worldly affairs. I am neither strong, nor knowledgeable. I have neither any companion nor even my body is my own. Please hold my hand and take me out of this mess. There is darkness all around, kindly show me the light. I am at your mercy."

"O Goddess of Holy Fame, grace my miserable self too in spite of my being far removed from thee for lack of devotion. My humble self will feel blessed while to thee it involves no loss. The rays of the moon fall alike on mansion and on wilderness."

"O *Māṃ*, I have taken refuge in Thee. Hold me by the hand and let me stray no more."

"I am deficient in every form of spiritual discipline. I am a sinner. I am full of shortcomings but you are compassionate. I am in the darkness of omissions and errors but you are the Light of pardon. You have shown me your grace, O Gracious One."

"O *Māṃ*, this world is only a cosmic drama in which I have a temporary role to play. While I enact my role, teach me to be anchored in your changeless Consciousness as I behold all the sorrows and joys of life."

"O Saviour of the Universe, you have assumed innumerable forms from time to time for the deliverance of the fallen souls. Reveal thyself to me in one of these forms."

"I wandered far away in quest of thee.
I found thee at last within the Heart.
Grant thou to me a new mind,
So that in renouncing all
I may cling forever to thee in faith.
I am lost in this world
And I come to you, O *Māṃ*,
for your protection. SAVE ME."

"O glittering moon and stars, are you also in search of *Māṃ*? If you find Her, please tell Her, I am also waiting to see Her. I cannot bear the agony of separation anymore. Why are you indifferent to the heartbroken call of this child, O *Māṃ*? You cannot remain hidden any longer. I long for your loving caress and a pat on the back. Please come, embrace me and take me in your lap. I shall wash your lotus feet with my tears of joy, O Kātyāyani. Hurry, come O *Māṃ*."

"Immersed in dangers, O Durgā, I turn my mind to you. Please don't consider this as my deceitfulness since children remember their mother only when they suffer from thirst and hunger."

"On the theatre of existence all play is yours. Through your grace and mercy, I see my path, O *Māṃ*."

"*Māṃ*, thy *līlā* (play) is so enjoyable for those who know thee but it is equally agonising to those who know thee not and forget the role assigned to them on the stage of this world."

"My soul likes nothing but your presence and pines for a vision of your holy feet, O *Māṃ*. Shall I be fortunate enough to enjoy Divine Bliss?"

"You enslaved me, O *Māṃ*, by binding me in the chains of the senses. Now I wish to break these chains and be free, and then bind you with the chain of my love."

"I do not ask, O *Māṃ*, that life may be a pleasant road and I do not ask also that flowers should always spring beneath my feet. I only plead: Lead me to Light."

"To those who adore you, O *Māṃ*, you grant them boons. You are the origin of Veda-s and all the worlds. Be pleased to shine in my heart and accept my adoration. Bathe me in your light and dye me in your hue."

The true devotee embraces both the ever-affectionate and the terrible aspects of the Divine Mother in totality and bows in reverence before the known Unknown.

Śrī Rāmakrśna Paramhansa lived and died this ideal. When the disciples and devotees asked him to pray to the Divine Mother for relief from the pain (he was suffering from throat cancer), he said, "Do you think I undergo this suffering voluntarily? I should like to see it cured. Everything depends on the sweet will of the Mother." And when it was pointed out to him by a learned *paṇḍita* that perfect souls like him have to merely concentrate their mind on the affected part to cure it, his reply was: "I have given my mind once for all to the Lord. How can I take it away and concentrate it upon this cage of rotten flesh and blood?"

"Thou art knowledge, thou art conduct, thou art heart, thou art soul for thou art the life in our body. It is thy image we raise in every temple. To thee I bow. I bow to thee, O Divine Mother."

"Be You our Saviour, O *Māṃ*, looking after and showing mercy to your devotees. You are our divine Beloved. Dye us in your own hue."

"*Māṃ* could be a mere word of mouth with many but for me it is the very agony of my soul. It is not only a sound uttered but the very flame of my heart. When that agony smoulders in a *jīva*, the goal is not far away. Her name heals my sores. I belong to her for eternity. If I think of Mother and remember her, it is because She thinks of me and remembers me."

"O
Mother,
Thy Light doth shine
On herb and grass, on flower and fruit,
On drops of dew, on beauty of the clouds,
On running streams, on falling rains,
On winds and on wheeling fires,
On every silence of night
and sleep."

"My search for *Māṃ* will never cease, my longing will never end. I revel in this killing thirst. The misery of the hunger is my life and joy for ever."

Mother Divine made us not because SHe knew what we would do but to find out what we would do.

The Goddess is the possessor of the wealth of bliss. He who constantly sings her glories and worships her with devotion will enjoy pleasurable experience to the extent of his desires and ultimately attain union with Her. She nullifies sorrow, suppresses evil, destroys difficulties.

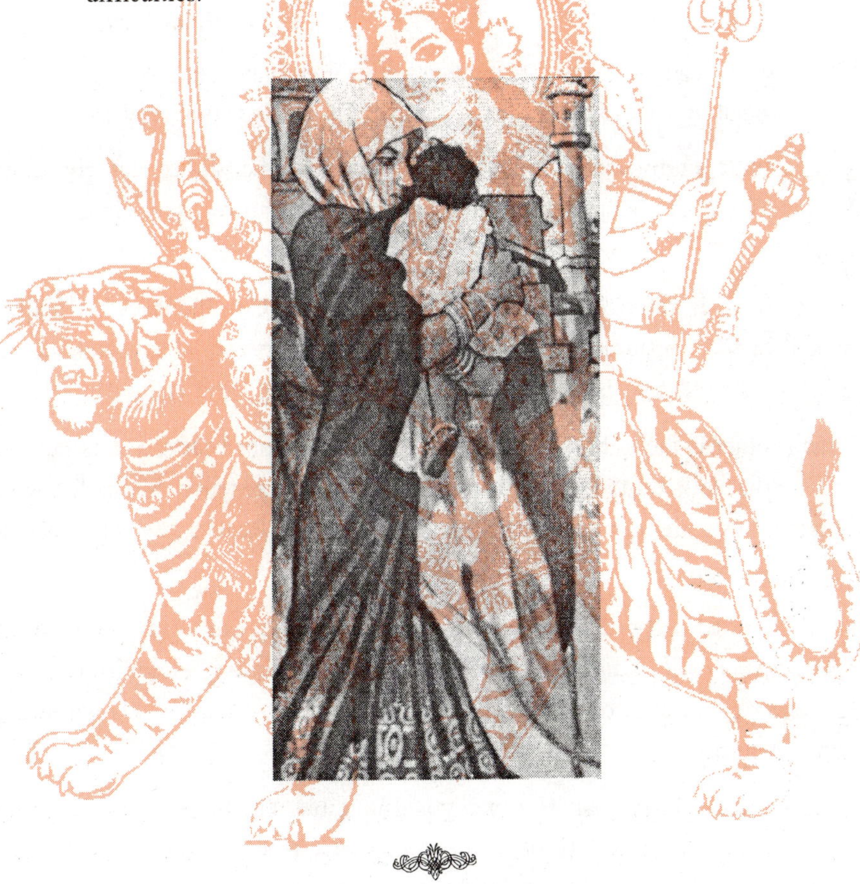

To earn Mother's grace one has to lead a pious life.

CHAPTER THIRTY FOUR

IN PRAISE OF MOTHER DIVINE

(Her Glory)

> "TO ME Mother's grace is hundred thousand times more valuable than Father's. Mother's grace, Mother's blessings are all paramount to me. Please pardon me. I am a little bigoted here as regards Mother."
>
> Swami Vivekananda.

> WORDS cannot express Thee; Intellect cannot know Thee; Senses cannot find Thee; Mind cannot conceive Thee; Thou art beyond all.

THE countless universes are only dust of Divine Mother's holy feet. Her glory is ineffable, Her splendour is indescribable. She showers Her Grace on the devotees.

Mother Grace is referred to as Pure Consciousness. Consciousness is a light which always keeps burning and is self-luminous. This is Her Absolute character. She is In Herself, She is by Herself, She is to Herself, She is for Herself.

Divine Mother is the light that dispels the darkness of our hearts. She is the rain of nectar that falls on the parched soil of our earthly existence. She is the wind that drives away all our misfortunes. She is the ultimate Reality, the One invisible but tangible Spirit.

She is accordingly described as eternally One and eternally many *(Ekanekasvarūpa)*, eternally Being and eternally Becoming, eternally manifest and eternally unmanifest *(avyakta-vyaktarūpa)* and eternally all-pervading *(sarvavyāpaka).*

Mother's grace is boundless. Her mercy is illimitable. She is pleased with a little purity of heart. When the devotee of Divine Grace reaches in her arms (Being-Consciousness-Bliss, *satcidananda*), he attains his goal.

We can hug Mother, be at her feet, confess our woes and feel the warmth of her love provided we dispense with our ego. Mother is thus a *kalpa* tree to the devotees yielding all their wishes. She incarnates from time to time to dispel their woes. Mother is the word for selfless love.

Divinity is our essence. We are its expression. If She would not be, I would not be, nor you would be.

"*Māṃ*, thou art the Self that pulsates within every heart. Both thy aspects, the external universe and the inner soul are full of thy supreme bliss and beauty. This insight enables one to see unity in diversity. Reality is nearer than the nearest to the immanent Self of human beings."

Who knows what the Mother Divine is like? Comprehension is possible only if Mother is gracious enough to lift the veil and reveal herself. She knows our feelings and fulfils our longings.

Māṃ is a mere word of mouth with others but She is the very agony of the devotee's soul. It is not just a sound so uttered but the very flame of the heart. When that agony smoulders in the soul, the destination is not too far away. Her name heals. We are Hers for eternity. If we have thought of Mother, Certainly the Mother has thought of us.

Glory to the Divine Mother who triumphs over every obstacle. Glory to the Divine Mother who forgives and forgets the misdoing of her devotees. He who accepts *Māṃ*, has been accepted by *Māṃ*.

A lamp lit in the home dispels the darkness. The lamp of Mother Grace lit in the heart with devotion, dispels ignorance of ages.

As She was installed in their hearts to keep their spirits evergreen, Brahmā, Viṣṇū and Maheṣa sing Her glory in celestial strain. Śrī Rāma invoked Her aid to kill the ten-headed Rāvana. Arjuna was told by Śrī Kṛṣṇa in the battlefield to worship the mighty Mother and pray for victory.

In the market place of this world, the Mother keeps flying her kite. In the hundreds and thousands of kites She cuts the strings of some. And when the kite soars up into the Infinite, oh ! how She laughs.

The lion She rides is the ferocious animal that mercilessly devours its helpless victims. Desires which consume human beings without ever been satiated, can be compared with the lion. That the Devī rides the lion shows She has complete control over the world. She is reassuring Her fear-stricken children through the *abhay-mudrā* saying, 'Don't be afraid'. Also She grants boons through the *varadān-mudrā*.

There is no language barrier as far as Mother is concerned. When the mother and the child communicate with each other, it is not through any language but the heart speaks to the heart.

Life is but a game of Hide and Seek with Mother Grace and if in its course we chance to touch her feet, the divine energy that flows into us is immeasurable.

"O Mother, it is most difficult to find an opportunity to think of you, to remember you, to speak of you, to utter your glorious names, to realise you and recognise you, without your grace. As the dew-drops vanish helplessly before the rays of the sun, so do all the fallacies vanish after attaining you."

With the axe She cuts off the attachments of her devotees and with the rope She pulls them nearer and nearer to Truth.

She is called *brahman* in the Veda-s, Viṣṇu by the Vaishnavite-s, Śiva by Sivaite-s and Śakti by Śākta-s. Infinity is our heritage.

"O Mother Grace, The scholars who know the real meaning of the scriptures describe you as Sarasvati, the goddess of Learning who bestows true knowledge on her devotees. Besides, they speak of you as the lotus-born Lakṣmi who bestows prosperity and qualities conducive to the spiritual uplift, and also as Pārvati, the daughter of the Mountain, who destroys the evil propensities that lurk in the mind of the devotees. But you are beyond all. You are the unique Power which revolves the wheel of this world."

The individual is enchanted by the excellent attributes of the Mother such as love, beauty, generosity, goodness and compassion. The Mother too is enchanted by the same attributes of her devotees. She showers grace and is Grace personified. When Mother Yaśodā lifted a rope to bind Kṛiṣṇa, many spiritual powers attempted to intercede. How can the Infinite come within the compass of a finite? The Mother Grace was then smiling. Kṛṣṇa baby was bound. The devotee ties God by a rope. Wherefore does the devotee derive the authority? Graciously, Kṛṣṇa allowed himself to be bound not by rope but by the love and devotion of the devotee. The Divine Mother too looks forward to her devotees for love and devotion.

"O *Māṃ*, knowing thy grace, experiencing thy love, singing thy glory, perceiving thy greatness, observing thy light, feeling thy presence and realising thy wisdom, my tongue loses its power to express the bliss that I experience. Pray, bless me and grant me grace."

Mother Divine rescues us from dangers and difficulties, bestows prosperity and emancipation and helps us to cross the ocean of existence *(saṃsāra).* She resides as the Force Incarnate in all actions.

"To those who adore you, O *Māṃ*, you grant all boons. You are the origin of Veda-s and of all the worlds. Be pleased to shine in my heart and accept my adoration. Bathe me in your light and purify my mind. You redeem the depraved, liberate the sinners like Vālmīki and Piṇglā."

Mother's nature is love. Her form is love. Her substance is love.

She has a variety of names consistent with her attributes, forms and roles. Four great aspects of the Mother are Maheśvarī, Mahākālī, Mahālakśmī and Mahāsarasvatī.

Imperial Maheśvarī is the mighty and wise One who opens us to the grandeur of supreme Light. Tranquil is She for ever. Nothing can move her because all wisdom is in her. Nothing is hidden from her. She is above all and bound by nothing.

In Mahākāli there is an overwhelming intensity, a mighty passion of force to achieve, a divine violence rushing to shatter every limit and obstacle. The aspirations that mount in flame are the motions of Mahākāli. Her love is as intense as her wrath.

There is no aspect of the Divine Śakti more attractive to the heart of embodied beings than Mahālakśmi. She throws the spell of the intoxicating sweetness of the Divine. Wherever She fixes her wonderful gaze, the soul is seized and made captive. And yet it is not easy to meet the demand of this enchanting Power.

Mahāsarasvati is the Mother's power of work and her spirit of perfection and order. She bestows intimate knowledge to those whom She chooses worthy. A mother to our wants, a friend in our difficulties.

> Mothers are like cooling shade.
> Sons have lapses; mothers never do.
> Look after us, Māṃ, we adore you.
> You shower us with happiness,
> Rid us of desire, hunger, and thirst.
> Salutation to you, Hail, hail, hail.

It is an irrefutable fact that whenever oppression of righteousness is ascendant, the Divine Power incarnates to quell it. Devi's incarnation was for the protection of the *deva-s* who were defeated and tortured by the *asura-s*.

> LIVE constantly in the Presence of the Mother; live in the feeling that it is the Presence which moves you and is doing everything you do.

Even gods invoke Mother divine, when in trouble.

CHAPTER THIRTY FIVE

THUS SPAKE MOTHER DIVINE

"MY CHILD, you need not know much in order to please Me. Only love Me dearly. Speak to Me as you would like to speak to your mother when she has taken you in her arms."

Divine Mother.

THE GODS assemble near the Goddess and with great respect and folded hands asked Her identity as to who She was. SHE spake thus in Durgā Sapataṣati (The Devī Mahātmya):

"I am the intrinsic nature of the Consciousness. From me this world of true existence and untrue appearance, has taken birth. Mind, spirit and body are my temples for the self to realise in them my supreme Being and Becoming.

"I am the Sovereign, the supreme Consciousness, the all-pervading Soul of the abundant Being. Through Me alone all beings eat, see, breathe, hear. They know Me not, yet they dwell beside Me. I blow all beings of the universe like the wind. Beyond the heavens and beyond the earth extends my domain. Hear the truth with faith as I speak to you:

"I perform the functions of great devotion, creative intelligence, search for truth and realisation. I perform the functions of the all-pervading Consciousness, the creative Capacity and the Lord of beings.

"I am the form of bliss and sorrow. I am the form of wisdom of unity and lack of wisdom as well. I am the great elements of existence as they unite in forms and in their individual aspects as well. I am this entire perceivable universe.

"I travel with the relievers of suffering, with the finders of the wealth, with the sons of enlightenment, as also with all gods. I hold aloft friendship and equanimity, the rule of the Pure, the light of meditation and the divine urge of Union."

And In Srimad Devi Bhagavatam, the Devī *uvāc* (speaks):

"BEFORE creation, I, only I, existed. My Self is known by the names *cit, samvit* (intelligence), *parā-brahman* and others. My *ātman* is beyond mind, beyond any name or mark, beyond birth and death or any change. My Self has one inherent power called *māyā*. This *māyā* arises as heat comes out of fire, as the rays come out of the sun. I am the cause of this world. *Māyā* has the power of hiding Me, the Originator.

"I am verily the *brahman*. It is from Me that the entire universe, both *Puruṣa* and *māyā,* existent and non-existent, emanated. The atoms of the universe may be counted, but not My manifestations, for, eternally I create innumerable worlds.

"I have an inherent power called *māyā*. This *māyā* is not existent nor is it non-existent, nor can it be called both. *Māyā* can be destroyed by *brahmajñāna*, so it cannot be called existent; again if *māyā* doesn't exist, the practical world cannot exist. So it cannot be called non-existent. Of course it cannot be called both, for it would involve contradictions. This *māyā* arises naturally as heat comes out of fire, as the rays come out of the sun, and as the cool rays come out of the moon.

"I am *nirguṇa,* I am *saguṇa*, the great cause of this world. This *māyā* is divided into *vidyā* and *avidyā*. *Vidyā-māyā* reveals Me whereas *avidyā-māyā* hides Me. *Māyā* united with *chaitanya* (Intelligence) is the efficient cause of this universe; whereas *māyā* united with the five original elements is the material cause. Some call Me *ajā* (unborn) while others call Me *Śakti.*

"You are but a little spark, O soul, and yet you extol yourself so much. I own the whole universe, but I remain silent in the background. I am looking after you through your father and mother."

"Hear now about the *parā-bhakti*. He who always hears My glories and recites My name and whose mind dwells always in Me, like the incessant flow of oil and who always meditates on Me, does not think himself separate from Me. He worships Me with intense feelings as the Mother of the universe and gets dissolved in My nature of Consciousness. This is *Parābhakti* or the highest devotion."

"Arise, my child, and go forth a man. Think not life as serious. What is destiny but thy Mother's Play. Come, be My play-fellow awhile, meet all happenings merrily. My sport is unerring. Shrink not from defeat, embrace despair. Pain is not different from pleasure, I will both. Rejoice. When the sun sets and the game is done, you will know well that I, the giver of manhood, am your Mother. Give Me your heart and let Me alone govern it. This world cannot exist without the sub-stratum and that sub-stratum is my existence. By the wheel of time, the beings are led sometimes into happiness, and sometimes into pain. Be the witness of earth's joys and sorrows, sharing them not. Thus you can be free from worldly cares and ultimately attain peace."

"I am of the nature of pure Consciousness and Bliss supreme. I am the one Reality behind everything. I am Śiva, the Auspicious."

"I am the dweller of the Innermost. I am Spirit untouched by thoughts or form. I am *ātman.* I am *paramātman.* I am *brahman.*"

"Waking is for one who is sleeping and sleeping is for one who is awake. But I am beyond both. It is this ever-present Presence, that I am."

"Through Me a man eats. He sees, He breathes, He hears, He speaks through Me. I blow forth like the wind grasping all worlds beyond heavens, beyond this earth."

THE way to love is the little way: To tread the little way is to be humble as dust, that is, to realise your nothingness, for, the heart must be emptied before it can receive the treasures of the Spirit.

Salutations to the Deity who is One without a second.

CHAPTER THIRTY SIX

Prayers and Praises : Solemn Address

(A bouquet of the choicest hymns.)

"O Śive, You are the auspicious
of all auspicious things,
And the fulfiller of all purposes.
You are the refuge, O *Tryambake*,
O *Gaurī*, unto you, O *Narayani*,
My Salutations."

Prayers and praises are the first means to be adopted for spiritual growth. By prayers we do not seek to change what God ordains. We get a spiritual charge into our frame by being in His benign presence. Then comes reason, reflection, contemplation and meditation. They have the power to emancipate the soul.

We pray to avoid emotional sufferings, gain practical advantages, obtain intellectual satisfaction. These following selected prayers uttered with full faith and truthful sincerity will definitely shorten the projected distance between the devotee and the deity.

"We pray that we may know the Divine and be more and more like Him. The *jñāni* who knows God as He is, loves God for what He is, lives in the Divine. God is dear to him as he is dear to God. The *jñāni* has the purity of heart and singleness of will to see the plan of God and ask for its realisation. It is *jñāna*, integral wisdom, divine life."

S. Rādhākṛśnan.

"O Divine Mother, creator, preserver and destroyer of the universe, your real face is veiled by your self-effulgence. Pray remove that covering and reveal yourself to your devotees. Stricken with grief I pray to thee: Do not believe me insincere. A child who is seized with thirst and hunger thinks of his Mother only. Be gracious."

"I meditate on the glorious light of the cosmic Sun. O all-wise, all-merciful God and Mother, pour the bright beams of thy light into my soul and guide me into thy eternal Truth."

Lord Kṛṣṇa, for the sake of Arjuna's well-being, advised him to recite the *Durgā-stotra* and extol the *Devī*. Arjuna descended from the chariot with folded hands in reverence, and uttered the hymn thus:

"Salutations to you, O virtuous One who dwells on Mandār. O young virgin, O Kālī, O Bhadrakālī, hail to you. O Caṇḍi, the fierce One, O Kātyāyanī, the Illustrious One, Salutations to you. O Umā, O Śākambarī, destroyer of Kaiṭabha, hail to you. O One, well-versed in the Veda-s, who has knowledge of all beings, hail to you. O blessed Mother of Skanda, O Durgā, who dwells in all places, salutations to you. You are *Svahā*. You are *Svadhā*, O Sarasvati. Through your grace, may victory be mine, O luminous Sāvitri, the Prosperity of the prosperous, hail, hail, hail."

The Divine Mother who is kind and gracious to her devotees, acknowledged the prayers of Pṛthā 's son, stood in front of Arjuna and said, "You will conquer your enemies, O son of Prthā. You are invincible, for you have Nārāyaṇa to assist you."

"O Mother Divine, I desire no honour from men, I desire no pleasures of the flesh, only let my soul flow into Thee as the permanent confluence of the Gaṇgā, Yamunā and Sarasvati. Mother, I am without *bhakti*, without *yoga*. I am helpless and friendless. I desire no praises. Only let my mind always dwell in thy lotus feet."

"O *Māṃ* the divine One, grant me love and devotion. Cast away my doubts. See that you do not forget me. Cleanse me of my sins. May I develop deeper attachment to thee who is the dearest of the dear."

"O *Māṃ*, the embodiment of love, take away the burden of my wicked deeds that weighs upon me. Banish all my illnesses, take away my troubles and sins and my grief."

"O Wish-fulfiller, shower on me your compassionate love. O Saviour of mankind, forgive my sins. A wicked son is sometime born but an unkind mother there cannot be."

"O radiant Divinity, cause of all manifestations in the universe, may you remove all evils from our path and let us attain whatever is noble."

"Guide me, lead me, show me the goal, instruct me the path. I know nothing. Give me the strength to walk the path. I want thee. Give me a surer sign of Thy Grace, O Mother Divine."

"O *Māṃ*, manifest yourself in a form perceptible to our senses. We meditate on you as Bhagvati, the supreme Deity of the universe, the luminous and self-effulgent *brahman*. Illumine us, O *Māṃ*, to enable us to meditate on your real *svarūpā*."

"I now bow to the Devi of the nature of *Hrīṃ*, of everlasting existence, intelligence and bliss, who stimulates our activities. I ask you this boon: that my devotion may remain constant, fixed and unflinching towards you."

"Praise to the Divine who abides in all creatures in the form of faith. May SHe endow me with the keen desire for divinity."

"Mother, may I attain that love for you that the worldly people have for the objects of the world. I do not beg for a kingdom nor for gold nor for jewels. Do reveal yourself unto me."

"Let my deeds be according to your commands, O Adorable Mother Mercy."

"Grant us inner spiritual strength to resist temptations and to control the mind. Free us from lust, anger, greed, hatred and jealousy. Fill our hearts with divine virtues, O Mother Grace."

"Be gracious to those who have bowed before you. Grant them grace, faith, love, wisdom, protection and compassion, O gracious One."

"Again and again I bow to *Śri Māṃ* who delights the whole world, removes all adversities and bestows prosperity. O Mām̐, guide me and take me straight to my destination."

"May the Goddess *Śri* take abode in my person, fulfil my desires, materialise my utterances. Pray, Her all-auspicious presence shine in my heart day and night."

"Be gracious, O Mother Divine, to thy children who have taken refuge in thee and give them shelter at thy feet, O compassionate One, Salutations to Thee."

"Before fire burns this body to ashes, rain down on me a shower of your cool blessings, O Mother Divine. Strip me naked and re-robe me with the splendour of your grace, O Mother Grace."

"You are the Deity of deities, O *Māṃ Śri*. May my debts, poverty, ailments and sins perish for ever."

"O *Māṃ* Sarasvati, you delight in white flowers. I bow to you who is fond of purity. You are the source of learning, the source of all the sacred books, the fountainhead of all faculties, the purifier of mind, speech and vision. May you be the source of inspiration and accomplishment for all our benevolent acts."

"O blessed and beloved *Māṃ* Durgā, protect us always from the malignant departed spirits, ghosts, gods and demons who are ill-turned, and from all sorts of fears. Destroy our sins, afflictions, sorrows, calamity, misery, disease, anxiety."

"O *Māṃ* of radiance, you have dawned in the narrow horizon of my mind and revealed to me a chamber alive and warm. I can now safely retire there and find refuge in your living Presence. Thus my aim in life will be fulfilled."

"O *Māṃ,* I wish to perform a servant's duty at your glistening lodge at Maṇidvīpa: I shall comb your hair, dust your shoes, sweep your room and serve you every morning milk and honey. Send for me."

"*Māṃ,* open the door of thy heart. My mind has tried again and again but not has it succeeded once. I am tossed between pain and pleasure. Have mercy, O gracious One, and give me the boon of thy love, although it is the privilege of the rare few and the fortunate."

"O *Māṃ*, destroy my arrogance, curb the evil propensities of my mind, bring to cessation this mirage, the world of sense objects."

"The shade of death and immortality, O *Māṃ*, are thy grace supreme. May thy gracious face never be turned away from me, thy child."

"O *Māṃ*, bless me that I develop all the seeds of spiritual potential that are within me, and that I use them to please thee whom I love more than all thy gifts. Be thou mine for ever."

"Illumine the dark in me, raise and support what is low."

"O beloved Mother, an ocean of mercy art thou.
May thy mercy be showered on me, thy child,
May thy mercy purify my mind and heart,
May thy mercy grant me calm and tranquil vision,
May thy mercy fill my heart with *bhakti*, love,
May thy mercy fill my soul with the endless joy. "

"With folded hands I make obeisance to thee, O Mother, whose nature it is to do that which we cannot understand."

"O *Māṃ*, you are at home deep into my heart. Enable me to join you and be with you."

"O wise and benevolent One, endow me with happiness."

"I beg of you, O *Māṃ,* that I may remain always at peace with myself. Bestow thy gracious glance on me, thy son, thy servant, O Bhavāni."

"Praised by manifold hymns, fully meditated upon and revealed to the heart, may the Supreme Being, Mother Grace, be eager to grant spiritual strength to the devotees and annihilate all obstructions to Self-realisation."

"O Divine Mother, how long will you make me go about like a bull with blinkers on, round and round the oil press? True, I cannot see you. Yet I am not a lost child. I still cry *Māṃ, Māṃ.*"

"Salutations to thee, the most auspicious, the Consciousness of the three states, destroyer of demons but merciful to devotees, invisible but tangible Presence, the One only, the supreme Truth, cosmic Intelligence, great Void, silent Witness, kindly Light, known Unknown, homogenous Existence, highest Cause."

"Salutations to you, O undifferentiated transcendental Power, Unborn, Eternal, Infinite, divine Spark of life. Salutations, Salutations to you again and again and yet again."

"O *Māṃ*, thou art Purity, Silence, Harmony, Peace, Felicity, Knowledge, Wisdom, Equanimity, Perfection, Oneness, Eternity, Infinity, Immortality, Consciousness, Intensity, Light and Truth. Take possession of this body and mind and manifest in it, O my Love and my Soul."

"Alas, I do not know either the mystery of thy Presence everywhere or the words of praise of thee. Owing to my ignorance of the injunctions relating to thy worship, I might not have done what I ought to have done. So O Auspicious One, forgive me for whatever faults of omission I might have committed."

The glory of Mother Divine is sung by Adi Śankarācārya, a great teacher of *advaita* (non-duality) in some of his hymns. He was a passionate devotee of the Mother Divine. He has glorified the Impersonal *Brahman*, as also of many other divinities in the Hindu pantheon knowing them to be the manifestations of the One and non-dual ultimate Reality. In his famous hymn '*Saundarya Lahari*', he sings the glory of Śakti, the Mother Divine, and asks for forgiveness from Devī for the mistakes and sins committed by the son:

"kuputro jayeta, kvacidapi kumātā na bhavati."

(there may be a kuputra, a bad son, but never a kumātā," a bad mother).

He even ascribes the undisputed status of Śiva as the Lord of the universe to the grace of Bhavānī, "This is only because of Her being married to You." Again he sings in his *Tripurasundari Ashtakam* :

Seek I shelter in *Tripurasundari,*
Who is roaming in *Kadamba* forest,
A bank of clouds to the galaxy of sages,
Whose eyes rival new-born lotus,
And swarthy like the nimbus newly formed !

Seek I shelter in *Tripurasundari*,
Wearing a necklace of gems priceless,
A face deeply aglow with ambrosia,

Through mercy bestowing prosperity,
Clear-eyed, the wandering One !

Arrayed we be in panoply,
By her *Kadamba* forest abode,

Seated on the golden disc,
Who resides in lotuses six !

Vinā gracing the bosom,
Adorned with curly tresses,
Scorning the evil-minded !

Who bears the first flower of *Manmatha*,
Clad in garments blue, spotted sanguine.

In *japa* I remember the Mother,
Smeared with vermilion,
Bearing arrows, bow, snare and goad,
Deluding all people !

I salute the Mother of the world entire,
Who has the celestial queen for plaiting tresses,
Brahmā's consort skilful for anointing *sandal* paste,
Viṣṇu's spouse for adorning with lustrous gems,
And heavenly damsels for servant maids.
Seek I shelter in *Tripurasundari*.

"Immersed in dangers, O Durgā, I turn my mind to you, O Ocean of Mercy and spouse of Śiva; please don't consider this as my deceitfulness, since children remember their mother only when they suffer from hunger and thirst."

Śri Rāmakṛṣna loved to sing to Kālī, the Divine Mother:

"Is Kālī, My Mother, really black?
The Naked One, of blackest hue,
Lights the lotus of the Heart.... "

The philosophy behind all myth and legend seems to be that the Consciousness (*cit-śakti*) is the ultimate Reality behind the universe and that it is masculine-feminine e.g., *Brahman-māyā*, *Śiva-Śakti*, *Puruṣa-prakṛti*. It is the integral unity of *nitya* and *līlā,* space and time. Nearer one comes to God, more will he realise that God has neither form nor name nor sex. Every human being is free to choose his *Iṣṭa*, the object of worship and adoration.

❄

Asato mā satgamaya,
Tamaso mā jyotirgamaya
Mṛtyor mā amṛtamgamaya,
Aum śāntih śāntih śāntih.

[From untruth, O Lord, lead me to Truth. From darkness (of ignorance) lead me to light (of knowledge). From death lead me to immortality. Aum, Peace, Peace, Peace].

❄

Om pūrṇamadah pūrṇamidam, Pūrṇāt pūrṇam udachyate,
Pūrṇasya pūrṇam ādāya, Pūrṇamevā vaśiṣyate,
Aum śāntih śāntih śāntih.

(That the invisible Substratum is Absolute. This, the visible manifested creation, is infinite. The infinite creation has sprung up (through *māyā*) from that Absolute *(brahman)*. Comprehending the absoluteness of the Absolute, the Absolute verily remains the Absolute even when (if) the creation appears or disappears. Aum, Peace, Peace, Peace).

Consciousness is eternal. Its non-existence can never be experienced. The Divine exists in fire and water, herbs and trees, is immanent in the whole universe - to Her I make my repeated salutations.

No one belongs to anyone, O man, only Mother belongs to all.

DURGĀ SAPTAŚATI - DEVĪ MĀHĀTMYAM

DURGĀ SAPTAŚATI deals with the concept of God as Mother. This spiritual truth is inculcated through many a myth and legend. The philosophy behind this myth and legend is the truth that energy of Consciousness is the ultimate Reality out of which the universe has evolved as infinite Pure Consciousness. Sri Rāmakṛṣṇa spoke of the ultimate Reality in its two-fold aspect: *Nirguṇa-saguṇa*, the Impersonal-Personal; *nirākāra-sākāra*, the Formless-with Form, as *Brahm-Māyā*, as Śiva-Śakti. It is the integral unity of Eternity and Time.

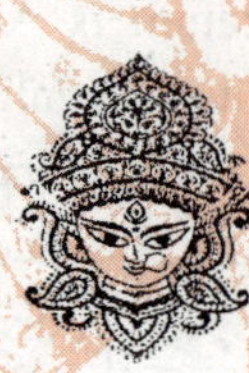

Prostration unto Thee, O Mother Divine, the Supreme Being, the Lord of Love and Mercy, the In-dweller of all beings, the effulgent One.

CHAPTER THIRTY SEVEN

Durgā Saptaśati

(The Essence)

> "Through Me a man eats. He sees, he breathes, he hears, and he speaks through Me. I blow forth like the wind grasping all worlds, beyond heavens, beyond this earth."
>
> Divine Mother.

Śrī Durgā Sapatśati constitutes a portion of Markandeya Purāṇa wherein the *deva-s* (gods) invoke the Divine Mother and sing Her glory. The worship of the Mother in Her three aspects as sublime glory of Mahālakṣmī, pristine beauty of Mahāsarasvati and carnal image of Mahākāli, has its base on this *Purāṇa.* In self-exploration there is always a thrill of discovery and inspiration to search for more and more meaning in each *Purāṇik* story.

Durgā Saptaśati describes how Divine Mother using numerous forms annihilates all the aspects of evil, ne-science, ignorance and the cosmic delusion *(malīṇtā, vikṣepa* and *āvarṇa).* And at the end, the supreme victory to the power of truth, wisdom and knowledge is achieved and the *jīva* is freed for the epic march of the human soul to its freedom.

The Glory of the Mother unfolded by Sage Medhas in *Śrī* Durgā Saptaśati:

The story begins with a king named Suratha, who is deprived of his kingdom by his foes and is forced to flee from home. Deeply afflicted and dejected, cursing the bitter fate, he comes to the hermitage of a sage named Ṛṣi Medhas, and takes shelter there. During his stay in the hermitage he meets another man named Samādhi, a merchant, who had also been robbed of his riches by his own offspring and was thus forced to run to the forests. He also took shelter at the feet of the sage. Both King Suratha and Merchant Samādhi were in a similar situation. In spite of the high-handedness and cruelty of their own people, they were intrigued to find that their minds go back to the very people and things which have been the cause of their sorrow and misery. What is this mysterious nature of the mind which runs back again and again and clings to those transitory things?

Unable to solve this riddle, they humbly go to the sage and entreat him to throw light on the matter. Ṛṣi Medhas explains thus: "O my children, a mysterious delusion dwells in the mind of man by which his pure reason is blinded. This delusion makes him go back time and again and cling to those very objects and persons from which he is subjected to so much torture and suffering. This delusion is the mysterious power of the Divine Mother. This veiling power is indescribable, invincible and plays a mysterious role. The formless seems to have taken many forms and the unmanifest has become manifest. It is *Mahāmāyā*, the great cosmic illusory Power. The remedy for your sorrows lies in obtaining the grace of the Mother of the universae."

The king Suratha and merchant Samādhi wanted to know more about the *śakti* which Ṛṣi Medhas had referred to. In response to their request, the Ṛṣi goes into the detailed exposition of the nature of the Divine Mother. The Ṛṣi said:

"The Goddess is eternal, without beginning and end. The entire world issues forth from Her. She abides in everything from the subtlest to the grossest. Though unborn, She manifests in the world in response to the prayers of gods and pious souls for arresting the decay of the world order and restore righteousness. I shall narrate to you such manifestations of the Mother."

And thus he went on to narrate the episodes relating to the incarnations of the Divine Mother as Mahālakśmī, Mahāsarasvati and Mahākālī. These three are not different but one Devī worshipped in different forms or aspects.

THE FIRST EPISODE begins before the creation when the world is covered by water, and Viṣṇu, merged in *yoganidrā* during dissolution, is floating on the serpent Śeṣa and Brahmā is seated on the lotus emerged from Viṣṇu's navel. Two demons, Madhu and Kaiṭabha, born from the dirt of Viṣṇu's ears also appear on the scene. The demons attack Brahmā who in turn extols *yoganidrā*, the personification of Sleep, the queen of cosmos, the cause of sustenance and dissolution of the universe, to awaken Viṣṇu so that he can slay Madhu and

Kaiṭabha who had come out from the dirt representing lower nature, thus:

"You are *Svahā*., and *Svadhā*. You are the Nectar, O Eternal and Imperishable One. You are Sāvitrī, the Indescribable Supreme Mother. You are the Substratum, the Protector and great Delusion of the world. You are the great Knowledge as well as the ne-science. You are the goddess of good fortune, intelligence, contentment, nourishment, tranquillity and forbearance. Armed with spear, club, discus, conch, bow, arrows, noose and mace, you are terrible. You are also most pleasing and exceedingly beautiful. You are the soul of everything. How can then I extol you? Even Viṣṇu is brought under the influence of sleep by you. O Devī, May you be praised and pleased. Destroy these two unassailable *asura-s* with your invincible powers. Let Viṣṇu be awakened from sleep to slay these asura-s."

After being praised thus by Brahmā, the Goddess *(Yoganidrā)* who was in her *tāmasik* mood, withdrew from Viṣṇu's body and appeared before Brahmā. Viṣṇu who was thus freed by the Goddess, woke up and saw the demons of immense prowess. "Be welcome, mighty ones. I shall grant you a boon for I am pleased with your valour", said Viṣṇu to the demons. The haughty demons replied: "Ask us a boon instead, O Viṣṇu, we are your benefactors. We shall surely give you a boon". The Lord said, "I accept your boon. I wish that the two of you may be killed by my hand." The demons had no choice. They agreed to give the boon but with certain strings: "Do the killing at a place where there is no water." "So be it", said the Lord. He looked at his own uncovered thighs, took the demons on the thighs and cut off their heads with the sharp edge of his discus.

Remember: It is the Goddess as the great Illusion who deludes the two demons into thinking that they can outwit the Divine. Madhu-Kaiṭabha myth provides a ready entry-point for establishing the Goddess's cosmic transcendent status. It is solely through Her graceful withdrawal that Lord Viṣṇu could act.

THE SECOND EPISODE centres around the Divine Mother's appearance in her aspect as Mahālakśmī and the killing of Mahiṣāsura, the buffalo demon. In a long-drawn battle between the gods and demons, the gods were vanquished and the demon Mahiṣāsura became supreme. The gods approached *Viṣṇu* and *Śiva* and told them their tale of woes. *Viṣṇu,* and *Śiva* got very angry and there issued forth from their mouths a *tejas* (brilliance) rising like a mountain whose flames seemed to touch the sky. The other gods then followed suit and released similar energies possessed by them individually. The whole mass gathered together and assumed a charming female form. The gods were pleased and each of them offered a weapon too to Her. *Śiva* gave her a trident, Himalaya a lion as her vehicle and so on. Mounted on the lion, She roared and challenged the enemy who takes on to varied forms of a buffalo, a lion, an elephant and a buffalo again, in the course of the battle. At last the Goddess leapt on the *asura,* struck him with her spear and cut off his head with her sword. The lion devoured the dead bodies.

After the Goddess vanquished Mahiṣāsura and his army, Indra and the host of other gods assembled together and sang praises and thanksgiving for their deliverance in this manner:

"We bow down with devotion to the all-powerful Goddess Ambikā, worthy of worship by gods, seers and sages. May She grant us auspicious things! May Caṇḍikā, the ineffable Power, take care of the entire world and destroy the fear of evil! We bow before the Devī who dwells as good fortune, intelligence, faith and modesty in the hearts of the virtuous and as misfortune in the hearts of the vicious. May you protect the universe! We cannot describe your inconceivable form, your valour, your feats in battles with *asura-s*. You are the origin of the world. You transcend the three *guṇā-s* You are unfathomable even by Viṣṇu. You are the original *prakṛti*. You are chanted as *Svahā* and *Svadhā*, the utterance of which brings satisfaction at all sacrifices, O Divine Mother."

"You are Bhagavatī, the supreme *vidyā,* the cause of liberation. You are the soul of *brahman*. Slightly smiling, your face resembles the full moon's orb, as beautiful as the lustre of gold. O Devi, be propitious. You destroy the *asura-s* in a trice. You are always bounteous. By your grace, O Devi, the blessed ones

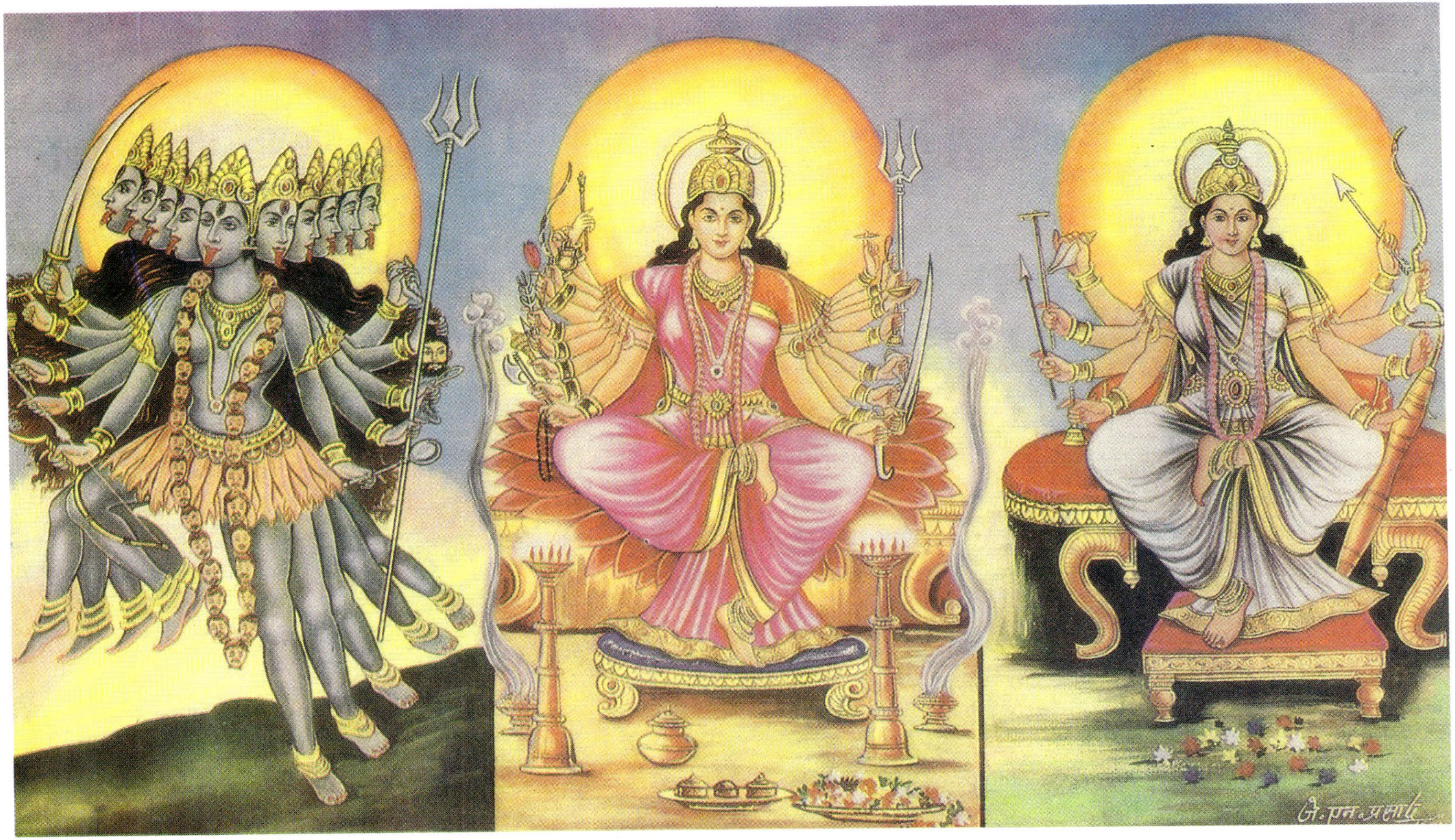

Three major mani festations of Devī : Mahākālī, Mahālakṣmī, Mahāsarasvatī (p.163)

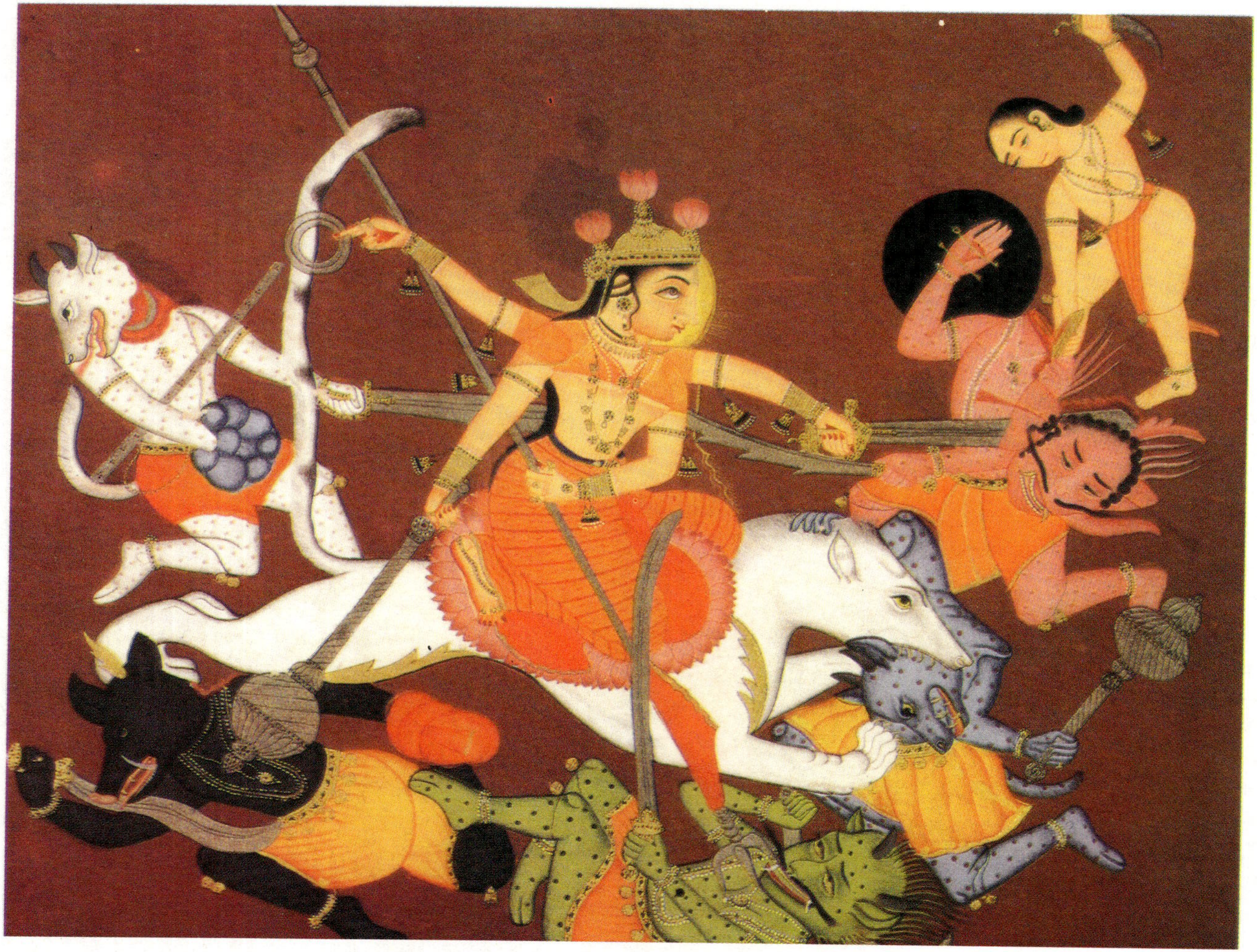

Mahiśasurmardinī, the Goddess Durgā, slays Mahiśasura's army. Salutations to Her.
SHe keeps the world free from ills and affilictions (p.163)

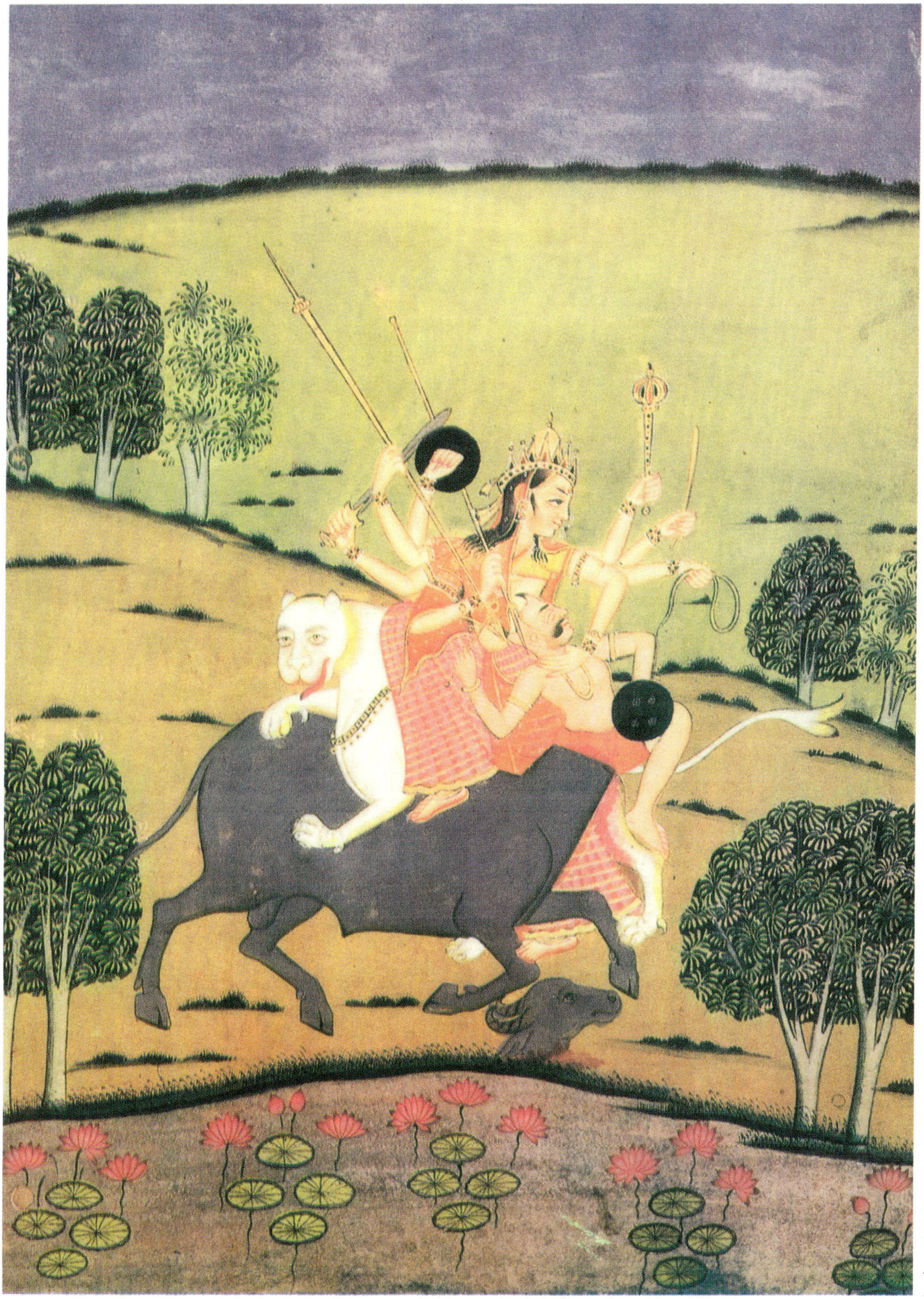

Mahiśāsurmardinī piercing the trident into the neck of the demon (p.163)

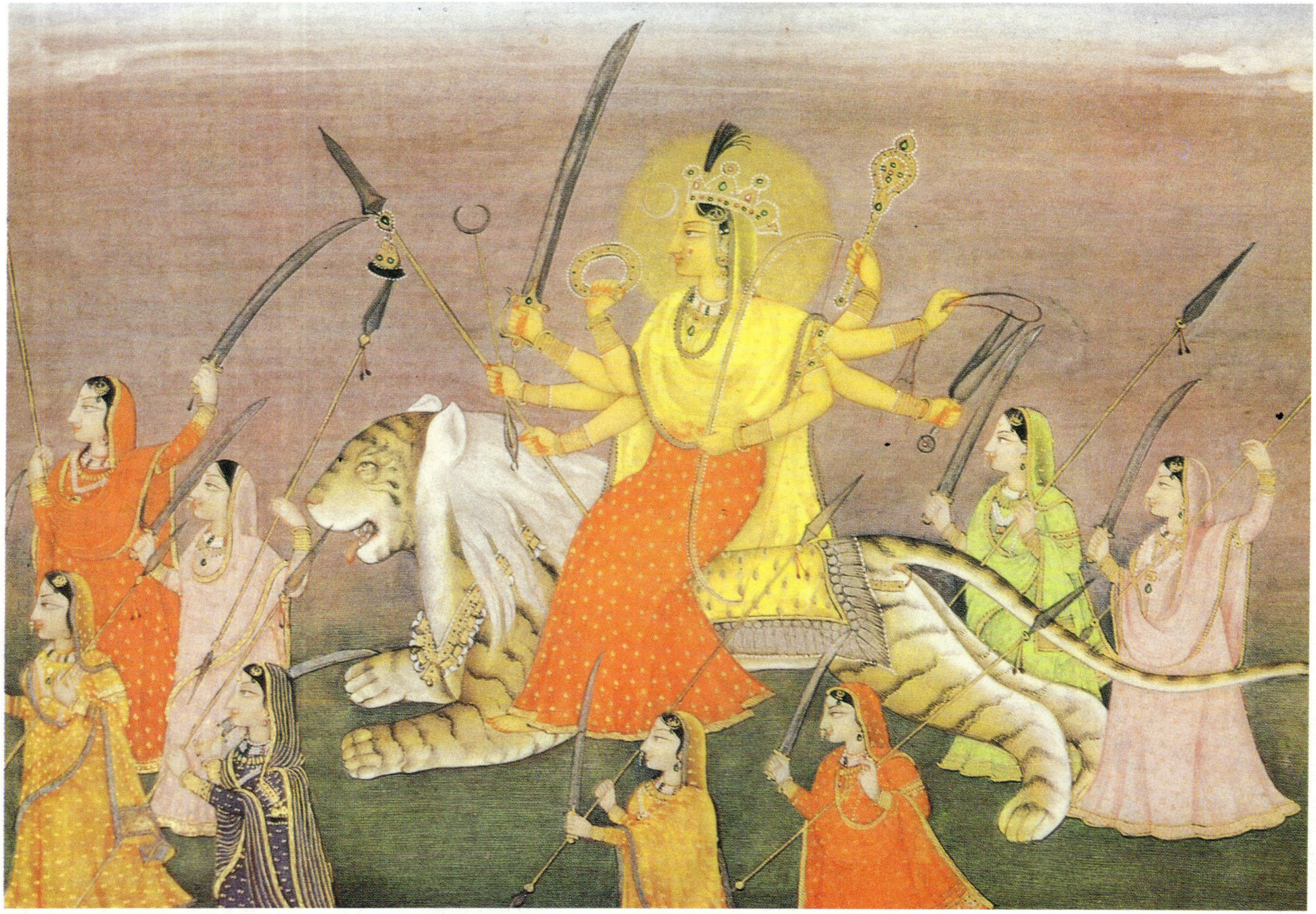

Goddess Durgā with *Śaktian* (different forms of cosmic energy) at Her beck and call. (p.163)

always do all righteous actions and attain to heaven. "You alone destroy misery and remove fear of all creatures who call you to mind. The world attains happiness after these foes are slain. You can reduce to ashes all *asura-s* by the mere sight. But you direct your weapons against them so that they are purified by the weapons and may attain higher worlds. You think of them so kindly and are gracious to them. Your nature calms the actions of the wicked and this your peerless disposition is incomprehensible by others. This compassion in heart and relentlessness in battle are seen in you alone. O Goddess, grantor of boons, O Ambikā, O Caṇḍikā, protect us. Protect the earth."

Thus the Supporter of the three worlds was praised and worshipped by the gods with devotion. Gratified immensely with hymns of glory, She spoke to all the obeisant *deva-s*: "Choose whatever you desire of me. I grant it with pleasure." The *deva-s* said, "Since our enemy, Mahiṣāsura, has been slain, everything has been accomplished. Still if you are pleased to grant us a boon, O *Maheṣvari*, then whenever we think of you again, come and destroy our calamities."

"Be it so" said Bhadrakālī and vanished from their sight.

THE THIRD EPISODE is the longest of the three and introduces numerous manifestations of the Supreme Mother, who are so well integrated in the whole show.

Once again the beleaguered divine beings run to the greatest of all the gods, Brahmā, Viṣṇu and Śiva, to plead for help because the demons, Śumbha and Niśumbha, have conquered the three worlds rendering gods totally helpless. The Trinity realised as to what the demons were up to and decided that there was only one recourse and that is to meditate on the Supreme Goddess to seek Her blessings. They recalled also the promise of the Mother. Thus they went to Mount Himāvat and extolled the Devī thus:

"Salutations to the Devī, the auspicious, the *prakṛti* and who is eternal. Salutations to Her again and again. We bow to Her who is Prosperity and Success. Hail to Durgā, the charioteer of the existence, the essence, the author of everything."

"Salutations to the Goddess who is known as Consciousness in all creatures."

"Salutations again and again to the Devi who abides in all beings in the form of Hunger, Sleep, Shadow, Power, Thirst, Forgiveness, Birth, Modesty, Peace, Faith, Loveliness, Fortune, Activity, Memory, Compassion, Mother, Sorrow, Calmness, Self-restraint, Patience, Austerity, Purity, Charity, Virtue, Knowledge, Devotion, Love. Hail, Hail, Hail."

"Salutations, salutations, salutations again and again to thee, O Goddess Grace who, pervading this entire world, abides in the form of Consciousness."

"Invoked of yore and adored by the gods for the sake of their desired object, may She, the source of all good, accomplish for us all auspicious things and put an end to our calamities. She is now revered by us, the gods who are tormented by arrogant *asura-s.*"

At this moment the auspicious Goddess sprang forth and asked the gods their problem. At once from Her body issued forth Ambikā. This new goddess was surpassingly beautiful. She illumined the whole sky with her lustre and reports of Her presence spread far and wide. She is incredible. But 'ego' must possess Her! Śumbha thereupon sent a message to Her and proposed for marriage. The goddess replied that She would marry only the person who could vanquish Her in battle. He is enraged. Dhūmralocana was sent to capture the Lady alive but She slays him. Caṇḍa and Muṇḍa then attack with armies of demons. A bloody battle ensued. At one stage the Goddess grew so dark with rage that out of Her forehead issued forth Kālī with a terrible form, lolling out her tongue for the blood of the enemy, Raktabīja, whose fame was that each time a drop of his blood touches the earth, it leaps up as a warrior. She sucks all his blood drops and roams about on the battlefield crushing the demons. Kālī destroys Caṇḍa and Muṇḍa. She is thus called Cāmuṇḍā. As the battle continued, more *śakti-s* emerged and with their help the Goddess killed Niśumbha and his entire army. Śumbha stood alone and taunts the Goddess that She is receiving help from so many other women. The Goddess replied, "O evil one, I am One only. There is no second to Me. Look, these my manifestations enter back into me." All the *śakti-s* thus entered into the Goddess and disappeared. Śakti alone then destroyed Śumbha.

When the great lord of the *asura-s* was thus slain by the Goddess, the gods rejoiced and praised Kātyāyani:

"O Devī who removes the sufferings of your supplicants, be gracious. O *Māṃ* of the entire world, be gracious. Protect the universe. You are the sole Support of the world, for, you abide in the form of earth. You are the power of Viṣṇu of endless valour. Deluded is this entire universe, O Devī, If you become gracious, you become the Cause of the final emancipation on earth."

"By you alone, O Divine Mother, this world is filled. You are beyond praise, the ultimate utterance. Salutations to You, O Devī Nārāyaṇi who abides as Intelligence in the hearts of all individuals, and bestow liberation and heavens. Praise be to you, O Nārāyaṇi. You have the power to create, sustain and destroy. You are eternal. Praise be to you, who are intent to save the dejected and distressed who take refuge in you. Praise be to you who carry the trident, conch, discus and bow. Be gracious."

"O Devī who set out to slay the demons in the fierce form of man-lion, who slew the mighty army of demons and having the form of *Śivadūti* whose mouth is terrifying with its teeth, who are ornamented with a garland of skulls, O Cāmuṇḍā. Praise be to you, O Great Illusion. Salutations to You."

"May this benign countenance of yours, adorned with three eyes, protect us from all fears, O Kātyāyanī. May the trident protect us from all dangers, O Bhadrakalī. Praise be to you. When pleased, you destroy all afflictions but when angered, you frustrate all desires longed for. No calamity befalls on those who have taken refuge under you. This slaughter of immoral *asura-s*, which you have wrought, O Ambikā, no other goddess could accomplish. Be gracious. May you bring the sins of all the worlds to tranquillity. Be a boon-giver, O *Māṃ*. Praise be to You."

The Devī thus extolled and praised by the gods, appeared before them and granted a boon: "Whenever trouble arises due to the advent of the *dānava-s* (demons), I shall incarnate and destroy the foes."

Here the paramountcy of the Goddess is obvious. She is able to accomplish what the male deities could not. This episode establishes Goddess's origin on earth. The Śumbha and Niśumbha episode recounts in glorious details Mother's diverse mundane forms and accomplished activities. When we ignore the eternal and focus on the temporal, the Goddess seems to be shown the Ultimate.

And at the end, Ṛṣi Medhas advised Suratha and Samādhi to practise *yoga*, worship the Divine Mother, pray, meditate and propitiate Her. They performed as advised. Pleased by their devotion, the Mother appeared before them, bestowed Her grace upon both of them and fulfilled their heart's desires. The King was granted "Manū-ship" and the Trader who had developed sufficient discrimination and dispassion, sought self-knowledge and liberation. The Mother lovingly bestowed it upon him. Thus blessing them both, the Mother disappeared.

In the *Śri Durgā Saptaśati,* Devī is primarily conceived as the war goddess. In Her perfect nature, She has been described as the most beneficent but Her fierceness as a martial goddess dominates in the main episode and we always find Her killing the demons. For anything to exist, the power *(śakti)* is necessary. In the *Purāna-s* the possessor of power, construed as male, is seen to exist in varying relationships to this power*(śakti)* personified as female. What we have in Śri Durgā Saptaśati is not only the identification of many local goddesses with the supreme Goddess, but also the recognition of the paramountcy of the supreme Goddess. It is not right to consider this *śakti* as a mere spiritual entity. She is the all-powerful - spiritual, moral, mental and physical. Whatever there is, is due to Her. Whatever works, works due to Her.

Thus we learn from the Śri Durgā Saptaśati that the ultimate Reality is feminine as the Divine Mother who is transcendent, an inward phenomenon, immanent, operative both as the material world and in the material world. The forms of *śakti* are many but the Reality is one. The Goddess is affirmed to be both māhāmāyā and māhāvidyā.

The worship of Śakti, the Supreme Being, the primordial power underlying the universe, personified as female deity, is one of the most ancient religious expressions. The cult of *Śakti* has been closely associated with that of Śiva. In the Śri Durgā Saptaśati, however, the Goddess is associated more with Viṣṇu as in Her epithets Nārāyaṇī and Viṣṇumāyā, than with Śiva who is mentioned only once in the role of a messenger. The text shows that the Goddess can be represented as the *śakti* or the creative power of male gods but not as a consort to them. Also, the Goddess can produce Her own *Śakti-s*. She does not need a male counterpart. She resolves the cosmic Order that has been threatened. Other frequent epithets Ambikā and Caṇḍikā, reveal the motherly and destructive aspects of the Goddess respectively.

Every character mentioned in the book is within us. The forces which impel us to realise our own divinity, fill our lives with love and joy and a sense of meaningful purpose as well as the forces which incline to diminish that perception, can be all experienced in our day-to-day life.

Mother Divine, the Supreme Being resides in the image or idol of our worship. She is manifested in the physical body of the worshipper. Her feet cover the earth and Her crown extends to the farthest reaches of the universe. On every level the scripture is a commentary on the evolution of consciousness. By reciting the verses we offer to the Mother all our troubles and afflictions and one by one She cuts them down and purifies them. We must dispel the darkness of egotism in order to realise that 'I am divine being of infinite perception.'

In this beautiful allegory, the dual responses of desire and aversion (*rāga* and *dveṣa*) are pictured as two demons, Śumbha and Niśumbha. The leader of the army of *asura-s,* Raktabīja is fierce in his power that allows him to multiply as soon as a drop of blood from his body falls on the ground. This represents the inimical quality of desire to give birth to numerous progeny, even if allowed to take root only for a fraction of an instant. The divine Goddess finally succeeds in destroying these powerful demons only when She drinks up their blood before it falls on the ground. The virtues in us must remain a tenacious observer for even the slightest encouragement or resistance will only result in the feelings of likes and dislikes taking root.

On every level the scripture is a commentary on the evolution of Consciousness.

"*YĀ DEVĪ*" HYMN

या देवी सर्वभूतेषु मातृरुपेण संस्थिता
नमस्तस्यै नमस्तस्यै नमस्तस्यै नमो नमः

"Yā Devī Sarvabhuteṣu Matṛ Rūpeṇa Saṃsthitā,
Namastasyai, Namastasyai, Namastasyai, Namo Namaḥ"

(As sung by the gods to glorify the supreme Deity
in Śri Durgā Saptaśatī.)

Salutations to Thee, O supreme Deity, Mahādevī, who abides in all things as Mother, Hail to *Prakṛti*, the Auspicious.

O MOTHER, ever benevolent, we bow down to Thee. We bow down to the Divine Mother abiding in all beings, the charioteer of all existence. We bow to Her, we bow to the eternal Gaurī, the Protector, again and again.

HAIL to Durgā who removes all difficulties, the Invincible, Hail, Hail, Hail. Prostrations unto Thee, O Devī. Hail, Hail, Hail.

O Mahādevī, Primordial Cause, Salutations to Thee, the Moon Deity, Hail, Hail, Hail.

SALUTATIONS to the One who is gentle, beautiful and terrible, fierce who is Prosperity and success, Hail, Hail, Hail.

SALUTATIONS to the Mother Divine who is known as Viṣṇūmāyā (perceivable Cosmic form) in all creatures, Hail, Hail, Hail.

SALUTATIONS to the Mother Divine who is Consciousness (spiritual Power), Hail, Hail, Hail.

SALUTATIONS to the Mother Divine who abides in all beings in the form of intelligence *(buddhi)*, Hail, Hail, Hail.

SALUTATIONS to the Mother Divine who abides in all creatures in the form of Sleep (*nidrā*), Hail, Hail, Hail.

SALUTATIONS to the Mother Divine who abides in all creatures in the form of Hunger *(kṣuddhā)*, Hail, Hail, Hail.

SALUTATIONS to the Mother Divine who abides in all creatures in the form of Appearance *(chāyā)*, Hail, Hail, Hail.

SALUTATIONS to the Mother Divine who abides in all creatures in the form of Energy *(Śakti)*, Hail, Hail, Hail.

SALUTATIONS to the Mother Divine who abides in all creatures in the form of Desire *(tṛṣṇā)*, Hail, Hail, Hail.

SALUTATIONS to the Mother Divine who abides in all creatures in the form of Forgiveness *(kṣamā)*, Hail, Hail, Hail.

SALUTATIONS to the Mother Divine who abides in all creatures in the form of All living beings *(jāti)*, Hail, Hail, Hail.

SALUTATIONS to the Mother Divine who abides in all creatures in the form of Modesty, Humility *(lajjā)*, Hail, Hail, Hail.

SALUTATIONS to the Mother Divine who abides in all creatures in the form of Peace *(śānti)*, Hail, Hail, Hail.

SALUTATIONS to the Mother Divine who abides in all creatures in the form of Faith *(śraddhā)*, Hail, Hail, Hail.

SALUTATIONS to the Mother Divine who abides in all beings in the form of Radiance, Beauty *(kānti)*, Hail, Hail, Hail.

SALUTATIONS to the Mother Divine who abides in all beings in the form of Affluence *(Lakśmī, wealth)*, Hail, Hail, Hail.

SALUTATIONS to the Mother Divine who abides in all beings in the form of Activity *(vṛtti)*, Hail, Hail, Hail.

SALUTATIONS to the Mother Divine who abides in all beings in the form of Memory, (recollection, *smṛti)*, Hail, Hail, Hail.

SALUTATIONS to the Mother Divine who abides in all beings in the form of Compassion (*karūṇā*), Hail, Hail, Hail.

SALUTATIONS to the Mother Divine who abides in all beings in the form of Contentment, satisfaction *(tuṣṭi),* Hail, Hail, Hail.

SALUTATIONS to the Mother Divine who abides in all beings in the form of Mother *(mātṛ),* Hail, Hail, Hail.

SALUTATIONS to the Mother Divine who abides in all beings in the form of Confusion (*bhrānti),* Hail, Hail, Hail.

SALUTATIONS to the Mother Divine who, pervades the entire world, in the form of Mind (*mānas),* Hail, Hail, Hail.

SALUTATIONS to the Mother Divine who constantly presides over the senses of all beings, pervading all existence. We bow to Thee. We bow to Thee again and again.

The conception of the infinite divinity as Mother is significant in as much as it is purposeful. The *Ṛgveda* bears testimony to the fact that the Ruler is the all-compassionate Mother. Mother is the personality that appeals most to the human heart, the mother being nearest to filial affection to the child. In the spiritual field also the aspirant has very intimate relations with the Mother Divine.

The recitation of this hymn and the repetition of the word *'namaḥ'* done out of pure devotion and with meaningful understanding helps the mind to get rid of its dross (worthless stuff) progressively and the devotee will attain self-realisation and the knowledge of *brahman*.

> Śri Durgā Saptaśati is said to be a Training Manual. As human beings we have become habituated to being beset with thought. Through the study and practice of this work, we seek to free ourselves from the ego 'I' and from the chronic disease called attachment (*moha*), and to expand our awareness beyond the relationships of this physical body so as to intuit by direct perception the bliss of the Universe."
>
> Swami Satyananda Sarasvati.

Śakti is not something that a deity possesses, but something that the deity is.

"You are in everything and everything is in you; how can then you be adequately praised, O Mother of the universe"?

❄

Oṁ aiṃ hrīṃ klīṃ Cāmuṇḍāyai vicce
Oṁ aiṃ hrīṃ klīṃ Cāmuṇḍāyai vicce
Oṁ aiṃ hrīṃ klīṃ Cāmuṇḍāyai vicce

❄

Mātṛ devo bhava namah
(Mother is none other than God, We bow to our mothers)

Iṣṭadevatābhyo namaḥ
(We bow to the chosen deity of worship)

Sarvebhyo brāmaṇebhyo namaḥ
(We bow to all the knowers of divinity)

The worship of the Highest One in the form and *svarūpa* most cherished in one's heart, puts an end to sorrow, attains prosperity and spiritual progress simultaneously. *Premabhakti bhāva* (attitude of loving devotion) stems from it.

❄

The Goddess who is the possessor of the wealth of bliss, will give command over the three worlds to those who will praise Her with songs and worship Her with devotion. She pervades the entire universe of movable and non-movable objects. He who constantly sings the glories of the Goddess will enjoy pleasurable experience to the extent of his desires and ultimately attain union with Her.

She nullifies sorrow, suppresses evil, destroys difficulties and confusion. She is the Mother who nourishes. She is the rays of light, the remover of darkness. The Mother of the universe, the energy which tears apart thought, known as the cow which satiates all desires. This is the supreme secret worth to be known by one and all.

By merely reciting the seven hundred *mantras* in praise of the Goddess, contained in the Śri Durgā Saptaśati removes all difficulties, all impurities and sins. Thus the greatest of esoteric secret of the meditation of the Goddess as Mother Divine, have been described. Therefore, if a full and devoted effort is made, all desires will be fulfilled.

Epithets earned by the Goddess
in Durgā Sapatśati (Devī Mahātmya)

Aindrī	Ambā	Ambikā	Bhadrakālī
Bhagavatī	Brahmānī	Buddhi	Cāmuṇḍā
Caṇḍikā	Dhātrī	Durgā	Gaurī
Īśvarī	Iṣā	Kālī	Kalyānī
Katyāyanī	Kaumārī	Lajjā	Lakṣmī
Māheśvarī	Mahādevī	Mahāmāyā	Mahāvidyā
Medhā	Nārāyanī	Narasiṃī.	Nityā
Pārvatī	Paramā	Parameṣvarī	Prakṛti
Puṣṭi	Śānti	Śakti	Sanātanī
Śivā	Śivadūtī	Śraddhā	Śrī.
Sthitā	Svadhā	Svahā	Tāmasī
Tuṣṭi	Vārāhī	Vaiṣvavī	Varadā
Viśveśvarī	Viṣṇumāyā	Yoganidrā	

Come out of the silent sky,
Come out of the mountain glee.
Come out of the secret Soul,
Come out of my cave of Silence.

I say to Divine Mother, "O Mother, I do not need to understand. Please grant me love for thy lotus Feet and grace my devotion."

The Lord is my mother, father, relative; There is none other than the Lord. O my mother, I feel the pains of love and yearn for the Lord. If only someone would come and unite me with Her.

"I do not ask of thee, O Mother, riches or salvation. My only prayer to thee is that as the breath of life forsakes me, I may still be chanting thy holy name."

Ādi Śaṅkarācārya

जयन्ती मंगला काली भद्रकाली कपालिनी।
दुर्गा क्षमा शिवा धात्री स्वाहा स्वधा नमोस्तुते।

(She who conquers over all, all-auspicious, the remover of darkness, One beyond time, the reliever of difficulties, loving forgiveness, supporter of the universe, oblations to you. We bow.)

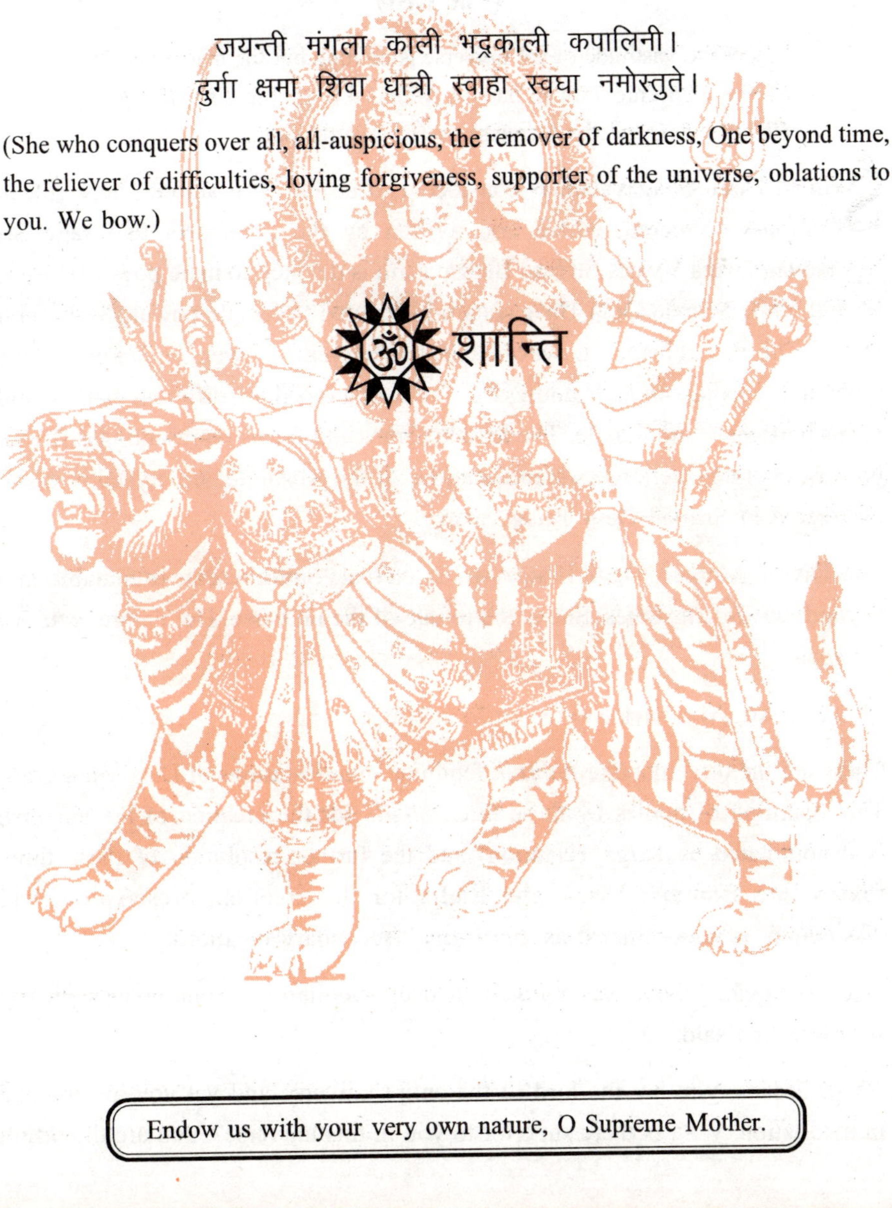

ॐ शान्ति

Endow us with your very own nature, O Supreme Mother.

CHAPTER THIRTY EIGHT

ŚRIMAD DEVI BHĀGAVATAM

(The Gist)

THE entire vastitude of the universe is nothing but the manifestation of the Supreme Power named Māhāśakti in the *Śrimad Devī Bhāgavatam*, and this universe as Her playful field.

Śrimad Devī Bhāgavatam is considered to be the fifth among the eighteen *Purāna-s* collected, edited and written by the great seer and sage Śri Kṛṣṇadvaipāyana Vyāsa. Śrimad Bhagavatam is devoted to male power (*Puruṣa,* Kṛṣṇa) while Śrimad Devī Bhagavatam is devoted to female power (Māhāśakti Devī). The fact remains, however, that the Supreme Power, *brahman*, is One without a second, though addressed and worshipped in different names and forms both male and female. The female names and forms representing different powers, energies, actions as manifestations of the Absolute, are crystallised and elaborated in Śrimad Devī Bhagavatam.

The Divine Mother, Devī Bhagavati, is eternal, omnipresent, immutable and beyond *māyāic* attributes. She is the refuge of the universe. Her nature is *turīya caitanya*.

MAHĀLAKŚMĪ, MAHĀSARASVATI AND MAHĀKĀLĪ:

These are the three popular *purānik* feminine manifestations of Devī Bhagavati. The assuming of bodies by these three *śakti-s* for the creation of the universe is denominated as *'sarga'* (creation) and the further resolution of these three *śakti-s* into Brahmā, Viṣṇu and Rudra for the creation, preservation and dissolution, is denominated as *'pratīsarga'* (secondary creation).

Once Bhagvān Viṣṇu was merged in deep meditation. Brahmā was greatly surprised and said:

"O Janārdana, you are the lord of the entire universe and yet you are merged in meditation. Who is there superior to you in this universe? You are the origin of all, cause of all causes. By your command, the sun shines, the clouds shower rain. Then whom are you meditating?"

Hearing Brahmā's words, Bhagvān Viṣṇu spoke thus:

"O Brahmā , though the *deva-s* (gods) and *dānava-s* (demons) and *jīva-s* (human-beings) know that you are the Creator, I am the Sustainer and Rudra is the Destroyer, yet it is to be known that the saints have come to the conclusion by inference from the Veda-s that the creation, preservation and destruction are performed by the Prime Power *(ādyaśakti)* alone. We are always subordinate to that Power. Under Her command I am engaged in *tapasya* and fighting battles with demons like Madhu and Kaitabh. By Her grace only I killed those demons. By Her Will I assume Tortoise, Boar, Man-lion and Dwarf incarnations. In ancient days you said that my head was cut off when the bowstring gave way and then you brought a horse's head and stuck that on my headless body. Since then I am known by the name of 'Hayagrīva'. Therefore, I am not independent. I am in every way under that Mahāśakti."

❄

The *ṛṣi-s* ask Sūta more about the Śakti and he replies thus:

"The *Vedānta Śāstra-s* say that the Supreme Being *(parābrahman)*, the prime cause, cannot be comprehended by any proof or reasoning. It is stated in the *purāna-s* that the prime Force (*śakti*) is present in Brahmā as Creative Force, in Viṣṇu as Preservative Force, in Rudra as Destructive Force, in Fire as Burning Force, in Air as Moving Force. She is present everywhere, in everything, in various manifestations, in the universe. The sages called this omnipresent Śakti as *parābrahman*. She alone is present in cause and effect and is doing every action. Know this fully that It is the highest Divine Force that is playing and residing in everything. The Supreme Śakti is worshipped by all the *deva-s* (gods) and *dānava-s* (demons). There is nothing above that Adyaśakti, the Supreme Power."

Brahmā extolled Devī thus:

"You are the only One cause of this *brahmāṇḍa*, the Player in the minds of all beings. You have brought Viṣṇu under the control of sleep. O Mother, you are reigning in all as *kīrti* (fame), *mati* (intellect), *kānti* (beauty), *śraddhā* (faith) and *rati* (enjoyment). I am extremely ignorant of your nature. Even Veda-s do not know it. As a dramatic player you play in this world theatre assuming many forms."

When Vedvyāsa saw that his son Śukadeva was strongly inclined to take to *saṃyāsa*, he recommended him to read auspicious Bhāgavata Purāna written by him and spoke thus:

"In days of yore at the end of a *kalpa*, Bhagvān Hari was lying as a small child on a floating leaf of *banyan* tree and was thinking thus: 'Who is the intelligent one that has created me? What is his object and how am I created?' At this moment the Devī Bhagavati who is *chaitanya* (Consciousness) spoke out in the form of celestial voice: All this that exists is I, Myself."

Vedvyāsa continued:

"Bhagvān Viṣṇu began thinking deeply as to who uttered those words and became anxious to know what the words implied. At that time Devī appeared before Hari in the form of Mahālakśmī. Hari was very surprised to see Devī standing on the water without anything to rest upon, and thought within: What is this I am witnessing? Is it *māyā?* Whence has She appeared? Who has placed me here in the form of a child? Is this my Mother? Why has She made Herself manifest before me now?"

The Devī Mahālakśmī spoke thus to Hari smilingly:

"O Viṣṇu, there had been many a dissolution (*pralaya-s*) and creations (*sṛṣṭi-s*). At the beginning of every creation, you come first into existence and every time I am united with you; but now you have forgotten me under the spell of that Māhāśakti. The Māhāśakti is transcendent of all the *guṇa-s*. Know me as the *Śakti* of *sattva guṇa* who is known as Mahālakśmī. After this the Prajapati

Brahmā, full of *rajo guṇa*, will come into existence from your naval lotus and acquire the excellent energy *(śakti)* to create the three worlds. You will be the Preserver of the universe. Then Rudra will appear from the centre of your eyebrows. Rudra will practise severe *tapasyā* (austerities) and will get the *saṃhāra-śakti* who is of *tamo guṇa* and will dissolve this universe of five elements at the end of the *kalpa*. I have come to you for this work of creation. Take me as your Vaiṣṇavi Śakti of *sattva guṇa*. O four-armed one, it is because I have come to you with form and endowed with *guṇa-s* that you have come to know me; but you have not known that *Ādyaśakti*, the Prime Force, transcending all the *guṇa-s* though She is the substratum of all the *guṇas*."

❄

In Maṇidvīpa, Brahmā, Viṣṇū and Rudra had seen Devī Bhagavatī Bhuvaneśvari sitting on the cot known as *śivakāra*. Bhagvān Viṣṇu recalled and spoke to Brahmā and Rudra thus:

"This is the Devi Bhagavati, *māhāvidya, māhāmāyā*. She is eternal (*brahman*). She is the Creator of this world. At present, She is residing in the form of a Seed of the universe. Behold, on Her sides are seen all the *vibhūti-s* (manifestations). Today we are blessed and highly fortunate that we have got the sight of this Devī. She is the mūl-*māyā*. She creates the *brahmāṇda*. She is *māyā* assuming all forms. She is the Goddess of all. It is this excellent Lady I saw in the great Ocean. When I was sleeping on the cot made of *bunyan* leaves and licking my toes, this Lady rocked my body to and fro singing songs like a mother. I recollect and recognise that She is the Bhagavati, our Mother."

❄

Once on an occasion, Bhagvān Viṣṇu chanted hymns in praise of the great Devī, Śri Bhuvaneśvari thus:

"Salutations to the Devī Prākṛti, the Creator. You are all-auspicious and grant the desires of your devotees; I bow down to the world Mother who is of the nature of everlasting Existence, Intelligence and Bliss. You are the great efficient and material cause of the changeful. You are the Supreme Soul *(paramātman)* and you are the individual soul *(jīvātman).* Salutations again and again to you. The creation of this universe shows your infinite power. O Mother, were it not for you, no object would be visible. You pervade the whole universe. You did save us from the hands of Madhu and Kaiṭabha. Then you had brought us to this Manidvipa and showed us your form. When Śaṅkara, *Brahmā* and I myself are unable to fathom your inconceivable glory, who else can then ascertain it? Your glory is infinite. May this relation of ours as mother and sons always exist. O Mother, it is through your will that we create, preserve and destroy. O granter of boons, it is through your power and lustre that the sun is lustrous and visible. O Mother, destroyer of the greatest difficulties, I always take refuge unto you. Obeisance to you, O Devi Māhāvidyā. I fall prostrate at your feet."

After Viṣṇu stopped, Śaṅkara, the Destroyer, stepped in and bowing down to the Devī, said:

"O Mother, you are the earth, water, air, fire and ether *(ākāśa)*. You are the organs of perception and the organs of action. You are intellect *(buddhi)*, mind and ego *(ahaṅkāra).* O Mother, Brahmā, Viṣṇu and I execute our duties by taking the dust of your lotus feet. Hari, Hara and Brahmā whom you have created as the cause of the three worlds, is simply your will. Austerities, O Unborn One, control of passions, enlightenment, performance of sacrifices as ordained in the Vedas, cannot save mankind from this ocean of *saṃsāra*. It is the devotional worship only of your lotus feet that can make one attain beatitude. O Devī, be pleased and gracious to initiate me in that holy *mantra* of yours."

Then Brahmā fell down on the feet of the Devī and spoke thus:

"O Devī, It is you that has been extolled in this universe as the universal Consciousness, all-knowing and all-transcending. Those who do not know your nature, think that I am the creator of the universe. Those who do not worship you and worship other *deva-s* (gods) are certainly ignorant of your glory. O Bhavāni, no one has seen or heard of you taking birth; nobody knows whence you are born. You are indeed the One and only Śakti. You are the *brahman*, the

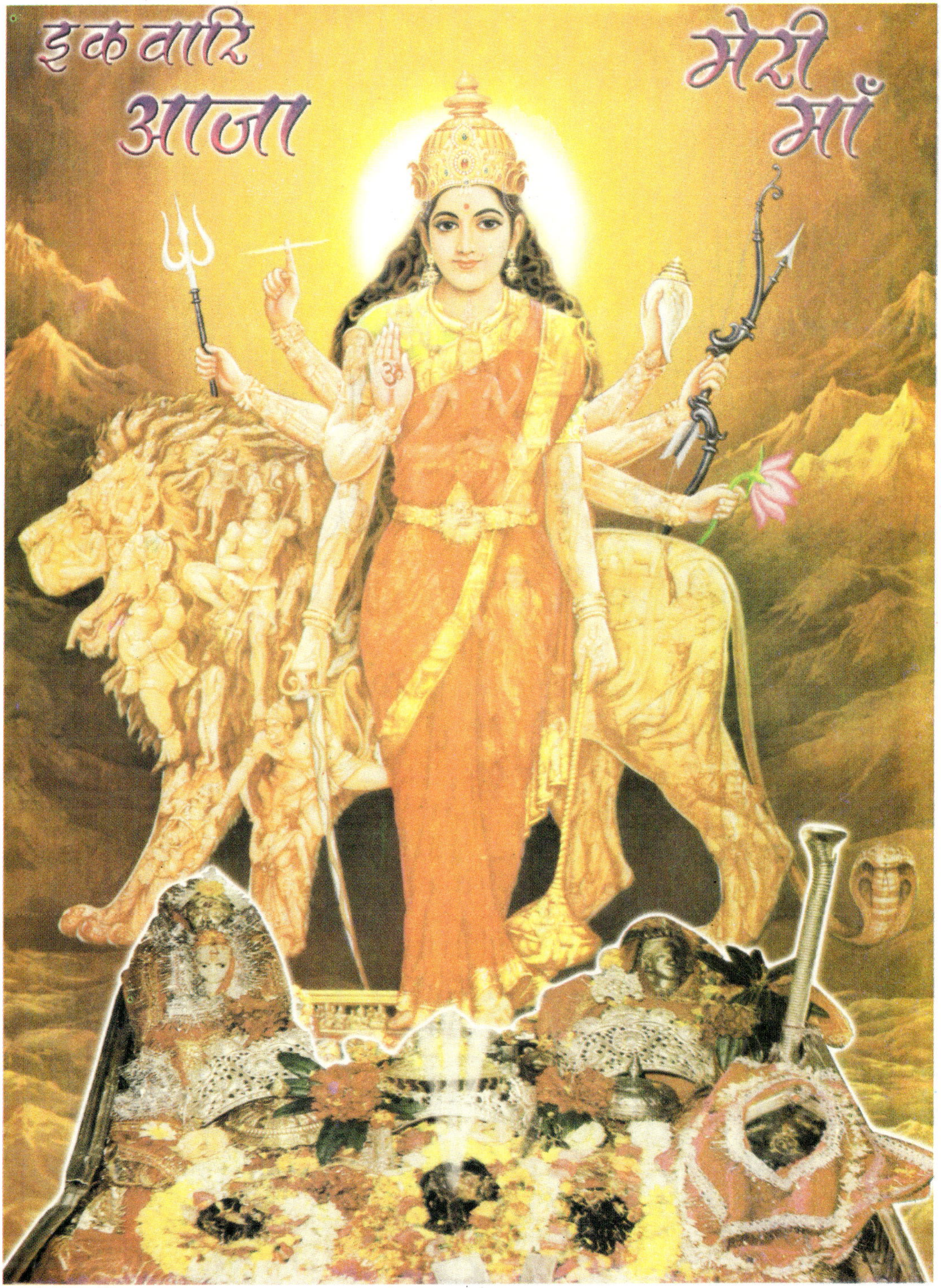

Obeisance to Thee, O Mother Divine, the Supreme Being (p.178)

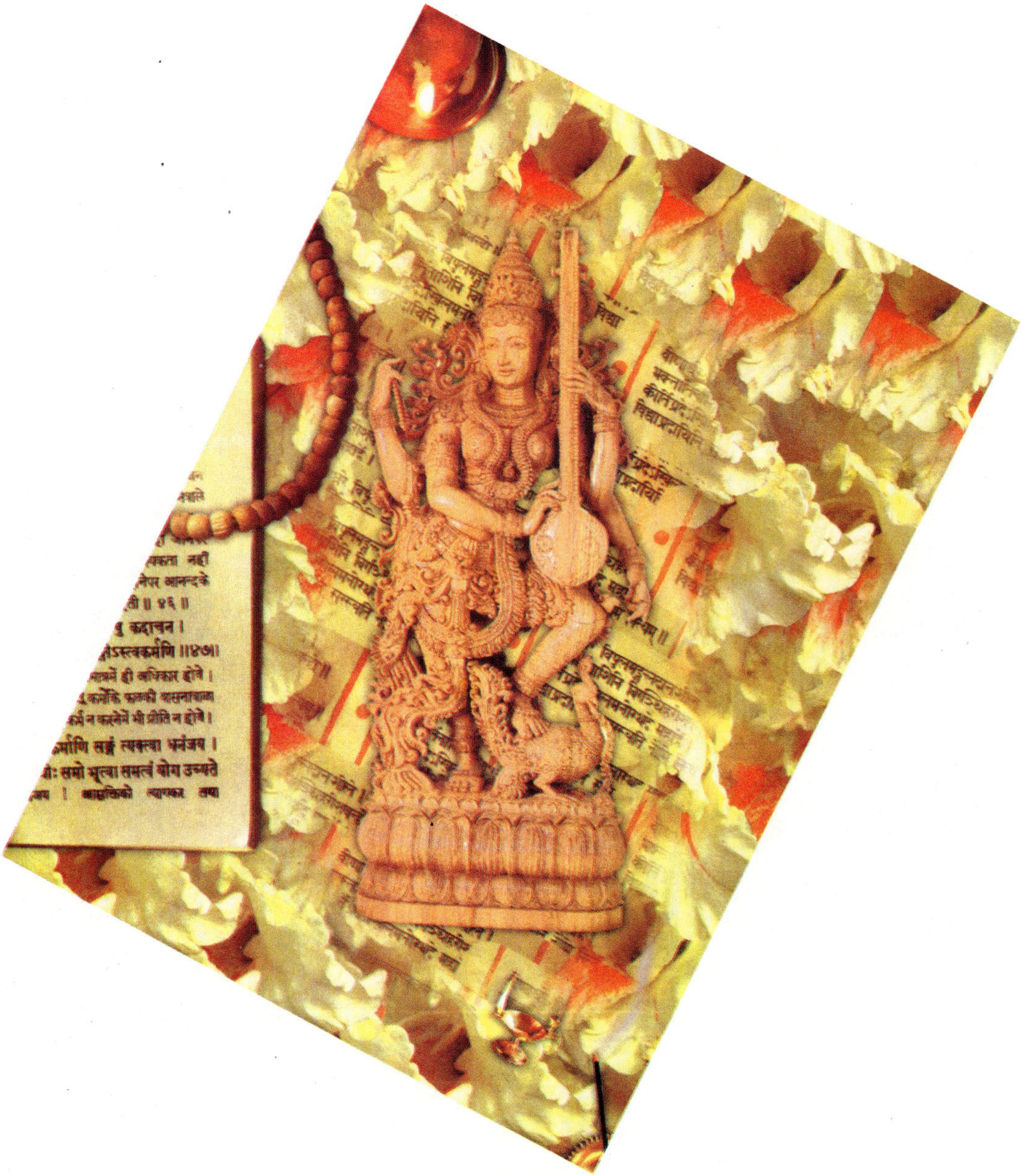

Prostrations to Thee, O Devī, manifested as Mahāsarasvatī, the abode of all learning.

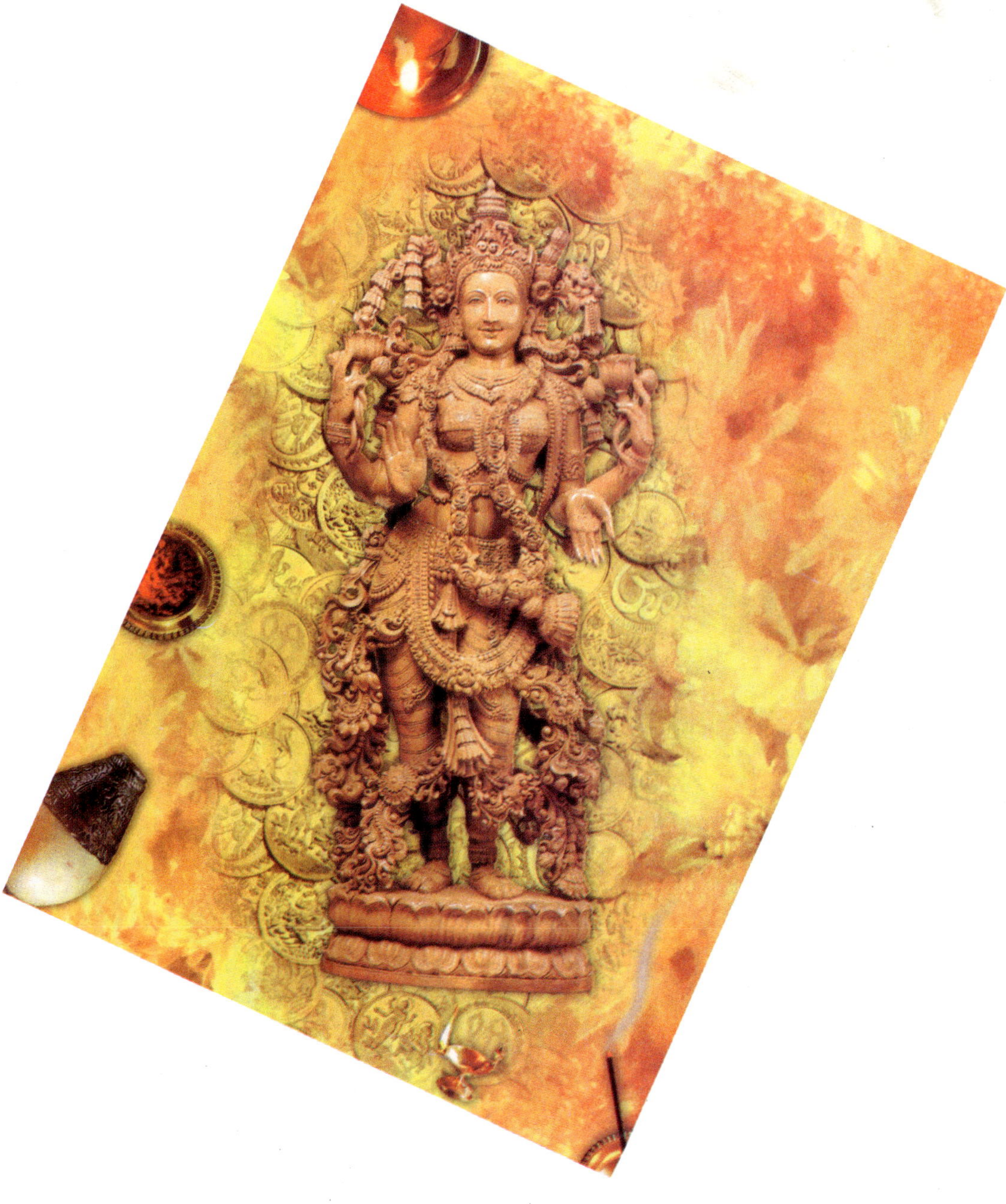

Adoration unto Thee, O Devī manifested as Mahālakṣmī.

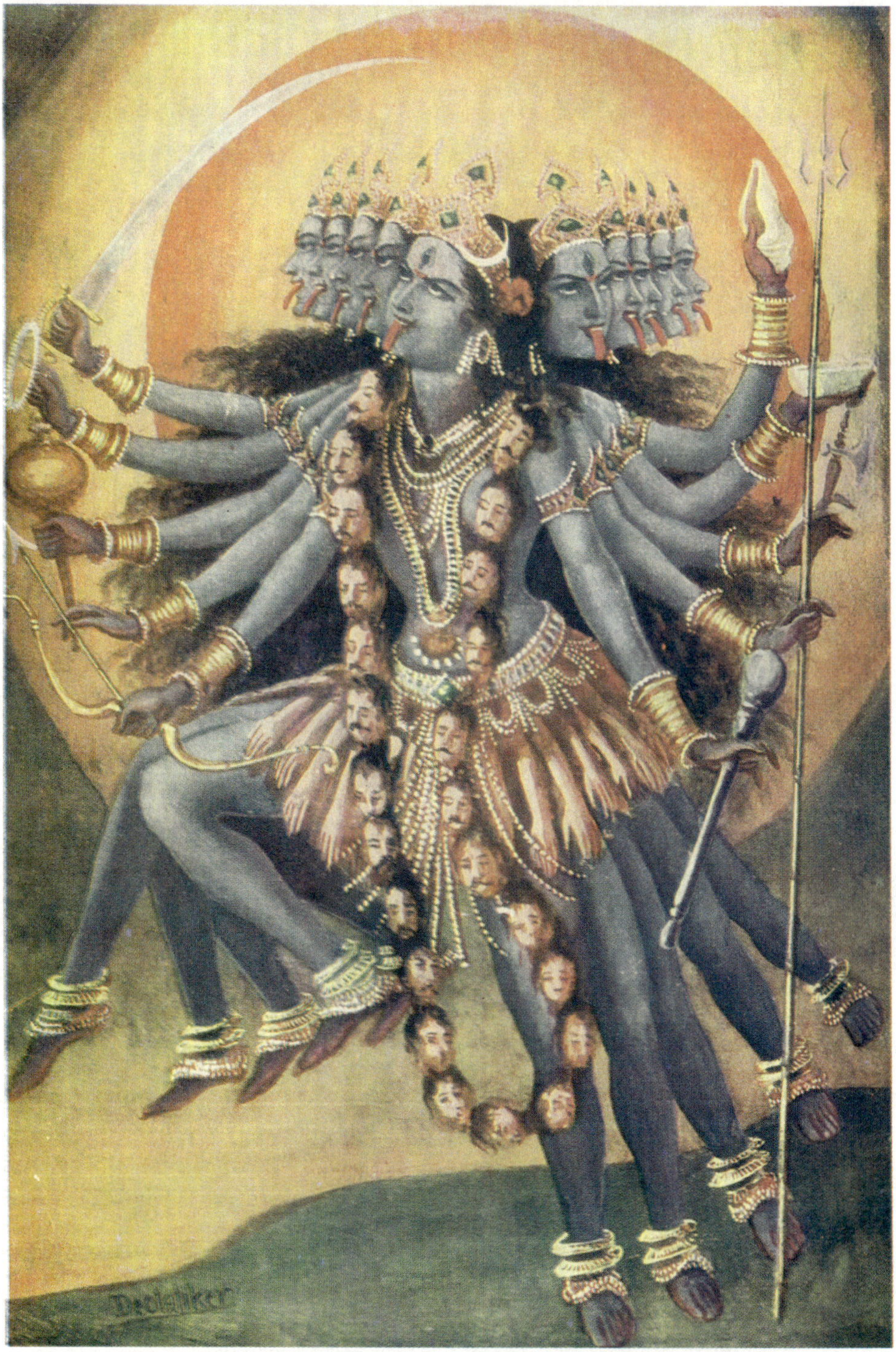

I bow down unto the lotus feet of Devī, manifested as Mahākālī, the Goddess of time,

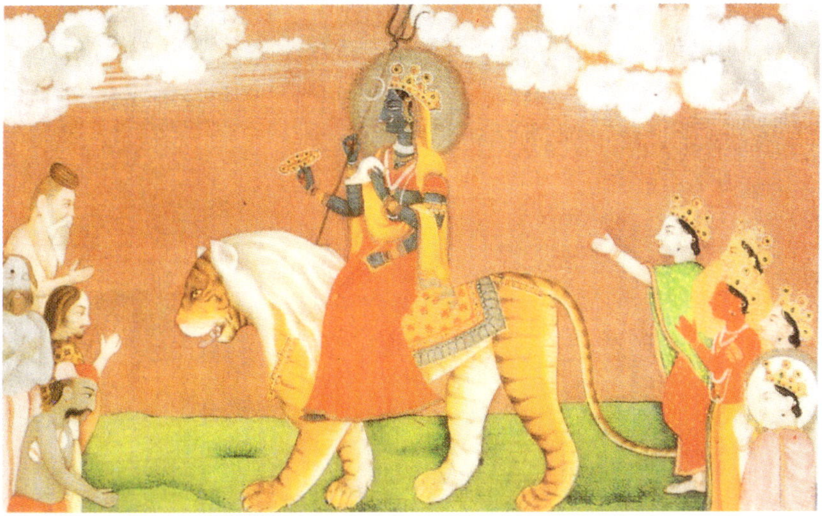

THE MOTHER DIVINE GODDESS DURGĀ

I bow down at the lotus feet of the nine emanations of the Mother Divine : Shailputrī, Brahmcārnī, Caṅderghanṭā, Kūṣmāṅḍā, Skandh Mātā, Kātyayānī, Kālrātrī, Mahāgaurī and Siddhātrī - called urgā-s Durgā-s

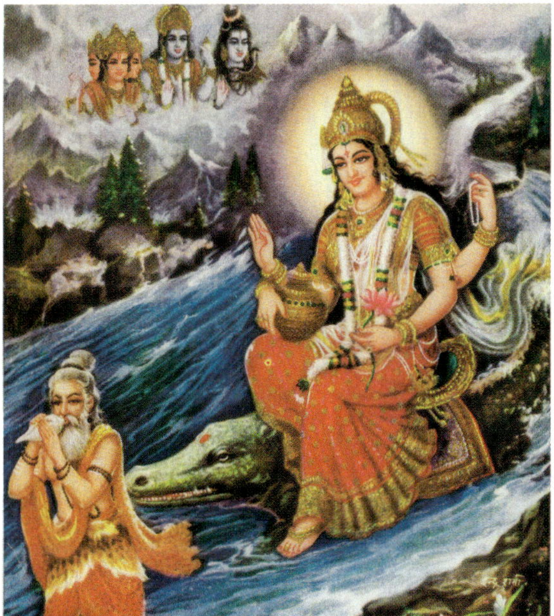

Bhagavatī Gaṅgā blesses

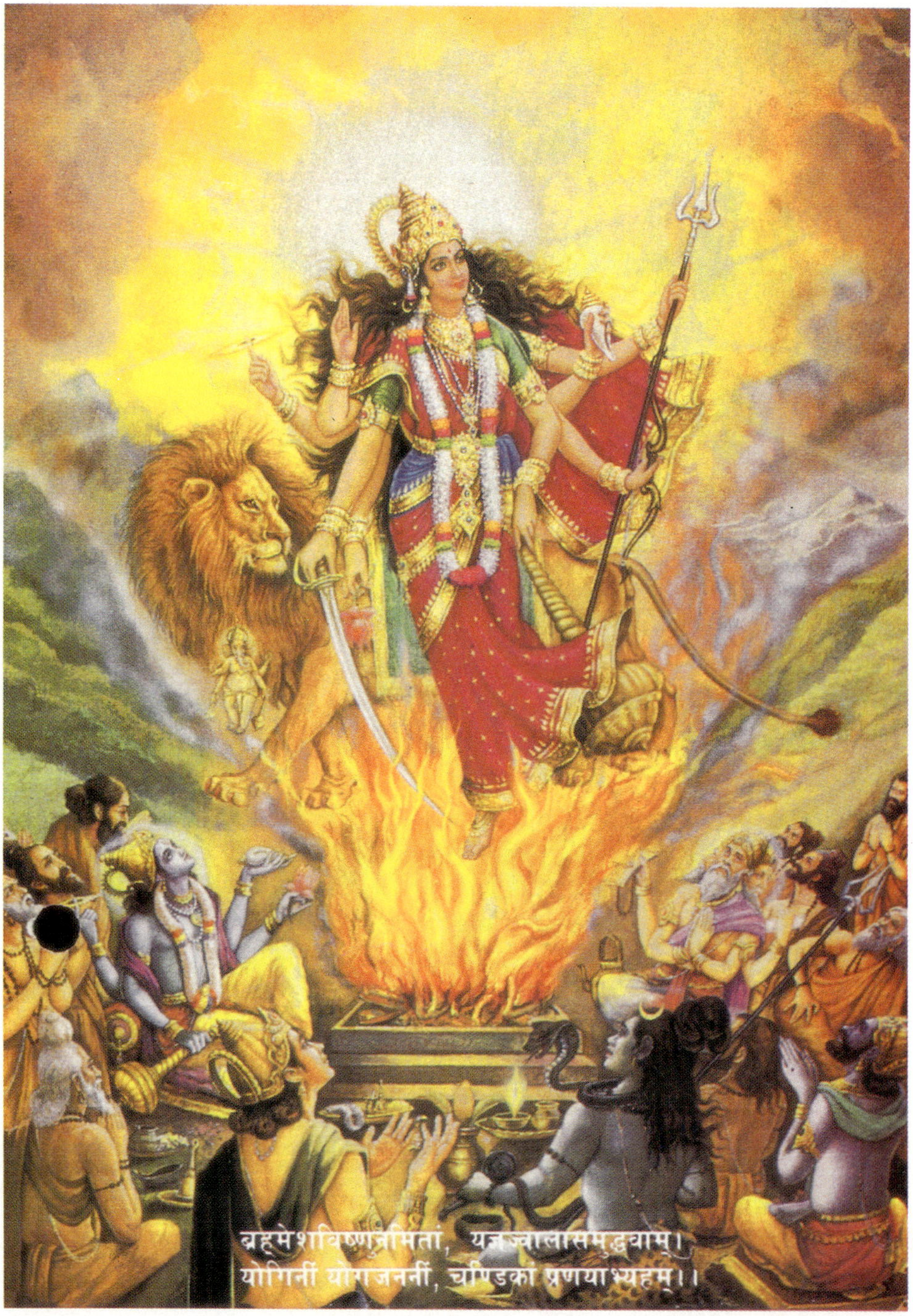

Caṇḍikā Mātā, Yogni and Yog Jananī rising from the Yajna's Flame adorned by gods. (p.178)

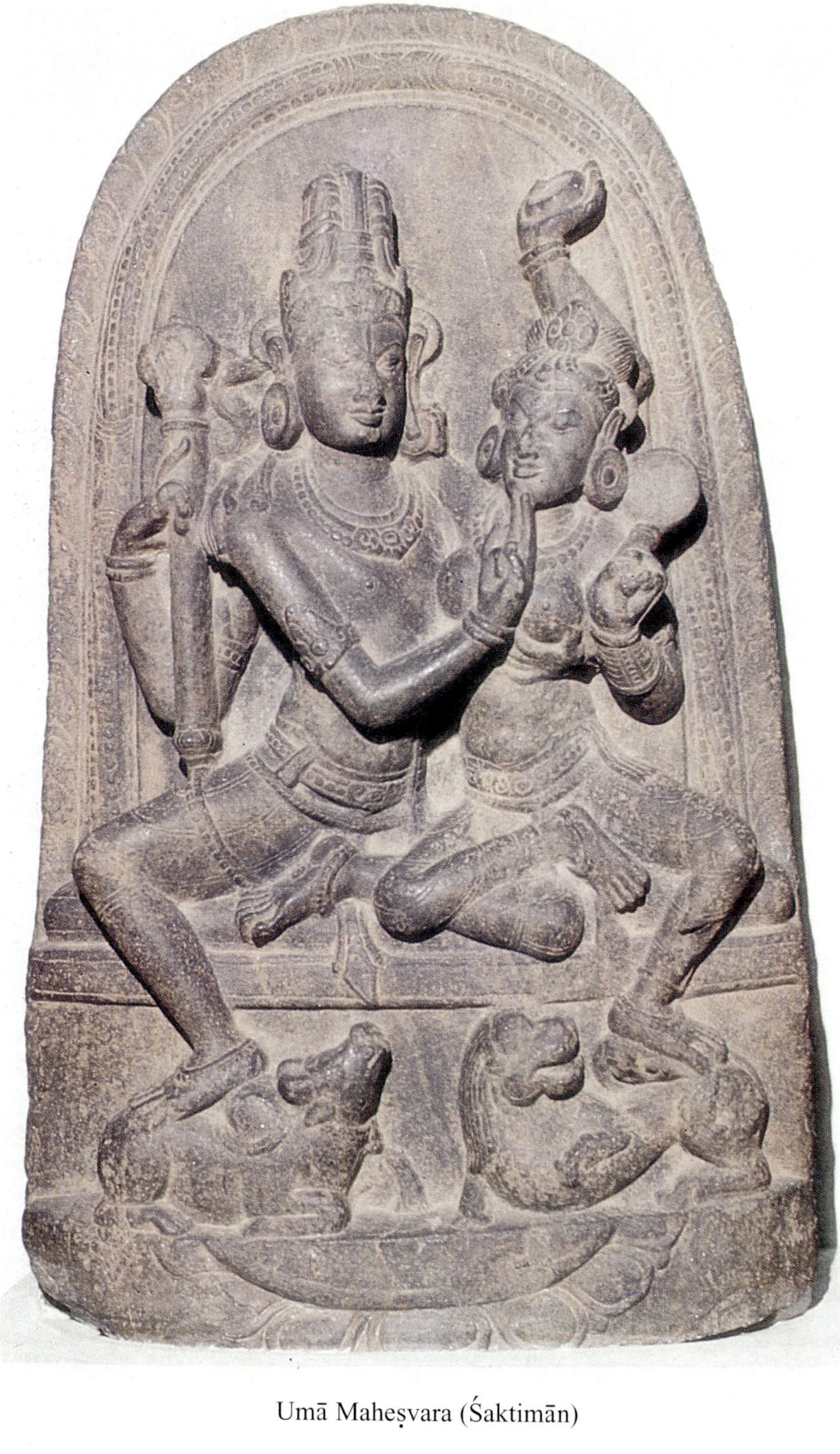

Umā Maheṣvara (Śaktimān)

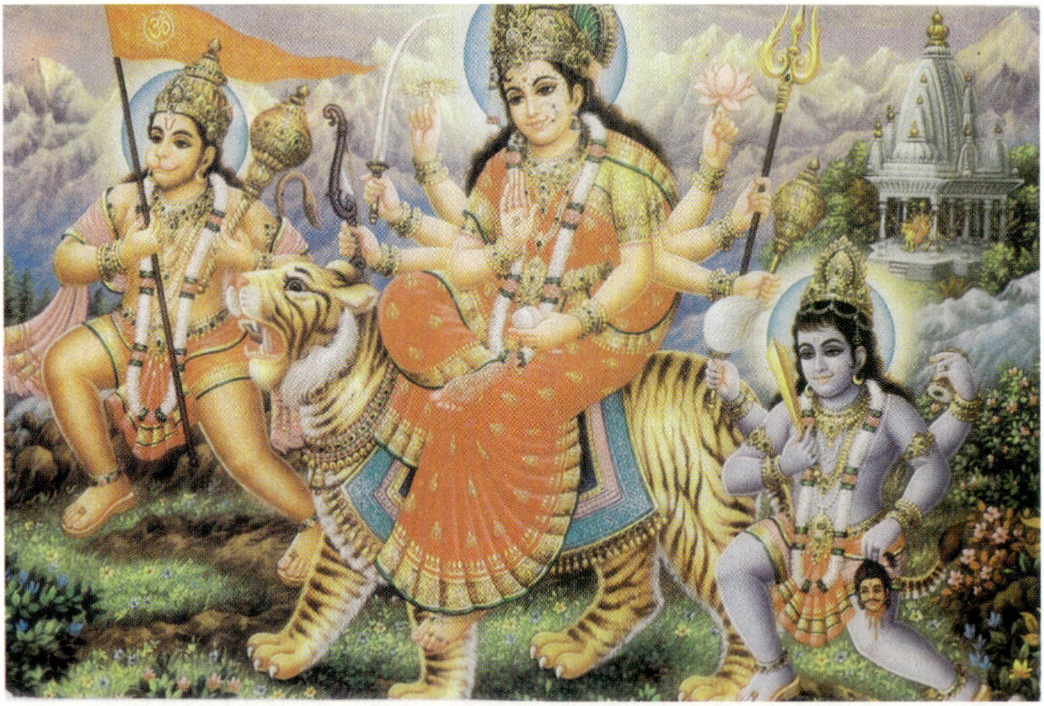

Māṃ Sheraṅvālī

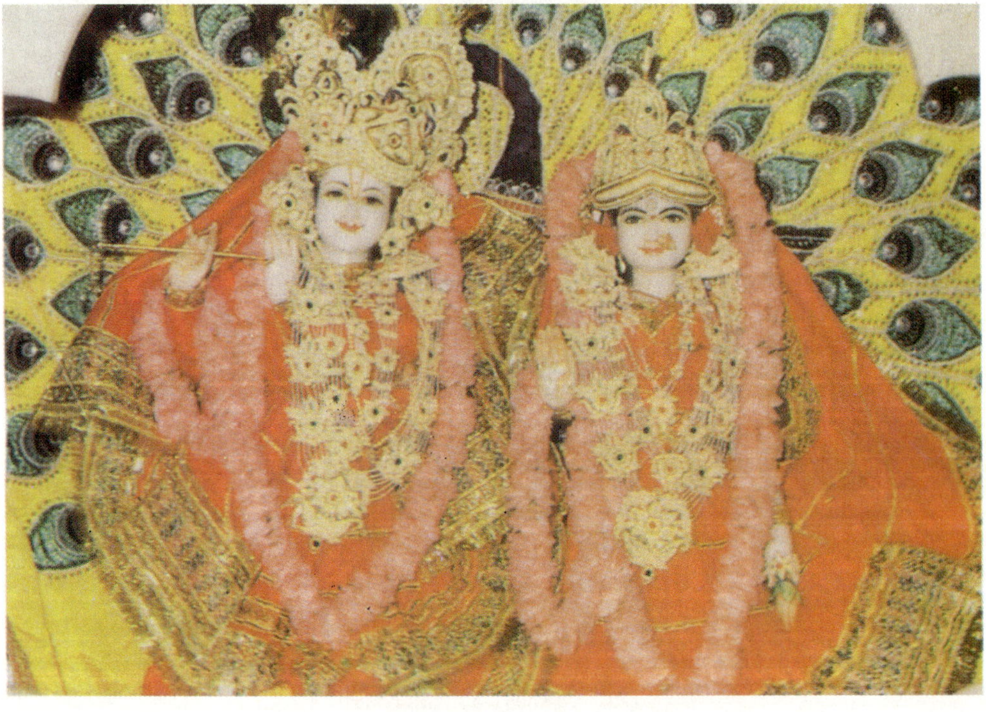

Rādhā Kṛṣṇa

One without a second. That is mentioned in the Veda-s."

❄

Lord Brahmā asked Devī Bhagavati:

"Are you the *brahman* that is mentioned in the Veda-s? My mind is not completely free from doubts. Is the Reality dual or one? Are you male or female? Pray describe in detail."

The Devī Bhagavati addressed Brahmā thus:

"There is oneness always between Me and the *brahman* (*puruṣa*, the supreme Self). Who I am, that is Puruṣa. Who Puruṣa is, that I am. The difference between Power and the Possessor of power is due to *bhrānti* (error). The One without a second, the eternal *brahman* becomes dual at the time of creation; just as a face, though one, becomes two when reflected in a mirror; and just as one man becomes double by his shadow. So I become many by virtue of different *antāhkarṇa* (mind, intellect, ego) created by *māyā*. *Brahman* is the efficient cause, the basis. Without *brahman* the existence of *māyā* is simply impossible. *Brahman* is interwoven in *māyā* and *māyā 's* actions."

"I am not male. I am not female. I remain as *brahman* with *māyā* latent in it. Know this for certain that It is I that, assuming the names of the various *deva-s* (gods), manifest in so many forms of *śakti-s*. I manifest that power and wield it too."

"I enter in everything of the nature of effect. A weak person is often considered to be without any *śakti* (strength); Why is he not said to be without Rudra or without Viṣṇu? He is only short of strength *(śakti)."*

"O Brahmā, now you go to Satyaloka. Take this beautiful great Śakti, Mahāsarasvati full of *rajo guṇa*, and of a smiling nature, and create the universe. This śakti will always be your boon companion. Consider Her as my *vibhūti* (manifestation) and most worshipful. Never show any disrespect to Her."

"Viṣṇu is prominent in *sattva guṇa* and hence superior to you. So, you should always respect and worship him. Whenever you will face any difficulty, Viṣṇu will come down to earth to meet your ends. You utter and repeat my nine-lettered *mantra* and do your work. Śiva, the Incarnate of *tamo guṇa* will be revered and worshipped by all persons. When the *deva-s* are frightened by demons, then Varāha, Vaiśnavī, Gaurī, Nara-siṅghī and my other *śaktī-s* will assume forms and destroy them."

❄

After addressing Brahmā, Bhagavatī turned towards Viṣṇu thus:

"O Viṣṇu take this beautiful Mahālakśmī with you. She will always reside within your heart. For the good of the world, I unite Lakṣmī and Nārāyaṇa. For your sustenance I create *Yajña*. You three will act together in harmony and will be respected and worshipped in the world."

Now Devī began to address Mahādeva, Rudra, thus:

"O Śaṅkara, accept this beautiful Mahākālī Gaurī, build a new Kailāśa and live there happily. Your primary *guṇa* will be *tāmas. Sattva* and *rājas* are your secondary *guṇa-s.* Have recourse to peaceful *sattva guṇa* when you reflect on the Supreme Self and practise austerities. Everything that is visible is endowed with the three *guṇa-s* and nothing can exist without them. Only the Supreme Self is beyond these *guṇa-s*. I am the *parā-māyā*. At times I appear with *guṇa-s* and at others I remain without any *guṇa-s*."

"Now go to your respective places and fulfil your respective duties. Whenever you get into any dire distress, remember Me."

❄

Nārada to Brahmā:

"Father, you have seen the Śakti (the Prime Energy), the *saguṇa sākāra,* the Supreme Goddess, having hands and feet, but I cannot understand of what kind is that *nirguṇa nirākāra śakti* which cannot be seen and which is devoid of all *māyāic* qualities. O lotus-born, be good enough to describe to me the real nature of Māhāśakti."

Brahmā smiled and spoke thus:

"*Nirguṇa-nirākāra puruṣa* (the Supreme Spirit) is not visible. Everything that comes within the range of sight is transitory. The eternal Spirit is formless. She has neither beginning nor an end. The universal Consciousness that is felt in all the beings is the highest Self. The *Puruṣa* and *Prākṛti* pervade everywhere and exist in all the things in this universe. Both of them are the highest intelligent Self (*nirguṇa)* free from all material qualities, without any tinge of impurity. What is Śakti is the highest Self and what is the highest Self is the highest Śakti. Nobody can ascertain the subtle difference between these two. The *jīvas* are *saguṇa* (with qualities). How can the *saguṇa* see the *nirguṇa* with their physical eyes? Until one cuts asunder all connections with *saguṇa*, the seeing of that *nirguṇa brahman* is impossible."

Vyasji sums up and tells Janmejaya:

"The essence of all that has been said in the *Śāstra-s* is that the highest Energy, the Supreme Force, the greatest Goddess, who is pervading the universe, is always with qualities and without qualities. That Māhāmāyā is Mahālakśmī is Mahāsarasvati is Mahākālī is the Cause of all causes. This Supreme Power is to be worshipped with the greatest devotion."

❄

When the great Mahiśāsura was slain by the Devi Bhagavatī, Indra and all other *devata-s* (gods) were very glad and chanted hymns in the glory of world Mother:

"O Devī, you are undoubtedly the prime Cause of all causes. You are *śakti* of Rudra, you are Girija, you are Umā and all other forces in this universe. Everything rests on you. O Mother, were you not this earth, could all this world-load of things have rested on the sky?"

"It is a great wonder that to kill these *asura-s* you had to assume this divine body. You could not have done so by your will. It seems that this act of yours is but a mere pastime."

"You are *vidyā* (blissful Intelligence) and you grant pleasure and liberation. You are *avidya* (delusion) and thus you cause bondage and pain in this world. This universe has been created by you. You are thus its Mother."

"May we always recollect your lotus feet, and may our devotion be firm and steadfast towards you. It is only the Mother that bears the thousand offences of the son. O Mother, whether in times of distress or happiness, you are our Saviour. There is no other means of our security than by the grace of the dust of your feet."

"O Devi, your names are endless, your forms are innumerable. None can count them. You reside always as the Force Incarnate in all actions. You are the Memory, Intelligence, Peace, Prosperity. You are the eternal seed. No action can be without cause. We therefore ascertain by reasoning and inference that you are the supreme Cause of this whole universe."

❄

Vyāsaji to Janmejaya again:

"That omnipresent Bhagavatī is ever the cause of bondage of all when She casts Her spell of delusion and She is again ever the cause of liberation when She imparts Her knowledge to them. She is eternal without beginning, and Cause of all causes. She resides in all the beings as the essential vital Force. The form of the Śakti is the form made up of Consciousness Itself, the *brahman*. Whenever the *deva-s* and men worship Her, She makes Her appearance to destroy their pains and sufferings. She assumes various forms and possesses various powers. She is not under the influence of time, space and causation. The Devī is the Mother of all that is witnessed. She is the manifested, She is the unmanifested and She is the Effect. This is the greatness and glory of the Divine Mother, Ādyaśakti."

❄

The Devī describes to Himālāya Her real Essence *(tattva):*

"Before creation, I, only I, existed. My Self is known by the names *cit*, *saṃvit*

(Intelligence), *parā-brahman* and others. My *ātman* is beyond mind, beyond any name or mark, beyond birth and death or any change. My Self has one inherent power called *māyā*. This *māyā* arises as heat comes out of fire, as the rays come out of the sun. I am the Cause of this world. *Māyā* has the power of hiding Me, the Originator."

"I am *nirguṇa.* United with my *śakti* I become *saguṇa,* the great Cause of this world. This *māyā* is divided into *vidyā* and *avidya. Avidya māyā* hides Me; *vidyā māyā* reveals Me. *Māyā* united with *caitanya* (Intelligence) is the efficient cause of this universe; whereas *māyā* united with the five original elements is the material cause. Some call it *māyā,* others call it *śakti.*"

"O Giriraja, this whole universe is created by Me (My *śakti,* My *māyā).* The *māyā* is conceived in Me. It is not, in reality, different or separate from Me. So I am the only *cit,* Intelligence. Viewed from the point of *brahman,* there is no such thing as *māyā*; only One *brahman* exists. I am that *brahman* of the nature of Intelligence. This world cannot appear without a substratum. And that substratum is My Existence. The Great Self is the only Supreme thing in this world of *māyā* (Illusion). Ignorance or *avidya* is the cause of this *saṃsāra.* Desire comes out of it and action flows thence. So men ought to try to get rid of this ignorance. The goal of life is attained when this Ignorance is destroyed. *Vidyā* alone can destroy this ignorance as darkness cannot destroy darkness."

The Devī continued:

"O Chief of the Mountains, hear now about the *parā-bhakti.* He who hears always my glories and recites My *nāma* and whose mind dwells always in Me, like the incessant flow of oil, who always meditates on Me, does not think himself separate from Me and worships Me with intense feelings as the Mother of the universe, gets merged in My nature of Consciousness. This *bhakti* is called *parā-bhakti* or the highest devotion.

"*Māyā* is of the nature of *brahman.* She is eternal. There is no distinction between *ātman* and its *śakti* between *puruṣa* and *prakṛti*. The highest *yogi-s* do not recognise any difference between a male and a female. All is *brahman* - the *mūla-māyā*., the Great *Devī* Ishvarī (the Controller of the Universe). By Her command manifest many forms from Her for the purpose of creation and for bestowing grace to the *bhakta-s* (devotees):

Durgā, the Mother of Ganeśa, the most auspicious, loved by Śiva, comes first. She is the presiding Deity of all the *deva-s* and therefore worshipped and praised by Brahmā and other *deva-s, muṇi-s* and *maṇū-s*. She is *mūlmāyā*, *viṣṇūmāyā* and of the nature of *purṇa brahman*. Bhagavatī Durgā destroys all the sorrows and troubles of the *bhakta-s* who have taken Her refuge and come to Her for protection. She has infinite qualities."

"The second *śakti* is Padmā *(lakṣmī).* She is of the nature of *śuddha sattva* and is the presiding Deity of all wealth and prosperity. She is of a very peaceful temper. She is the source of life of all beings. She is worshipped by all."

"The third *śakti* is named Sarasvati. She is all the Learning of the universe. She is Intelligence, Memory, Wit, Splendour and inventive Genius. All the beings earn their livelihood by taking recourse to Her. She is peaceful and holds in Her hand *vīṇā* (lute). She is the Goddess of speech."

"Now hear the glories of Gāyatri, the fourth *śakti.* Herself an ascetic, She is the *tapas* (austerities) of the brahmins. She is the *tejas* (fire) and embodies in Herself all sorts of *saṃskāra-s.* She is the *japa* and of the nature of highest bliss, bestower of *mokṣa.* The whole world is purified by the touch of whose feet, is this Devī Savitrī."

"The fifth *śākti* is Devī Radhikā. She is the life of all, dearer than life even to Śri Kṛṣṇa. She is higher than the Highest, the Essence of all, Eternal, of the nature of the highest Bliss and worshipped by all. She is the presiding Deity of *rāsa līlā* of Śri Kṛṣṇa. Her abode is in *Goloka* and from Her have come all the *gopikā-s*. She transcends the three *guṇa-s* and is *nirākāra*. She assumes forms only to show Her favour to Her devotees. She incarnated Herself as the daughter of a cowherd and earth was blessed by the touch of Her feet."

Now hear about those *śakti-s* that are parts of the *māyā:*

"The Gaṇgā sprang from the lotus feet of Viṣṇu. She is eternal. She is the fire that burns the sins of the sinners. Tulsi Devī is the consort of Viṣṇu, ornament of Nārāyaṇa. She is the Chief of all flowers, holy and able to give merits. All *tīrtha-s* (places of pilgrimage) desire to have Her sight and touch for purification. And the lotus-eyed Maheśvari, Kāli, who, when angry, can destroy the whole universe in a moment, sprang from the forehead of Durgā to slay the two demons Śumbha and Niśumbha. The beauty and splendour of Her body make one think as if the millions of suns have arisen simultaneously. When pleased, She can grant the four fruit: *dharma, artha, kāma* and *mokṣa."*

"Devī Vasundharā (Earth) is again the part of *mūlmāyā.* All sorts of best things come from Her. She is the refuge of all. Without Her, where to stand on? The Devī Svāhā is the wife of Agni (fire). The whole world worships Her. Devī Śraddhā is the wife of Pitries. Devī Svasti is the wife of Vayudevatā. Puṣṭi is the wife of Gaṇapati. Tuṣṭi (contentment), Sampatti (Prosperity), Dhṛiti, Dayā, Kīrti, Kriyā, these are all the manifestations of the mūl-māyā."

❄

Thus it is most desirable to worship the Devī. King Suratha worshipped the mūl-māyā, Durgā, destroyer of all evils. Śri Rāma worshipped Her when He wanted to kill Rāvana. Since then Her worship is extant in the three worlds. She destroyed the *daityā-s* and *dānava-s.* King Aśvapati worshipped Sāvitri Devī and since then the *deva-s, muni-s and* all began to worship Her. Bhagvān Śri Kṛṣṇa, worshipped Devī Rādhā in the region of Goloka. Later, all followed suit.

It is by Her command that the wind blows, the sun shines, Indra showers rains, death strikes the beings, moon revolves, the fire burns.

As the eternal space does not know its own extent, so perhaps Devī Herself knows not Her own glories. She is the Cause of all causes, the Lord of all, the Witness of all, the Refuge of all. She is with *māyā.* She is *mūlmāyā.* Though formless, She assumes forms for the gratification of the desires of Her devotees. This highest *śaktī*, the *mūlmāyā* is the only One without the second; It is the only One *nirguṇa* and the highest *Puruṣa*. This *mūlmāyā* appears as *jñāna śaktī* or the knowing Force who alone can recite Her glories. Devotees prefer *bhakti* (devotion) to *mukti* (liberation).

❄

Saint Nārāyaṇa to Nārada on Durgā:

"Durgā presides over the *buddhi.* She is the Mother of all and *śaktī* of Mahādeva. She removes the difficulties and dangers of all and is worshipped by all. She is the mūlmāyā. "*Oṁ aiṃ hrīṃ klīṃ Cāmuṇḍāyai vicce*" is the nine-lettered *bīja mantra* of Śri Durgā."

The Glory of Divine Mother is sung thus:

"O Divine Mother, O Śri Sandhyā, Omnipresent, Infinite, I bow down to you. You are Gāyatrī, Sāvitri and Sarasvati. You are Brāhmi, Vaiṣṇavī and Raudri. O Bhagavati, you are always meditated by *muni-s.* Obeisance to you. You are seen by the *tapasvi-s* (ascetics) as Brāhmi, riding on *haṃsa* (swan), as Sarasvati riding on *garuḍa*, and as Sāvitri riding on bull. I bow down to you. O Devī, you show your favours to the mortals and immortals. You are *māyā*. You grant boons to your devotees. O *Māṃ*, you are recited by a host of names. You are Bhagirathi in this world, the Bhagavati in the *pātāla* and the Mandākini in the Heavens. You are all-enduring Earth, the Vayu*śaktī.* You are *tejas* (Energy), Great Siddhi, Tapasvini. You are Truth. O Gauri, you are sung as *māyā*. You are *parāśaktī*. "

MANIFESTATION OF BHAGAVATI DEVI, THE MOTHER DIVINE

Vedvyasāji narrates: "In ancient days, the *asurā-s* (demons) maddened with pride, fought against the *devā-s* (gods) a grave battle for one hundred years. They were bent upon destroying the whole world. By the mercy of the greatest *Śaktī*, the battle was won by the *devā-s* who were all delighted and equally inebriated and proud as a result. They boasted of their own prowess and glories and were thus deluded. The Divine Mother noticed their plight and took pity on them. She appeared before them in the form of the Most Worshipful, the Great Holy Light. Never was this witnessed before. Seeing this extraordinary Beautiful Light, the *devā-s* were wonder-struck and taken aback. "What is this, what is this?" they spoke amongst themselves. Then they decided to approach the Adorable Light to ask as to what It was.

"Indra called upon *Agni* and asked him to go and ascertain what that Light was. *Agni* went to the Light and said, 'I am *Agni,* the power of burning everything resides in me.' The Light offered him a straw of grass and asked him to burn that. *Agni* tried but failed to do that. He got ashamed and went back. Indra then sent Vayu to ascertain the reality behind the Light. Now Vāyu approached the Light and said: 'I am Vāyu and I can move anything and hold everything.' But when asked to move the petty straw of grass, he too failed to do that. Vāyu gave up his pride and returned to the *devās* and spoke thus: 'O *devā-s*, our pride is vain. In no way we can ascertain the nature of that Light. That Holy Light is beyond comprehension.'

"Indra then himself went to the Light with great pride. The Light gradually began to disappear and ultimately vanished from Indra's sight. He could not even speak to the Light. Felt so ashamed he gave up his pride and took refuge into that Great Light."

"At that time a celestial voice was heard from the Heavens: 'O Indra, go back and do the *japam* of the *bīja mantra*.' Indra obeyed. And after a period of time there appeared suddenly a Great Mass of Light as was seen earlier. Indra saw within that Mass of Light, a Virgin Form, the Devī Bhagavati. Indra felt ecstatic and fell prostrate unto the feet of the Devi and then asked Her, "O Fair One, are you that Great Mass of Light? If that be so, state the secret of your appearance."

The Bhagavati replied:

"This, My form is *brahman*, the Cause of all causes, the seat of *māyā,* the Witness of all, of the nature of the Great Holy Light. The sages declare that *brahman* is revealed by (ॐ) *Oṃ* and *'Hrīṃ'* - My two foremost *mantra-s* wherein I remain hidden. 'ॐ' *bīja* is denominated as *sat-cit-ānanda* and *'hrīṃ' bīja* is *māhāmāyā*, the undifferentiated Consciousness made manifest. Know that *māyā* as the highest *śākti*, and know Me as That Omnipresent, Omnipotent Goddess at present revealed before your eyes. As moonlight is not different from the moon, so this *māyā śākti*, in the state of equilibrium, is not different from Me. The powerful man and the power he wields are not different. They are verily One and the same."

"When this *māyā* exists latent in Me as potential, It is termed unmanifested and when it becomes kinetic and is *bāhirmukhi*, It is believed to have manifested. I am known as *turīya* transcending the *guṇa-s*. I am the *brahman*, Inner Controller of all. Know verily my two forms: *saguṇa-sākāra* and *nirguṇa-nirākāra.* That which is beyond *māyā* and *māyāic* qualities, is called *nirguṇa* and that which is within *māyā* is *saguṇa.* O Indra, after creating this universe, I enter within that as the Inner Controller of all and It is I that impel all the *jīva-s* to their efforts and actions. Brahmā, Viṣṇu and Rudra are performing their functions under my command and other *devā-s* too perform their respective duties under my instructions. Through my grace you have achieved victory over the *daitya-s* (demons). You have been deluded by your vain egoism. Henceforth banish for ever from your heart all your vain boasting. Take refuge wholly unto Me, My *Sat-cit-ānanda* form, and be safe."

Thus saying, the *mūlmāyā*., the Great Devī Mother Divine, the Supreme Being, vanished from the sight.

THE MANIFESTATION OF BHAGAVATI: ANOTHER VERSION.

Mahiśasura (the demon) was granted a boon that he could not be killed by any man and had thus become unconquerable. The terror-stricken gods approached Viṣṇu for help and refuge. Viṣṇu proposed to create a beautiful Lady out of the collective energy *(śakti)* of each of the *deva-s*, who could kill the haughty demon. "I ask you all now to grant boons of *śakti* which when manifested will assume the form of a Lady. We will then bestow her all the divine weapons we possess individually. That Lady will fulfil our ends and liberate us."

And lo, there appeared a dazzling mass of hallowed light having a beautiful female form. An exquisitely beautiful Lady was thus manifested out of the united mass of Light and Fire. SHe was Devī Bhagavati, the destroyer of all sorrows and hardships.

Viṣṇu then addressed all the *deva-s* to give the Devī their auspicious ornaments and weapons created out of their own weapons and endowed with divine strength.

Visnu created discus *(chakra)* and presented the same to the Devī. The mountain Himalaya offered her various gems and a beautiful lion. Sankara gave her trident *(triśula),* Varuna, a conch. Fire offered *Śataghani*. Maruta delivered a bow and arrows. Indra came forward with a thunderbolt as well as a bell. Yama presented a staff and Brahmā, a *kamandalu*. A pāśa, an axe and a shield, a lotus and many more offerings were thus made by other *deva-s* to the female Deity.

The beautiful Lady adorned and decorated with auspicious ornaments and divine weapons and mounted on the lion, began to look splendid. The *deva-s* began to praise and chant hymns to the auspicious goddess.

The nine-lettered *bīja mantra* of *Mām̐ Bhagavati*:

Oṃ Aiṃ Hrīṃ Klīṃ Cāmuṇḍā *Yai Vic Ce Oṃ*

Oṃ:	The Infinite Being, *Brahman*, *Ādyaśakti* (beyond conception)
Aiṃ:	Creation, *rajoguna*, energy of Desire, Mahāsarasvati.
Hrīṃ:	Preservation, *sattvaguṇa*, energy of Action, Mahālakśmī.
Klīṃ:	Destruction, *tamoguṇa*, energy of Wisdom, Mahākālī.
Cāmuṇḍā:	The slayer of Caṇḍa and Muṇḍa.
Yai :	The granter of boons.
Vic :	In the body of knowledge and perception.
Ce :	Of Consciousness.

O Reliever of difficulties, Exposure of Goodness, Cause of Peace, Infinite Consciousness, Beloved of those who know Consciousness, One who motivates and guides the three worlds, the Mother of the universe, Invisible Existence, Light of Purity,

Your divine effulgence is beyond thoughts and reflection, O Holy One.

CHAPTER THIRTY NINE

108 TRIBUTES TO MOTHER DIVINE

SALUTATIONS to the Divine Mother who is without dependence. *(nirādhāra).*

Salutations to the Divine Mother who is unattached, bound to nothing. *(nirañjana).*

Salutations to the Divine Mother who is free from all impurities arising from action. *(nirlepa).*

Salutations to the Divine Mother who is eternal. *(nitya).*

Salutations to the Divine Mother who is formless. *(nirākāra).*

Salutations to the Divine Mother who is beyond three gunas of Nature. *(nirguṇa).*

Salutations to the Divine Mother who is peace. *(śānti).*

Salutations to the Divine Mother who has no desire. *(niṣkāma).*

Salutations to the Divine Mother who is unchanging. *(nirvikāra).*

Salutations to the Divine Mother who confers happiness. *(śamadāyiṇi).*

Salutations to the Divine Mother who is attained only through devotion. *(bhaktigamya).*

Salutations to the Divine Mother who is embodiment of benevolence. *(bhadramūrti).*

Salutations to the Divine Mother who confers prosperity. *(saubhāgya dāyini).*

Salutations to the Divine Mother who is attainable through *bhavana,* feelings, sentiments of love. *(bhāvanāgamya).*

Salutations to the Divine Mother who grants all wishes. *(kāmadāyini).*

Salutations to the Divine Mother who bestows all that is auspicious. *(śiva).*

Salutations to the Divine Mother who is the auspicious Mother. of all. *(śrī mātā).*

Salutations to the Divine Mother who is chaste. *(sādhvī).*

Salutations to the Divine Mother who is peaceful. *(śāntīmati).*

Salutations to the Divine Mother who is eternally pure. *(nityaśuddha).*

Salutations to the Divine Mother who is ever wise. *(nityabuddhi).*

Salutations to the Divine Mother who is all-pervading. *(nirantara).*

Salutations to the Mother Divine who is without cause. *(niṣkāraṇa).*

Salutations to the Divine Mother who has no protector. *(nireśvara).*

Salutations to the Divine Mother who destroys desires, passions. *(rāgamathani)*

Salutations to the Mother Divine who destroys pride. *(madanāśini).*

Salutations to the Divine Mother who is without the concept of 'I' and 'mine'. *(nirahaṅkāra).*

Salutations to the Divine Mother who is free from delusion. *(nirmoha).*

Salutations to the Mother Divine who destroys delusion in Her devotees. *(mohanāśini).*

Salutations to the Mother Divine who is imperishable *(nirnāśa).*

Salutations to the Mother Divine who is incomparable. *(nirupamā).*

Salutations to the Mother Divine who destroys sorrows. *(dukhahantrī).*

Salutations to the Mother Divine who is giver of happiness. *(sukhapradā).*

Salutations to the Mother Divine who is Omniscient. *(sarvajñā).*

Salutations to the Mother Divine who shows intense compassion. *(karuṇā).*

Salutations to the Mother Divine who has all the divine powers. *(sarvaśaktimayi).*

Salutations to the Mother Divine who rules over all the living and non-living. *(sarveśvari).*

Salutations to the Mother Divine who protects and rules everything. *(iṣvari).*

Salutations to the Mother Divine is the greatest object of worship. *(mahāpūjyā).*

Salutations to the Mother Divine who is the great illusion. *(mahāmāyā).*

Salutations to the Mother Divine who is the root of the world. *(jagatīkanda).*

Salutations to the Mother Divine who is the bliss, supreme bliss. *(paramānanda).*

Salutations to the Mother Divine who is Consciousness Itself. *(cinmayi).*

Salutations to the Mother Divine who has the whole world as Her form. *(viśvarūpa).*

Salutations to the Mother Divine who is. in the form of Sound. *(brahmvidyā).*

Salutations to the Mother Divine who is Intelligence. *(cit).*

Salutations to the Mother Divine who transcends all. *(parā).*

Salutations to the Mother Divine who is witness to the whole universe. *(viśvasākṣiṇi).*

Salutations to the Mother Divine who is supreme sovereign. *(parmeśvari).*

Salutations to the Mother Divine who is the sum-total of the effulgence of all the Deities. *(kātyāyani).*

Salutations to the Mother Divine who has three eyes *(tryambakā).*

Salutations to the Mother Divine who is in the manifested and unmanifested forms. *(vyakta-avyakta svarūpiṇi).*

Salutations to the Mother Divine who is Self-effulgent. *(svaprakāṣa).*

Salutations to the Mother Divine who destroys all obstacles. *(vighnanāśini).*

Salutations to the Mother Divine who is the supreme End. *(parāniṣṭhā).*

Salutations to the Mother Divine who is the knowledge of the Self. *(ātmavidyā).*

Salutations to the Mother Divine who is not immeasurable. *(ameya).*

Salutations to the Mother Divine who is Self in all. *(ātman).*

Salutations to the Mother Divine who contains the whole universe in Her womb. *(viśvagarbha).*

Salutations to the Mother Divine who is the One. *(ekānkiṇī)*

Salutations to the Mother Divine who is *pure Love.* *(premarūpa).*

Salutations to the Mother Divine who is giver of liberation. *(muktidā).*

Salutations to the Mother Divine who is transcendental. *(parākāśa)*

Salutations to the Mother Divine who is the supreme Light. *(parama jyotiḥ).*

Salutations to the Mother Divine who is Truth Itself. *(satyarūpa).*

Salutations to the Mother Divine who is full of awe-inspiring wrath. *(prakanḍa).*

Salutations to the Mother Divine who is the Foundation. *(pratiṣṭhā).*

Salutations to the Mother Divine who is the Playful. *(lalitā).*

Salutations to the Mother Divine who is giver of life. *(prānadātrī).*

Salutations to the Mother Divine who is to be attained through the yoga of knowledge. *(jñānagamya).*

Salutations to the Mother Divine who has no birth. *(ajā)*

Salutations to the Mother Divine who is Reality Itself. *(tattvamayī).*

Salutations to the Mother Divine who is benign. *(somayā).*

Salutations to the Mother Divine who abides in Herself. *(svastha)*

Salutations to the Mother Divine who is fond of hymns in Her praise. *(stotrapriyā).*

Salutations to the Mother Divine who is in the form of mind. *(sanomayi).*

Salutations to the Mother Divine who transcends the world. *(lokātīta).*

Salutations to the Mother Divine who is eternal. *(śāśvatī).*

Salutations to the Mother Divine who is adorable. *(vandaniyā)*

Salutations to the Mother Divine who is beyond the three *guna-s* of *Prakṛti*. *(guṇātīta).*

Salutations to the Mother Divine who assumes the form of the *jīva* in the waking state. *(jāgariṇi).*

Salutations to the Mother Divine who assumes the form of the *jīva* in the dream state. *(svapanti).*

Salutations to the Mother Divine who assumes the form of *jīva* experiencing deep sleep. *(sūptā)*

Salutations to the Mother Divine who is the Creator. *(sṛṣṭikārtṛi)*

Salutations to the Mother Divine who is always whole, without growth or decay. *(pūrṇa).*

Salutations to the Mother Divine who is in the form of sound. *(nādarūpa)*

Salutations to the Mother Divine who resides in the heart of all. *(hṛdayastha).*

Salutations to the Mother Divine who grants boons generously. *(varada).*

Salutations to the Mother Divine who is ever victorious. *(vijayā).*

Salutations to the Mother Divine whose deeds are marvellous. *(adhibhūta caritra).*

Salutations to the Mother Divine who is in the form of cosmic whole. *(virāṭarūpa)*

Salutations to the Mother Divine who is the Absolute Supreme Being. *(brahman).*

Salutations to the Mother Divine who is knower of all thoughts and sentiments. *(bhāvajñānī).*

Salutations to the Mother Divine who is both *parā* and *aparā*. *(parāparā).*

Salutations to the Mother Divine who is essence of all scriptures. *(śāstrasāra).*

Salutations to the Mother Divine who is of the nature of Existence, Consciousness and Bliss. *(sat-cit-ānandarūpiṇi).*

Salutations to the Mother Divine who is great illusion. *(mahāmāyā).*

Salutations to the Mother Divine who is Mother Earth. *(dharā).*

Salutations to the Mother Divine who is not perceived by the sense organs. *(adṛśya).*

Salutations to the Mother Divine who dispels fear. *(bhayāpāhā)*

Salutations to the Mother Divine who ends all sins and sorrows. *(akanta).*

Salutations to the Mother Divine who is in the form of language. *(bhāṣa rūpa).*

Salutations to the Mother Divine who gives knowledge of the Self. *(jñānadā).*

Salutations to the Mother Divine who is the absolute as She is independent and without any attributes. *(kevalya).*

Salutations to the Mother Divine who is the Ruler of all worlds. *(sarvalokeśa).*

Salutations to the Mother Divine who depends on none. *(nirlamba).*

Salutations to the Mother Divine who has no form. *(amūrta).*

Salutations, salutations to the Mother Divine. *(lalitā ambikā).*

Is there any vibration that is not your song? All movements are the steps of the Truth, all beings are souls and powers and bodies of divine Light . But we dwell in ignorance and remain separated from source. Pray, dispel that veil of ignorance and bless your children.

LIKE a child cling to the Divine Mother; like a child surrender to Her. Practise greater faith; cultivate more devotion, constant love and care *(Māṃ's maṃtā)* which only a mother will afford to give and which the child would take for granted at all times. Sweet Surrender.

Cure me, O Mother Grace, of all my ailments.

Chapter Forty

Śri Rāmakṛśna Paramhansa

(An Enlightened Soul)

The title of this work will not justify itself without a specific mention of *Śri* Rāmakṛśna Paramahansa, a unique and rare devotee of Mother Divine. It is one of his greatest contribution to Indian religious tradition that his spiritual experience has identified the Śakti not as a mere female counterpart of the Absolute, but as the Absolute Itself.

He put up his heart and soul into the worship of the Goddess. Though he was worshipping an image, he began to feel that he was worshipping a living Goddess. The worship intensified his yearning for a living vision of the Mother Kālī. He was seized with a burning passion to visualise in the stone image a living entity.

Śri Rāmakṛśna became actually Her child and began to behave like one. He clung to Her with the earnestness of a babe. He saw the Mother everywhere, in everything, and in everyone. A learned ignorance is the end of philosophy and the beginning of religion, said Swami Vivekananda. Soon the scales fell completely from his eyes, and Śri Rāmakṛśna required neither a trance nor a meditation to invoke the vision of the Mother.

"When I think of the Supreme Being as inactive - neither creating nor preserving nor destroying - I call Him *brahman* or *Puruṣa,* the Impersonal God. When I think of Him as active - creating, preserving and destroying - I call Him *Śakti* or *Māyā* or *Prakrti*, the Personal God. But the distinction between them does not mean a difference. The Personal and the Impersonal God are one and the same, like milk and its whiteness, like the diamond and its lustre, like the snake and its wriggling motion. It is impossible to conceive of the one without the other. The Divine Mother and *brahman* are one."

"I worship the Devi. She stands before me as the manifold *jīva-s* and objects of this universe. Bhagavati and Iṣvara are one and the same. You cannot

THE ENLIGHTENED SOUL
A unique Devotees of Mother Divine, the Supreme Being

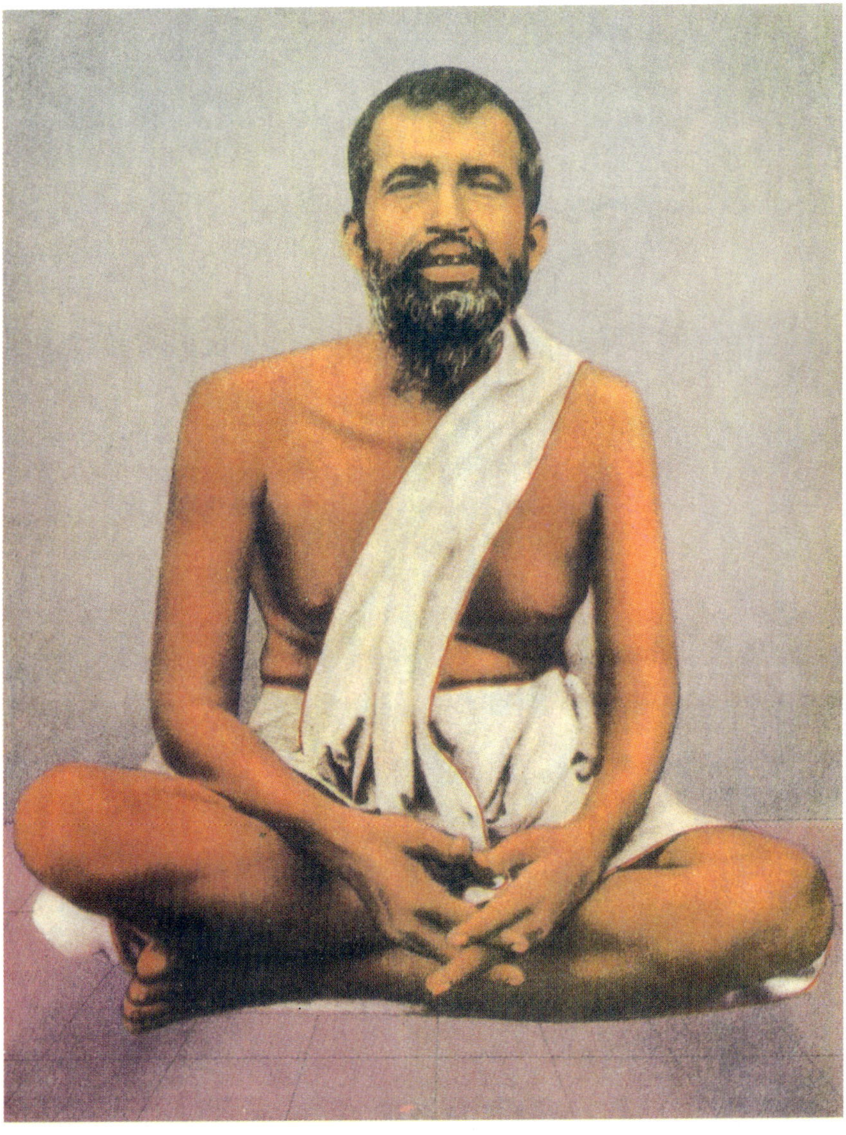

Bhagavān Śri Rāmakṛṣṇa Paramhansa (p.200)

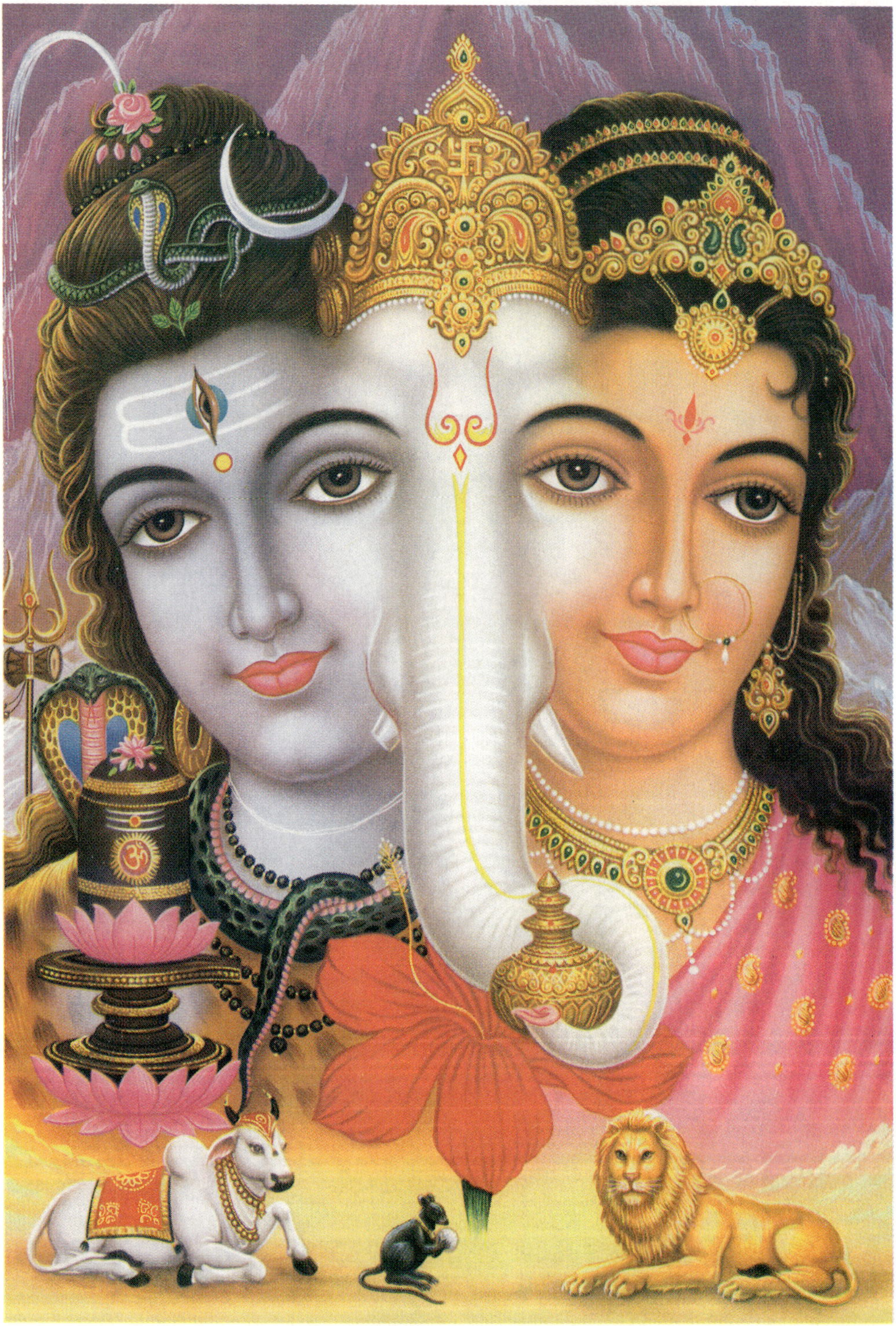

Lord Ganesha and Śiv-Śakti

differentiate between the two. The Devī whom I worship is the *brahman*, the one without a second."

"When we see a beautiful woman, we must think of Devī, the Mother of the Universe. She is an incarnation of Devī. Can the Mother of the universe be anything but beautiful? We should become like a little child. She is the form of the all-pervading Supreme Being. Her beauty and her smile signify maternal tenderness."

"You adore the decorated image of the Devī in the shrine. The women are the living forms of the same Devī. One should keep one's heart steadfast in purity and bow to them. The lust will vanish."

There are several instances in the life of *Śri* Rāmakriśna Paramahansa of the most tender concern for his worldly mother, Candra Devī. Once he went on a pilgrimage to Vrindavan and was so taken in by the spiritual atmosphere there, that he wanted to stay there itself. But he had a consideration for his old mother who would be left without care if he stayed there. So he returned home. Another instance showing his concern for his mother is recalled here. One of his brothers died quite young. *Śri* Rāmakriśna was afraid that the news would break the heart of his mother. He went to the Kāli temple and prayed to Divine Mother to give his mother necessary strength of mind to bear the loss.

His relations with his wife may be said to have been unparalleled. They converted their wedlock into a purely spiritual companionship without any trace of carnality, a divine mystic relationship which grew into a union of one pure soul with another and remained so throughout the life. The wife learnt to love that Divine Mother in her husband and the husband discovered the same cosmic power in the person of his wife.

He had the brilliant intellect of Śaṅkarācārya and the soft heart of Śri Caitanya. He was the fulfilment of the Indian sages, one whose teaching is most relevant in the present time. He practised what he preached. He taught more by his life than by his words. He never wrote or lectured. He proved that the spirit of man is capable of progress without what is commonly called education and learning.

Given the inner urge, it can progress on the path of spirituality almost unaided. He showed that spiritual teaching can be given not by logic or eloquence but by living the spiritual life. He had given up everything for God. "God can be seen and spoken to just as I am seeing you and speaking to you."

Śri Rāmakṛśna, the prophet of harmony of religions, held that all religions lead to the same goal of God-realisation. Righteous conduct and equanimity of mind are necessary gifts. He was a *Mahātmā* who saw God in his heart and in all things in the world outside.

"I have practised", *Śri* Rāmakriśna had said, "all kinds of *sādhanā*: *jñāna-yoga,* and *bhakti-yoga.* I have even gone through the exercises of *haṭha yoga*. There are many views, many paths and I have seen them all. But I don't enjoy them any more. They all quarrel. I have come to the final realisation that God is the Whole and I am a part of Him and that God is the Master and I am His servant. Furthermore, sometimes I feel that SHe is I and I am SHe."

> IT IS no use merely muttering *'Śivohaṃ.'* That consciousness can arise only when the ego is completely rooted out by devotion. Till then to utter "I am Śiva" is not apt. The truth is that I am Lord's slave; I am the instrument of Her Will.

Drunk with a draught of celestial wine, the yogi reels and yet falls not. Communion with God is the true wine, the wine of ecstatic love.

PART FIVE

TOWARDS EMANCIPATION OF SOUL

(All-Bliss)

(The state when the mind neither grieves nor desires.)

YOU cannot omit the outward if you wish to know the inward. The inward is reflected in the outward.

Genuine spiritual awakening is a shift in the perception and attitude from the gross to the subtle.

It is the destiny of all souls to evolve towards perfection.

He who is happy rejoices within and is illumined within; that person has attained freedom, *mokṣa.*

> THERE is no holier sanctuary than a purified mind, the region of Peace - Peace wherein the voice of God is heard, audible within the Silence. Purity, bliss and blessings make up the true state of meditation. The spiritual consciousness dawns in these silent sacred hours. The soul is close to its source, the Oceanic Consciousness of God.

❄

Your Grace is infinite, O Supreme Being.

CHAPTER FORTY ONE

Is Worldly Life A Hurdle?

Worldly life is not an obstacle for pursuing spiritual *sādhanā*. In fact, it is helpful. God has created the world with love and for the sake of love.

The entire talk of truth and wisdom is to make man peaceful, quiet and free. It is not to destroy his worldly life or to rob him of the so-called gains and pleasures. True spiritual science does not interfere with the life as such. It tries to remove the difficulties caused to life by agitated mind and immature knowledge.

Enjoyment of the good and beautiful things of life, both material and spiritual, is not only encouraged but enjoined. All that has been created is for man and he should be thankful for the bestowal.

Each part of our personality has a function to perform for life's fulfilment. Body is not to be despised and neither the necessary comforts. Giving up wholesome food, discarding of clothes or footwear for practice of austerities has no intrinsic merit. Simply to renounce the world and become a hermit is not renunciation.

It may be advisable in the beginning to seek renunciation, dispassion and observe certain other related austerities and disciplines in order to divert the mind inward for introspection leading to knowledge and devotion which further leads to purification of mind leading to the achievement of *sthitaprajña* (equilibrium, equanimity, equipoise). Once the mind is sublimated, there is no comeback. The world is no more a hurdle for spiritual growth.

You may attain divine perfection and yet not turn your back upon the world.

We have split minds. A split mind does not possess an integrated ego. Integrity of ego is essential for fruitful human activity. We erroneously think that every kind of instinctual enjoyment is evil and forbidden. This conviction produces a sense of guilt. One should therefore acquire the ability to resolve these conflicts and liquidate the guilt. Single-minded devotion to God is compatible with the enjoyments of worldly things.

There is always a conflict in man's nature: whether to go after the sensual pleasures or turn towards God. God's grace resolves that conflict and both the thoughts work harmoniously because under the changed state of mind even worldly inclinations are used in the service of humanity and God.

Ramana Mahāṛṣi did not encourage ascetic isolation. There is no need to renounce worldly objects, your chosen profession and other obligations to the family and the society. Life-active and life-meditative can well be reconciled. The individual is transformed when he is made to realise his true identity by self-enquiry. When one resolves to achieve the goal of self-realisation, every situation seems helpful for the purpose.

The Vedāṇtic thesis is not that the world is an illusion, but that our belief in its permanence and the attendant fear of extinction and attachment to its appearance, are delusions.

To feel disgusted with the objects of the world is wrong. To indulge in their company too is equally unjust. Instead, mind must have the skill to remain free of both the disgust and indulgence. Live in that stable state in which you give yourself to the world without losing yourself in it.

Aṣṭāvakra.

Life here in this world is neither a banishment nor a punishment, but is a blissful play. Live life fully in a spirit of sportsmanship and, when the time is up, quit the arena gracefully.

?

Heaven lies at your feet. It holds true that pure thought can grasp reality.

CHAPTER FORTY TWO

PRAY, SAVE THE SOUL

AS WAVES, foams and bubbles are not different from water, so the universe emanating from the Self is not different from It. *Ātman* is the only substance of the universe, just as clay is the only substance of the pot. The pot is nothing but clay with names and forms superimposed on it.

Ashṭavakra.

"WISDOM and spiritual maturity consist in being alert, inwardly aware and watchful of making the right choice at all times and in all circumstances."

Śri Raman Mahāṛṣī.

This soul is overcome by *māyā* (Nature's qualities). Now, because of being overcome, man goes on to more confusion and sees not the blessed Lord, the Cause of action, who stands within oneself. Unsteady, wavering, bewildered, full of desire, distracted, he goes on and on to the state of self-conceit. In thinking 'This is 'I' and 'That is mine', the man binds himself with his self, as does a bird with a snare.

Maitrī Upaniṣad.

Be the child of poverty, have an intense passion for purity, root out lust and greed out of your nature, study your mind as though it was a thing apart from you, tear off the masks with which the body hides its shames and wash your mind clean from all impurities. Avail the spiritual opportunity which is a rare privilege.

The *ātman*, hidden in all beings, is not manifest to all. But It can be realised by all who are determined to inquire into subtle truths by means of their sharp and subtle reason.

Kaṭha Upaniṣad.

The cultivation of genius requires restraining the greedy and lazy part of the soul from doing what it wishes.

The Self is of the nature of perfect peace: serenity, calmness, stillness, purity. As it is unveiled with the process of knowledge, it becomes like the child, simple and pure. God is the Mother of such a child. In this state we experience the sweetness of the most personal relationship with the Mother Grace. The Self is manifest; it is not concealed. The reason why we cannot perceive it with our ordinary senses is that the Self is itself the perceiver.

The Self is both light and awareness. As light it illumines everything and as awareness, it is the power of understanding which makes us aware of what something is. Light illumines the pot; awareness makes us realise that we are seeing the pot made of clay. Being both, the Self illumines the mind, the intellect and all the senses.

The Self has the awareness that it exists everywhere; whereas the individual Self *(jivātman)* believes that it exists only in its body from head to toe. The reason for this could only be ignorance. To expect a spiritual technique to reveal the Indwelling Lord is like expecting a flashlight to illumine the sun. The Self, like the sun, is always shining with its own effulgence. We meditate and perform spiritual practices only to make the mind pure enough to reflect the effulgence of the Self.

In this body which is made of inert matter dwells a conscientious and immortal entity, the eternal spark of life and light called the soul, the deity in a temple. The body and the brain are like a computer whereas the soul programmes it and uses it.

When a soul gives up the body, it takes the *saṃskāra-s* with it on its journey into the next body. The *saṃskāra-s* initially determine the personality traits and the state of happiness/sorrow of the Self in the new body. All the thoughts that occur in the mind are due to *saṃskāras.* Personality, the most fundamental feature of each individual, is determined by these *saṃskāra-s.*

The soul is a traveller from another world into this world where the basic law of action is that it will have to reap as it has sown.

The soul that is attached to anything will not achieve divine union. Whether it is a wire rope or a delicate thread that binds the bird, it matters little. So long it really holds fast and is not broken, the bird cannot fly. The soul held by human bonds and affections, however slight they may be, cannot make its way to God.

It is given to man alone to know and realise Self. If a man dies without realising the unity of the individual Self with the Supreme Self, he has not achieved his life's mission.

Kabir wanted to know the real Reality behind the apparent reality, the unknown in the known, the formless in the form, the emptiness of the whole. Spirit is the essence of the phenomena of the existence. It is characterised by Being, Consciousness and Bliss *(sat-cit-ānanda)*.

Only discriminating souls practise spiritual disciplines. Great is the glory of the self-luminous being, the Inner Reality. Be devoted. Unite the light within you with the light of *brahman*.

> THE Self is ever untouched by pain and pleasure; but thinking itself to be the body, it undergoes the experience of the body. The abandonment of this ignorant belief is liberation, freedom from conditioning.
>
> Sage Vāśiṣṭa's Precepts to Śri Rāma.

✷

It is the destiny of all *jīva-s* to evolve towards perfection.

CHAPTER FORTY THREE

MORE FOR THE TRUE SEEKER

SPIRITUAL growth is gradual. There is progressive evolution. One should not be in a feverish hurry to enter into *samādhī*. Ascend the ladder step by step, stage by stage.

Swami Sivananda

THE TRUTH-SEEKER's battle goes on for ever. It never ceases. There is intense desire, earnest wish and strong resolution to execute everything to its very best.

Kabīra.

THERE are two forces of nature working in us. By one we decide that in this lifetime we will make spiritual advancement but at the next moment, the other force, *māyā*, or illusory Power, says, 'what is all this trouble you are taking for? Just enjoy this life and be easy with yourself.'

What counts in *sādhanā* is the stubborn resolve to seek the Truth. This do-or-die frame of mind is itself proof enough that the *sādhaka* is already possessed by the Divine.

The committed seeker of course ceases to look to the objects and objective considerations in his attempt to discover the supreme Source of eternal bliss. He retires into himself to search and find out whether there is anything within, which holds the vital answer to his vexing question. The great glories of this world pass away in the twinkling of an eye. The in-gathering of the mind solves the bulk of seeker's problems.

Watch if there is any tendency in you which you do not like. This could probably be hindering your spiritual progress. Progress depends on the free flow of spiritual thought-power within us. We have allowed these channels to become blocked by wrong thinking. Recognise this fact and you are on the path.

Cultivate spirituality from a good example and then become a good example yourself.

The discriminating thought 'I am not the doer, all actions are only the reactions of the body, mind and senses', is an aid for turning the mind back to its pristine state and keep it fixed in the Divine while engaged in the mundane activities.

Enter not the doors of any organised religion. Religion is only between you and the Lord, and no third person should come in between.

Māyā presents many temptations to you when you are on the path. Resist them.

No matter how many times you fall. Always get up smiling and keep walking. Generally, seekers are assailed by doubts even when they are at the threshold of light. The struggle with darkness will continue until the light fills one's whole being. The life and its experience is an ongoing process of perfection.

If the divine virtues are gaining strength in life, the mind is recoiling from the pleasures of senses, the attraction for the divine is developing, and mental peace and joy are increasing.

The sunshine is one and the same wherever it falls but only bright surfaces like water, mirrors and polished metals can reflect it fully. So is the divine light which falls equally and impartially on all hearts but only the pure and clean hearts can fully reflect it.

The birds in the air, fish in the water and the arrow leave no track behind. None can see the path pursued by those who sought and reached the destination. Those who are liberated, fly in the sky of truth, but neither are any footprints left behind, nor is any path created. Everybody has to light his own lamp and create his own path to Truth.

Some read to think, these are rare; some to write, these are common; some read to talk about and these form the great majority. Esoteric study proposes to reawaken spiritual awareness through self-discipline, inner work and outer action.

Despite the best efforts of the seeker there remains always an unexplained residue. The soul must go beyond this point all alone. Of course the solitary part of the journey will be illumined by a steady development within.

We may not be able to change the events but we can change our attitudes. That should be our ideal which infuses in us high qualities (*lakṣanā-s*). Changing our inner world of ideas changes the outer world of events.

Sinning would appear to be certainly not as bad as the brooding over the sins because brooding drives the impressions deeper and deeper into the mind where *saṃskāra-s* of such hardness are formed that greater subsequent effort is required to clean the system.

Ignorance disables man to discriminate. Because of ignorance man identifies himself with the body and whatever he says or does, he invariably starts with the subject 'I'.

You must invite a *'bhāva'*, a divine attitude, into your life. *Buddhi* means intellect, and *medhā* means intellect illuminated by love full of *rasa*, of joy, of inspiration. The objective is to illuminate your wisdom with *bhakti*, divine love.

Purity of mind is a must for Self-realisation. The only impurity of mind is bad thoughts. Mind borrows its light and intelligence from the Inner Ruler, the *ātman*, that is Self-effulgent, just as the iron rod borrows its heat and brilliance from the fire. Reflection can only be on a reflecting surface.

Just as an iron rod may be hot at the end close to fire and cold at the other end away from it, even so the mind is pure and strong when it is turned towards the indwelling presence of God, and impure and weak when it is turned towards the external world of objects.

Man alone can visualise the evidence of things unseen by the physical eyes. The subjective experience alone is the final culmination of all spiritual seeking because Self is the very light that illumines all our experience.

For an earnest seeker wanting to make a success of his life's mission, there are no small things which can be neglected and big things which are to be given more importance. Rather, it is the small which prepares you to handle the big.

A stream can never go backward. When the stream of faith once begins to flow, it washes clean of all alien matter. One who knows his alliance with divinity never loses his courage or his faith. Let's be silent and full of faith so that we can hear God's voice.

Maintain a rapport with the world but keep a distance at the same time.

The goal of man is partly achieved on the realisation of Self. In this state man comprehends his Self as a fragment of the Holy Spirit, a spark of the Holy Fire, abandons the vain idea of his separate existence, and begins to grow spiritually to unify himself with the eternal Spirit.

The spiritual journey is often agonisingly painful until the hungry soul finds its original Source. It is not easy to develop one's instincts to act like the calf that finds its mother's udder even blindfolded. Every sincere devotee must find the great Goal eventually. But those who want to earnestly speed up the process should shut out the distractions from the external world and focus the mind on the Self.

Mahāṛṣi Ramana compared *samādhi* to a bucket of water tied with a rope and immersed in a well; the self is immersed in the greater Self but the rope which is symbolic of the ego, is there to pull it back again.

Silently that Light is observing everything that is going on.

CHAPTER FORTY FOUR

An Elevated Soul

(Characteristics)

In order to understand an enlightened soul we must know the way as he lives in the world, not as he sits under a tree lost in contemplation.

The first sign of an enlightened person is that he is not blinded by false identification of the body with his true Self. He knows perfectly well that he is not this body but a part and parcel of the Supreme Personality of Godhead. He is therefore not joyful in achieving something, nor does he lament in losing anything which is related to his body. This state of mind is called *sthira-buddhi* (equipoise).

In a realised soul the common factor is peace and tranquillity. He neither praises nor criticises anybody, talks ill of none. Like the sun shining impartially upon all things, he looks with an equal eye upon all. He moves about in the world as a liberated soul released from all attachments.

He does not care for the dead past, nor worry about the unborn future and is indifferent to the never-to-be present.

A *yogi* is a person who is aware of the direction in which he has to move, no matter how gloomy the day, how cloudy the sky. His mind shines in the light of the sun despite all those thick clouds. All his desires have been consumed in the fire of knowledge. The beauty of a form does not captivate a yogi. He only appreciates it.

He remains verily ever calm and tranquil in mind, thought and deed, unaffected by *māyā* and *moha, and* has renounced all greed. Such evolved souls are like ordinary people but they are highly superior in terms of sublimation of soul, illumined intelligence, refined emotions and dedication to higher ideals.

A saint carries the word of God in his heart. He is divine because he possesses godly attributes. He is above lust, greed, anger and hatred. He is indifferent to pain and pleasure. He is unassuming and humble.

The true saint goes in and out amongst the people, eats with them, buys and sells in the market, marries and takes part in social interaction. He never forgets God for a single moment. He is a *jīvanmukta*, even when the body continues to exist.

Victory to you, O saint

- who renounced the life's affairs by enjoying them all.
- who offered the bodily senses to the fire of repentance.
- who revealed the faith in dispassion.
- who chose the peace by losing ego and affection.

The enlightened one signifies a spiritually aware individual in whom the personality is in alignment with the soul, and the soul and spirit are unified.

A true *yogi* considers all ordeals, trials, tribulations and crisis in his life as a storm in a tea-cup. He is not overawed by them. He maintains the equipoise of mind as a rope-dancer keeps his balance. Illusory joys cannot evoke any response from him.

The saint gives and forgives. He remains ever in silent contemplation of the eternal Reality. His presence will increase one's hunger for God. This hunger is the dire need for realisation of Truth.

"When you no longer make any distinction between ditch water and the Gaṅgā water, then you will know that you have the perfect knowledge."

A *faqir* (saint)

You can get anything from the enlightened souls: They will fill you with prosperity, immortality, joy, bliss. But they are rare to find.

❄

Silence is the core, In the total silence there is always an absence of thoughts (tranquillity of mind) and the self comes closer to divinity.

CHAPTER FORTY FIVE

In the Hours of Meditation

There is no holier sanctuary than a purified mind, the region of Peace wherein the voice of God is heard, audible within the silence. Purity, bliss and grace make up the true state of meditation. The spiritual consciousness dawns in these silent sacred hours. The soul is close to its Source, the oceanic consciousness of the Absolute.

Know your self to be the substance of Truth, the substance of divinity. You are the Reality within which no change abides. The form is a dream. Life is but a play. The soul is stationed in the formless divinity.

By knowing your self, you can know Him. God and soul are one, indestructible, imperishable, indivisible. All else wanes. There is no becoming for you, O soul. Progress is in time but Perfection is within eternity. You are not of time, you are of eternity. 'Thou art That.'

The pure in heart alone sees God. Death is everywhere swallowing up the forms of life. Death and change ensnare and blind all things save the Spirit. Let the tempest blow over. But when the desire burns and the mind vacillates, then call on Him. Purity is the pathway to the divine Presence. Retreat from the world. It is the embodiment of dreams.

Peace dwells in the silence. Silence comes when the tumult of senses has been drowned in the powerful stillness of renunciation. Renouncing all, go by those paths which lead you into the solitude of your own insight. Plunge into sanctity. Divinity is the end. True dependence on God solves all difficulties.

Behold. There is an inner as well as an outer world. There is a world of spirit as well as a world of form. The outer world is only a semblance of the inner world. In this inner world your true nature abides. Turn within. Fly on the wings of ardent love.

Silence is the nature of love. Deep within the deepest folds of silence there is

God. Abandon all outer concerns. See the divinity in form as well as in the formless. There is no greater good than the mercies of the Lord. Divinise everything that you do. God is the very substance of the soul. He is the Knower of all thoughts and of the most silent aspirations of the heart. Go into the chambers of the silence; come into the presence of Reality.

Outward things are like arrows that bruise the soul. Reflect on the smooth flow of mental experience. A spiritual sort of indifference is likewise necessary. Why take notice of the thousand and one irritating details that the day may bring forth?

Divine is the nature of the self and freedom is the goal. The goal is Here and Now.

Meditation is a fight between thoughts. Thoughts order the mind into a definite pattern and this determines the texture, behaviour, efficiency, sincerity and quality of the mind. The attempt of the spiritual seeker is to destroy the undesirable thoughts and maintain that state of mind for all times. Worthless thoughts abound like trees in a jungle. If allowed to be fed on them, the mind becomes a wild elephant. So long as the ego (the acting self) lasts, effort is necessary. When the ego ceases to exist, action becomes spontaneous.

Meditation is a process of purifying and transforming the normal human nature into divine nature and thereby achieving a mental state of equilibrium, equanimity and equipoise *(sthitaprajñā)*, the final goal of the seeker who hungers for lasting peace and happiness.

The true meditation consists in the mind perpetually attuned to the inner music. It involves a positive flow of thoughts meant ultimately to take the individual soul to prime heights and explore avenues of union with the Supreme Soul, the *Paramātman*.

Meditation in the deep silence of the mind and uttered with the tongue of the thought alone is capable of bearing a fruit. Prayer is the essence of spirituality. It affords a wonderful recreation to the body, mind and soul.

Meditation is for bliss, for relaxation, for experience of the divine love and peace with one's own self in union with the Creator for overall enhancement of personality. It is helpful for eradicating past impressions as a new song erases the old one in a magnetic tape or as a needle pushes out a thorn from the body. It strengthens one's moral sense, restores inner peace and harmony, improves one's outlook and attitude.

The way is shown. The initiative needs to be taken. Learning without practice is of little use. Having found the path, march bravely on. Once the inward journey is resumed and continued in a steadfast manner, the Truth will reveal Itself and the goal will not be far away. Everything becomes spiritual. Even a blade of grass speaks of the Spirit. The path to salvation lies in the constant touch with the Supreme Power. The enlightenment is not a thing to be sought after but a voyage into the spontaneity of life.

> Self is the effulgence transcending darkness and light. It is spontaneously shining as the Absolute. This enquiry into the Self in the form of devotional meditation, evolves into the state of absorption of the mind into the Self and leads to liberation.
>
> Mahārṣi Ramana

It is no use closing your eyes. Close the mental eye, all will be right.

CHAPTER FORTY SIX

THE SOUL'S LONE JOURNEY

(A Palatable Narrative)

O MAN, you are blessed with a body to reside in and are enrolled in a full-time school called life. You have the opportunity to learn. You have all the requisite resources for the purpose. What you make of your life and the available resources is left to you. Learning knows no end.

The Body.

The body is like a machine which needs to be powered to make it run and function. That power is the Self, the Soul *(ātman).* The body without Self is a dead matter.

The Mind.

As part of the body, the mind too is considered inert, insentient, just like a mass of materials shaped into an engine which cannot run and function without fuel. In order to act and function, it draws its strength from the Self.

The human mind seems to be functioning as a dividing line between the outer world and the world within. It is associated both with the knower (subject, the Self) and the knowable (object, material world) giving rise to duality.

For all creatures, the mind alone is the cause for bondage and freedom. Muddied with agitation (*rājas*), the mind binds man to his passions and possessions, while the same mind, purified from passions and impressions, is instrumental in liberating man from all his inhibitions and bondage.

Although the mind is inert, it has the ability to function like a mirror and reflect Consciousness. For instance, when a pot is placed before the eyes, one's mind takes its form. One cannot experience or perceive anything without the light of Consciousness.

To become deeply aware of the nature of the Knower (the Self), the discriminating mind will have to forsake all those activities relating to the world of objects and seek within its source of the nature of perfect Self. The mind runs in three parameters e.g. space, time and objects, and can rebel any time.

The Body-Mind Identity-Crisis.

The mind identifies itself with the body, family, race, country etc. (self-imposed limitations, a mistaken Self-identity). All these multifarious affiliations exert their pulls and pushes on the mind and demand certain loyalty, which is a disintegrating factor. Identifying the Self with the non-self is the bondage of man.

Individuality arises by identification with the elements through ignorance. Where there is consciousness of the Self, individuality disappears in divine illumination.

The problem is that the man identifies himself with the heterogeneous rather than with the homogeneous. Submerged in material consciousness and false adjuncts (*upādhi-s*), he thinks himself the doer of all actions and activities, and this makes him forget his indebtedness and gratitude he owes to the Creator.

It is not possible to maintain the identification with one's individuality and at the same time experience the vision of the Whole. To hold on to the ego and talk of infinite *brahman* is to remain at the level of mere thought.

The Ego *(ahaṅkāra).*

The ego is the sense of 'I am' which is born of the mind. The mind, out of its own experiences, abstracts an entity which may be termed 'identified ego'. This ego, the mistaken Self-identity, is due to its assuming affinity with three material components (body, mind and intellect) which make up our shell, and is the root cause of dualism, the seeming separation between man and his Creator. In all these affinities 'I-s' are many but 'Am' (existence) is one without a second.

This wretched 'I' is almost indestructible. It is like a hydra. You cut off one head and another head replaces it. I-identity is the root of life in the manifest dimension. The appearance of this delusive 'I' (ego) between the sentient and the insentient (shell) is a mystery. Ego survives in us as long as it is not enquired into and pushed out, by whatever means. Ego is calamitous because it sprouts desires, man's worst enemy.

Scriptures distinguish the individual soul from the universal soul. In the Upaniṣads two selves are depicted as two birds perched in the same tree. One is the empirical self attached to the fruit of the tree, while the other is the eternal Self, a detached observer *(sākśi).* Caught in the bewildering and tempting multiplicity of the world, the individual soul as a resident in the body, goes through many sorrows and joys. But it also has the idea of liberation, however vague, at any given time, and it expresses itself, 'Save me, O Lord'. It would also seem from this portrayal that the *ātman* is only a witness.

In me there are two 'I-s'. The small 'I' which is identified with the body, *prāṇa* and mind; and the big 'I' which is common in all beings. *Ahaṅkāra* manifests as the *jīva bhāva.* The stimulus.from the sense organs leaves impressions on the mind and with every subsequent thought a new *'ahaṃ'* is created.

Ego is the simulated self-forgetfulness of the soul of its own eternal nature. It disregards the prompting of the soul, and believes in living for sense-gratification and glorification aided by greed, lust, anger and other similar vices. The ego which is dependent on its relative partners, and on the self for its play, deserves no sympathy or respect.

A human being has many personalities because the ego has many facets. In the *sātvik* state the ego is the true knowledge of Self; in the *rājsik*, ego is a desire for power; and in the *tāmsik*, it is mere selfishness. The true ego is also the 'I' but it is veiled for the time being.

Ego is consciousness boosted by the props of status, learning, accomplishments, name and fame. It is in fact a barrier to spiritual growth and development.

The *Jīva* (living entity).

The *jīva* is the individual personality which undergoes rebirth. It is the individual spirit which imagines itself trapped in a physical form subject to the limitations of embodied existence. Each *jīvātman* is considered to be individual and separate and remains so until it realises its identity with the Supreme Soul. It is exemplified by the space in a jar *(ghatākāśā)* which when smashed, the space within the jar unites with all space *(mahākāśā)*. The seeming gap between the universal Self and the individual soul is created by the ego, the mistaken Self-identity, which stands in between the two like a stick on the surface of the water making it appear divided into two parts while in reality it is one.

The Soul *(ātman)*.

The soul meaning 'God within' is often translated as Self. This Self is our basic personality or nature.

Thus the soul is the indwelling spirit, the true and immortal nature of the cosmic person and of all living forms of life, an emanation of God, an inextinguishable spark of heavenly flame, an overflowing wave of God-ocean, identical with the ineffable Transcendence. It animates and makes the physical structure (body, mind, *prāṇa*) pulsate with its warmth, touch and presence, and enables the same to perform and perceive the world of objects. The true nature of the soul is Being-Consciousness-Bliss (*sat-cit-ananda*).

The soul is a non-physical, imperishable, indescribable entity and becomes the central point of our existence. It is unsullied by thought, word and deed.

The Self animates the body-mind equipment (*antāhkarṇa*) even as a small lamp kept in a room lights up the whole room. Consciousness level of a *jīvātman* is directly proportional to the intensity of the lamp lit within. *Jīvātman* is considered different from *brahman* in the state of bondage and becomes one with Him in the state of liberation. When it realises that it is free from all contacts with *prakṛti*, it is released.

We cannot objectify the Self as we can objectify our eyes before a mirror. All the times one speaks of 'I', 'I', yet when questioned, one denies the knowledge of it. If the Self is not there, *jīva* is not there. 'I think I think', 'I think I act', but who thinks and who acts will have to be differentiated and determined.

Vedānta visualises the Self in us as the witness of all our actions and activities, and records them like the detached observer both during the day and at night. It remains awake when we go to sleep and reports to us on our dreams. He who dwells in the mind but is separate from the mind, and he who controls the mind from within but whom the mind does not know, is the Self, the Inner Ruler, the Immortal.

The Self and *prāṇa* are inseparable. *Prāṇa* is born of the Self like a man and his shadow. *Prāṇa* is fire and therefore he whose bodily heat has gone out, is dead.

Everyone is conscious of his existence. 'I am'. That is the Self which speech cannot express but that which makes us speak, that which cannot be felt but that which makes the mind feel, that which shines within as 'I' but that which is never seen. It is this 'I' which is the essence of *jīva*. In truth, the Self, the mystic spiritual Presence, exists everywhere at all times. The Self is self-revealing and cannot be negated.

Consciousness.

Empirical mode of consciousness is always intentional, which means that it goes out of itself to relate itself to the object that is out there. Therefore, we may say that consciousness is the relationship between oneself and one's environment. It is the awareness of one's thoughts, feelings, emotions and actions.

Consciousness (with capital 'C') is the Reality that is inherent in existence. It is the innermost Self *(ātma-tattva)*, the 'Thing-in-Itself', the Light of lights. It is the Spirit in us which propels, motivates and causes the body (matter) to function. It is self-revealing, indivisible, all-pervading.

Brahman, the Absolute.

Behind all this seeming multiplicity of existence, the One unchanging substratum persists in all its splendour. This Supreme Being is the dynamic Truth that pervades the cosmos in the form of an indescribable substance. This Presence beams with full sentience. This one Existence is spoken of differently using a host of names. The divine energy, also known as Spirit, is the effulgence transcending both darkness and light. It is the illuminator of everything. Being all-pervasive, the Absolute *(brahman)* cannot be limited by time, space and causation. The Supreme Being is both the transcendent and immanent Spirit of the Cosmos, the unmanifest and the manifest Being, the invisible but tangent Presence.

As the indwelling Consciousness of all insentient and sentient beings, the Lord imparted their essential nature and identity to them. Like the distinctive sweet taste of sugar gives it its unique nature, the Lord imparts this quality to it.

See in this scene of changing shows, there is a changeless One that glows. He is *brahman,* the Absolute.

Spirit hides as movement in the air, as hardness in stone, as liquidity in water, as emptiness in space, as huge serpent in the egg, as tree in the seed. So is the world latent in the *brahman*, the Mother Divine. The Supreme Being is seen in Nature as a flash of lightning, like the invisible electric current functioning through bulbs and tubes. Truth pervades in the untruth just as awareness pervades in the inert body. The divine energy pervades everything but we are not always aware of it. If in the inner silence one's spiritual eye opens, the Invisible becomes visible.

Kabīr wanted to know the real Reality behind the apparent reality, the unknown in the known, the formless in the form, the emptiness in the Whole. Spirit is the essence of the phenomena of the existence. It is characterised by Being-Consciousness-Bliss (*sat-cit-ananda*).

Saṃskāra-s.

Each thought that is thought out, each word that is spoken, each deed that is done, every incident that has taken place in one's life, creates an impression *(saṃskāra)* in the inner growth of man. Some *saṃskāra-s* exist for a short period while others remain for longer duration. These *saṃskāra-s* influence and counter-influence among themselves. They undergo changes in their nature and character. A sudden experience in the life of a person may bring a turning point.

Man's consciousness is bound with *saṃskāra-s*. Good ones counterbalance or counteract or even neutralise bad ones.

What went Wrong?

The *ātman*, in its pristine glory, is essentially divine, possesses limitless knowledge, bliss and power. How is it then that It came to be known as imperfect, veiled and identified with the body?

Apparently, something seems to have gone wrong after its brush with the phenomenal world. The *jīva,* enticed by the fascination of the visible and the tangible world, gets involved in it, and finds itself tied down to it totally oblivious of its true nature and original abode. The 'divinity' thus appears 'veiled' by unbroken series of desires, passions, dispositions in the proximity of *prakṛti* (Nature). *Avidyā* (Ignorance), *karma-s* (actions) and *vāsanā-s* (impressions) too play a vital role. Just as a clear crystal assumes the colour of another object when brought near it, so is the *jīva* influenced and affected by the material world as it passes through various incarnations. The *jīvātman* gets lost in the turmoil and deviates from the Truth. During the course of its repeated journey in the world, and under the heavy burden of *vāsanā-s* which it carries along, the *jīva* becomes defiled, and loses its spiritual stature.

"Just as clouds born of the sun's rays cover the sun, so the mind and ego born of the Self, veil the Self itself, and play as though there were no Self behind them."

Śaṅkarācārya.

Thus when the *jīva* becomes associated with mind (senses), it belongs to the class of men and matter. Its separation from the Divine becomes pronounced. Its union with God, its identity with God, and its original nature and behaviour with God, suffer an impairment. The *jīva* which is thus far-removed and distanced from its original source, comes, after the death of the body, to the womb of the mother, derives the available material benefits, weaves a body around itself and is born again.

Death.

Everything in the world dies inevitably but nothing dies absolutely. Things look lively but they are ephemeral. Nothing appears to live for ever. The body dies. The Soul does not.

It is one of the persistent beliefs of humanity that when the physical body dies, the *jīvātman* continues to be and the residual impressions, the sum total of tendencies (*saṃskāra-s*) of the past lives, remain bound to it. Desires with motives and attachments, when attempted to be fulfilled, develop *saṃskāra-s*, even though they may be noble and religiously inspired. The vehicle of astral body which survives death is commonly referred to as the *ātman* itself. The *ātman* carries the astral body just as the air carries the odour. The astral body is a mental construct and not a physical matter. Man's nature is dependent upon his affiliations. We are governed by our appetites, our shortcomings, our desires. Possessiveness and cravings are seen as the root cause of repeated reincarnations. As long as soul remains under the spell of ignorance which is another name for spiritual self-forgetfulness, it will continue to undergo the wheel of transmigration *(saṃsāra cakra).*

Consciously or unconsciously, we seek, throughout our life, an aesthetic completeness, a perfection. But we die with a sense of non-fulfilment. Whatever thoughts become dominant at the dying moment, those will determine the character and combination of the next birth. It must reincarnate again and again until its earthly longings are worked out and it is free from all *vāsanā-s*. Only an emancipated soul jumps out of this cycle of life and death to embrace divinity. This happens though in the rarest of rare cases. Nevertheless it does happen.

An Analogy.

The traveller (*jīva*) is lying 'asleep' in the chariot (body) which is being driven by an inebriated driver (the ego-ridden mind) who is obviously incapable of controlling the horses (senses) each pulling in different directions. The chariot diverts from the main path into muddy pits and ultimately collapses midway. The journey remains unfinished. The traveller, however, is given another chariot (body). But again he gets drunk and goes to sleep The chariot obviously veers away from the right path once again. Thus the journey remains unfinished. So the cycle of birth and death continues. This is the tragedy of human life which is repeated over and over again. The destination is so near and yet so far. Only if the *jīvātman* awakens and disciplines the mind (driver) to shake off the ego's drunken stupor and regains control over the senses (horses), the long journey may finally culminate in a state of everlasting bliss in the warm bosom of Mother Grace.

The Way Out.

To many it is not given to hear of the Self. Others, though they hear of it, do not understand it. Intelligent is he who learns of it. Blessed is he who is able to understand it. Man has a divine destiny to fulfil. Few know the goal of their existence; fewer still seek to attain the goal.

Only with the spiritual input, the mind can be trained to shun worldly pleasures and seek eternal bliss. When the mind is purged of its impurities, it will become indifferent to earthly activities and get equipoise. Attachment *(moha)* is an unyielding fetter but the same attachment, if directed towards the Divine, serves as an open door to liberation.

Just as Nature creates favourable circumstances for a seed to transform itself into a huge tree, It also creates necessary situations through which the individual soul *(jivātman)* can reach the Supreme Being, its original abode. Only discriminating souls practise spiritual disciplines.

We all come into this world gifted with innocence and silence but gradually, as we grow and evolve, we become more intelligent and take to speech leaving the silence and innocence far behind. As time passes, we move from our hearts into our heads. It is ultimately the reversal of this journey i.e. from head to heart, from words to silence, and from intelligence to innocence, that ends in enlightenment. Knowledge should lead us to that beautiful point of 'being' that says, 'I don't know'. The individual soul of the enlightened one loses its individuality and becomes one with the Supreme Being.

Till such time man realises the eternal Presence within, he is carried away helplessly in the currents of *karma-s*. Does it take any special efforts to know that 'I am'? None is ignorant of this 'I'. None admits that 'I am not'. Self-knowledge, therefore, is the answer.

Self-knowledge is the primary *sādhanā* and is emphasised by our seers. The mind is the footstep. Through it, one knows all about spiritual life. The single belief that soul and body are two separate entities is the paradigm to change the whole outlook of a person. To seek is to find. What is being sought is the greatest Reality within us. Self is to be listened to, reflected and meditated upon, and ultimately visualised and seen.

Self-knowledge is progressive evolution and starts from being true to oneself. It needs courage to be true to oneself. Often we are dauntless with the world but we are cowards with ourselves. We keep lying to ourselves, refuse to own our follies and to admit our faults. It is our fundamental weakness. Our strength is in proportion to our being true and honest to ourselves. We have to be true 'within' not only for worldly duties but for the spiritual fulfilment also, which is in harmony with the Perfect Law and in union with the Eternal.

The Self is the source of all creativity and intelligence. To know the Self, one has to sink within the mind and reach the source of all thoughts and feelings. The Thinker, the source of all thoughts, is indeed the Self.

The goal of man is partly achieved on the realisation of Self which may once again turn to the Divine. In this state man comprehends his Self as a fragment of the Holy Spirit, a spark of the Holy Fire. He abandons the vain idea of his separate existence, and begins to grow spiritually to unify himself with the Eternal Spirit.

Śandogya Upaniṣad.

❄

The whole of the Vedanta Philosophy is in this story: Two birds of golden plumage sat on the same tree. The one above, serene, majestic, immersed in his own glory; the other below, restless and eating the fruits of the tree, now sweet, now bitter. Once he ate an exceptionally bitter fruit, then he paused and looked up at the majestic bird above; but he soon forgot about the other bird and went on eating the fruits of the tree as before. Again he ate a bitter fruit, and this time he hopped up a few boughs nearer to the bird at the top. This happened many times until at last the lower bird went to the place of the upper bird and lost himself. He found all at once that there had never been two birds, but that he was all the time that upper bird, serene, majestic, and immersed in his own glory.

Swami Vivekananda

Maharṣi Ramana compared soul to a bucket tied with a rope and immersed in water in a well. The soul (bucket) merges in the ultimate Self (water) but the rope (ego) pulls it back again.

What surprises you most about human kind? A dreamer asked God. "That they are bored with childhood and rush to grow up. And when they grow up they long to be children again. Also that they live as if they will never die," quipped God.

By self-forgetfulness, by selflessness, by self-giving, without asking anything in return, one finds the inner peace and joy which is ever-lasting.

The Supreme Being appears in diverse forms to shower Its grace in the manner we invoke it. The energies attributed to these manifested forms for the purpose of creation, sustenance and dissolution, are subservient to the primordial Absolute, Mother Divine.

The knot of his heart is cut asunder, all doubts are dispelled and *karma-s* are exhausted, when the Supreme Self is seen by the seeker.

PART SIX

Wisdom Dispensed

(Wisdom is more precious than Pearls)

"There is nothing more sanctifying than *jñāna*. Not everything that you try to do, even in hundred births, will be of any avail unless you awaken *jñāna* within yourself. The end and aim of spiritual wisdom is repentance and good deeds."

Ādi Śaṅkarācārya

Our *ṛṣi-s* minimised their food intake in the beginning and gradually reduced it to naught. Reducing the food signifies not only the food taken through the mouth, but more important, the food on which the mind thrives, namely thoughts and desires which cause the wandering of the mind.

Knowledge is a unifying thread that weaves the bits together. Call it scientific knowledge. Cultivate into a sane rational being. Rationality is a spontaneous flow from the eternal to the state of consciousness. There is another plane termed emotional intelligence which is not born exclusively of reason. Emotions create their own realm. Still deeper and subtle is the spiritual knowledge which transcends the earlier two. Use the rationality as a pole-vault to take a high jump on to a higher self and leave it behind.

Thoughts To Ponder.
Meditative Quotes.

?

Every cradle asks us 'whence?' and every coffin 'whither?'

CHAPTER FORTY SEVEN

Thoughts to Ponder

(Consider and Contemplate)

Knowledge is a sacred cow. How can we milk it and keep clear of its horns and dung is our problem.

These crisp, instructive, appropriate, relevant and thoughtful notes on some of the common thoughts, terms, views and concepts often heard, talked about and discussed during spiritual discourses and studies are picked up from wherever available and added here for the benefit of the aspirants to read and contemplate and relate them to their own personal experience thus widening the horizon of their knowledge. These views are however not exclusive by any means.

On...

Ajñāna (Ignorance).

Musk forms in the navel of the deer. Being fascinated with its smell, the deer runs hither and thither. He does not know where the fragrance comes from. Likewise God resides 'within' man but he does not know it. That is *ajñāna* (ignorance), the cause of suffering.

Aspiration.

Aspiration is the courage that has the taste of a supreme adventure, that seizes you entirely and throws you without calculation, without reserve, towards the great discovery of the Divine, the great adventure of realising the Divine.

Attitude.

The definite sign of a spiritual-minded person is his silent and tolerant attitude.

Austerity.

Austerity is usually confused with mortification. It is mainly for the discipline of the mind to conserve energy from dissipating into unproductive channels and

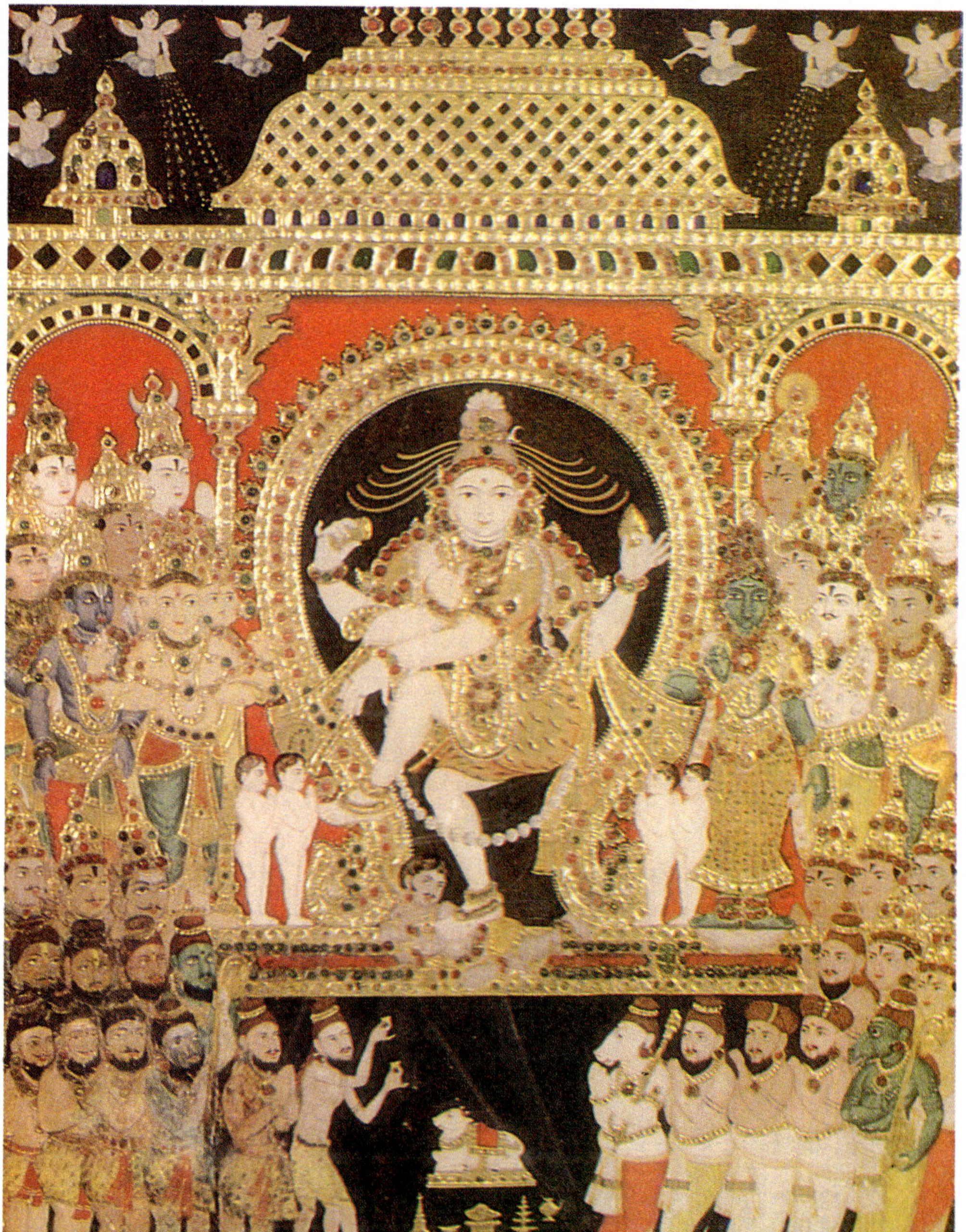

Natrāja (the dancing Śiva)

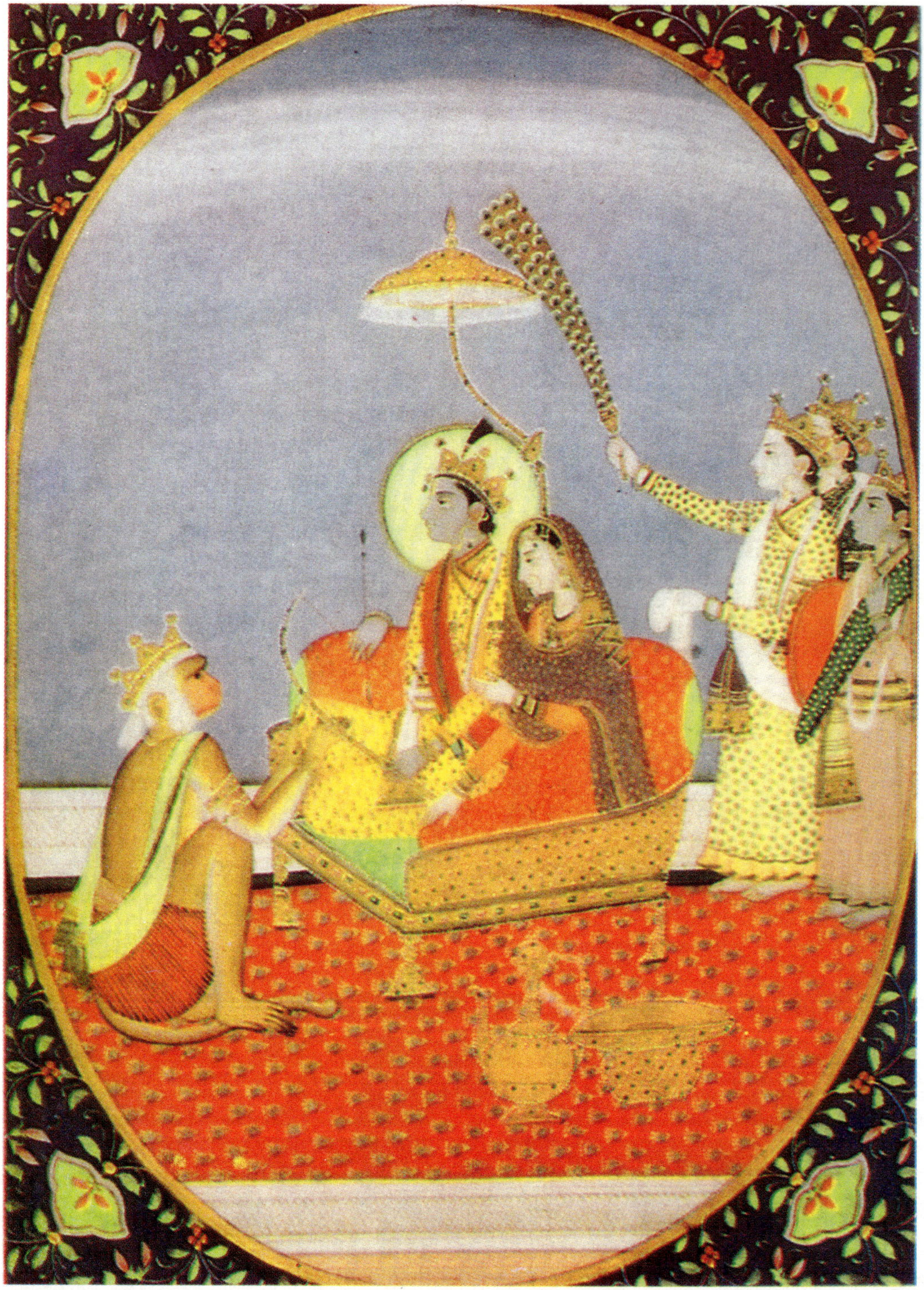

Divine Sri Ram Darbar in celestial Goulok Midst Saket Celestial Ayodhya

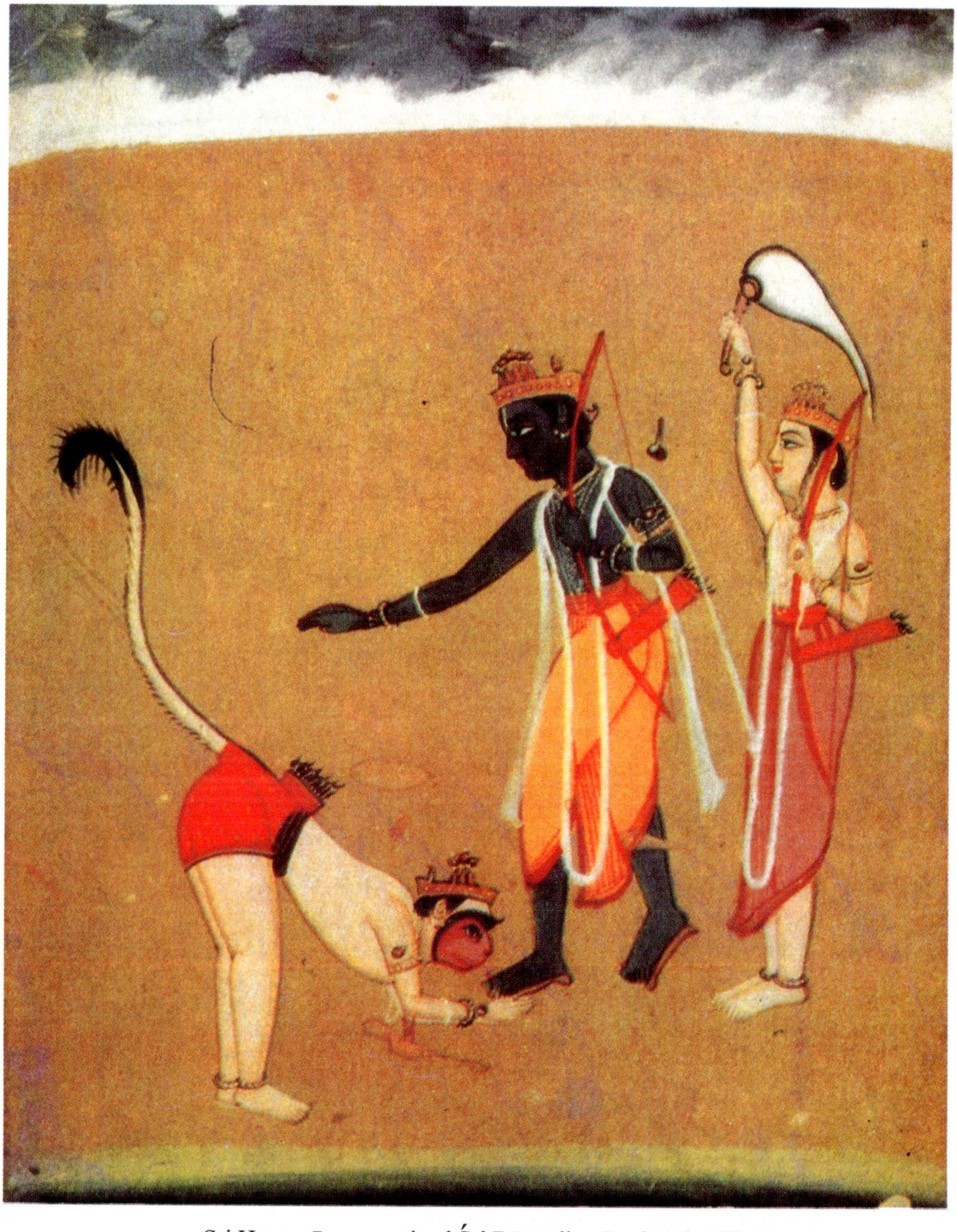

Sri Hanumān recognized Śri Rāma ji at Ryshmuk Hill,
fell on the ground and clasped His feet. (p.39)

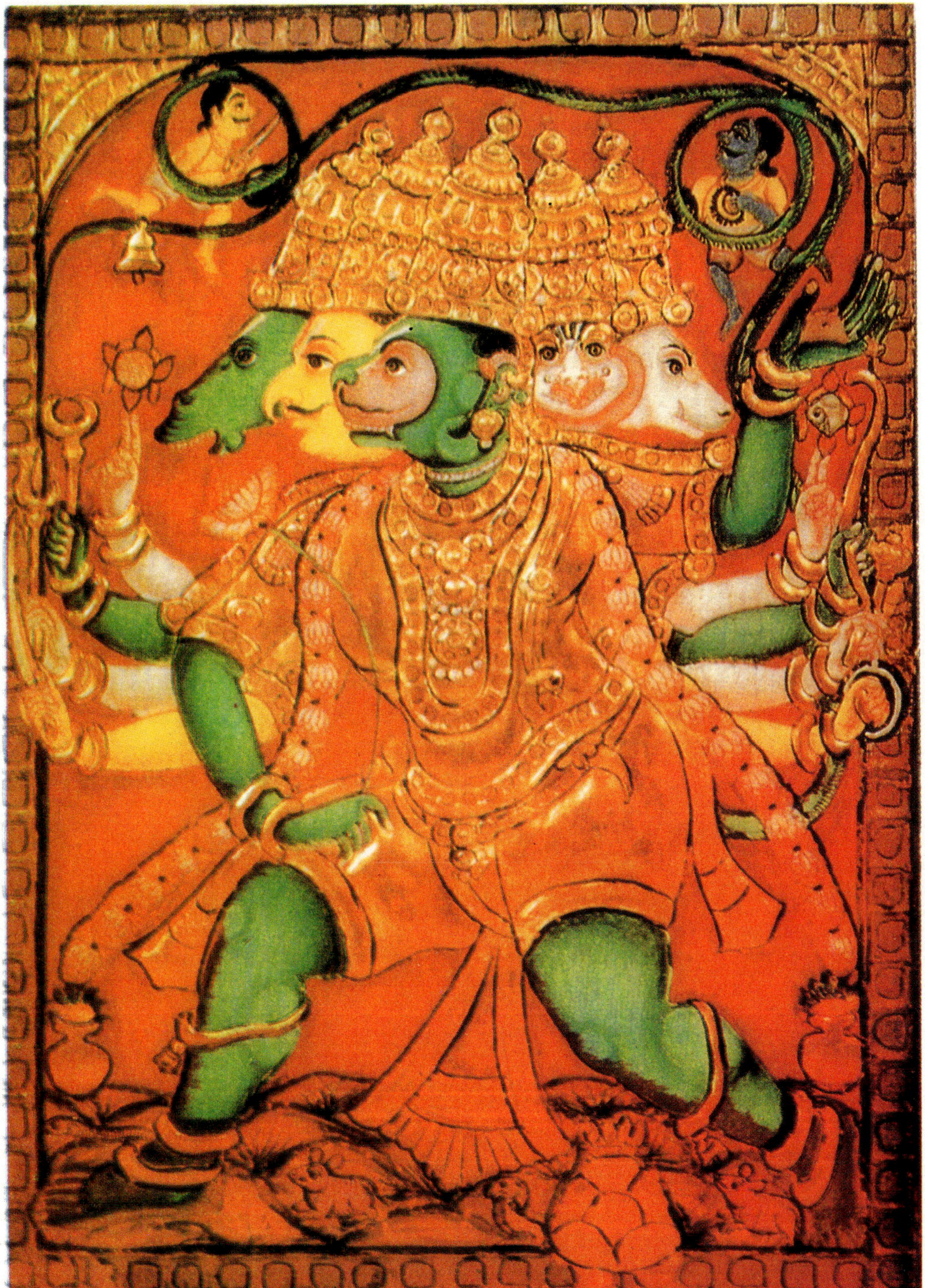

Pancmukhī Hanumān

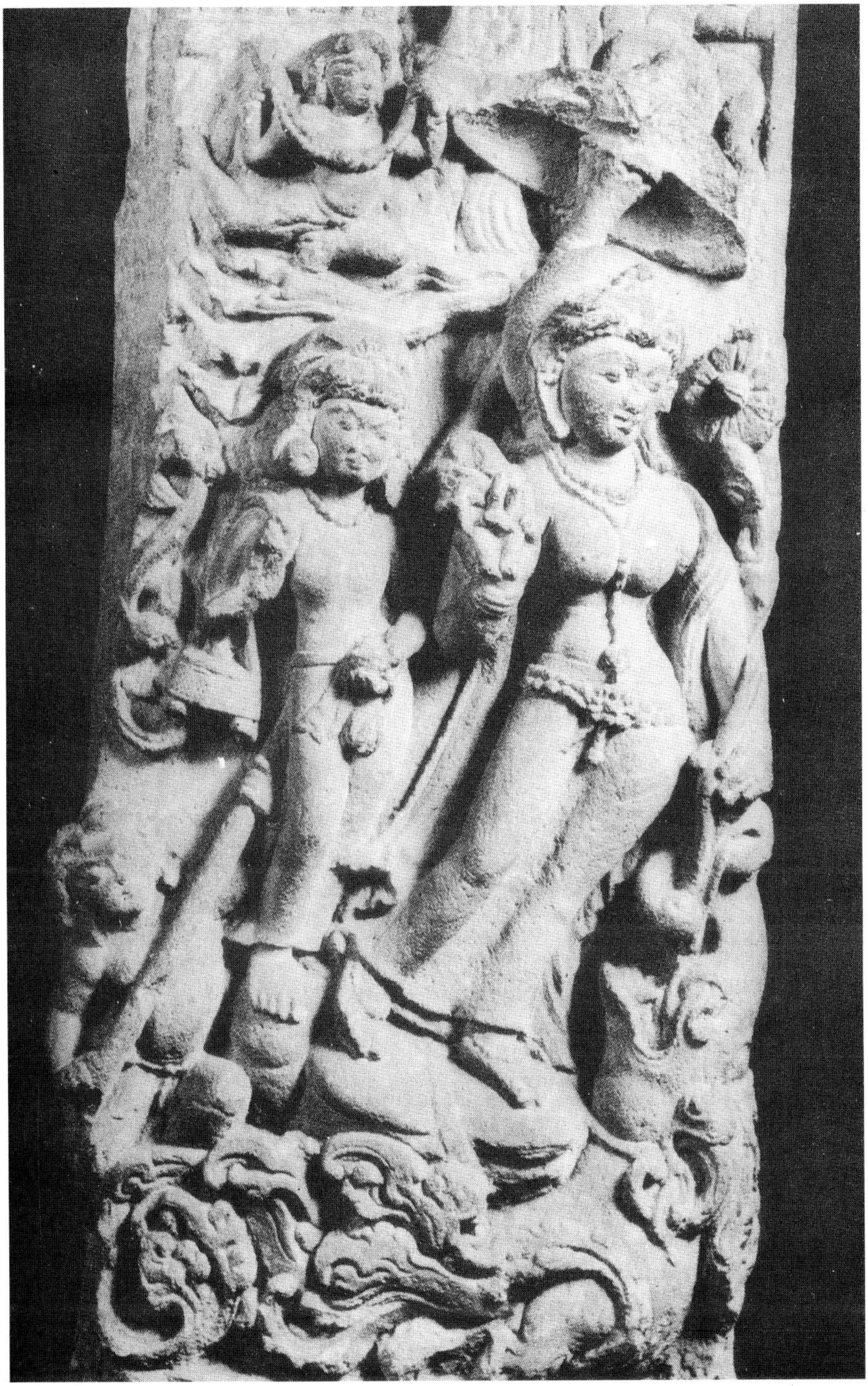

Ganga on temple doorway from Buxar, Bihar

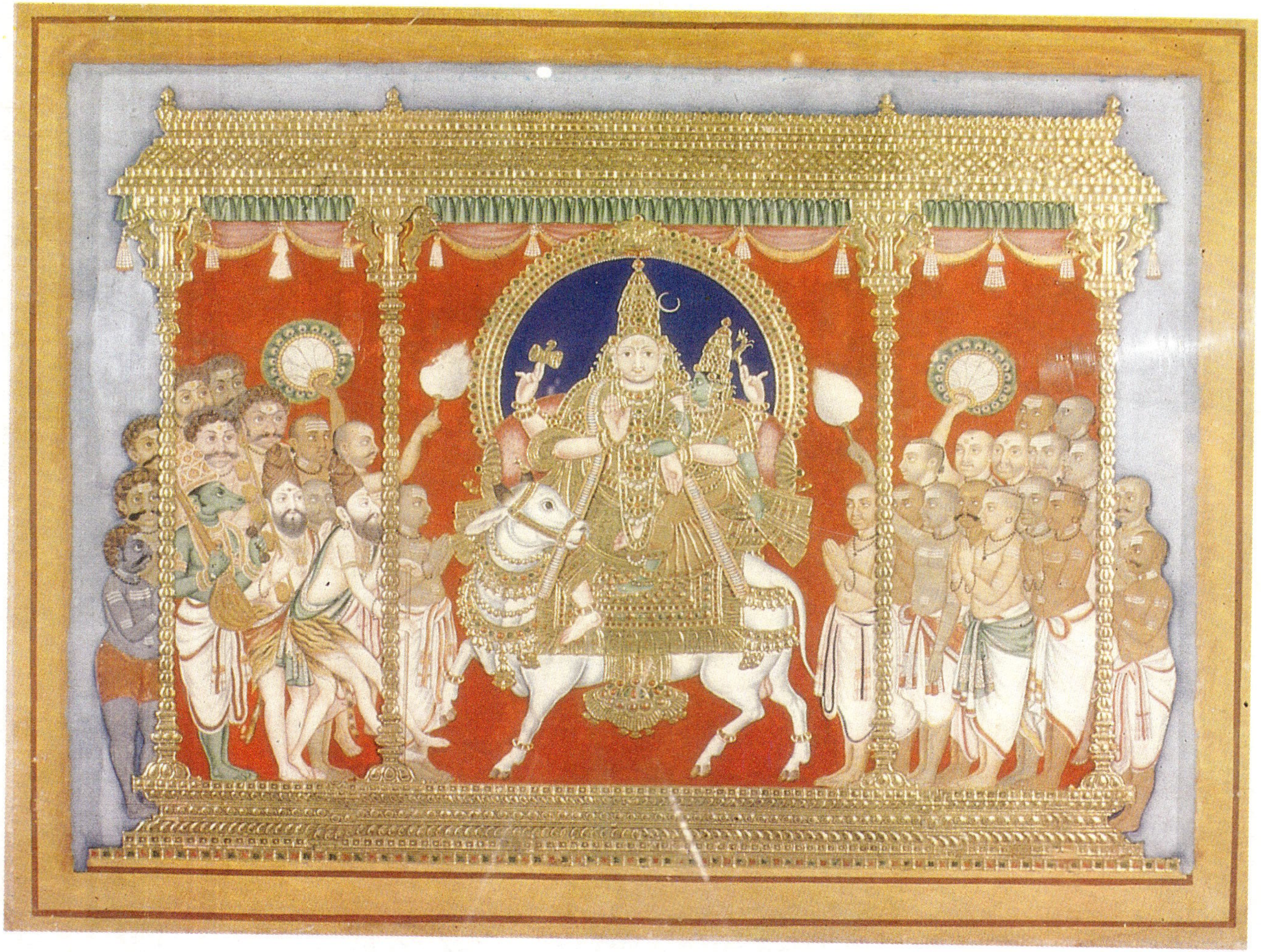

Vrisabhandhū Śiva and Pārvatī

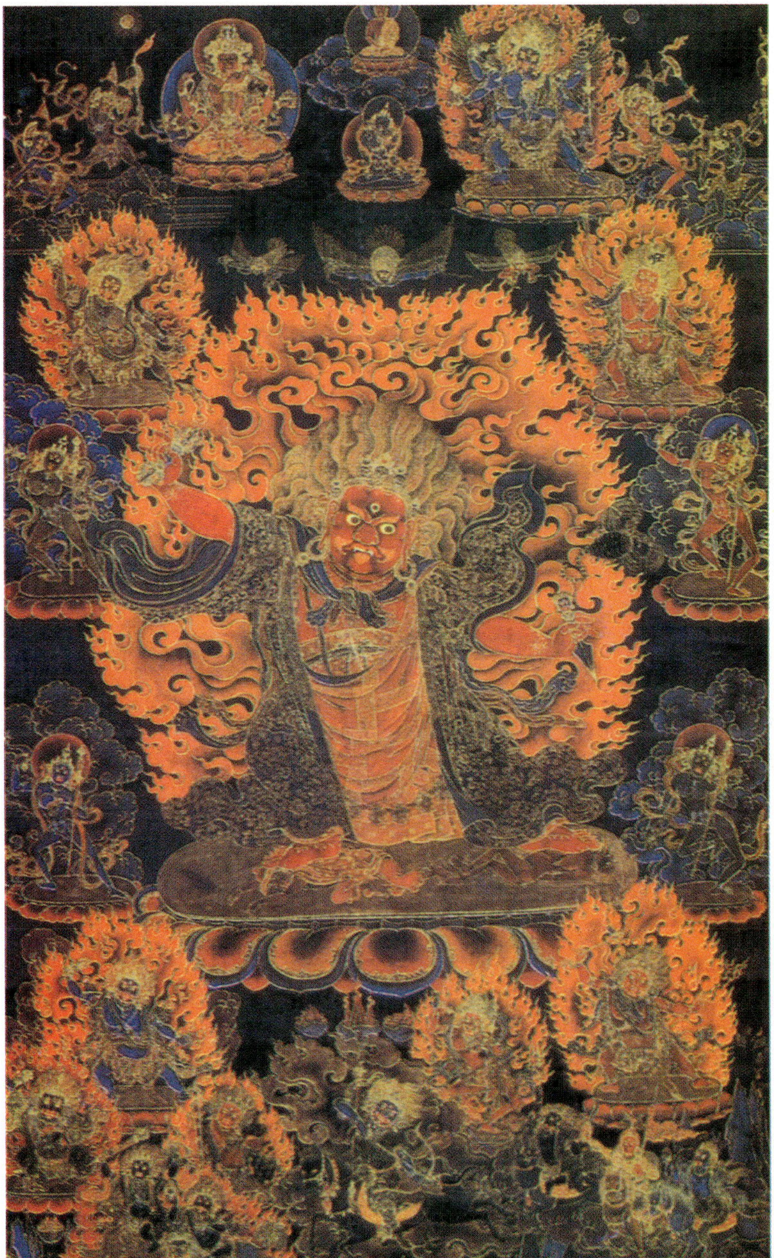

A Tankha painting conveying mystical and miraculous powers.

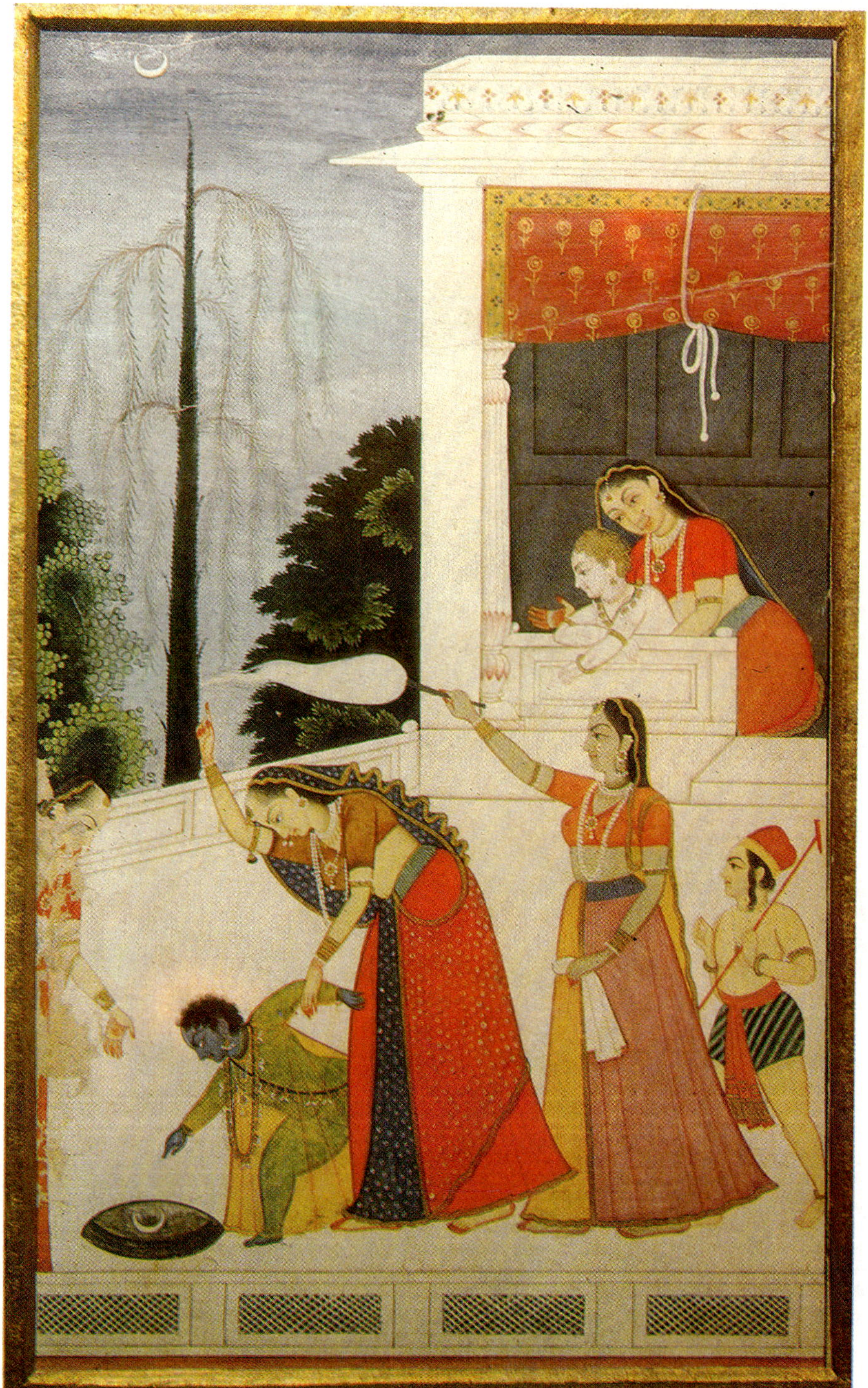

Kṛṣṇa demanding moon *(vatsalya)* (p.39)

redirecting it to a higher goal

BEING.

Existence is abstract. That which exists is creation. Being is present in all strata of creation. Water cannot wet It nor can fire burn It. Wind cannot dry It and weapons cannot slay It. It is all-pervading, the omnipresent divine Being. God is at hand for anyone to realise. One needs only to Be.

BETTER.

Things do not become better, said Swami Vivekananda. They remain as they are. We grow better by the changes we make in them.

BLESSINGS.

Blessings come in disguise. An illness gives us time to be holy, time to think and reflect on the purpose and direction of our life. Destruction on any level means turmoil and this is essentially true on the spiritual level. A turning point in the course of anything is a crisis, but some time it proves to be an auspicious turning point! True human spirit may grow out of it.

BONDAGE.

Bondage and liberation are for intellect only and not for the individual Self (*atmān*).

CONSCIENCE.

Conscience is the light of the soul that is burning within the chambers of one's heart. It is the inner voice of the Self which says 'yes' or 'no' when you are involved in a moral struggle and shows you the path of virtue and value.

CONSCIOUSNESS.

Consciousness is the Reality that is inherent in existence. It is the innermost Self, *(ātma-tattva),* awareness, knowledge, the 'Thing-in-Itself', the Light of lights. It is the Spirit in us which propels, motivates and causes the body (matter) to function.

CONTROL OF SENSE ORGANS.

Control of sense organs is nothing but the separation of sense organs from the passions so that they do not defile the perceptions. Do not allow the passions to colour your perceptions. Change the mental attitude. You cannot change the sense organs.

***DARŚANA* (A Vision).**

Higher spiritual vision by the inner eye, made easy by a process of Truth-realisation, according to seers and saints.

DESIRE *(Kāmanā)*

Time is having its sport, life is being spent away; yet the vain desire does not go. Man can progress towards God-realisation either by perfect renunciation of desire or by perfect satisfaction of desire, though the latter alternative remains a remote feasibility. Desire never rests by enjoyment of lusts as fire surely increases with more fuel added to it.

DESTINY.

Destiny must have its go. Its edge, however, can be blunted by devotion to the Almighty. Eschew vanity and take refuge in Him. He will spontaneously take charge and guide you to the higher state.

DETACHMENT *(anāsakti).*

Detachment means not simply giving up something one has or wants, but giving up the desire for it.

Retirement means abidance in the Self. Nothing more. What does it matter where and how you are placed? The essential point is that the mind must remain in its Source. If the mind is active, even the solitude becomes like a market place. There is no use closing your eyes. Close the mental eye and all will be right.

Mahārṣi Ramana

DIVINE DISPENSATIONS.

God's favours cannot be snatched from His hand. Most, even when awake, attain them not. On others SHe confers these, shaking them awake. Like the waves in rivers there is no turning back of that which has already passed. The *jīva* is bound with the fetters made of the fruit of good and evil previously earned.

DIVINE LOVE.

When Love made me Her own, my life became pure and holy. Love is Mother Divine, I am Her child - ever free and happy. It is invisible mystic touch.

DIVINITY.

Divinity is the very nature and essence of man but it lies covered under the hard surface of thoughts and *upādhi-s* (adjuncts). When the thoughts cease to erupt and *upādhi-s* eliminated, man attains Godhead.

DUALITY *(dvaita).*

Sat (being) is an idea in relation to *asat* (non-being), *Cit* (consciousness) in relation to *jaḍa* (inert), *ānanda* (bliss) in relation to *dukha* (pain), *ananta* (infinite) in relation to *alpa* (limited), *prakāśa* (light) in relation to darkness (*tāmas*). Every qualitative concept involves relations and every thought creates duality.

ECSTASY.

Ecstasy is commonly understood as a physical sensation. In mystical terms it signifies the blissful state in which spiritual awareness, cosmic consciousness and visions replace the normal awareness of one's surroundings.

EMANCIPATION.

A state of mind when the mind neither grieves nor desires.

ENLIGHTENMENT.

Enlightenment is as much an intellectual state as it is spiritual awakening. A pure mind that regards selfish ends with distrust and hatred is indispensable for enlightenment.

A state of spiritual maturity in which one's self is unshakeable by any adversities, worldly attractions, sensual pleasures. Nothing whatsoever can rob him of his smile.

EQUILIBRIUM.

A person who neither rejoices on achieving something pleasant nor laments upon obtaining something unpleasant, who is self-intelligent, and who knows the science of God, is to be understood as already situated in Transcendence.

Bhagavadgītā

ETERNITY.

A period of time that seems to go on for ever.

EVIL.

Is evil created by the Divine? Light, not darkness, is coming from the sun. When we turn our face from the divine Consciousness, darkness (ignorance) arrives and gives rise to ego. The ego cannot see the Almighty and thinks itself powerful. This creates the complexities of evil thoughts and troubles. Suffering is also a great purifying agent.

EYES.

Closing the eyes unconsciously, without having any content in the mind, is sleep. Closing them consciously is a part of meditation. A yogi closes his eyes to withdraw his senses from the objects of the world. For him closing the eyes means opening the inner eye.

FLUSH OF LIFE.

Souls that are entangled in worldliness, rarely come to their senses. They lie in the net but are not even conscious that they are entangled.

FORGIVENESS.

Forgiving is a choice and not an emotion. The beauty of forgiveness is that it frees a person from the need to get even.

GOD-CONSCIOUSNESS.

God-Consciousness means to remain mentally, emotionally and spiritually conscious of the Self at all times and in all places. *Ananda* (bliss) within is one of the signs of God-vision. The waves roll over the surface of the ocean but deep expanse of water lies unruffled beneath.

Guṇā-s.

Three thought-conditions under which the human mind functions: the *sattva* (good, pure and noble), *rājas* (the passionate, the agitated, ego-centred) and *tāmas* (the dull and inactive) states. Combination of these three states of mind in various proportions determine the individual personalities. All objects, all situations, all choices, all persons, all things in this world are composed of these three possible attributes. There is an incessant tussle between these three *guṇā-s* (qualities) for gaining supremacy over one another in all the shades and walks of life.

HAPPINESS.

A simple-abiding mind picks up joy. It generally happens when we experience something desirable. I am never tired of happiness but I am tired of being sorrowful. I complain of being sad because happiness is my nature. What is natural is not a matter for complaint. Blessed is the person who has something worthwhile to do and does it wholeheartedly.

HEAVEN.

The aim of life is not to reach heaven but to bring the state of heaven down to earth where one may live happily in peace.

HOLY PLACES.

It is true that the whole world is filled with God. Holy places are, however, like the cow's udder, a sanctity of their own. The milk of the cow permeates her whole body and is mixed with her blood. Can we get it if we press her ears? It is only from the udder that it comes out. Cows graze in the pastures and chew the cud leisurely. So do we ruminate our thoughts after visiting the holy places.

HUMILITY

Humility exalts man to the heaven of glory and power. It is the virtue of the cultured. Erring and annoying is part of the human activity. But how quickly can one regain one's original poise, reflects his spiritual achievement. True humility is free from any traces of humiliation, dejection, self-reproach.

IDOL WORSHIP.

Idol worship means attributing forms to God and pouring out everything to that Godhead. These are the props used for eternal enquiry and there is nothing wrong with it. Let's carry on struggling in this make-belief ocean of the world holding on to the only available life-boat e.g. Love. Love is the fastest means of communication to God.

IMAGES.

An incorporeal thing is reflected in the body. The intelligible cosmos is reflected in the sensible cosmos. Worship the statues of the gods, seeing that the statues too have in them forms which come from the intelligible cosmos.

***KARMA* (Actions)**

As long as we have even one desire we can still be caught in the wheel of *karma* and take rebirth in this world to try to satisfy that desire. We will play again in the 'three cities' known as the gross, subtle and causal bodies.

Karma means action or deed. Bhagavadgītā emphasises the importance of *karma* to be the duty of every individual which should be carried out without any fear or expectation of reward. *Karma* thus performed is known as *puruṣārtha.* Reward is in the hands of God.

KNOWLEDGE (jñāna)

True knowledge is the practical wisdom of purified beings. Neither the practice of austerity, nor resort to places of pilgrimage, nor repetition of *mantras*, nor charity, nor any other spiritual discipline, can add to the perfection already attained through knowledge.

LOVE FOR GOD.

The pathway of love is the ordeal of fire. Those who take the plunge into the fire, attain eternal bliss. Those who stand afar looking on, are scorched by the flames. Love for God is ecstatic making us go out of ourselves. It does not allow the lover to belong to anyone. He belongs only to the Beloved.

MEDITATION.

Meditation is the process of purifying and transforming the normal human nature to the divine nature. Concentrate on the Knower. Know that there is only one Existence every where. When you give up attachment, anger and pride, you do not have to pose for meditation anymore. The life would seem to be a sort of meditation by itself.

MENTAL CALM.

"The aspirant reaches this state of mind after having the vision of the Supreme Being. When a boat passes by a magnetic hill, its screws and nails become loose and drop out. Lust, anger and other passions cannot stay with an enlightened soul."

Śri Rāmakṛśna

***MOHA* (Delusion).**

Moha (delusion) is a mysterious working of an illusory power called *māyā*, about which we know nothing! We only posit its presence because of its effects. We know that millions of human beings are totally deluded.

***MOKṢA* (Salvation, Liberation).**

Mokṣa is a state of mind of endless calm bereft of all impure *vāsanā-s* in which purified and realised souls dwell. They realise God in the world and through the world. When the flame of desires is blown out, one achieves absolute peace.

MORALITY.

Morality is human. It demands the right understanding of what is good and bad and expects that the right is done and abided by. Moral conduct is the basis of spiritual life. The pure alone will find the Divine.

MYTHS.

The primitive mind does not invent myths; he experiences them. Myths are not mere allegories of physical processes, they have vital meaning - (Jung). Myths embody supernatural but not unreal level of existence. They present a sacred history- (Eliade). The world of symbols and myths is not separated from that of metaphysics or even that of science.

PAIN AND PLEASURE.

Pleasure tends to make you forgetful. Pain is a remembrance, an awareness, and a meditation. Body pain is possible even for an enlightened one, but psychic anguish *(dukha)* is not. The realised soul can avoid it or live with it without being aggrieved.

PASSIONS.

Truth cannot dwell where passions live. When a tree is burning in flames, how can the birds assemble there. The ultimate non-existence of passions is the desired purity of mind. And that is the intrinsic nature of mind.

PATH.

The path is long and arduous strewn with snares and problems. It is like the explorer's trek through virgin forests in quest of an unknown land. Birds in the air, fish in water and the arrow in space leave no track behind. Nobody could see the path pursued by those that sought to realise God as none has left any footprints behind. There is no predetermined path. One has to light his own lamp and determine the appropriate path.

PERFECTION.

Wise, self-controlled and tranquil souls who are contented in spirit and who practice austerity and meditation in solitude are freed from all impurity and attain to the truly changeless existing Self. He would attain to divine perfection and yet not turn his back upon the world.

PRAYER.

Prayer is an urge to call for the Divine. It depends on faith on the ultimate Power. It is that spontaneous craving of the soul to possess that priceless treasure which the thieves cannot steal and death cannot snatch away.

Prayer does not change God but changes the one who prays. All the great prophets and great teachers of the world attained their enlightenment through prayer only.

QUIESCENCE.

The state of mind where there is not the slightest trace of the 'I' thought. That is the true being of oneself. When the mind becomes absorbed in the heart and the ego vanishes, the pure Consciousness alone remains.

RITUALS.

Rituals were meant to discipline the mind and to develop love for God. After a while rituals drop away as the devotee succeeds in concentrating on the *Iṣṭa* during *sādhanā*. A guard is needed when the plant is younger; it is no more needed after the plant grows into a tree.

Give up, give up your unholy thoughts. If you bathe in the waters, without giving up these, it is like bathing in a stream that has run dry. The whole world is lost in empty rituals.

Saṃskāra-s (Impressions)

Saṃskāra-s are impressions, tendencies, psychic traces left in the mind after an experience. *Vāsanās* (mental dispositions) act like seeds and have a tendency to germinate into action. What we are at any moment of life is determined by the sum total of the impressions in the mind. We are like a machine driven by these tendencies.

SAMĀDHI

Experience of *samādhi* is indicated by the quality of life - the purity of character, cessation of desires, perfect mental equipoise, radiant happiness, clarity of vision towards the nature of things, a life well above the mundane state of existence.

SAT-CIT-ĀNANDA.

Being-Consciousness-Bliss is a state of existence of the Divine. *Sat*, divine existence, *cit*, divine consciousness and *ānanda*, divine bliss, are three divine aspects and together they are regarded as one Absolute. From this divine state of existence evolves a condition which can be called the seed of divine Self.

SEED AND PLANT.

Plants grow and develop according to the seeds sown. We cannot sow lime and reap mangoes. In other words we cannot have a bull from a buffalo mother. Of course if the soil is rich, we can improve the quality by nurturing but we cannot change the nature of the produce.

SELF-RESTRAINT.

Self-restraint is not self-denial. It is attaining mastery over the senses. All emotions must be filtered through the intellect which must be in control of every activity.

SPIRITUALITY:

Spirituality, in its true essence, is an awakening to the inner reality of our being (Spirit, Self, Soul) which is other than our mind and body. It is an inner aspiration to know, to feel, to be that, to enter into communion with that and desire union with it. A transformation of our whole being is the result. It advocates limitations of wants, self-discipline and renunciation of abundance.

SUFFERINGS.

Just as an ordinary stone can be fashioned into a beautiful image worthy of adoration and worship only after it has received many a stroke of the chisel, so also a distorted and inharmonious life has to pass through many an ordeal, suffering and tribulation, before the life of ignorance could be transmuted into a life of immortal splendour and joy, fit to be revered and adored.

Swami Ramdas

THE SNAKE AND THE ROPE.

The world appears from the ignorance of the Self and disappears with the knowledge of the Self, just as the snake appears from the non-cognition of the rope and disappears with its recognition.

TRANSFORMATION.

Transformation is a change of consciousness so conceived as to bring about a strong and assured step forward in the spiritual evolution of the being. One cannot entirely realise the Divine if there is no transformation. We must become truly what we are essentially. We must live integrally the truth, the beauty, the perfection, the power that are hidden in the depths of our being and then all becomes the expression of the sublime divine Joy.

Śri Aurobindo.

TRANSCENDENCE.

God is transcendent, beyond perception, beyond understanding and beyond time, space and causation.

TRINITY.

The Trinity *(trimūrti)* is said to be the union of the three distinct divine Personalities, Brahmā, Viṣṇu and Śiva, together with their divine Consorts

Sarasvati, Lakṣmī and Pārvatī respectively: The three function as the Creator, the Preserver and the Destroyer. Their oneness is the soulful song in our scriptures; and this song is heard and sung by only a few most evolved souls.

TRUTH.

The Truth which is God cannot be expressed in words but it is the Truth which enables us to speak whatever we say.

Truth means the final Reality, ultimate Existence, the *brahman,* the Absolute. If you take these worldly things as true, it is because that Reality which is Truth is behind them. So numerous are the suggestions of Truth, so varied are the presumptions of God that almost anybody may seek in them what he wants and find in them what he seeks, said S. Radhākrishnan.

***TYĀGA* (Renunciation).**

Practical renunciation *(Tyāga)* means throwing off and casting overboard all anxiety, fear, worry, hurry and trouble of mind.

UNION AND SEPARATION.

Paradoxically the separation is more uniting than dividing. The solid wall that separates two rooms also joins them. Silence is the mark of solitude as speech is the mark of communion. Silence and speech have the same inner correspondence as do solitude and communion. One cannot be separated from the other. Speech comes out of silence and vice versa

***UPĀDHI-S.* (superimpositions).**

All the extraneous adjuncts of the *ātman,* such as body and mind and whatever attachments man develops relating to his worldly pursuits, his family relations, career, position in society, all these are man's *upādhi-s.* Lost in their attractions and aversions man forgets his real nature and this makes it possible for him not to feel the need for God. Honour and fame though agreeable and sweet, are poisonous in effect and ruin the spiritual progress of the practitioner.

VAIRĀGYA (dispassion).

Vairāgya does not mean aversion for anything of the world. Once *vairāgya* becomes a living inspiration, the illusory nature of the world comes to the surface. Nothing seems to belong to you. When the fruit of a tree is ripe, it will fall of its own accord. So, too, when *vairāgya* saturates your heart, you lose contact with the world and slip into the lap of the Mother

LOVE'S LABOUR EARNED

ALL VIRTUES lead to the purification of the mind, which is the first need in spiritual development and leads to self-realisation. The love of God is the greatest virtue that a man can ever cultivate. The path of love is like the relationship between a child and the heart of his mother. The child takes its first step towards his mother, her heart swells. Her happiness radiates and reflects on the child so that at each step he enjoys greater happiness and that again reflects in the heart of the mother. The mother's joy reaches its height when the child arrives in her arms and finds himself one with his mother's heart. May the Eternal Mother grant us grace, love, and devotion and lead us on and on.

ONE'S own thought is one's world. What a person thinks is what he becomes. That is the eternal mystery. If the mind dwells within the Supreme Self, One enjoys undying happiness.

Maitri Upaniṣad.

A REVERIE.

I am the child of divinity. I entered in this world at her will and shall depart when She pleases. The ticket for the return journey was issued and endorsed at the starting point itself but the date cannot be deciphered. The date of commencement of journey, duration of stay and the purpose behind this life will always remain a mystery.

The Mother Divine brought up her children and sent them to this wonderful world of delusion *(māyā)* to fend for themselves. They were given the option however to go back to the Mother if only they ever remembered her and realised the importance and need to do so! The authority to recall her progeny back at any time always remained with her. She was perhaps sure that the children would be so tempted to the attractive world of objects that they would totally forget the Source.

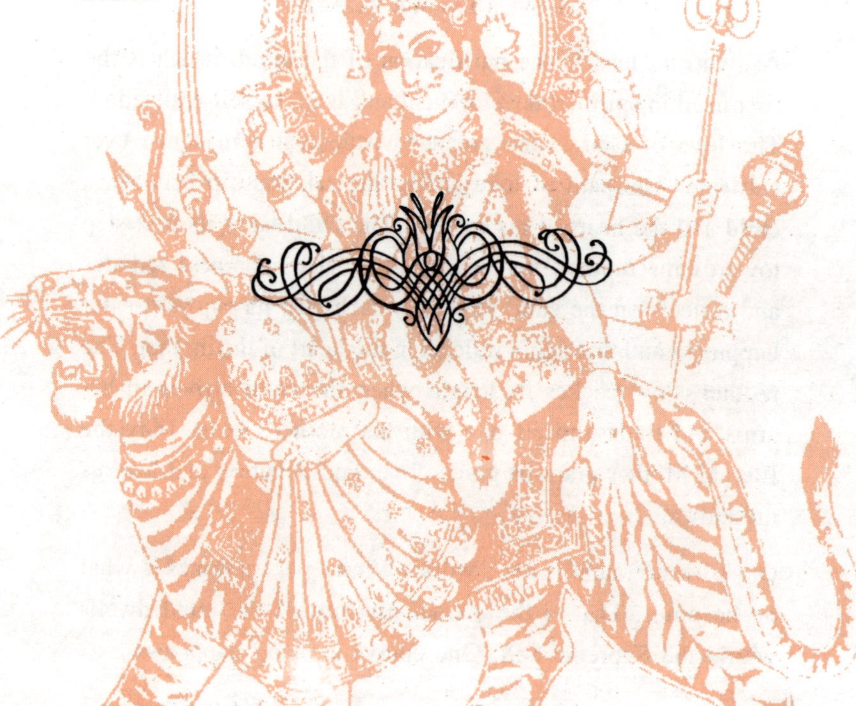

You are a pilgrim upon the earth, and have nothing to concern with the affairs of the world. Suspension of reaction is dispassion. Be a witness.

CHAPTER FORTY EIGHT

MEDITATIVE QUOTES

(Read and Reflect)

"THOUGHTS are a dynamic force. A good thought is like fragrance."

Mahatma Gandhi.

"LEARNING without thought is labour lost."

Confucius.

INNUMERABLE useful thoughts are being expressed, coined as quotations, recorded and preserved for everyday use for the posterity. These quotations speak more than mere words and serve as timely and emphatic expressions for which the mind at times aches. The following quotes are gathered from far and wide for reflection and action leading to high moral and spiritual life which should pave the way for attainment of eternal bliss. A thoughtful collection.

- A boat may stay in water but water should not stay in the boat. An aspirant lives in the world but the world should not live in him.
- A happy old age is the result of well-spent youth.
- A healthy person is he who is least conscious of his body.
- A holy thought is a voice which speaks when the tongue is silent.
- A journey of a thousand miles begins with a single step.
- A narrow mind and a wide mouth usually go together.
- A seed dies into a new life and so does the man after death.
- A smile is a tranquilliser without any side effects.
- A smile is a wrinkle which should not worry you.
- Absence makes the heart grow fonder.
- After having sublimated the mind, meditation ends by itself. Our attempts to sleep end when we start sleeping.
- All creation is the family of God.
- All Her glory and beauty come from within where SHe delights to dwell.
- All problems are focused in the Self - 'If I Am'.

- All see Her sport but none sees Her.
- All strive but each accomplishes as much as the Lord wills.
- All the problems of the world are the problems of mind. 'Out there' is also a thought 'here' in the mind.
- Ambition is a vice but it may be the father of virtue.
- As a solid rock is not shaken by strong winds, wise people falter not amidst blame and praise.
- As long as you run with the running mind, you cannot discover the Self. The silence of the Self is ever there waiting within.
- As passion without reason is blind, the reason without passion is dead.
- Be it anger, greed or ego - I reject none. I accept their challenge and strive to humanise them.
- Be like a rose wafting to all the sweet fragrance of goodness.
- Be sure of the sun, even when clouds gather.
- Before we learn to run we must learn to walk.
- Believe it or not, God aspires to love man and be his very own if there is a similar call from below.
- *Bhakti* (devotion) is a matter only for experience and not for words.
- Blessed are the pure in heart for they shall see God.
- Blessed is he who needs nothing, for, he will have all.
- Character is what you are in the dark.
- Children learn to talk, adults to be silent.
- Cling to His Name with leach-like tenacity.
- Communion with God is the true wine, the wine of ecstatic love.
- Consciousness is eternal, for its non-existence can never be experienced.
- Constant practice of knowledge purifies the Self stained by ignorance.
- Contentment swallows greed.
- Cosmos exists, life comes and goes. How does it happen that none of us knows?
- Covetousness is the source of discontent. Differentiate between necessary necessities and unnecessary necessities.

- Creative evolution aims at the emancipation of the soul.
- Desire eats the body as worm eats the wood.
- Discipline needs will and effort in the beginning but becomes a habit with practice.
- Divine love when possessed has to be concealed as a miser conceals his wealth.
- Do not correct others. You have enough to correct in yourself.
- Don't fight, don't flight, simply flow.
- Duty is what one expects from others!
- Education knows no fruition without intuition or love.
- Egoism is the knot of Spirit and matter. Egoism ends, divinity remains.
- Ends are achieved by endeavours alone.
- Enjoy the company of your real blood relations - air, water, light and earth.
- Even the gods cannot say how this creation was caused, for, even they were born after the creation.
- The Pure One is within you, ignorance is veiling It.
- Every anxiety, every violent exercise means that you are burning the lamp of your life quickly.
- Every contradiction is both false and true.
- Every failure is not a tragedy.
- Evil dwarfs man. Virtue exalts him to his full human stature.
- Existence is abstract. That which exists is creation.
- Faith is belief in the unknown. Belief is faith in the known.
- Faith is blind, experience alone is truth.
- Fewer the thoughts, greater the peace. Fewer the desires, lesser the thoughts.
- Follow one, hate none.
- From the invisible he made all things visible, himself being invisible.
- Give up those things which the mind likes best for a fortnight in an year.
- Giving never empties one, taking never fills one. The only way to experience fullness is to give away everything.
- Go where people hate you. Let them thrash the ego out of you. And you

will be nearer the God.

- God could not be everywhere, so He made mothers.
- God heals and the doctor takes the credit.
- God is one; gods are many. Enjoy any divine vision.
- God is rational too.
- God looks at the working of one's mind. He recognises the motive alone.
- God suffers with the poor and rejoices with the contented.
- God-realisation is a state of mind: equilibrium, equanimity, equipoise.
- Good is intermixed with evil, pleasure is blended with pain.
- Good is the conquest of evil, not the absence of evil.
- Grin and bear it, or, bear it and grin.
- Happiness: wanting nothing and knowing it.
- Happy is one who is drowned in the heavenly intoxication. Blessed is one who is drunk in the divine madness.
- He that loves not knows not God, for, God is Love.
- He who abides the law, rides the law. Divine laws are very exacting and unrelenting. One cannot escape them.
- He who has given up sense enjoyments for God's sake, has already covered three-fourth of his journey.
- He who truly fears a thing, flees from it, but he who truly fears God, flees unto Him
- Heaven itself is on earth, could one but realise it.
- Hold your head up and your temper down.
- Honesty pays but it does not suit some people.
- Humility cannot come as long as there is any egotism left.
- Humility is the essence of virtues.
- Idle people have no time to spare.
- I hold it true that pure thought can grasp Reality.
- I think too much of myself. How can I think so much of God?
- In most of mankind gratitude is merely a secret hope for greater favours.
- If a lie runs for ten years, truth takes one day to catch up.

- If I slow down, I give myself more time to do things properly.
- If the family lives in harmony, all affairs will prosper.
- If the mind is content what matters between rich and poor.
- If we realise the natural as natural, we realise the ever-existing divinity.
- If you put your hand in the fire, it will get burnt. Is it the fault of the fire?
- If you want honey, you should be prepared for the bee-sting.
- If you want to forget all your troubles, wear a pair of tight shoes.
- Ignorance obstructs the vision of Truth just as you cannot see your way in a thick forest.
- Immanence is the concept of God's presence within the whole of creation.
- God is with you in your ecstasies and agonies.
- Instead of 'falling' in love with the objects of the world, why not 'rise' in love with ever-blissful God, the Mother Grace.
- Irrational knowledge is faith.
- It is better to be maimed of the senses than to misuse them.
- It is better to light a lamp than curse the darkness.
- It is not difficult to realise God. It is difficult to be human.
- It is not that 'I think' and therefore 'I am', but 'I am' and therefore 'I think'. No one thinks 'I am not'.
- It is only when the want is there that the supply will come.
- It is this 'I' which is the essence of man - and this 'I' is never seen.
- It is with God's grace that deliverance is obtained.
- It is wonderful to live life without baggage in the head or heart. Travel light in the journey of life.
- It needs the tongue to speak out but it needs both the tongue and discretion to keep quiet.
- Keep cool; anger is no argument.
- Keep silent or say something better than silence.
- Keep your mind pointed towards God and the life's boat will sail smoothly.
- Know thyself. Embrace your original nature and hug solace.
- Knowledge comes with the perception of the Self.

- Knowledge must be experienced in order to be known.
- Learning is a treasure that follows its owner everywhere.
- Learn to be calmly active and actively calm while carrying on your daily activities.
- Let not life dismay you. The problems are meant to be solved.
- Let man transform his self (ego) into the Self (soul).
- Let the Self be sought and had; the world then be unsought and ultimately lost.
- Life is an unbroken series of experiences and a perennial search for Truth.
- Life is very easy if you have your priorities right.
- Life without love is like a tree without blossoms.
- Living with constant awareness of God is meditation
- Love is a soul-to-soul relationship.
- Love is the best and attachment is the worst part of life.
- Love is the price of God.
- Lust has to be sublimated if not eliminated.
- Lust in the heart is a cobra.
- Man begins to achieve when he begins to believe.
- Man gets and forgets. God gives and forgives.
- Man is a spiritual being learning to be human.
- Man rewards results. God rewards efforts.
- Man with clenched fists cannot shake hands.
- *Mauṇa* (silence) is constant speech.
- Meditation checks the impulse of wrong thinking.
- Men talk of killing time while time quietly kills them.
- Misery is hankering after pleasures of the senses.
- Moods are like cancer - they eat into the peace of the mind.
- More, more, more is the cry of a mistaken soul. Nothing less than all will ever satisfy it.
- *Mukti* is a state of desirelessness.
- Never can desires end by obeying them and fulfilling them.

- No one belongs to anyone, O man, only God belongs to all.
- No worldly relations are truthfully real. It is *moha*, not love, for selfish ends.
- No wants, no sorrows.
- Nobody loves selflessly. Only God has selfless love.
- Not providence but the man's desire to possess, mutilates his destiny and makes him suffer.
- Nothing is destroyed. Things appear and disappear only to reappear.
- O Truth, I love Thee. O Love, I am true to Thee.
- Of all acts of man, repentance is the most divine.
- One and only One, a vision of bliss, beauty and benevolence.
- One cannot realise God and also retain individuality.
- One who is born in fire will not fade in the sun.
- Our life is predetermined but remains undetermined.
- Our life is what our thoughts make it.
- Our little intellect is like shallow water in a little pond. If we stir it too much, the mire comes to the surface.
- Misery is desires unfulfilled.
- Pray to thank and not to demand.
- Prayer is not measured by the length of time but by its efficacy.
- Prayer is the sincere sighing of a penitent heart.
- Prejudices are hidden fetters that tie the soul and smother it.
- Purity and goodness belong to the mind, not to the body.
- Quest for Reality is devotion.
- Realise your worth and keep on deserving more and more, not desiring more and more.
- Reason should always be aided by tolerance and should not forget its own limitations.
- Regularities of nature are real. Without this assumption science is reduced to a meaningless charade.
- Reluctance to share is a vice; willingness to share is a virtue.

- Rely on Him. To believe is to embrace.
- Rest is meaningless for one who is doing nothing.
- See in this scene of changing shows, there is changeless One that glows.
- Self-experience rules out all proofs and considerations.
- Selfless people do not do different things but they do things differently.
- Serenity: To possess and not be possessed.
- Shoes cannot run faster than man. Illusion must be our footwear.
- Silence does not involve us in controversy. Where there is no fuel, there is no fire.
- Simplicity is the sign of a highly creative mind.
- Sincerity belongs to mind and speech.
- Skill to do comes from doing.
- Sometime you can make a very effective statement while holding your tongue. Silence is gold.
- Sorrow is seated on joy. Attraction wears the cap of repulsion.
- Spiritual dignity is also a vanity.
- Spiritual humility should be our nature and not dogmatic pride.
- Spirituality is not a social conduct. It is an internal transformation of consciousness.
- Strive to become rather than seem. You will be nearer to your goal.
- That deed is a blessed deed that pleases the Lord and that knowledge is true knowledge that unites our heart with God.
- That which binds one is the fruit of actions.
- The audience with the Supreme Being has to be in the harmonious synthesis of body, mind and soul.
- The child is happy through ignorance, the wise through knowledge.
- The desire determines the resolve, the resolve determines the action and the action determines the man.
- The devotee does not question the Will of God. He only carries out His dictates.
- The ego is the consciousness of possessions, qualities, status.

- The fact remains that we love to be flattered.
- The heart has reasons that reason does not understand.
- The heart emotionalises the intellect and the intellect intellectualises the heart. Truth stands above both.
- The illumined way of doing actions is to imitate the child.
- The inner coolness and composure are the one sure result of all spiritual austerities.
- The inner voice speaks when the mind is serene, and the thought is stilled.
- The light of Truth inebriates the heart of the beholder.
- The nature of poison is to kill whether taken deliberately or unknowingly.
- The process of meditation is exactly that of following the light to its source.
- The secret of bliss is dispassion.
- The Supreme Spirit is the vital content in every particle of this world.
- The ultimate fate awaiting everyone is loneliness.
- The veil of illusion conceals the vision of God from our sight.
- The venom of the superimposed serpent cannot poison the rope - the substratum.
- The way to fulfil a desire is to give it up.
- The whole world is contained in a small ball called head.
- The wise cannot make you see with his eyes. At best he can inspire you to use your own.
- There is evil in your mind. That's why you can't find peace.
- There is music in everything if you have ears to hear the same.
- There is neither life nor light in the absence of the Spirit.
- Thou and Thine is wisdom, Me and Mine is ignorance.
- Time is a construct of the mind; time is the space between two thoughts.
- To be angry is to revenge the fault of others upon ourselves.
- To define Truth is to defy Truth.
- To enjoy contentment, all the urges of your personality must be dispensed with.
- For an awakened soul to expel an obnoxious thought from his mind, should be as easy as to shake a stone from the shoes.

- To live is to love. To love is to live.
- To retire from active life to seek peace is no escape. Escape is no solution of a problem.
- To save ourselves from drowning we don't have to dry up the stream.
- To seek is to remember. This is devotion.
- To take is lust, to give is love, to give and take is business.
- Tongue is not steel, still it cuts.
- Traditions evolve. Faith varies. God endures.
- There is no road to divinity. It is made when you walk on it.
- Truth is often eclipsed but never extinguished.
- Under the shelter of the Supreme Being, not a whiff of hot air touches us.
- Union implies separation; acquisition implies loss.
- Vain indeed is all struggle for spiritual life if there is no love.
- War-mongers are more happy than peace-lovers.
- We can see God only if He turns His light on His own face.
- We learn not to love others but to love oneself and long to be loved by others.
- We should think of each extra day a gift from God.
- What if man had eyes to see the true beauty, the divine beauty?
- What is soil to a plant, faith is to the seeker of Truth.
- When intellect and mind are harmoniously wed we get heart whose function is *bhāvanā*.
- When one wants, one cannot give.
- When the 'I' dies, God shines as the Radiant Reality.
- When the passions are quelled, devotion dawns.
- When there is love in the heart, no language is necessary.
- When you learn to live for others, they will live for you.
- Whenever you say, 'this is mine', Nature says 'No, nothing is yours. This is given to you for use only.'
- Which hurt cannot be forgiven when a sincere smile accompanies an apology?
- Wise men learn more from fools than fools learn from the wise.

- Plus ego, all is 'mine'. Minus ego, all is 'yours'.
- You cannot add to or subtract from someone's destiny by worrying about it.

MAY the Merciful Mother bless Her children with the divine wisdom and lift them up to the magnanimous heights of eternal splendour.

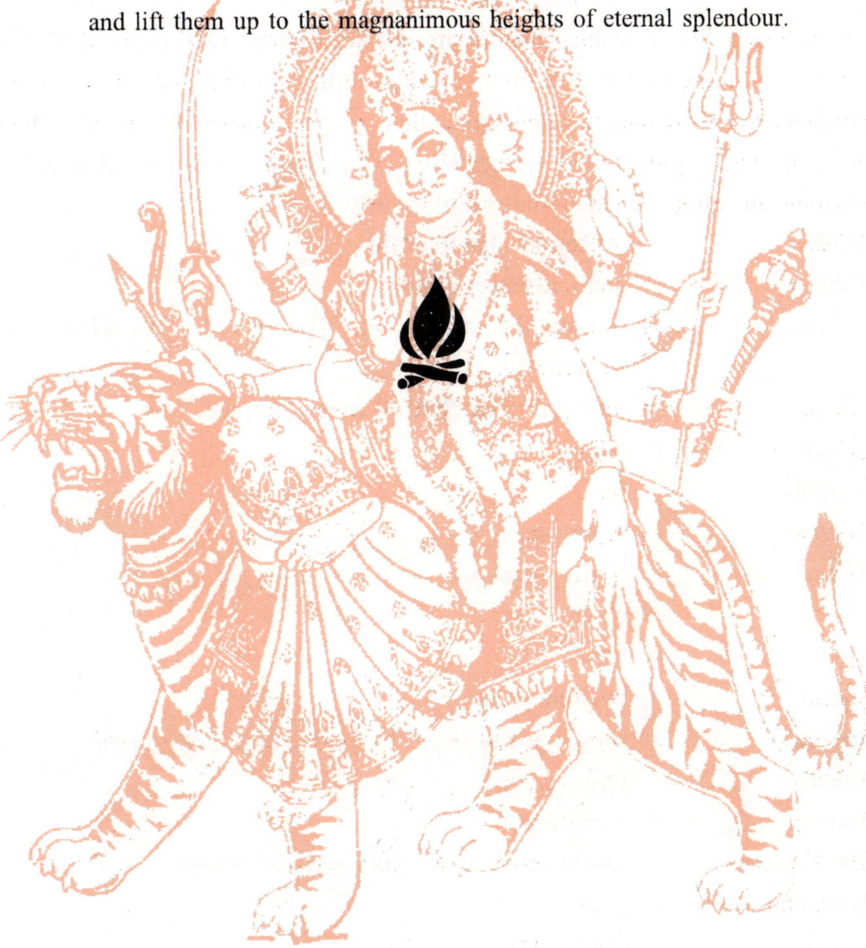

That Primordial Force we call Mother Divine, the Supreme Being, resides everywhere, in everything. Give all to Her.

PART SEVEN

APPENDIX 'A'

GLOSSARY

THE WORDS included in this glossary are not necessarily used in this text. One often hears these words used so frequently during spiritual discourses in both Hindi and English. The meanings given here are not exhaustive. However these are expected to prove useful especially to the English-knowing devotees in grasping the subject (under-study) fairly easily.

Ābhāsa	:	reflection, manifestation.
Abhāva	:	non-existence, absence.
Advaita	:	non-duality, where the *ātman* and *Paramātman* are regarded as one.
Aham	:	the pure inner Self; 'I' consciousness.
Āhaṇkāra	:	I'ness, ego.
Āhantā	:	I'ness.
Ākāṅkṣā	:	Expectancy
Ākāra	:	form, shape.
Ākāśa	:	ether, space.
Akṣara	:	Oṃ
Anādi	:	beginningless.
Anāhata	:	mystic sound heard by yogis, un-struck sound.
Ananta	:	infinite.
Anitya	:	transitory.
Antahkaraṇa	:	inner equipment: mind, intellect and ego.
Anugraha	:	grace.
Anurāga	:	divine love.
Anusandhāna	:	enquiry into the nature of *brahman*.
Aparokṣa	:	direct, immediate.
Ārādhanā	:	worship.
Ārati	:	waving of lights.

Arūpa : formless

Āsana-s : body postures.

Asmitā : egoism.

Āśrama : hermitage

Āstika : theist, believer in existence.

Asura : *demon*

Ātmabodha : knowledge of the Self

Ātman : Self, soul.

Atīta : beyond.

Avatāra : incarnation of God.

Āvāhana : invocation of a deity, respectful invitation.

Āvaraṇa : veil.

Avadhūta : A mystic, who has risen above body consciousness, all duality and all conventional standards.

Avidyā : ignorance.

Avyakta : unmanifest, indistinct, *brahman* in vedānta.

Bhakta : a devout person.

Bhakti : devotion to God.

Bhāṣya : commentary.

Bhāva : matured devotion.

Bhāvanā : feeling, idea.

Bhoktā : enjoyer.

Bhūta : element.

Bodha : awareness.

Brahman : the impersonal Absolute, Existence or Godhead.

Caitanya : Consciousness.

Caraṇāmṛta : the water that has washed the feet of an idol.

Cit : Consciousness.

Darśaṇa : vision.

Dāsya : the devotee's attitude toward God as servant to master.

Dayā : mercy.

Deha : body.

Devī : Mother Goddess.

Dhāranā : an effort of fixing the mind on an object.

Dhyāna : meditation.

Dikṣā : spiritual initiation.

Divya cakṣu : divine eye.

Divyadṛṣṭi : divine perception.

Doṣa : defect, weakness

Draṣṭā : seer.

Dṛṣṭi : look, sight, attitude.

Dveṣa : envy.

Ekāgratā : concentration.

Guṇa-s : the three primal qualities that form the nature of things, *sattva*, *rājas* and *tāmas*.

Guṇātīta : one who has transcended the guṇā-s.

Guṇagāna : praises, glory.

Hiraṇyagarbha : a name of *brahman*, first manifestation of *brahman*, also called *sūtrātman*.

Iṣṭadevatā : A representative symbol of Truth conceived as a deity, chosen deity.

Japa : the repetition of a divine *Name* or a mantra.

Jijñāsā : inquisitiveness.

Jīva : the individual soul, the ego.

Jīvanamukta : liberated while still living.

Jivātman : individual soul

Jñāna : knowledge

Jñāna yoga : the yoga of knowledge; a spiritual path based on continuous contemplation and self-enquiry.

Jananī : creatrix mother.

Kaivalya : the state of liberation, isolation.

kāla : time.

Kāma : desire, lust.

Kāraṇa śarīra : causal body.

Karma	:	any action, physical, verbal, or mental.
Karmayoga	:	the yoga of action.
Koṣa	:	sheath or covering.
Kṛpā	:	grace
Kūtastha	:	the soul standing immovable in the midst of the moving multitude of body, mind, etc.
lakṣanā	:	characteristic mark, feature.
Līlā	:	divine play.
Liṇga śarīra	:	subtle body, astral body.
Mahāta	:	cosmic intelligence, the first product of Nature.
Manana	:	thinking over what has been heard.
Māyā	:	Primordial nature. The power which veils the true nature of the Self.
Moha	:	delusion.
Mokṣa	:	liberation from bondage.
Nididhyāsana	:	uninterrupted contemplation.
Nirākāra upāsanā	:	meditation on the formless.
Nirguṇa upāsanā	:	worship of the impersonal aspect of God
nirvāṇa	:	freedom, liberation.
Niṣkāma karma	:	selfless action
Nitya	:	eternal.
Nivṛtti	:	renunciation.
Niyama	:	practice, principle, injunction.
Om	:	the primal sound from which the entire universe emanates.
Parā	:	higher, beyond.
Paramahansa	:	a Self-realised person.
prāṇāyāma	:	regulation of breathing.
Parokṣa	:	Indirect.
Prapatti	:	surrender.
Pravṛtti	:	attachment, outward-going thoughts.
Prasāda	:	a blessed or divine gift.

Pratyāhāra : psychic practice of withdrawing the mind from the sense objects.

Puṇya : merit.

Puruṣa : Supreme Person.

Rāga-dveṣa : attachment-hatred.

Rajo guṇa : one of the three primal qualities in which passion, activity and restlessness predominate.

Ṛṣi-s : seers., saints.

Sadācāra : righteous conduct.

Sādhaka : a spiritual aspirant.

Sādhanā : spiritual practices.

Saguṇa : with attributes.

Sahasranāma : 1000 names of the Lord.

Sākāra : with form

Sākṣātkāra : direct realisation.

Samādhi : a state of meditative absorption, ecstasy.

Saṃskāra : impressions in the subconscious mind.

Samvīt : Consciousness.

Sanyāsa : formal vows of renunciation.

Saṇkalpa-vikalpa : thought and counter thought.

Śānta bhāva : attitude of peace and serenity,

Sat-cit-ānanda : the nature of Absolute Reality, Being- Consciousness-Bliss.

Satsaṇga : a spiritual meeting or discussion, company of truth.

Sattva guṇa : one of the three primal qualities in which purity, equanimity and wisdom predominate.

Śāstra : scriptures.

Sevā : service

Saṃhāra : destruction

Smṛti : what is remembered, memory.

Śraddhā : devout faith in God and the scriptures.

Śravaṇa : listening.

Śruti : what is heard or revealed; *veda-s*.

Siddhi : psychic powers.

ŚṛṣṭI-s : creation.

Sthūla śarīra : physical body.

Sūkṣma : subtle

Svabhāva : nature.

Svarūpa : essence, essential nature of *brahman*.

Tamo guṇa : one of the three primal qualities in which lethargy, ignorance and inertia predominate.

Tanmātrā-s : elements in their subtle forms.

Tapasyā : austerity; self-discipline of body, speech and mind.

Tat tvam asi : That Thou Art.

Tattvajñāna : knowledge of the *brahman*.

Tejas : effulgence.

Turīya : beyond waking, dreaming and deep sleep states of consciousness.

Tuṣṭi : contentment.

Tyāga : sacrifice, renunciation.

Upādhi : limiting adjuncts.

Upāsanā : meditation.

Upāya : means.

Vairāgya : dispassion.

Varadāna : boon.

Vāsanā-s : habit of the mind; latent tendency or impression.

Vātsalyabhāva : a devotee's attitude toward God, of parent toward child.

Vidyā : knowledge.

Vikṣepa : tossing of mind.

Vinaya : sense of propriety.

Virakta : a man of detachment.

Virāṭa : macrocosm.

Viṣaya : object of perception.

Viveka : discrimination.

Vyakta : manifest.
Vṛtti : a wave in the mind lake, modifications.
Yogi : one who has attained perfection through *yogik* practices.
Yajña : sacrifice.

KNOWLEDGE is a unifying thread that weaves the bits together. Call it scientific knowledge if you wish. There is another plane termed emotional intelligence which is not born exclusively of reason. Emotions create their own realm. Still deeper and subtler is the spiritual knowledge which transcends the earlier two.

Transliteration guide for Hindi/Sanskrit words.

a as **a** in organ or **u** in but.	ā as **a** in master
c as **ch** in cheese	d as **th** in father
ḍ as **d** in dove	e as **e** in they
g as **g** in give	h as **h** in hand
ḥ as **h** in aha,	i as **i** in pin
ī as **ee** in feel	j as **j** in jar
k as **k** in kite	l as **l** in light
m as **m** in man	ṃ as **m** in simple
n as **n** nose	ṅ as **n** in monkey/sing
ṇ as **n** in under (hard)	ñ as **n** in lunch
o as **o** in go	p as **p** in put
r as **r** in run	ṛ as **r** in Kṛṣṇa
s as **s** in stand	ś as **sh** in shut
ṣ as **sh** in show	t as **t** in French (tu)
ṭ as t in touch	u as **u** in push
ū as **oo** in fool	v as **w** in wine
y as **y** in yes	ai as **ai** in aisle
au as **ow** in now	bh as **bh** in abhor
ch as **chh** in staunch-heart	dh as **th** in breathing
ḍh as **dh** in godhead	gh as **gh** in ghost
kh as **ckh** in Eckhart	ph as **ph** in photo
th as **th** in throat	ṭh as **th** in anthill,

Divine laws are very exacting and unrelenting. One cannot escape them.

APPENDIX 'B'

Acknowledgements and Remembrances

I greet and make obeisance to the Eternal Preceptor in the form of Divine Mother, the Supreme Being, the Source of All-Learning, without whose Grace and Will this Project would have never seen the light of the day. "Thy goodness is infinite. I bow before Thee in gratitude, O Mother Grace. I have taken direction from You."

I am indebted to the following compassionate hearts and elevated souls who were instrumental in the process of writing this volume at various stages and thank them all from the core of my heart :

Shri Vachaspati Upadhyaya, Vice Chancellor, Shri Lal Bahadur Shastri Rashtriya Sanskrit Vidyapeeth (Deemed University), New Delhi, who showed keen interest in reviewing the book and contributed a thoughtful Foreword.

Late Shri Amir Chandra Shastri, my spiritual guide, who was a great source of divine inspiration, aspiration and moral support. His blessings, love and admonitions, scriptural feedback, patient hearing and appreciation of a job well done, have gone a long way in building this project.

Acharya Sharad Chandra Kushal who read the Mss. at various stages, made valuable suggestions and offered helpful comments. He played an anchor role and also wrote the Introduction to this Treatise.

Dr. Kreet Joshi, Chairman, Indian Council for Philosophical Research, and *formerly* Special Secretary in the ministry of Human Resources Development, Govt. of India, who very patiently reviewed my first sketchy manuscript and rightly advised me to hold on to it for some time and make it more cohesive. The suggestion was adhered to for obvious beneficial results.

Swami Sarvanandji Saraswati, Founder President of International Bhajansukhsewa Mission, Mahashakti Peeth, Sukhdev Vihar, New Delhi, who, on seeing the manuscript, blessed me for the work 'well-done' and urged me to get it printed without further delay and also let me take some photographs from the temple.

Swami Gokulanandaji; Swami Anubhavanandaji; Prof. S.P. Singh; Paramacharya Shri Vishwanath Rameshji; Dr. Balbir Singh; Shri M.P.K. Kutty; Prof. Makarand Pranjape; Shri Shrikrishan Semwal; Dr. Badri Narain Pancholi; Acharya Prabhakar Mishra; Dr. Veeracharya Shastri; Pt. Subhash Chandra Shastri; Swamini Purnanandaji; Swami Satyamitranandaji; Swami Adveshanandaji; Mahant Surinder Nath Avdhutaji; Prof. S.R. Bhatt; Swami Asanghanandaji; Swami Atmachaitanyaji; Swami Brahmanandaji; Swami Pragyanandaji; Swami Bodhanandaji; Swami Servanandaji; Shri Narender Chanchal Ji: They were all so kind to find time to review the Mss. and give their stimulating comments and shower their blessings. *(Excerpts are endorsed as Reviewers' views in the book).*

Swami Chinmayanandaji, Swami Bhoomanandaji Tirtha, Sri Sri Ravi Shankarji, Swami A Parthasarathyji, Swami Tejomayanandaji, Jyotirmai *Māṃ* Bhagyawanti, Rev. Anandmurti Guru *Māṃ*, Acharya Sudhanshuji Maharaj, Swami Bodhanandaji, Rev. Murari Bapuji, Sant Asa Ramji Bapu, Swami Sivanandaji, Swami Dayanandaji Saraswati, Swami Vishwasji: Spiritual discourses and writings by these saints sharpened my mental faculties and generated self-awareness, serenity of mind and acute thirst for knowledge. I prostrate unto their holy feet.

Now my heart goes all out to remember the Preceptors, Saints and *Pandita-s* whom I heard at Deer Park *Satsang*, Haus Khas, New Delhi and held long enlightened discussions with most of them. It helped develop my sensitivity and grasp on the subject. I would like to remember some of them here: Swami Acharya Bhagwatanandaji Saraswati; Sant Balak Ram Sharanji; Swami Raghvindrananda; Swami Namonarayanacarya; Pt. Vijay Shankar Chattarvedi; Acharya Pt. Siyaram Saran; Pt. Brajesh Pathak; Dr. Ram Vashishtha; Pt Ram Gian Pandey; Dr. Shrimohan Pradip; Pt. Trilok Mohan; Shri Acharya Devji; Pt. Ram Babu Pathak. I feel obliged and thank them all for their bit of indirect contribution.

I also owe my gratitude to Dr. Vijay Shankar Shukla, a devotee of *Māṃ*, who was kind enough to spare his valuable time to provide the diacritical marks for Hindi/Sanskrit words in the Text.

I owe my sincere gratitude to Acharya Moti Ram Pandit, Editor, Samata Yog Samachar (Monthly) who very patiently carried out the editorial work of this Treatise at the final stages and rendered me the much needed help and advice. He is a distinguished author of over a dozen of books on philosophy, spirituality, religion, etc.

I also salute my ever-smiling *'Bare Bhai'* Shri R.S.Bhardwaj, who provided warmth and companionship in *tete-a-tetes* during my lonely hours of writing.

Last but not the least, I admire my son, Raja, who so willingly and readily drove me to any destination I wished - be it day or night, for attending a spiritual discourse, a seminar or a discussion with enlightened souls- thus contributing indirectly to the subject Project. Pray *Māṃ* bless him and grant peace.

And finaly I owe my grateful thanks to the publishers M/s Aravali Books International (P) Ltd. New Delhi, who readily accepted the book for publication. I marvel at their keen insight and wider outlook and congratulate them on the task accomplished which speaks volumes about their planning and practices.

the Author

Let Her be wherever She wills. My search shall never cease. My longing for Her will never end. I revel in this torturing thirst and mad craving.

APPENDIX 'C'

REVIEWERS' VIEWS

Swami Satyamitrananda Giri

(Ex. Jagadguru Shankracharya)

Founder President: Bharatmata Mandir

Date: 13.9.2001

The Supreme Being is always considered as impersonal, formless and beyond comprehension. It is, by nature, absolute, without attributes and beyond all qualities. The theory accommodates the differences of opinions, disputes of forms, and quarrels of superiority. Since time immemorial and going back right upto the point when the individualistic 'ego' might have found its existence, there have been unending discussions dwelling upon the exact nature of that Supreme Being which appears to be existing behind all the worldly and unworldly happenings – whether they are perceptible or imperceptible.

But we Hindus are undoubtedly fortunate because our religion very happily and open-heartedly allows the concept of the 'ISHTA', i.e., the acceptance of the Personal God or Goddess, in accordance to the suitability of our individual nature. Thus we are free to worship God either as The Divine Mother, Lord Vishnu, Lord Shiva, Sri Ram, or in any other way.

One may feel that all these multitudes of Gods and Goddesses might create chaos and confusion in the minds of the 'lesser souls'. So it is mandatory that the background behind all such personal Gods must be understood thoroughly in order to avoid any such confusion. This is exactly what is done by Shri Chaman Lal Kaushalji, the author of 'MOTHER DIVINE – THE SUPREME BEING'. The treatise is a laudable endeavour, which deals with the theoretical part in detail, in the early sections of the book and then he shifts to the Mother Form of The Supreme Being. He perceives the Feminine Energy as the Executive Divinity of the universe which is personified in the forms of Durga-Lakshmi-Saraswati, manifesting as Mother of courage, strength, wealth, wisdom, joy and bliss.

I extend my best wishes to such attempt in order to promote the basic values such as devotion, divine surrender of the will and submission to the Divine Grace. May The Divine Mother Bless One and All.

In The Service of The Almighty,

Swami Satyamitranand

(Swami Satyamitrānand Giri)

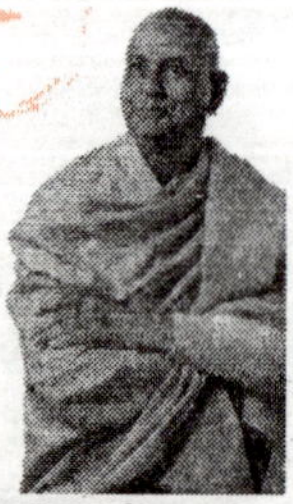

Samanvaya Kutir, Sapta Sarovar, Haridwar (U.P.) India
Tel: (Residence) 426535 • (Office) 426256

RAMAKRISHNA MISSION
RAMAKRISHNA ASHRAMA MARG ☐ NEW DELHI - 110055

PHONE : 52-7110
FAX : 3544985

Bhagawan Sri Ramakrishna had divided human beings (JIVA) in four categories. He has described this by giving the example of a fisherman who casts his net to catch fish. The first category are those who are always away from the net (Maya) and are never caught. Such are called Ever free, Nitya Mukta. The second category are those who get caught in this net (Maya) but are able to free themselves. These are called Muktas. The third category consists of those who are constantly struggling to get out of this net. These are called Mumukshas. The fourth category are those who burrow into the mud, and while being trapped in the net, they foolishly feel secure. This category are the bound souls (Baddha Jivas).

Shri C.L. Kaushal's book "Mother Divine – The Supreme Being" is a very appropriate treatise to help the Jivas of the third category, viz., Mumukshas. This category of aspirants have faith in the existence of God and strive hard to attain God realization. It is they who need help and guidance to attain the goal.

Shri Kaushal has struggled for 25 years and has put in very serious and consistent efforts for ten years to prepare this treatise. It is very clear that all what has been put down in the book is not merely an intellectual study of scriptures or religious literature, but is also backed by his sincere self-effort, meditation and constant contemplation on the Supreme Being.

The book has very clearly highlighted and succeeded in establishing the Truth that the Reality is one, though it may be called by different names. The Divine Mother is not different from the Supreme Being; the absolute Truth. As indicated in part-IV "Matru Devo Bhava", Mother is a personality that appeals most to the human heart. Therefore, the worship of Supreme Reality as Mother Divine helps in concentration.

Bhagawan Sri Ramakrishna says that one can attain the vision of God by repeating His name, singing His glories and keeping Holy Company. Holy company implies not only meeting holy men and saints but also constant study of scriptures, religious and devotional writings which help devotees to keep their minds fixed on God. Sri Ramakrishna has further stated that holy company promotes love of God in human beings. With love of God a man develops a sense of discrimination which helps him to discriminate between what is real and what is unreal and ultimately man realizes that only God is real and all else is unreal, and God dwells in all beings. Shri Kaushal has dealt with this thought process in detail.

The book is indeed very valuable and I recommend it for the serious aspirants since it will help them in their pursuits of spiritual wisdom.

Swami Gokulananda

Swami Gokulananda
Secretary

Narender Chanchal

प्रियवर

आध्यात्मिक जगत की अद्भुत बड़ी उपलब्धि है, आपका यह विशाल ग्रन्थ। माँ की लीला तो माँ ही जानती है पर आपने जिस प्रकार ममतामयी माँ का चित्रण किया है यह सराहनीय है। हमारे प्राचीन ग्रन्थों की रचना ऋषियों मुनियों ने की जो विशाल हिन्दु समाज की अमूल्य धरोहर है। आपने उसी कड़ी को आगे बढ़ाते हुए "MOTHER DIVINE THE SUPREME BEING" की रचना करके हम सब पर उपकार किया है कितना अच्छा होता अगर इस महान ग्रन्थ का हिन्दी में भी एक साथ ही प्रकाशन होता ताकि सर्वसाधारण माँ भक्त भी इस महान ग्रन्थ का अवलोकन करके अपने जिज्ञासु मन की जिज्ञासा शान्त कर सकते। और अन्त में — जिस प्रकार देसी-विदेशी बड़े-बड़े होटलों के हर कमरे में BIBLE रखना लगभग अनिवार्य सा है उसी प्रकार यह ग्रन्थ भी अनिवार्य रखा जाए।

माँ जगदम्बा आपको शक्ति दे। आपकी लेखनी निरन्तर चलती रहे आप दीर्घायु हों।

जय माता दी

आपका

"नरेन्द्र चंचल"

15/1 SARVA PRIYA VIHAR
NEW DELHI
110016
INDIA
2574 4642
2571 8703
FAX [illegible]
फै.: 26865656

चिन्मय सद्भावना केन्द्र
CHINMAYA CENTRE OF WORLD UNDERSTANDING

50 years CHINMAYA MOVEMENT 1951-2001

Swamini Purnananda

Hari Om

Brahman – the Absolute and its Power to manifest – Shakti, are inseparable as much as fire and its heat are. Fire cannot be without heat and heat cannot be without fire. Similarly, when we talk about Brahman, it includes its Shakti to manifest and Shakti has no separate existence other than that of Brahman.

This Shakti is the Primordial Energy – the Divine Mother. Unless we accept Shakti, we find it difficult to understand the manifestation. Existence-Knowledge-Bliss Absolute is One, and only One. But It is associated with different limiting adjuncts on account of the different degrees of Its manifestation. The Divine Mother is all these! Wherever we see actions like creation, preservation and dissolution, there is the manifestation of Shakti. Water is water, whether it is calm or full of waves and bubbles. The Absolute alone is the Primordial Energy, which creates, preserves and destroys.

The prayerful compilation of ideas and feelings of the Seeker-devotee, Sri C.L. Kaushal in this book 'Mother Divine, The Supreme Being' leads the reader to the perfect understanding that, the veiling power of Maya hides the Reality; the projecting power of Maya creates the manifold universe of the names and forms. May this Maya – the Primordial Energy – the Shakti of Shiva – The Divine Mother – bless Her children with the vision of the Absolute.

Sri Kaushal's feelings in the words on page 108 – "God could not be everywhere! So He made mothers!" have touched me the most!

Sri Purnananda

Swamini Purnananda
Acharya
Chinmaya Centre of
World Understanding
89, Lodhi Estate
New Delhi 110 003

89 लोदी रोड, नई दिल्ली 110003. दूरभाष: 4643301. टैलिफैक्स: 4643290.

89, Lodhi Road, New Delhi - 110003. Ph: 4643301. Telefax: 4643290
email: hhs_purnananda@hotmail.com

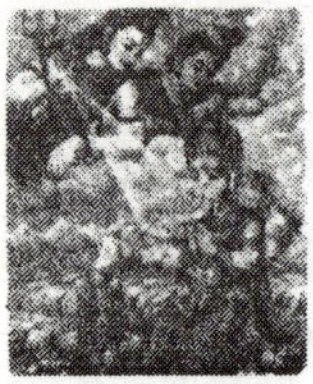

महन्त सुरेन्द्रनाथ अवधूत

Ph. : 6436405
6430191

पीठाधीश, मन्दिर श्री कालिकाजी

महन्त निवास, श्री कालिकाजी मन्दिर परिसर, नई दिल्ली-110019

परम सौभाग्यशाली है वे जन जिन पर मां की कृपा होती है। कोई बिरला ही शक्ति के मर्म को जान पाता है। **"सोई जाने जेहि देहि जनाई"**, यथार्थ में मां की कृपा से ही शक्ति तत्व को जाना सकता है। जिसकी व्याख्या करने में स्वयं ब्रह्मा, विष्णु महेश भी करने में असमर्थ है, उसकी व्याख्या मानव क्या करेगा, फिर भी चमन लाल कौशल का प्रयास स्तुत्य है। उन्होंने इस मर्म को समझा है। यथाशक्ति सटीक विवेचना भी की है। भारतीय संस्कृति में शक्ति की परंपरा को सही रूप में जानने, समझने के लिए आंग्ल भाषा के जानकारों के लिए मार्गदर्शिक सिद्ध होगी। मां इनके इस प्रयास को सफल करे।

इसी शुभकामना और मंगलकामना के साथ मां का सेवक

महंत सुरेन्द्र नाथ

---

* सर्वभूतहिते रताः *

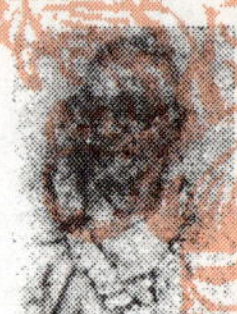

महामण्डलेश्वर स्वामी
असंगानन्द सरस्वती
एम० ए० वेदान्त साहित्याचार्य

परमार्थ निकेतन
पो०-स्वर्गाश्रम - 249 304
वाया-ऋषिकेश (हिमालय)
फोन : (0135) 434303

दिनांक २६. ५. २००१

आज आदरणीय श्री चमन लाल जी द्वारा लिखित माँ के प्रति समर्पित पुस्तक देखने का अति हर्ष हुआ। ऐसा प्रतीत हुआ कि लेखक की माँ के प्रति अनुभूतियाँ उपस्थित की गई हैं।

सम्पूर्ण वैदिक वाङ्मय में शक्ति की साधना के रूप में निर्विशेष-निर्विकल्प एवं निराकार रूप से मूल तत्व की सुविचारित स्थापना की गई है। वह मूलतत्व ही साक्षात् ब्रह्म का शब्द है। पुराणों में कहा गया है कि वह मूल-आद्या "न स्त्री न पुमांश्चैव तथैव न नपुंसकः। केवलं ज्ञान मात्रं तत् तस्मिन् सर्वं प्रतिष्ठितम्।" स्त्री-पुरुष आदि भावों में नहीं है तथापि उसी में सब है। वही पराम्बा - ब्रह्म की शक्ति आदि रूप में प्रतिपादित है। तत्वदर्शी समस्त ऋषियों ने उसी एक तत्व का अनुभव किये हैं।

श्री चमन लाल जी ने उसी सत्य को अनुभव के रूप में किया, तथा उसी के प्रकाश से ही लेखन कार्य किया। इनके ऊपर निश्चित ही माँ की कृपा है इस पुस्तक के द्वारा आध्यात्मिक साधकों को निश्चित ही पाथेय प्राप्त होगा, ऐसा मेरा विश्वास है।

शुभाकांक्षी -

असंगानन्द सरस्वती

(Excerpts from the pre-publication Reviews)

I WAS quite enthralled by Sri Kaushal's open-ended depiction of the female Divine. He has tried to portray the mystic aspect of Mother Divine into a living reality. I am sure this book is all set to make a mark in the field of devotional literature.

VISHWANATH RAMESH,
Chairman, Mystik Healing Foundation, New Delhi.

❄

In modern times Swami Ramakrṣhna's name is associated with the worship of Mother Kāli, described as Umā, Durgā &c. She is also associated with the functions attributed to *Prakṛti* and *Puruṣa* in our *Vedic* metaphysics. It is good that Mr. Kaushal also brings out the impersonal notion of *brahman* as the Absolute Spirit beyond all human characterisation.

Nowhere in the book 'MOTHER DIVINE, THE SUPREME BEING' has he sought to twist things to suit his own thesis. His ideas are clear and he has no intention to interpret the ideas of others as a peg on which to hang his own.

The book deserves a careful reading and one is well assured that the author has the gems of the matter in him.

DR. BALBIR SINGH,
formerly, Postgraduate Department of Philosophy,
Hindu College, University of Delhi, Delhi.

❄

'MOTHER DIVINE, THE SUPREME BEING' by Shri Chaman Lal Kaushal, is an inspired and unique work. What makes it different from several other books on spirituality and mysticism is that it is the outpouring of a genuine devotee and therefore filled with the *rasa* of *bhakti*.. I believe that it will not fail to move and elevate those in whom the sacred spark has been struck by the Divine. It was indeed a privilege to read the book.

PROF. MAKARAND PRANJAPE,
Jawahar Lal Nehru University

❄

THE BOOK 'MOTHER DIVINE, THE SUPREME BEING' visualises a deeply rooted organic relationship obtaining in the Reality beginning from the mundane to the Divine. In the course of this long stride of ideation, the author has had to face various dichotomies naturally involved in it, such as those of the subject and the object, time and space, name and form, *saguṇa* and *nirguṇa*,....The author has tackled all these problems quite aptly by making use of faith as well as reason.

The author's attempt accords, incidentally, very well with the *Ṛgvedic* seer Gotama Rahugona's vision of Aditi, the Mother Divine, embodied in the following *mantra*:

अदितिर्द्यौरदितिरन्तरिक्षमदितिर्माता स पिता स पुत्रः।
विश्वे देवा अदितिः पञ्चजनाअदितिर्जातम दितिर्ज नित्वम्।।

Meditative Quotes given towards the end of the book are highly illuminating and indicate to the wide range the author has covered in putting them together. They indeed are an apt supplement to making it a book of constant reference to traversers of the path of spirituality.

PROF. S.P. SINGH, Senior Fellow
M.S. Rashtriya Veda Vidya Pratisthan, New Delhi.

❄

THE WORK certainly would evoke great devotion in the reader and the style of approaching the divine in utter humility, could again promote '*bhakti*" and full surrender in the devotee. Am I entitled to comment on a labour of love that lasted nearly 12 years?

The style is elegant and I am sure it would be received well by the overseas readers.

M.P.K. KUTTY,
Chief Sub-Editor,
The Times of India, New Delhi.

❄

SPIRITUALLY it is really enlightening and rewarding to go through this book. Intellectually what is impressive is the order of arrangements of topics, the thematic organisation, systematic presentation, eloquent style and lucid expressions.

The averments in this book are revelations received by the author in meditative trance. For a spiritual seeker and aspirant for perfection, this book is highly valuable.

S.R. BHATT.
former Head, Department of Philosophy,
University of Delhi, Delhi

❄

SIMPLE FEELINGS lead the seeker to Mother-Divine, the source of pure Love. A world weary of intellectualism is turning to the Mother for belonging and nourishment. Hinduism has a rich tradition of spiritual wisdom and experience in Mother worship, the study and practice of which unlocks the wellsprings of Bliss. The author, Shri Chaman Lal Kaushal, having dived deep into that Divine source has brought up pearls of insights which he has strung meticulously in the form of this treatise "Mother divine, The Supreme Being". I enjoyed reading this book.

SWAMI BODHANANDA SARASWATHI,
Sambodh Foundation (Regd), New Delhi.

❄

THIS BOOK is a monumental work. It will inspire the seekers of Divine Power to develop vision and devote themselves to have practical realisation of Her Grace.

SWAMI PRAGYANANDA,
Pragya Mission International, New Delhi.

❄

THE BOOK should be of great help for the real Shakti worshipper if he can catch a spark from this roaring flame.

ACHARYA AVDHESHANANDA ॐ
Shri Harihar Ashram, Kankhal, Haridwar

❄

They who follow the tradition of religious theism look at God as a Person. Shri Kaushal has explored the devotional aspect of religious theism with great acumen and depth. This perspective of God enables the devotee to form an intimate relationship with the Transcendent. God as Mother is seen to be the ocean of love and grace. Hope this book will greatly enhance the spiritual depth of those who are desirous of exploring the unknowable realms of spirituality.

MOTI LAL PANDIT,
Editor, Samata Yog Samachar

❄

A wonderful success in establishing and highlighting the nature and form of the Supreme Being as Divine Mother. This study is really "नाना पुरकार निगमागम सम्मतं" in the words of Goswami Tulsidasa. It is a deep spiritual, devotional and meditational study. The style is epigrammatic, apt and chaste. Kudos to this scholarly approach!

PROF. KRIPA NARAIN MISRA,

❄

या देवी सर्वभूतेषु शक्तिरुपेण संस्थिता।
नमस्तस्यै नमस्तस्यै नमस्तस्यै नमो नमः।।

शक्ति के बिना राम–शिव–विष्णु आदि देवों का सगुण साकार विग्रह नहीं हो सकता है। अतः समस्त देवों में शक्ति रूप में विद्यमान है। भगवती की ही शक्ति सम्पूर्ण प्राणियों में विद्यमान है। अतः "या देवी सर्वभूतेषु शक्तिरूपेण संस्थिता"। इस भगवती के स्वरूप का तथा गुणों की महिमा का वर्णन श्रीमान चमनलाल कौशल जी ने किया है। यह पुस्तक आधुनिक शिक्षित लोगों के लिए अति उपादेश है।

स्वामी ब्रह्मानन्द जी गिरि
SWAMI BRAHMANANDA GIRI
श्री गिरीशानन्द आश्रम ट्रस्ट, कनखल (हरिद्वार)

❄

ॐ नमोनारायणाय ।।

देवी पुराण में भी चिन्मयी ईश्वरी को दुर्गा नाम से कथन किया है। उस उपास्य तत्व को कहीं पुरूष के रूप में कहीं ब्रह्म–ईश्वर–भगवान के रूप में वर्णन करते है। भक्त लोग उस तत्व को कहीं जगन्माता तो कहीं जगतपिता के रूप में भजते हैं। भक्ति मार्ग एक सोपान है। आज की सगुण साकार की या सगुण निराकार की भक्ति कुछ काल के बाद निर्गुण निराकार को प्राप्त कराती है। यही वास्तव में जीवन का लक्ष्य है। यही प्रेरणा देने के लिए श्री चमनलाल कौशाल जी का यह दिव्य प्रयास है।

महामण्डलेशवर श्री स्वामी आत्मचैतन्यपुरी जी
MAHAMANDLESHWAR SHRI SWAMI ATMACHAITANYAPURI.
आत्मशाक्ति पीठ, कनखल (हरिद्वार)

❄

परात्परायै नमः

पराम्बा भगवती शक्ति की वात्सल्यमयी कृपा, प्रेरणा तथा ममता के सहजभावों से अनुप्राणित, स्वाध्यायपरायण भावुक भक्त श्री चमन लाल जी कौशल ने अपनी भावानुभूति की स्वान्तःसुखात्मक अभिव्यक्ति अपनी कृति "मदर डिवाइन द सुप्रीम बीइंग" में की है। इस में शक्ति की महिमा, परात्परा आद्याशक्ति की वरदायिनी अनुकम्पा करुणा और वात्सल्य के विविध अवदानों को मौलिक शैली में प्रस्तुत किया गया है। पावन विश्वास, अकृत्रिम श्रध्दा और अटूट कियात्मकता की श्रृंखला पूरे ग्रन्थ में ओतप्रोत है। उल्लेखनीय, सुखद तथा सन्तोषप्रद पक्ष यह है कि श्री कौशल ने भावों के अंकन के लिये जिस आंग्लभाषा का चयन किया है उसकी प्रांजलता प्रवाहशीलता और सुस्पष्टता पाठक को भावविभोर कर देती है। साथ ही वह स्वयं भी मातृचरणों की शरण ग्रहण करने के लिये सोल्लास, सोत्साह लालायित हो जाता है।।

मैं श्री कौशल को ऐसी अनुपम रचना के लिये हार्दिक साधुवाद देते हुए आशान्वित हूं कि इस पुस्तक से अधिकाधिक मातृभक्त लाभान्वित होकर जीवन धन्य कर सकें इस दृष्टि से इसका हिन्दी में अनुवाद यथाशक्य शीघ्र उपलब्ध करवाने का सत्प्रयास करेंगे।। शुभाशंसा पूर्वक। स्वस्तिरस्तु।।

डा॰ वीराचार्य शास्त्री।
DR. VEERACHARYA SHASTRI,
Editor: Lok Alok (Monthly)

❄

आपकी पुस्तक MOTHER DIVINE, THE SUPREME BEING का अध्यन करने को मिला। आज की बदलती हुई परिस्थितियों में यह ग्रन्थ सभी के अन्दर संस्कृति एवं संस्कारों को जन्म देगा। यह पुस्तक आंगल भाषा में है। अतः यह सिद्व करता है कि यह पुस्तक विश्व की मानवता को सच्चे राह पर लादेगी कियोंकि आपने खुले विचारों का समावेष किया है। अतः आपकी लेखनी दुर्गासप्तशती के इस मंतर को सर्वथा करती है।

सर्वरूपमयी देवी सर्व देवीमयं जगत।
अतोहं विश्वरूपां तां नमामि परमेश्वरीम्।।

(The Goddess pervades every form and the entire universe is the form of the Goddess. Therefore I bow down to the Supreme Sovereign who is the form of the universe.)

SWAMI SARVANAND SARASWATI,
Mahāśakti Peeth, Sukhdev Vihar, New Delhi

❄

आपकी पुस्तक Mother Divine, the Supreme Being को आद्वंत देखा। आध्यात्म की जिस गहराइ तक पुस्तक में तथ्यों को प्रगट किया गया है, वह बहुत महत्वपूर्ण है। आपने श्री मां की आभा का जितना सुन्दर विवेचन किया है, वह अन्यत्र देखने को नहीं मिलता। आपके हृदय में जो जिज्ञासा है, उसकी आभा इस पुस्तक में दृश्टिगत होती है। ब्रह्म और जीव के शाश्वत रुप का विवेचन बहुत ही आकर्षक है। आशा है, आपकी इस कृति का आध्यात्मिक जगत में स्वागत होगा।

राम जन्म शर्मा, न्यासी,
Prof. Ram Janma Sharma, Trustee,
श्री आध्या कात्यायनी शक्तिपीठ मंदिर, छतरपुर, नई दिल्ली।

❄

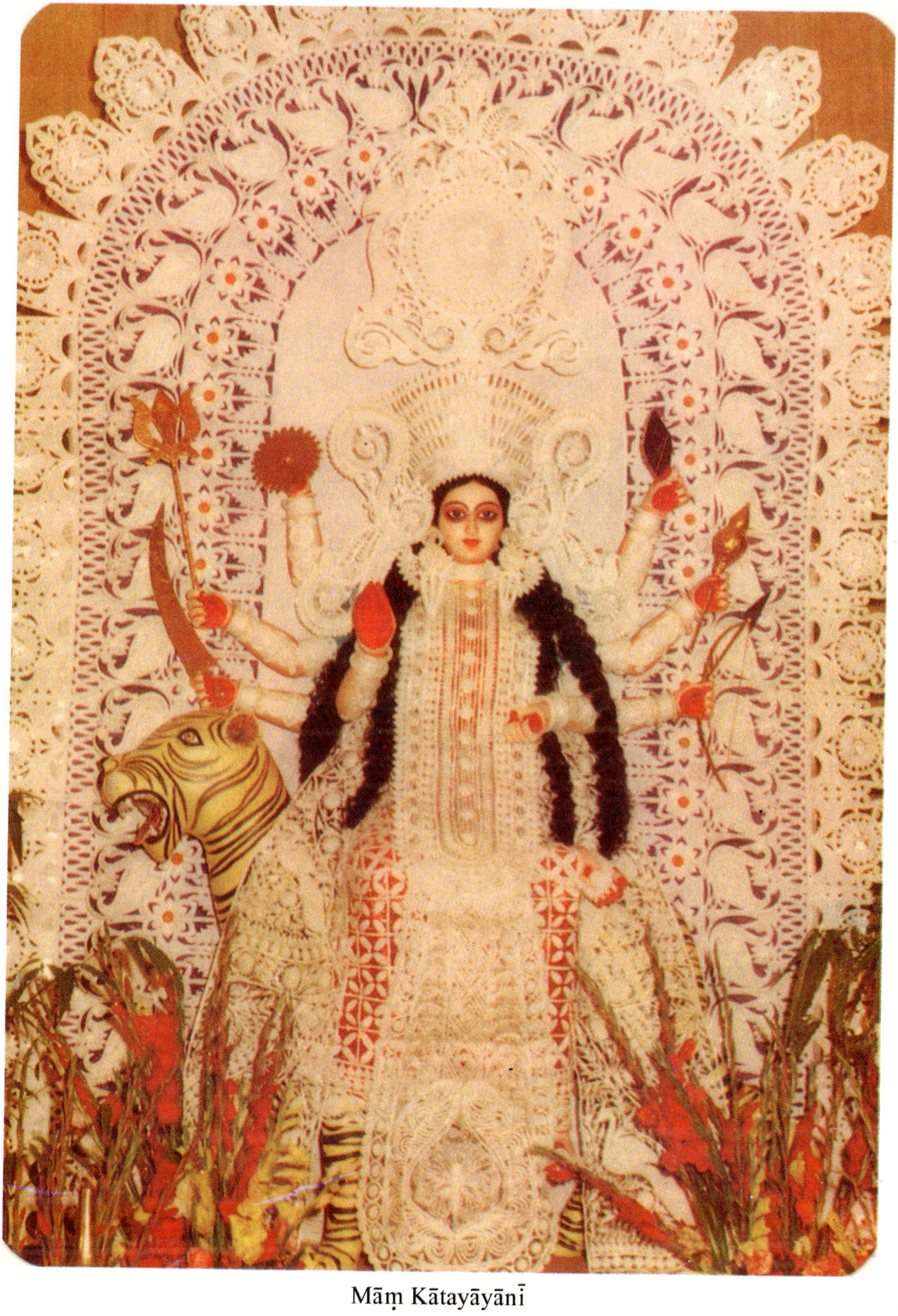

Māṃ Kātayāyānī

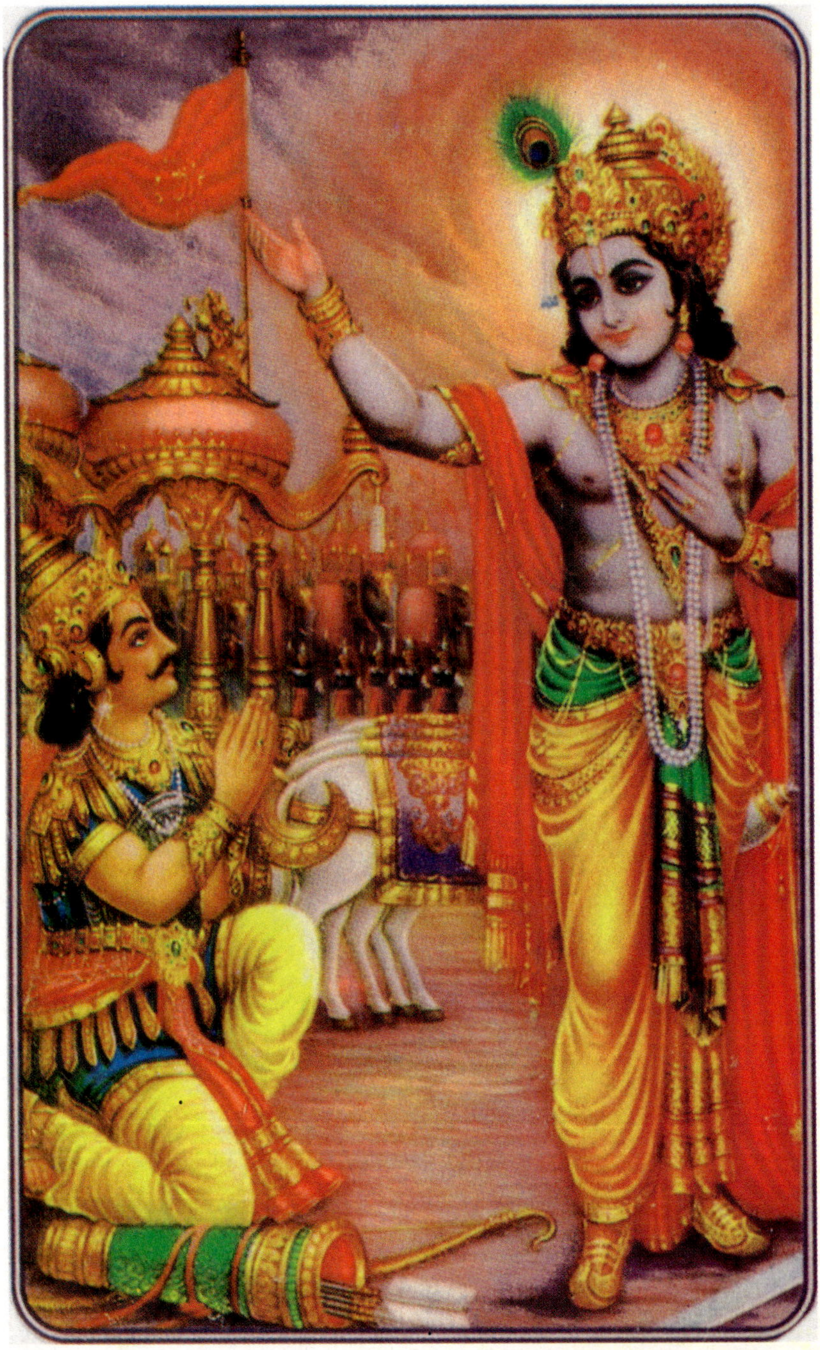

Lord Kṛṣṇa speaks to Arjuna in Bhagvad-gītā

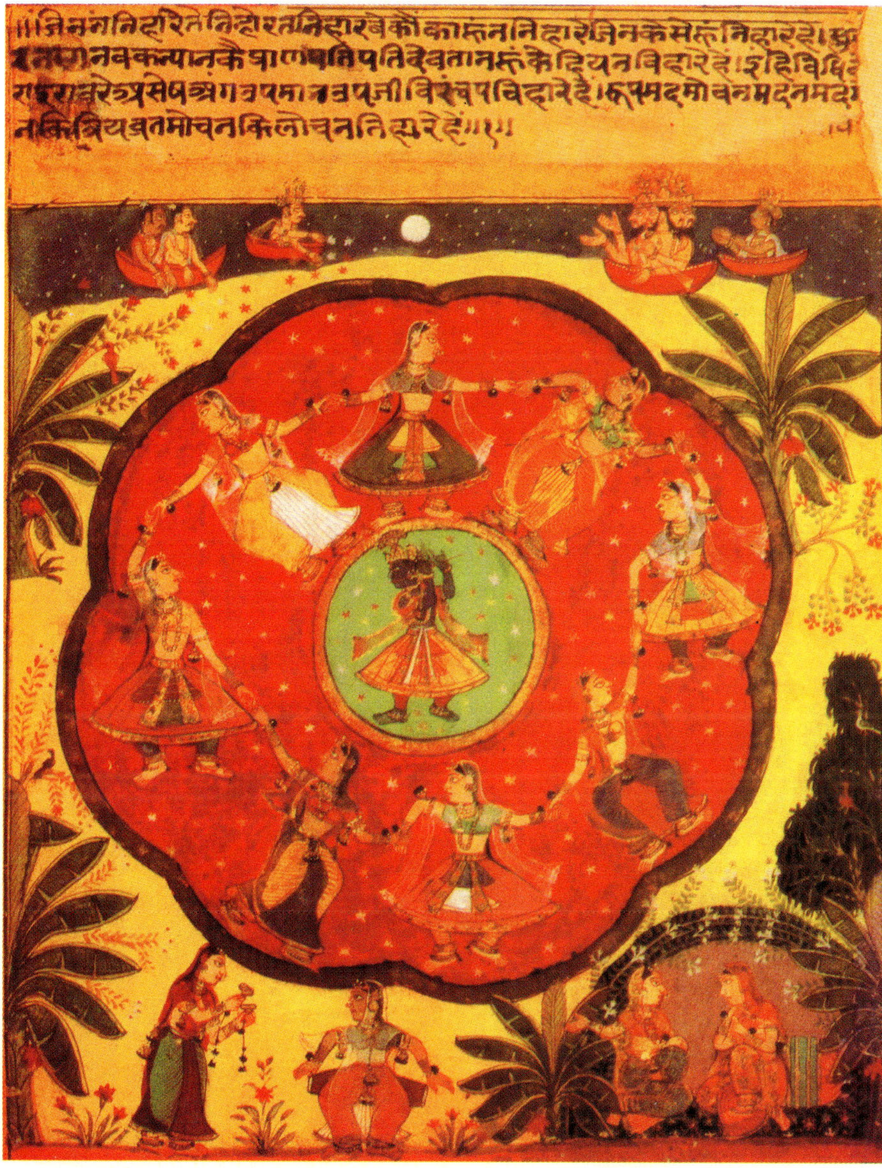

Rāsa Maṅḍala : *Gopi-s* in a trance

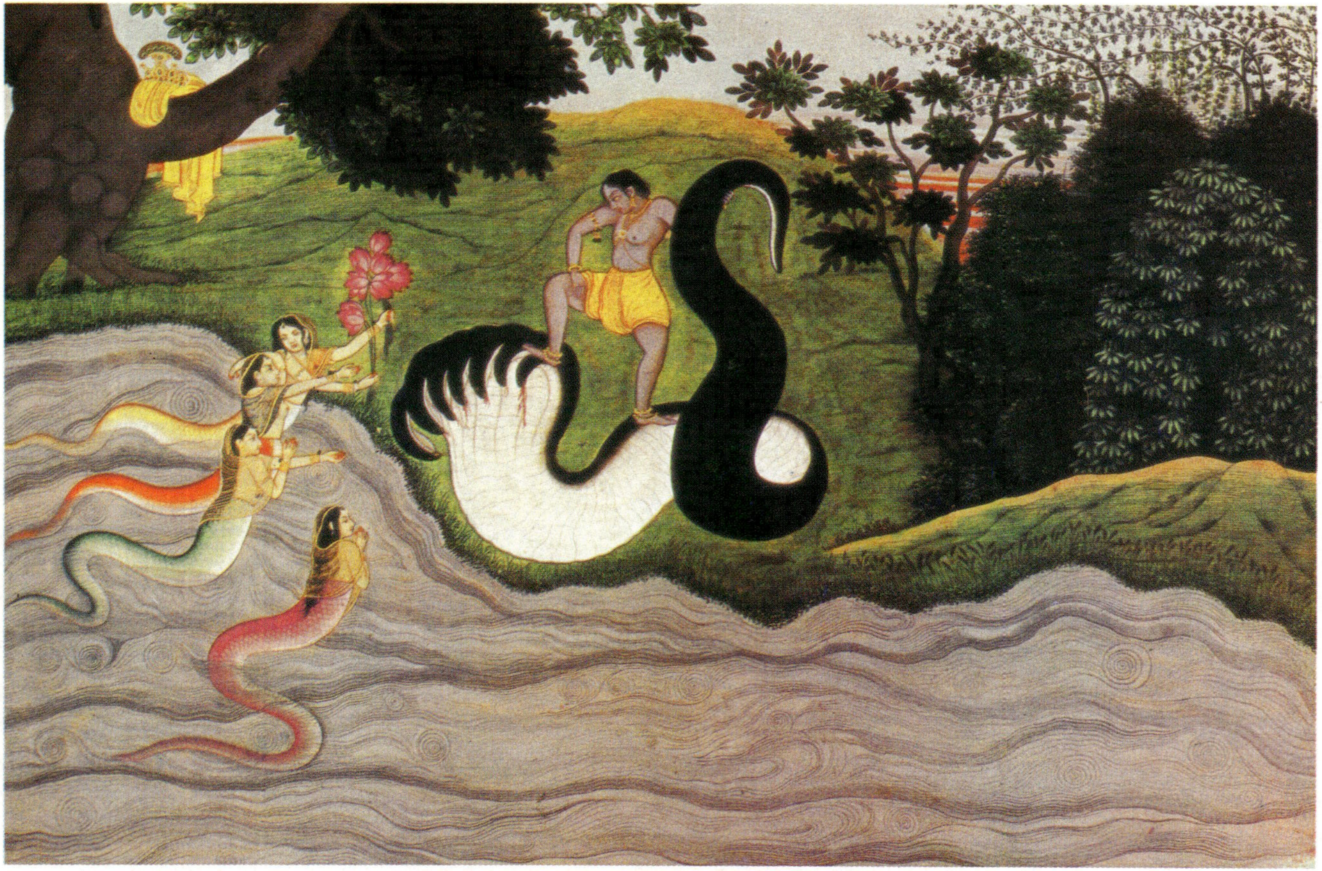

Kṛṣṇa subduing the Serpent Kāliya

Prayer for Forgiveness

O Mother Divine, the Supreme Being, on several occasions must have I committed grave mistakes. I have erred and strayed. My imperfections are many. I am guilty and full of apologies. But I yearn for you, O Merciful Mother. I take refuge in you. A *jīva* who commits a hundred faults, yet calls for the Mother's grace. I beseech your forgiveness, O *Māṃ,* for all my ignorance, errors, omissions and commissions. Pray, forgive me. May you be so gracious.

O *Māṃ*, ocean of love and bliss, accept this song of your glory as my humble offering and be pleased. My devotion to you may be far short of worldly standards. I am your fickle child. If you don't show your benevolence, where shall I go to seek refuge? A child can be bad but the mother can never be!

Praise to You, O *Māṃ,* I bow down in obeisance and pray: "Let my mind always dwell in the lotus of your feet. Let my soul flow into you. Grant me grace, love, devotion and inner spiritual strength to resist worldly temptations. Free me from vices. Fill my heart with divine virtues. Cast away doubts. Wash away my afflictions and tears with your pure love. Saturate me with your Presence. Reveal your Self and illumine me to meditate on you. Bestow your gracious glance. Be you mine for ever."

O *Māṃ*, Teach me to be anchored in your changeless Consciousness as I behold the sorrows and joys of life. Bestow on me equilibrium, equanimity and equipoise in this woe-be-gone world. May I remain always at peace with myself, O Compassionate Mother. I am your own. Bless us all. ...CL

Jai. Māṃ

❄

"सर्व खल्विदमेवाहं नान्यदस्ति सनातनम्"
(I alone am this universe. There is none other eternal like me.)
Devi in Srimad Devi Bhagavad

THUS FAR AND FURTHER

माता निर्माता भवति

(Mother is the architect of the child)

सर्वे भवन्तु सुखिन्ः, सर्वेसन्तु निरामयाः
सर्वे भद्राणि पश्यन्तु, माकश्चिद्दुःखभाक्भवेत।

(Lord! In Thee may all we happy. May all we be free from misery. May all realise goodness, and may no one suffer pain.)

Satyam Jñānam Anantam brahman
Nityānanda svarūpam brahman

(Brahman is Truth, Knowledge and Infinite, Brahman is the form of eternal Bliss.)

ॐ पूर्णमदः पूर्णमिदं पूर्णात्पूर्णमुदच्यते।
पूर्णस्य पूर्णमादाय पूर्णमेवावशिष्यते।।

(THAT (Universal Soul) is Perfect. From the Perfect is the Perfect born. Taking the Perfect from the Perfect, verily, the Perfect remains. The absolute nature of Brahman persists even when it takes the garb of the individual soul or universe by its mysterious power.)

Aum śāntih, śāntih, śāntih.
Aum Peace, Peace. Peace.

ॐ

No one can arrest the passege of time. Life appears and disappears to reappear like a jugglar's tricks. Pleasure when pursued, flies beyond reach as an arrow that has left the bow.

YOU ARE ONE WITHOUT A SECOND, O

YOU ARE OMNIPRESENT, OMNIPOTENT, OMNISCIENT

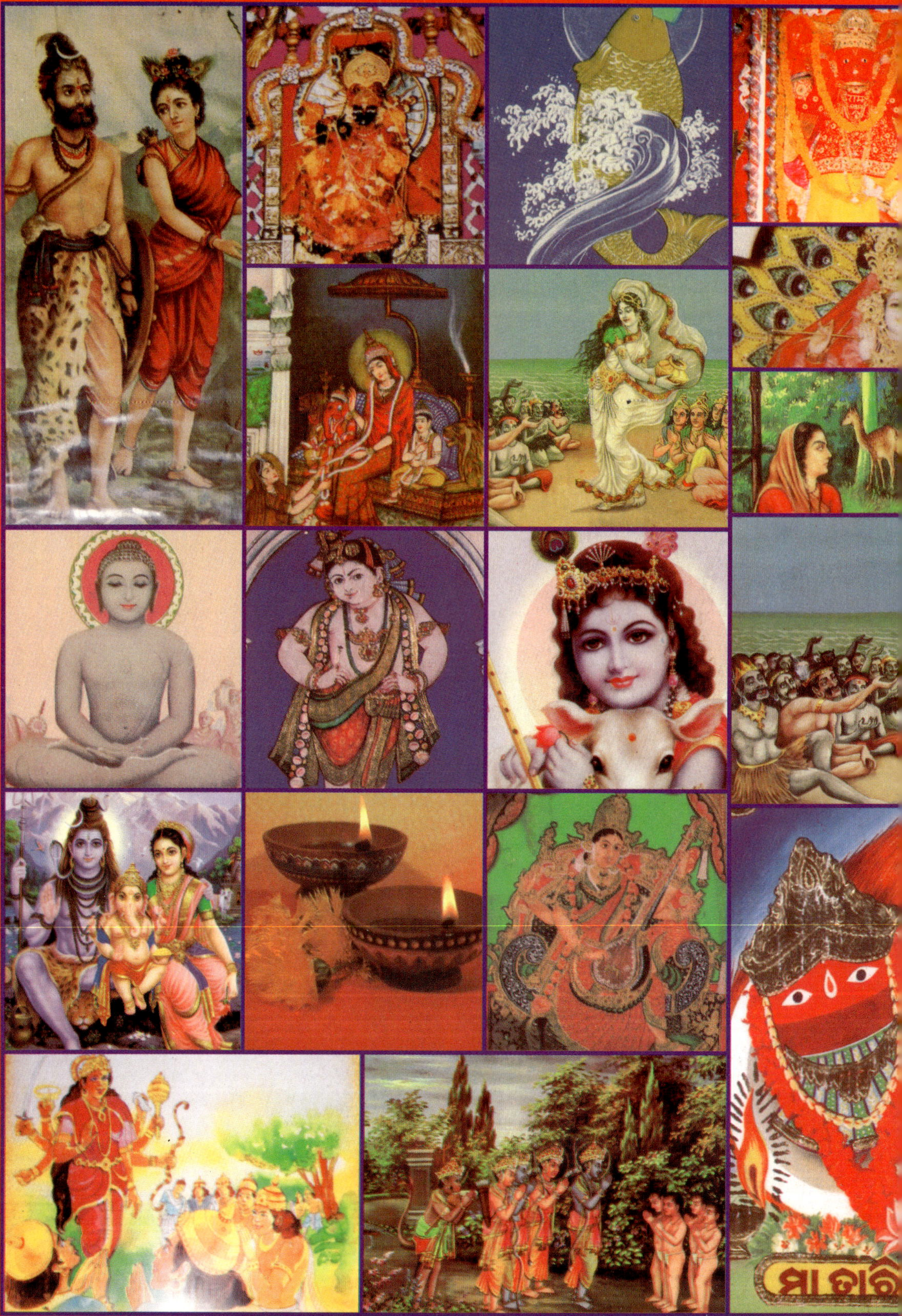

INFINITE ARE THY INCARNATIONS, MA